Of the many different kinds of anti-Semite, Eliot was the rarest kind: one who was able to place his anti-Semitism at the service of his art. Anthony Julius's study looks both at the detail of Eliot's deployment of anti-Semitic discourse and at the role it played in his greater literary undertaking. Starting with an analysis of Eliot's anti-Semitic poems that situates them in the context of arguments about the dramatic monologue, the supposedly non-propositional nature of poetry, and the aesthetic expectations conventionally brought to the experience of works of art he then moves to the prose work and an examination of the figure of the 'free-thinking Jew' based on close readings of *After Strange Gods*, *Notes Towards the Definition of Culture*, and other works. In conclusion he considers whether, as has elsewhere been suggested, Eliot's post-war work made amends for this aspect of his earlier writings.

T. S. ELIOT, ANTI-SEMITISM, AND LITERARY FORM

T. S. ELIOT,
ANTI-SEMITISM, AND
LITERARY FORM

ANTHONY JULIUS

CAMBRIDGE
UNIVERSITY PRESS

Published by the Press Syndicate of the University of Cambridge
The Pitt Building, Trumpington Street, Cambridge, CB2 1RP
40 West 20th Street, New York, NY 10011-4211, USA
10 Stamford Road, Oakleigh, Melbourne 3166, Australia

First published 1995

Printed in Great Britain at the University Press, Cambridge

A catalogue record for this book is available from the British Library

Library of Congress cataloguing in publication data

Julius, Anthony.
T. S. Eliot, anti-semitism and literary form / Anthony Julius.
p. cm.
Includes bibliographical references and index.
ISBN 0 521 47063 3 (hardback)
1. Eliot, T. S. (Thomas Stearns), 1885–1965 – Political and social views.
2. Eliot, T. S. (Thomas Stearns), 1885–1965 – Characters – Jews.
3. Eliot, T. S. (Thomas Stearns), 1885–1965 – Religion.
4. Christianity and antisemitism – History – 20th century.
5. Antisemitism – England – History – 20th century.   6. Antisemitism in literature.
7. Prejudices in literature.   8. Judaism in literature.
9. Jews in literature.   I. Title
PS3509.L43Z6867   1995
821'.912 – dc20   95-41878   CIP

ISBN 0 521 47063 3 hardback

TAG

In memory of my father

It needs literary criticism to do justice to Eliot.

F. R. Leavis, 'Eliot's Classical Standing', *Lectures in America*, 52.

In Cape Town [Eliot] was entertained by Mr Justice Millin and his wife, Sarah Gertrude Millin, the novelist and biographer whose books were published by Eliot's firm ... That night before going to bed Mrs Millin was brushing up her acquaintance with Eliot's verse ... when her eye fell on 'Burbank with a Baedeker: Bleistein with a Cigar', and particularly these lines:

> The rats are underneath the piles.
> The Jew is underneath the lot.

Mrs Millin was a Jew. She went and rapped on Eliot's door, asked whether he acknowledged these lines (he did) and then asked him to leave her house next morning.

T. S. Matthews, *Great Tom*, 163.

Contents

Acknowledgments

This book began as a PhD thesis; that it reached a successful conclusion is due in large measure to my supervisor, Dan Jacobson. Many friends and colleagues provided help. Judith Julius made numerous valuable suggestions. Moreover, without her commitment to the project my plans for this study of Eliot's anti-Semitism would have come to nothing. My children, Max, Laura, Chloe, and Theo, helped the book along. My mother, Myrna Julius, was encouraging throughout. I have been lucky to have received such support, and I am very grateful for it.

Note on the text

Where a work's original date of publication is relevant to my argument, I give that date in square brackets if it differs from the date of the edition I have used.

In certain cases, where quotations are given as instances of a particular anti-Semitic theme, and the sources for those quotations are not the works of which they are part, then those sources, and not the works themselves, will be identified. For example, Leon Poliakov's *The History of Anti-Semitism*, vols. I–IV contains numerous quotations on which I draw from time to time. In such cases, each reference will be limited to the relevant volume and page of Poliakov's work.

All quotations from Eliot's poetry and plays are taken from *The Complete Poems and Plays of T. S. Eliot* unless otherwise stated.

CHAPTER I

Introduction

PRELIMINARY

Anti-Semites are not all the same. Some break Jewish bones, others wound Jewish sensibilities. Eliot falls into the second category. He was civil to Jews he knew, offensive to those who merely knew him through his work. He wounded his Jewish readers, if not the Jews of his acquaintance, to whom, apparently, he was 'not disagreeable'.[1] Though worth noting, this is not a distinction that yields a defence to the charge of anti-Semitism. If the work, or some notable part of it, is anti-Semitic, it is the work of an anti-Semite.

No Jew reading the following is likely to doubt its anti-Semitism:

> And the jew squats on the window sill, the owner,
> Spawned in some estaminet of Antwerp,
> Blistered in Brussels, patched and peeled in London.

These lines from Eliot's 'Gerontion' sting like an insult. Purportedly referring to one Jew alone, they implicate all Jews in their scorn. They are therefore lines to make a Jewish reader's face flush. Such a reader's indignation and pain would become acute if he then read:

[We must discover] ... what conditions, within our power to bring about, would foster the society that we desire. ... reasons of race and religion combine to make any large number of free-thinking Jews undesirable.

This is from Eliot's *After Strange Gods*. When George Boas, a friend of Eliot's, read this passage he wrote to him, 'I can rid you of the company of one.' He never received a reply,[2] the first snub aggravated by the second. These two extracts – part of a poem and a passage from a lecture – comprise verbal gestures of exclusion. Eliot's Jewish readers are insulted by the first passage, while they approach the second only to be turned away. When Eliot begins that second passage with 'we', he has left Jews behind. Like a propagandist, he

discriminates between his audiences. Jews comprise the targets, not
the readers, of these passages. *After Strange Gods* is not *for* them (in
either sense), it is *against* them. 'We' can mean 'you and I', or it can
mean 'I and they but not you'. Slipping from the one meaning to the
other violates the relation of trust and equality between writer and
reader. In place of trust, there is hostility; in place of equality, there
is the writer's contempt and the reader's dismay. 'Gerontion'
similarly violates the writer's implicit bond with the reader. The
poem, so to speak, does not want Jewish readers. Instead of one
audience there are at least two: the one embraced by the author, and
the other, Jewish, audience rejected by him. How does that second
audience respond? Probably with a reciprocal gesture of rejection.
We know, of course, that we should practice a certain 'ideological'
restraint when reading, but there is a difference between reading a
text that challenges the worth of one's ideas, and one that challenges
the worth of one's person. Eliot's anti-Semitic work constitutes this
latter, more radical, challenge to the Jewish reader. How else could
he meet these lines from 'Burbank with a Baedeker: Bleistein with a
Cigar' (hereafter 'Burbank')?

> The rats are underneath the piles.
> The jew is underneath the lot.
> Money in furs.

'Burbank' so resonates with anti-Semitic scorn that if my
hypothetical Jewish reader persisted with such a poem he would, I
suggest, feel compelled to answer back in a spirit of remonstrative
exegesis. He would read the poem adversarially. I am that reader,
and what follows comprises my adversarial readings of Eliot's anti-
Semitic poetry and prose. I hope thus to keep faith with both
quotations prefacing this book. Eliot's anti-Semitic poems demand
literary analysis, and that analysis must be informed by something of
Sarah Millin's outrage.[3] Indifference to the offence given by these
poems is, among other things, a failure of interpretation. They insult
Jews: to ignore these insults is to misread the poems.

ELIOT'S LITERARY CAREER

Eliot's major poetry begins with 'The Love Song of J. Alfred
Prufrock' (hereafter 'Prufrock') and ends with 'Little Gidding', the
last of the *Four Quartets*. Though the former was published just before
the end of World War I and the latter just before the end of World

War II, neither most usefully may be read as a war poem. In each, Eliot explores the limits of the dramatic monologue as a poetic form. In each he thereby resists self-revelation. Most of his other poetry emerges likewise from this tension between the dramatic and the confessional: 'Gerontion', *The Waste Land*, 'Ash Wednesday', the first three of the *Four Quartets*. There are exceptions. 'His poems are all dramatic monologues', said Edmund Wilson,[4] overlooking the bulk of Eliot's anti-Semitic poetry, written between 1917 and 1922. These poems dominate *Ara Vos Prec* (1920), Eliot's second collection. 'Gerontion' transgresses the formal boundaries of the dramatic monologue; the poems composed in quatrains subordinate monologic revelations to impersonal ironies.[5]

As a playwright, Eliot wrote nothing so interesting as *Sweeney Agonistes* (1926–7) or so dull as *The Rock* (1934) again. In *The Family Reunion* (1939) and his three post-war plays, he crossed the comedy of manners with Greek tragedy in a number of unhappy combinations. *Sweeney Agonistes* is elliptical, experimental in idiom, and resists stage performance. *The Rock* is prolix, employs Biblical cadences, and was written as a pageant. *Sweeney Agonistes* defies audiences, challenging their understanding; *The Rock* seeks to convert its audience into a congregation. *Sweeney Agonistes* was itself never completed, while Eliot described another experiment, *Murder in the Cathedral*, as a 'dead end'.[6] It is a dead end in another sense – it ends in a death. Death, or more precisely murder, is a theme that runs through several of the plays. In *Sweeney Agonistes* and *The Family Reunion*, it is the fantasy of 'doing a woman in'. In *The Cocktail Party*, it is the martyrdom of a woman who is dying in protracted and ugly pain. In the milder *The Confidential Clerk*, it is a pregnant woman dying before term. Atonement is a related theme in this drama, though *The Rock* is too pious and *Sweeney Agonistes* too impious to find room for it. It is a Christian drama. *The Rock* and *Murder in the Cathedral* directly engage their audiences as Christians, and the final four plays meditate upon sin and expiation, common themes that make of each of the last three a family reunion with the first of the group.

At the outset of his career, Eliot's criticism comprised short notices, longer review articles, and reports back to America on English literary life. Essays, and lectures subsequently published in book form, followed later. He wrote 'Commentaries' in the *Criterion* (1922–39). The bulk of his literary criticism is to be found in *The Sacred Wood* (1920; 1928), *Selected Essays* (1932; 1951), *The Use of*

Poetry and the Use of Criticism (1933) (hereafter '*The Use of Poetry*'), *On Poetry and Poets* (1957), and *To Criticise the Critic* (1965). Eliot's cultural criticism was given book form in *The Idea of a Christian Society* (1939) and *Notes towards the Definition of Culture* (1948) (hereafter '*Notes*'), though topics of cultural concern are also addressed extensively elsewhere in his published work. Indeed, *For Lancelot Andrewes* (1928) and *After Strange Gods* (1934) each make questionable the distinction between the 'cultural' and the 'literary' in this classification of Eliot's criticism. This criticism was at first of decisive importance, and later was nothing less than authoritative. It was always influential, and established a 'school'.[7] At its best, it enlarged a particular tradition. In the context of his poetic achievement, however, Denis Donoghue's remark that its 'flaws... or even its merits – are hardly worth talking about'[8] is just, and in accord with the tendency of my book. While he had the instincts of the controversialist, Eliot couched his provocations in conventional courtesies. At times, the courtesies so muffled the provocations that Ezra Pound, reflecting on his own tendency to magnify his provocations by discourtesies, was led to ask: 'Has Eliot or have I wasted the greater number of hours, he by attending to fools and/or humouring them, and I by alienating imbeciles suddenly?'[9]

Eliot was held in a measure of public and critical esteem unrivalled by any other poet or man of letters in modern times. Person and work were equally revered: Harold Nicolson said Eliot was 'selfless and saintly'.[10] His work was often read, or misread, for its 'therapeutic, cathartic appeal';[11] it was also appropriated to an Anglo-Catholic orthodoxy. He received the Order of Merit and the Nobel Prize in 1948. Later, he was awarded the Hanseatic Goethe Award, the Dante Gold Medal, and the American Medal of Freedom. Eliot was a celebrity. A crowd stood at the dock to greet him when he arrived in South Africa; in America, police had to control the crowds who came to hear him lecture; when he went to Rome to receive an honorary degree, students shouting 'Viva Eliot!' lined the route to the university.[12] The authority of his literary judgments amounted for Delmore Schwartz to a 'dictatorship'.[13] By 1934 Wyndham Lewis could assert that '[t]here is no person today who has had more influence upon the art of literature in England and America than Mr T. S. Eliot'.[14] Almost from the first, dissenting voices were rarely heard, and lacked influence. Arthur Waugh's description of Eliot as a 'drunken helot' helped to mark the poet's arrival on the literary scene;[15] Richard Aldington's 'Stepping Heavenward' (1931) confirmed his early eminence in the person of the 'recently beatified' Father Cibber;[16] in *The Anatomy of Nonsense* (1943), Yvor Winters condemned Eliot's critical inconsistencies, censuring both master and 'disciples';[17] R. H. Robbins attempted in *The T. S. Eliot Myth* (1951) to unmask the poet as a fraud; Kathleen Nott's *The Emperor's New Clothes* (1958) sought to expose the sham in the religious revival in modern letters led by Eliot and others; William Carlos Williams attacked Eliot for his 'subtle conformis[m]';[18] there were other attacks, and there was some sniping. Early hostilities made his reputation; subsequent attacks failed to diminish it.

Eliot's anti-Semitic literary work comprises the following. First, there is the *Ara Vos Prec* group: 'Burbank', 'A Cooking Egg', 'Sweeney Among the Nightingales', and 'Gerontion'. Next, there is a deleted poem ('Dirge'), and some other lines, from the pre-Pound version of *The Waste Land*, unpublished in Eliot's lifetime. 'Death by Water', the fourth part of *The Waste Land*, and 'A Song for Simeon', published in 1928, are related to this poetry but are not themselves anti-Semitic. Then there is the drama: *Sweeney Agonistes* sets some vulgar Jews against the visionary Sweeney. Krumpacker and Klipstein are oblivious to the play's darker themes; their glib bonhomie is rooted in banality. They are among the 'material, literal-minded and visionless' figures of which Eliot wrote in his account of the play.[19] Eliot's anti-Semitic prose, and related prose, principally comprise: a passage in *After Strange Gods*, initiating a theme later taken up in *The Idea of a Christian Society* and revisited in a footnote in the first edition of *Notes*, then revised in the second edition and the revision in turn discussed in the preface to that edition; a review of Freud's *The Future of an Illusion*, and certain remarks concerning psychoanalysis; a review of, and passing references to, Julien Benda; certain remarks concerning Spinoza; a review of a book on Nazi persecution of Jews; a reference to Isaac Rosenberg; an article on Vichy persecution of the Jews. These texts, and other miscellaneous scraps, can be organised around three themes: antagonism to the figure of the Jewish sceptic, or freethinker; indifference to Jewish pain, and relatedly, indifference to the anti-Semitism of others; Eliot's inability to confront his own anti-Semitism. Some say, however, that he abandoned it later in his life, though others propose that he merely took pains to conceal it.[20] One critic believes that Eliot should be given credit for the suppression of

the hating and hateful 'Dirge';[21] another praises Eliot precisely for
not suppressing his anti-Semitic poetry: 'I respect Eliot for not having
tried to edit out of his earlier poems views which he himself later came
to regard as reprehensible'.[22] It has also been suggested that Eliot
suffered remorse over his anti-Semitism: 'the awareness / Of things
ill done and done to others' harm / Which once you took for exercise
of virtue' ('Little Gidding').

There is no consensus on the number of references to Jews in Eliot's
work. Sometimes it is the absence of any reference to Jews in an essay,
or the refusal to acknowledge the anti-Semitism of a favoured writer,
which may be anti-Semitic. There is even disagreement about how
many anti-Semitic poems Eliot wrote. The inclusion of 'A Cooking
Egg' has been doubted; the exclusion both of 'Mr Eliot's Sunday
Morning Service' and 'the Burial of the Dead', the first part of *The
Waste Land*, has been questioned.[23]

'Mr Eliot's Sunday Morning Service' is an *Ara Vos Prec* poem.
According to one Eliot critic, Hyam Maccoby, it is anti-Semitic. In
his summary of the poem, it opens with three accounts of God. The
first two are disfigured by complementary errors – the Jewish account
is too materialistic, the Pagan, too spiritual. The third, Christian,
account is the correct one. Then, simplicity replaces obscurity,
theology is exchanged for art, and 'doctrine' becomes 'vision'. The
ellipses dividing the poem mark a true break. God is above the line,
man below it. The stanzas that follow concern the Church's
constituent parts – clergy and laity. The poem returns in the last
stanza to the Jews. Sweeney's indifference to the Church is linked to
that of 'the masters of the subtle schools', whom Maccoby identifies
as modern scientists. They are the Jews of the present, 'because of
their materialism, their over-subtlety and pride of intellect, and their
adherence to the Many rather than the One'.[24]

Maccoby's case depends on whether he is right to gloss 'sapient
sutlers' in the first stanza as referring to Jews. Jews are sapient, he
proposes, 'because of their pride in the wisdom of the Law'. They are
like sutlers because they are 'petty traders in food and drink'.
Maccoby argues that for Eliot, Jews were traders, and their religion
is one of food and drink because of their dietary rules, and their
sacrifices. This gloss is misconceived. 'Sutlers' are camp followers
who sell provisions. They are petty traders in food and drink, true,
but of a certain kind; the wider meaning Maccoby advances is
obsolete. Sutlers keep an army on the road. If the soldiers of that

army are taken to be the members of the Christian communion, then their sutlers are the clergy. 'Sapient' can mean either wise or would-be wise, aping sagacity. It is therefore suitable for a poem that places an ironic distance between itself and its subject. The poem is not about Jews. Maccoby seeks offence where none is given.

In his elucidation of 'The Burial of the Dead',[25] David Trotter identifies the voice in the second stanza as belonging to Ecclesiastes: 'What are the roots that clutch, what branches grow out of this stony rubbish?' The answer is: nothing grows. The prophet's dismal revelation is of 'fear in a handful of dust'. The Judean landscape is evoked, 'the prevailing impression [of which]...is of stone...the heaps and heaps of stones gathered from the fields, the fields as stony still'. What could a people formed in such a place create? Nothing. The Jews, a nomadic people, and therefore rootless, 'originate nothing'. Hence Ecclesiastes' 'extreme scepticism towards all religious speculation'. Among other works, Trotter relies for these characterisations on W. Robertson Smith's *The Religion of the Semites* (1889). The hopeless barrenness of the prophet's vision is to be related to the 'images of aridity' in 'Gerontion'. These images are associated with the 'jew' who 'squats on the window sill'. Trotter thus makes a connection between *The Waste Land* and the anti-Semitism of 'Gerontion'. Though he does not state expressly that the former is anti-Semitic, this conclusion is a necessary implication of his argument.

It is open to a number of objections. Eliot does not associate Jews with the sterile. On the contrary, they possess a reptilian fecundity ('spawn'), and the 'protozoic slime' is their element. Smith does not attribute Ecclesiastes' scepticism to a nomadic, desert people's aridity of imagination. This scepticism toward religious speculation rather displays 'the proper attitude of piety, for no amount of discussion can carry a man beyond the plain rule to "fear God and keep His commandments"'.[26] In any event, Ecclesiastes is not the only source of the stanza: Eliot draws from Isaiah and Ezekiel as well, and also from St Matthew. The voice in this part of the poem is 'prophetic' only in the most generalised sense; it is not a Jew who speaks in the second stanza of 'The Burial of the Dead'. Though the stanza is 'full of the Bible',[27] it is not about Jews.

The anti-Semitic poems reappeared, and continue to appear, in the collected editions of Eliot's poetry, as well as in *Selected Poems* (1954, and subsequent editions). They have therefore been in

practically continuous print since they were first published. There
has been no protest at this, and little protest at the poems themselves;
they have not provoked controversy remotely comparable to the
French 'Heidegger wars',[28] or the de Man affair in America. In these
instances, reflections on the authors' anti-Semitism has led to
inquiries into the very foundations of philosophical and critical
practice. The intellectual stakes have been high; not so in England.
Though Eliot's work has been at the centre of English literary studies
for decades, the partially anti-Semitic character of the one, even
when expressly acknowledged, has not prompted any doubts about
the 'social mission'[29] of the other. But of course the anti-Semitism of
Eliot's work rarely was acknowledged. In *New Bearings in English
Poetry* (1932), F. R. Leavis was oblivious to the anti-Semitic nature of
'Gerontion': 'the Jew who squats on the window-sill could not hear
the old man even if he spoke his thoughts aloud'.[30] Stephen Spender's
The Destructive Element (1935),[31] expressly critical of the anti-Semitism
of *After Strange Gods*, left unmentioned the anti-Semitism of the
poems. In *Modern Poetry* (1938), Louis MacNeice describes 'Burbank''s anti-Semitic lines as 'shots of the contemporary world'.[32] On
reviewing *Collected Poems 1909–1962*, Donald Davie enthused: 'The
extraordinary fact is...that Mr. Eliot has published between hard
covers not a single poem which he now needs to blush about
reprinting.'[33] Published near the outset of his literary career, Eliot's
anti-Semitic poems remained an identifiable part of his work. Those
who esteemed him did so in the full knowledge of their existence. By
contrast, say, with the posthumously discovered anti-Semitism of H.
L. Mencken's diaries,[34] Eliot's anti-Semitic poetry did not take his
admirers by surprise.

It would be wrong to attempt an assessment of Eliot's anti-
Semitism by reference to the frequency of its appearance in his work.
This would be to confuse quantity with centrality. It has been
dismissed as a matter of 'one or two phrases',[35] a familiar argument
advanced recently on behalf of another literary idol, Paul de Man.[36]
Roger Kojecky contends that it 'is difficult to construct a convincing
case for Eliot's having been an anti-Semite. To hold a racial
philosophy of this sort, and to permit a few ambiguities are, after all,
different things.' Against these 'few ambiguities', Kojecky weighs
Eliot's friendship with Karl Mannheim.[37] These arguments stem
from an understandable sentiment to protect Eliot's work from
adverse criticism. Who would wish to see such an œuvre compromised

by association with anti-Semitism? Especially, one adds, when the author of that body of work is a revered contemporary, as the de Man case demonstrates.[38] If the anti-Semitism is marginal, is it not making an unnecessary fuss to dwell on the few instances of its appearance? The few critics for whom the problem has not been entirely invisible have tended to think so. Linking the anti-Semitism to an objectionable but equivocal politics, and then detaching it from the poetic achievement, constitutes the standard treatment of the question. William Chace correctly attributes this to 'the benumbing power of the title "poet"' and the fear that close examination of the matter might disclose something 'distasteful'.[39]

It is only by resisting this motion of severance that one can begin to study Eliot's literary anti-Semitism. Unless it matters to the work, the investigation will be inconsequential. The question has been posed, in defence of Pound: 'do we bother much now whether Agrippa d'Aubigné, the baroque religious poet, was on the Protestant or the Catholic side, except for points of exegesis?'[40] I contend that we should 'bother' about Eliot's anti-Semitism; we should also be 'bothered' by it. Anti-Semitism as an allegiance of the poet may be overlooked; the anti-Semitism comprising the substance of certain of his poems may not. I endorse the following remarks of de Man, which are not compromised merely because, in the context of his own life, they now seem self-serving:

it is just as absurd to blame Rousseau for the French Revolution as to blame Nietzsche for Hitler. This does not mean that philosophers and poets have no moral or political responsibility even when their work is apolitical. But it means this responsibility should be evaluated within the full philosophical or literary context of their work, not their lives.[41]

I agree, subject to one qualification: the distinction between 'work' and 'life' in particular cases will always be a blurred one. Studying the anti-Semitism in the work is a way of studying the work. The failure to acknowledge, and study, that anti-Semitism leads to misjudgments about Eliot's œuvre. One underestimates the virtuosity of its range. The failure of others to grasp this proposition is itself noteworthy. John T. Mayer's examination of Eliot's unpublished poetry, *T. S. Eliot's Silent Voices*, is itself silent about 'Dirge'; 'Burbank' is invisible in Hugh Kenner's influential study, *The Invisible Poet: T. S. Eliot*. Similarly, Craig Raine's essay 'To Purify the Dialect of the Tribe',[42] which celebrates Eliot's ability to compose poetry out of clichés, overlooks Eliot's indebtedness to the anti-Semitic clichés of the tribe. Even when silence yields to an acknowledgment of the existence of anti-Semitism in Eliot's work, such acknowledgments are often summary and concessionary in nature. Robert Crawford's *The Savage and the City in the Work of T. S. Eliot* purports to rebut the charge of anti-Semitism by observing, *inter alia*, that Eliot 'selected for notice in the 1934 *Criterion* a book highlighting persecution of European Jews'.[43] This overstates the book's theme, and passes over the qualified nature of the reviewer's sympathies.[44] In any event, one may find other passages in the periodical hostile to Jews.[45] In A. D. Moody's *T. S. Eliot: Poet*, Eliot's anti-Semitism is relegated to an endnote; the treatment of the subject is awkward and uninformed. My object is to resist the approach of studies such as these without relegating the poetry to an endnote in the study of Eliot's anti-Semitism.

PORTRAIT OF AN ANTI-SEMITE

Christopher Ricks's *T. S. Eliot and Prejudice* is an honourable attempt to engage with Eliot's anti-Semitism. It fails. One reason for this is that it does not ask *how* Eliot is an anti-Semite; it takes the nature of anti-Semitism for granted, by implication holding it to be an undifferentiated hostility to Jews without history or discursive complexity. This hostility is characterised as a 'prejudice', which makes it amenable to scrutiny as part of a larger, more affirmative inquiry into prejudice in general in Eliot's work. Examining Eliot's anti-Semitism in this way is doubly disabling. It tends to neutralise and to trivialise the subject: neutralise it, because in the context of the book's theme, even a 'prejudice' like anti-Semitism can appear to have its benign aspects; trivialise it, because representing anti-Semitism as a prejudice reduces it to a contingency of personality, when it is in reality a component of our culture.

One can isolate for analysis a number of distinct, overlapping discourses about Jews. Among this number is anti-Semitism, of which there are several versions. Anti-Semitism has a delimitable existence, notwithstanding its internal contradictions and blurred margins; that it is incoherent, and in certain instances shades into discourses less unequivocally hostile to Jews, merely reflects its unstable position within the generality of these discourses. Indifferent to circumstance and unamenable to refutation, it is constituted by instances of characterisation and denial. So, typically, 'Jews' are said to be heretic, parasitic, subversive, and therefore, it is then said, they may not live as we do, or live with us, or live at all. Though such imaginary constructs are not to be confused with real Jews, they are 'the object of a dismissal', in J.-F. Lyotard's succinct formulation, 'with which Jews... are afflicted in reality'.[46] Anti-Semitism thus ends in persecution; it is a discourse that intends harm. Historically resilient, its versions are made up of certain themes; those hostile to Jews draw on these themes to create themselves as anti-Semites. In what follows, I analyse, by means of explication and comparative quotation, that version which was Eliot's anti-Semitism. Of the many different kinds of anti-Semite, Eliot was the rarest kind: one who was able to place his anti-Semitism at the service of his art. Anti-Semitism supplied part of the material out of which he created poetry. I do not ask the biographical question: what made Eliot an anti-Semite? Instead, I ask: of what was Eliot's anti-Semitism made, and what did Eliot make out of anti-Semitism? These are literary criticism's questions. His anti-Semitic poetry draws imaginatively on anti-Semitism's discursive repertoire; his anti-Semitic prose is a derivative of that repertoire. This does not mean that these applications are ethically neutral: 'anti-Semitism is never merely a trope to be adopted or discarded by an author as he might choose to employ zeugma or eschew personification. It is charged from the start with bad faith and irrationality.'[47] Anti-Semitism precedes the facts from which it is supposed to derive; no external factor can induce anti-Semitism in the anti-Semite.[48] It is thus as a choice and not as a fate that anti-Semitism presents itself.[49] One may have reason to hate or fear a particular Jew; hating or fearing 'the Jews' is altogether dislocated from reason. It is a free and total choice of oneself.[50] On reading 'Prufrock', Pound exclaimed of Eliot: 'He has actually trained himself *and* modernised himself *on his own*.'[51] Eliot also trained himself to be an anti-Semite. He did so chiefly by drawing on the anti-Semitisms of America, France, and England, and it is with these that I will begin.

National contexts

English anti-Semitism was, and remains, an affair of social exclusion. Jews have not been harried, but kept at a distance. The dominant note since their readmission in the seventeenth century has been one of fraught accommodation. The return of the Jews did not provoke substantial opposition. English trade, already developed, could face Jewish competition with relative equanimity. English Protestantism embraced the Jews as the descendants of the heroic Jews of the Old Testament. The diversity of sects, and the principle of religious freedom that they fostered, also helped. The early Sephardi Jews, remarks Leon Poliakov, 'troubled the imagination much less than their German and Polish brethren'[52] who arrived two centuries later; a precedent for the latter's admission, however, had been created. The anti-Jewish agitation of 1753, which forced the repeal of a naturalisation act easing Jewish settlement, resisted the extension of, but did not seek further to circumscribe, Jewish privileges. In the nineteenth century British Jews secured their interests without allying with the political 'left', and therefore were not identified as a revolutionary threat. Once acquired, the political rights of Jews in England were rarely, and never seriously, challenged.

English anti-Semitism is unreflective. It has lacked theorists and publicists, and has been deprived of any event around which it could crystallise. England's expulsion of its Jews was too remote to be exploited by modern anti-Semitism; it was also so complete a victory that it refuted the anti-Semites' admonitions against Jewish power. This precedent of expulsion, and the precedent of the blood libel,[53] comprised the English contribution to European anti-Semitism. Having defined the pre-Holocaust parameters of its slanders and menaces, England then withdrew to the sidelines, while maintaining an anti-Semitic tradition strong enough to produce two remarkable anti-Semitic works, *The Merchant of Venice* and *The Jew of Malta*, at a time when Jewish residence had been illegal for three hundred years.[54] It was a tradition in which Jews tended to be despised rather than feared. H. S. Ashton's *The Jew at Bay* (1933) is typical. While commenting that 'the average person... is filled with a tolerant disgust at many Jewish habits', and objecting to 'the unpleasing Jews of Eastern Europe with their greasy, verminous ringlets', Ashton is also able to dismiss the alleged Jewish peril: 'the old lion of Judah is a toothless, mangy, inoffensive old beast'.[55] This is the timbre of an authentic English anti-Semitism. In the novels and plays of this tradition, Jews are regularly outwitted by superior Christian cunning: see Sheridan's *The Duenna* and Trollope's *Mr Scarborough's Family*. It thus allowed for a relative indifference to Jews that exasperated vigorous, and thus exceptional, English anti-Semites such as Hilaire Belloc. 'It is not very long since a mere discussion of the Jewish question in England was impossible', he complained, the depth of his own antagonism leading him to overstate the mildness of the anti-Semitism around him (although toleration of Jews often fell short of acceptance[56]).

As with its English counterpart, American anti-Semitism failed to develop into a movement. Here, however, the failure was not due to any aversion to ideological positions, but to the aversion of American ideological positions to anti-Semitism. It could be characterised as 'un-American'. Such an aversion was one of a number of inhibiting factors. There was the constitutional separation of Church and State. The wealth and expansiveness of the United States limited social resentment; sectarian diversity made religious antagonisms diffuse. Diverse anti-Semitic interests failed to group around a single issue, or a single leader. And lastly, anti-Semitism was contrary to the received notion of the Founding Fathers' political ideals. Indeed, it is even possible to argue that anti-Semitism brushed against the grain of American history.[57] One can, however, overstate this American 'exceptionalism'. An anti-Semitism of exclusion, derived from European practices, became a feature of American civil society; in addition, certain anti-Semitic fantasies, such as the menace of an international Jewish conspiracy, were imported from Europe.[58] There was a vigorous populist anti-Semitism; anti-Semitism was also an aspect of that late nineteenth- and early twentieth-century anti-modernism examined by Jackson Lears in *No Place of Grace*. This dissent derived from a sense of dissatisfaction with and alienation from modern America. Jews were taken to be representative of a commercial society without culture.[59]

These anti-modernists were predisposed to anti-Semitism by their elevation of the soldier over the businessman, and the medieval over the modern. The Jews seemed to prosper while American civilisation declined. 'Like the clerical reactionaries of Europe', Lears comments, the model anti-modernists Henry and Brooks Adams, 'merged capitalist, usurer, and International Jew'; Henry Adams 'embraced the medieval soldier as the emblem of a culture undefiled by commerce or its allegedly Jewish agents'.[60] The anti-Semitic Santayana remarked that 'America in those days made an exile and a foreigner of every native who had a temperament at all like mine'.[61] Henry Adams insisted, 'in a society of Jews and brokers, I have no place'.[62] Two aspects of this patrician anti-Semitism can be found in Adams: its extremism of expression, and the self-disgust that often accompanied it. The inability to conceive of oneself as anything other than American was complicated by a parallel inability to live with oneself as an American, because of what America had become: 'I [am] different from all my contemporaries ... I detest them and everything connected with them, and I live only and solely with the hope of seeing their demise, with all their accursed Judaism'; and again: 'The Jew has penetrated my soul. I see him – or her – everywhere.'[63] Adams found his anti-Semitism mandated by the Virgin herself: 'she disliked Jews, and rarely neglected a chance to maltreat them'.[64] This hatred could turn back on itself; both Adams and his fellow Brahmin James Russell Lowell would sometimes liken themselves to Jews.[65] The parallels between his life and that of a typical Jew were, for Adams, both grotesque and instructive: 'Had he [Adams] been born in Jerusalem under the shadow of the Temple and circumcised in the Synagogue by his uncle the high priest, under the name of Israel Cohen, he would scarcely have been more distinctly branded, and not much more heavily handicapped.'[66] This form of American anti-Semitism was a European reflex: the American fear of what he is, or is becoming, and the snob variant that was part of being 'European'. The difference between the nativist, and the élite, anti-Semitic traditions in America is that while the first railed against Europe as the home of the Jews,[67] the latter admired it as the home of anti-Semitism.

French anti-Semitism differed both from the attenuated anti-Semitism of England and the problematical, derivative anti-Semitism of America. It was ideological, it had a newspaper, it had a National Anti-Semitic League and local anti-Semitic clubs, and it had a series of 'causes' of which the Dreyfus Affair was simply the best known.[68] English anti-Semites tried to exploit the Marconi affair to similar effect, but failed: its one literary monument was Kipling's poem 'Gehazi', admired by Eliot as 'passionate invective rising to real eloquence'.[69] Though both France and England had once expelled their Jews, only France developed a modern anti-Semitism that was innovative and highly dangerous. If asked in the 1890s to name the country most dangerous for Jews, one might easily have said France.[70] French anti-Semitism was an intensely literary affair. The collapse of a bank believed to be owned by Jews prompted works by Zola, Maupassant, and Bourget; French anti-Semitic literature of the period comprised countless titles.[71] In France, anti-Semitism was a game played for high stakes. It ran counter to revolutionary ideology, as it did in America. Yet while 1776 founded a nation, 1789 merely established a political form that remained controversial. Repudiating Jews did not entail repudiating the nation. Anti-Semitism was not 'un-French'. French Jews benefited more obviously from 1789 than did American Jews from 1776. With characteristic overstatement, Edouard-Adolphe Drumont insisted that only the Jews profited from the Revolution.[72] Though Jews were not prominent in either the Enlightenment or the Revolution,[73] the cause of Jewish emancipation became identified with the tendencies that both represented.

France has had several particularly brilliant expositors of anti-Semitism; in Britain and the United States, by contrast, anti-Semites have tended to be intellectually marginal.[74] Drumont, author of the huge bestseller *La France juive*, was one of the greatest publicists of nineteenth-century France. A campaigning anti-Semite, he understood 'how to fashion repeated lies into received ideas'.[75] Many French anti-Semites were also intellectuals, and some, like Maurice Barrès (the 'bard of anti-Semitism'[76]), had Jewish friends and admirers. Indeed, prominent Jews were received at the literary salon of Alphonse Daudet, an anti-Semite of rare verbal violence.[77] And one French Jew, Julien Benda, went even further, advancing anti-Semitism's intellectual pretensions in *Belphegor*. Though for Eliot this book exemplified the 'modern tendency ... toward ... classicism' and represented 'an almost final statement of the attitude of contemporary society to art and the artist',[78] it is a repetitive and anti-Semitic attack on irrationalism in art and culture, and on the regime of the Parisian salons. In it Benda asks, 'Whence arises this frantic effort of present French society to force intellectual work into the realm of emotion?' He denies first that the pressure comes from 'the presence of the Jews', but then, by a distinction between the 'severe, moralistic Jew' and the Jew 'who is always greedy for sensation', reinstates this anti-Semitic formulation.[79] This second kind of Jew dominates modern society and is responsible for its present state. Though Benda feebly observes that such Jews could not corrupt the unwilling, it is easy for the anti-Semite to respond that this is because Jewish influence has sapped the ability of society to resist. The Jews in Eliot's anti-Semitic poetry accord with Benda's analysis: they are 'greedy for sensation', and, unless contained, their influence would be malign.

While such a formulation risks understating the international nature of anti-Semitic discourse (an esperanto of hate), its historical continuities, and the relevance of other contexts, I propose to regard Eliot's anti-Semitism as a novel derivative of the traditions outlined above. One notes the patrician, anti-modernist strain within American anti-Semitism, the ideological, vanguard nature of French anti-Semitism, and the politically undeveloped nature of English anti-Semitism. American anti-Semitism fed Eliot's desire to identify himself with Europe, and therefore with European prejudices. France showed Eliot that a vigorous anti-Semitism could yet be thoroughly literary, and that it was compatible with cordial, salon relations with Jews.[80] English anti-Semitism made available to Eliot a literary tradition in which the adverse characterisation of Jews was consistent with creative work of the highest quality. In addition, it encouraged an hostility toward Jews that was largely free from fear of them.

An anti-Semitism of contempt

There are anti-Semites whose fantasies of Jewish power are such that, if attributed to Jews, they would seem like nothing so much as immoderate boasts.[81] These Jew-haters mix their hostility with awe, and every triumph over their enemy is won against the odds. They are thrilled by imagined terrors. They regard themselves as combatants locked in a struggle of uncertain outcome. For such anti-Semites, even when Jews do not attack, they menace. Their very bodies are weapons: 'the dirty Jewish talon';[82] 'instead of fingers, [the Jew's hands] were furnished with long, brown, bony talons';[83] 'He had ... eyes that had grown keen ... from long searching amid muck and debris; and claw-like prehensile fingers';[84] 'the great grapple-hook of Shylock' gathering in 'the profits of labor'.[85] To be in the power of such men! To be – literally – in their clutches! What frissons of pleasurable dread these passages must have provoked. This was not for Eliot. There is comic bathos in these lines:

> Rachel *née* Rabinovitch
> Tears at the grapes with murderous

... 'paws'. The last word, after a minuscule pause, surprises both because eight syllables are expected rather than nine and because 'claws' is the obvious concluding word. It is a small piece of literary and anti-Semitic bravado. Eliot plays a variation on an anti-Semitic topos and mocks the fears of fainter hearted anti-Semites.

Bleistein is even more of a joke, with his 'saggy bending of the knees / And elbows, with the palms turned out'. Imagine the figure – thick legs, stretched suit too big, the gestures placatory and ingratiating. By avoiding a physiognomic caricature, the poem gives new life to an old gibe. It is Eliot's version of Al Jolson. Most anti-Semites imagine Jewish hands, when not clawing, as clasped: 'Whenever he talked with anybody, he was always rubbing his hands together, as if he was washing them in invisible soap and water.'[86] This self-abasing gesture conceals a manoeuvre that is calculating and sinister. Sometimes, too, there was both clawing and clasping: '[the Jew] rubbed his claw-like hands'.[87] Bleistein, by contrast, makes himself vulnerable and ridiculous by his gesture. He is defenceless. He is a Jew of the kind who are scorned, rather than feared, by anti-Semites. Eliot draws from the vocabulary of those anti-Semites who are confident in their distaste of Jews: 'to shrug one's shoulders and turn up the palms of one's hands in a typically Jewish gesture'.[88] In the poem's fourth stanza, Bleistein is a comic figure, comparable to the Jewish pedlars mimicked by music hall artists in the last century.[89]

By placing the Jew underwater in 'Burbank' and 'Dirge', Eliot makes literal the commercial cliché of bankruptcy: Bleistein has 'gone under'.[90] The name itself represents a financial diminishing; 'Bleistein' means 'Leadstone', Eliot's substitute for the more expected 'Goldstein'.[91] This name, along with 'Silverstein', 'Loanstein', 'Diamondstein', and 'Sparklestein', routinely appeared in American business jokes of the period.[92] Jews were meant to be at home in commerce; Eliot's 'Bleistein' is not. 'Dirge' rehearses, with Bleistein's gold teeth, the supposed fondness of Jews for that precious metal. 'The Golden International' was an anti-Semitic slogan of the late nineteenth century; other anti-Semites execrated the Jews' 'sempiternal gold pursuit'[93] and their love of gold for its own sake;[94] 'we Jews', boasts Kipling's Kadmiel, 'know how the earth's gold moves'.[95] Yet Bleistein lacks even a pauper's grave. Eliot's anti-Semitic poems imagine Jews as business failures; they depart from those fantasies of Jewish commercial power that excite more conventional anti-Semites. Thus, Gerontion's landlord, a person who might be thought to be of consequence, is cut down to size. He is misshapen and cowering, and thus an object of contempt. Two exceptions, however, should be acknowledged. First, and trivially, the name of Klipstein, or 'Klip', in *Sweeney Agonistes*, evokes the anti-Semitic charge that Jews were responsible for the debasement of the currency.[96] Secondly, there is a Jew of considerable wealth in 'A Cooking Egg', but before Alfred Mond, the exemplar of imagined Jewish plutocratic power, the poem displays an ironic deference free of fear or anxiety. A comparison with Pound is instructive. He fulminated against Jewish wealth, raging against the Rothschilds in Canto LII, – passages blacked out as if in a frenzy of destructive execration.[97] He repeatedly attacked Mond in his Italian radio broadcasts, and in Canto CIV wrote: 'Mond killed the *English Review*'.[98]

Likewise, Eliot's underwater anti-Semitism inverts the commoner sort: 'the low Jew ... appears like one of those monsters of the deep in whose form Shakespeare saw humanity preying on itself'.[99] Sheva, the supererogatorily good Jew of Richard Cumberland's *The Jew* defends himself by declaring 'I am no shark to prey upon mankind'.[100] Eliot's Jew, however, is prey, not predator. He is also a victim of the sea, not its master. He is not Lord of Kipling's 'Secret River of Gold' (*Puck of Pook's Hill*).[101] While this belongs to 'Israel', Bleistein belongs to the sea. Eliot's poetry returns Jews to the primeval mire, as if they were the oldest and most degraded members of creation, the first, but least honoured, of the species. The 'jew' in 'Gerontion' is 'spawned', and Bleistein, whose 'lustreless protrusive eye / Stares from the protozoic slime' in 'Burbank', is picked over by crabs in 'Dirge'.

Though Jews are degraded in Eliot's work, they are rarely the agents of others' degradation. In 'Burbank', Bleistein does not corrupt Burbank, nor does Sir Ferdinand corrupt Princess Volupine. Even *After Strange Gods*, which worries about the social effects of Jewish doubt, does not propose that Jews conspire to achieve their hostile ends. Jews may be subversive, but they are not the wreckers imagined by other anti-Semites: 'There's a wrecking class of Jews – international – and it is at work in India, and there in Paris, in London, a little everywhere'.[102] Even in 'Burbank' the menace of the Jews, undercut by their contemptibleness, is not quite the Jewish Menace. Eliot was aware of the realities of international finance, and he respected commercial enterprise. He was a banker, and then a businessman. ('I seem', remarked Eliot, 'to be a petty usurer in a world manipulated largely by big usurers.'[103]) In 'A Cooking Egg', the jibe at Mond, politician, newspaper proprietor, and industrialist, is not a jibe at the phantom of Jewish domination. If the poem identifies Jews with capital, it does not thereby identify capital with Jews. For Sir Thomas Browne, modern Jews were 'that contemptible and degenerate issue of Jacob',[104] and Eliot, at least in his poetry, may be taken to agree. In consequence, a distinction has to be drawn between his anti-Semitism and the misogyny of much of his poetry.

Anti-Semitism, misogyny, racism

In late nineteenth-century Europe, misogyny and anti-Semitism were frequent partners. This alliance represented a reaction, in part, to a certain coincidence in demand by women and Jews for emancipation,[105] especially in Germany and Austria.[106] In France, it was proposed that 'the Semitic race' had the weakness of women, who were emotional, superstitious, rapacious, and catlike.[107] One may trace this overlaying of hatred of women onto hatred of Jews in certain leading personalities of the period. For example, it has been commented of Proudhon: 'Obsession with women, obsession with Jews: everything suggests that the subjection of one and the expulsion of the other took on a related significance for [him].'[108] Taking stock of the relation between misogyny and anti-Semitism, Wyndham Lewis noted that the same arguments could be deployed against anti-feminists and anti-Semites;[109] he himself, in an earlier book, had described Jews as '[f]eminine, and in many ways very unpleasant'.[110] This historical linkage was part of the context out of which Eliot wrote.[111]

For example, anti-Semitism and misogyny were connected in the thinking of Otto Weininger, the fin de siècle Viennese critic. He was, for a time, something of a culture hero. In his doctrine, woman represents sensuality, and is thus ethically inferior to man. The Jew, representing scepticism and the spirit of imitation, is equally inferior to the Aryan. Indeed the Jew is the lowest form of womanhood. The Jewish male possesses female characteristics. He partakes of the 'feminine idea', a wanton urge to sexual gratification. He is the source of all irrationality and chaos. The feminine–chaotic principle of non-being is embodied in the Jewish race and, above all, in Jewish culture. The Jew is a degenerate woman.[112] Weininger 'treated Jews and women', remarked Freud, 'with equal hostility and over-whelmed them with the same insults'.[113] Does Eliot do likewise?

Women may be found near Jews in Eliot's work, proximities not wholly without significance. In certain cases, Jews achieve a relation with women that is denied to others. Princess Volupine entertains Klein with a deference withheld from Burbank, and in 'Eeldrop and Appleplex', Scheherezade is imagined in the company of a Jewish stockbroker.[114] In each instance the relation diminishes the female; the Jewish figure domesticating her. Elsewhere, they are companions in the same sleazy setting: the 'jew' squats near the 'old woman' in 'Gerontion', and the assembly in 'Sweeney Among the Nightingales' is gathered in the one low dive. In other places it is a matter of proximity of appearance in the text. In early drafts of *The Waste Land* Fresca defecates and then goes to bed to write to a friend about Lady Kleinwurm.[115] These seem to be similarly ignoble activities, the text hinting at an association between Jews and sewers (on which 'Burbank' elaborates), and between Jews and the act of defecation (which 'Gerontion''s squatting Jew evokes). ('Going to write to the Jews' was slang in France for announcing a trip to the lavatory;[116] in anti-Semitic lore Jews had a special smell, the 'foetor judaicus', which 'like the smell of the sewers … was the smell of shit';[117] when his domestic plumbing crashed Delmore Schwartz told friends that he was to be known as 'Squatter Schwartz' in honour of 'Uncle Tom's great lines' in 'Gerontion'.[118]) Jews and women are often rendered as non-reflective, indeed barely sentient creatures. They are animal-like in their rank corporeality, in Pound's phrases 'an element … A biological process' (Canto XXIX). The Jewish and the female combine in Rachel *née* Rabinovitch, Lady Kleinwurm, and Lady Katzegg, whose names are ugly and betray their owners. Unlike Prufrock's women, however, these Jews do not intimidate. By making women Jewish, Eliot overcame them; by subordinating them to Jews, he diminished them.

The theme of 'Ode', an *Ara Vos Prec* poem, is a disastrous honeymoon, and the humiliating, desperate coupling of virgins.[119] It combines the confessional with the clichéd, allying the most personal with the least original. Its inability to unite the intimate with the allusive is the sign of its failure. It is alternately exaggeratedly recondite and nakedly direct. Its intrusive use of the third person singular is a defensive, self-concealing gesture. Following a stanza of considerable opacity, these lines follow, full of dismay and pained recoil at the sex act:

> When the bridegroom smoothed his hair
> There was blood upon the bed.

The smoothing of the hair is an attempt to recover a poise lost by participation in an act which the poem's protagonist is at pains to forget. Intensifying, and complicating, this expression of a primitive male horror of female blood is the awareness that the man was the certain cause of its appearance. This is only half-acknowledged. One wants to read the first line as 'when the bridegroom smoothed his hair *he noticed that* there was blood etc.,' because the literal alternatives – either that the combing of the hair caused the blood on the bed, or that the bridegroom had nothing to do with the blood on the bed – are each implausible. But such a reading would be a mistake. The poem is trapped between a refusal to admit responsibility for the blood, and an inability to deny it. Hence the 'When', which inaugurates lines that seek to substitute for a causal relation an innocent contiguity – as if the combing of the hair had nothing to do with the blood on the bed.

Though both 'Ode' and 'Gerontion' thus potently evoke fears of pollution by exposure to disease or human waste, these fears are to be distinguished. It is only in 'Ode' that the person at risk is author of that risk; it is only in 'Gerontion' that the polluting agent can be quarantined. 'Ode' is a poem about the complicities of men and women; 'Gerontion', in passing, glances at what separates Christians from Jews. If it is protested that the 'jew' is Gerontion's landlord, and that this is a relationship of sorts, consider the following: though landlord, the 'jew' is forced to squat on a window sill, separate from, and in conditions presumably inferior to, his 'tenant'. While Jews can be driven away, women cannot. Indeed, they may exercise a sordid fascination. Hence the prostitutes that appear in Eliot's poetry: Sweeney's 'nightingales', the 'woman / Who hesitates towards you in the light of the door' ('Rhapsody on a Windy Night'), and 'The ladies of the corridor' ('Sweeney Erect'). Women are also importunate, difficult to shake off: '"Perhaps you can write to me." / My self-possession flares up for a second; / *This* is as I had reckoned' ('Portrait of a Lady'); 'My nerves are bad tonight. Stay with me. Yes, bad. Stay with me. / Speak to me. Why do you never speak. Speak' ('A Game of Chess').

Again, in 'Burbank' as in 'Ode' there is a shrouding of slogan-simple lines in adjacent lines that are thick with allusions and obscurities of expression. The revulsion leaps off the page:

> The rats are underneath the piles.
> The jew is underneath the lot.

These two lines pivot 'Burbank', just as the lines quoted above pivot 'Ode'. In each case at the centre of the poem, the lines are startling in the clarity of their accusations. The 'protozoic slime', which is Bleistein's element, and the blood, which is the woman's element, similarly impugn that composed integrity of the body[120] which in 'Ode' the bridegroom ineffectually seeks to restore by the smoothing of his hair. (Self-control is a project that the narrator of Eliot's prose poem 'Hysteria' pursues to the point of madness. Hence the deliberateness of his account, his sensitivity to what is patently 'background' – white noise intrusively loud – and the menacing nature of the woman's body. These are signs of an overstraining towards an elusive composure.) But again, note the differences. While 'Burbank' embraces all Jews in its epigrammatic, summary injustice, 'Ode' dramatises an incident involving one man and one woman. The lines in 'Burbank' represent a departure from narrative. The lines in 'Ode', by contrast, are an emergence into narrative from allusive obscurities of mood. At the point that 'Burbank' breaks off from its tale of tourists in Venice to make a statement about Jews in general, 'Ode' breaks into its tale of virginal disaster.

While Eliot may imagine a relation with women, he cannot with Jews. And while the outcome of his contest with women may not be predicted and is full of hazards, his contest with Jews, though fraught with revulsion, is predictably triumphant. The poetry is engaged in a struggle with women. It wins a series of victories over Jews. The difference between misogyny and anti-Semitism in Eliot's poetry is thus the difference between a war glimpsed in the course of hostilities, and a landscape in the wake of a pogrom. The contempt for women, and for Jews, has distinct resonances. The scornful 'In the room the women come and go / Talking of Michelangelo' is a defensive gesture in a poem dramatising male panic about women. Jews, by contrast, do not induce panic in Eliot. The poet's contemplation of a Jew would not lead to a poem such as 'Hysteria'. Jews don't rattle the poet; women do. Women's eyes can 'fix you in a formulated phrase', Jews' eyes cannot. They are sightless or dull ('Dirge', 'Burbank'), 'red-eyed'[121] or 'heavy' ('A Cooking Egg', 'Sweeney Among the Nightingales'). This makes Eliot's literary anti-Semitism relatively unusual. Compare, for example, the Jewish Rosedale of Edith Wharton's *The House of Mirth*. He has eyes that give him 'the air of appraising people as if they were bric-a-brac'. The 'steady gaze of his small stock-taking eyes' makes the novel's heroine 'feel herself no more than some superfine human merchandise'.[122] Rosedale has powers that Bleistein lacks. Eliot's Jews cannot shame with their gaze, and 'shame' in this context 'is [the] feeling... of being an object; that is, of *recognising myself* in this degraded, fixed, and dependent being which I am for the Other'.[123] But it is Jews who are lifeless in Eliot's poetry, not the objects of their gaze. Thus while Eliot's poetry delightedly conceives of Jews as dead, it broods on the killing of women. In 'Dirge' Bleistein is already dead, but in 'Portrait of a Lady' and 'Hysteria' the death or dismemberment of a woman becomes an imaginative project to be pursued. The difference marks, among other things, a choice made by Eliot within anti-Semitism.

'Murders', remarks Peter Ackroyd, 'always seem to have fascinated' Eliot; one adds, 'particularly the murders of women'. Eliot once went to a fancy dress party dressed as Dr Crippen. On another occasion he praised the *Daily Mail*'s callous reporting of the Edith Thompson case.[124] 'Eeldrop and Appleplex' makes an existential hero of a 'man [who] murders his mistress'.[125] 'Elegy', which Eliot dropped from *The Waste Land*, is about an 'injur'd bride' restored to life by a dream 'as in a tale by Poe'.[126] 'The Death of the Duchess', another deleted poem, pairs 'husband' and 'victim' with 'wife' and 'sacrificial knife'.[127] *The Family Reunion* examines the conscience of a man who wished his wife dead and whose wife has drowned,[128] though whether the one is the cause of the other is left unclear; the discontinuity between his horror at the death and his responsibility for it parallels that in 'Ode'. In *Sweeney Agonistes* Sweeney talks about a man he knew who had done 'a girl in'; he hadn't been caught, and visited Sweeney from time to time (but Sweeney himself might be the murderer). These 'ferocious fantasies about female defeat'[129] parallel other such fantasies in the literature of Modernism.

The contemplation of murder is often a defensive strategy. In 'Portrait of a Lady', the speaker diminishes his fears by fantasising the death of the Lady ('what if she should die some afternoon'). Its instability of mood is established at once by the contrast between the epigraph, which quotes lines of brutal humour from *The Jew of Malta*, and its opening lines, which evoke the cloistered pathos of 'Juliet's tomb'. Eliot's work also betrays a sadomasochistic fascination with the erotics of murder and rape. In the unpublished 'The Love Song of St Sebastian', a woman is strangled by her lover: 'I should love you the more because I had mangled you / And because you were no longer beautiful / To anyone but me.'[130] In 'The Death of St Narcissus', the saint imagines himself to be 'a young girl / Caught in the woods by a drunken old man'. Eliot invokes another rape in *The Waste Land*: 'Philomel, by the barbarous king / So rudely forced' ('A Game of Chess'). The poem then returns to the phrase, as if brooding on it, in 'The Fire Sermon': 'So rudely forc'd / Tereu'. It is only in the case of the martyrdom of Celia in *The Cocktail Party*, which is comparable to the death of Thomas Becket in *Murder in the Cathedral*, that Eliot is wholly able to disengage his visions of female death from his misogyny. Celia's death does not derive from Sweeney's conviction that 'Any man has to, needs to, wants to / Once in a lifetime, do a girl in'.[131] Men, however, don't have it all their own way. There are poems of Eliot's that acknowledge a certain comic or sinister strength: think of 'Aunt Helen', 'Cousin Nancy', and indeed *The Waste Land*. 'Sweeney Among the Nightingales' conjures powerfully with the murder of Agamemnon.

Misogyny is a hatred, fear or contempt of women deriving from an adverse and false conception of them as a sex, and anti-Semitism likewise is a hatred, fear or contempt of Jews deriving from an adverse and false conception of them as a people. Hatred, fear, and contempt are versions of an hostility that derive from perceived positions of equality, subordination, and mastery, respectively. Eliot's misogyny accented the fear, while his anti-Semitism accented the contempt. In consequence, women lose some of their power in Eliot's poetry when represented in an anti-Semitic context. While Eliot's women are not to be found exclusively within a misogynistic context ('Marina', 'La Figlia Che Piange'), Eliot's Jews are those of an anti-Semite's. His accounts of women are predicated on the inescapability of involvement with them; not so with Jews. For this reason the violence of Eliot's poetry towards women is different to its violence towards Jews.

So Eliot's difficulties with Jews and women are not to be collapsed into a generalised hostility towards an undifferentiated 'Other'. They are not merely two versions of a larger heterophobia. Likewise, Eliot's racism, which also has its specific provenance. Thus: 'the differences here [in Virginia], with no difference of language or race to support them, have had to survive the immense pressure towards monotony exerted by ... industrial expansion'.[132] This bland, imperturbable passage from *After Strange Gods* overlooks the entire Black population of the South ('no difference of... race'). It becomes visible in 'The Dry Salvages' only at the price of its life:

> Time the destroyer is time the preserver,
> Like the river with its cargo of dead negroes, cows and chicken coops,
> The bitter apple and the bite in the apple.

These 'negroes',[133] part of the river's flotsam and jetsam, lack the gentle, somnolent grace of the drifting figures in Eliot's underwater seascapes. Without censure the lines invoke the heritage of a commercial ('cargo') slave culture. This racism of prose and poetry amounts to the adoption of the Confederate cause.[134] So, in *I'll Take My Stand* – a volume of essays published in 1930 by a group of Southern intellectuals, and very important to the Eliot of *After Strange Gods*[135] – Robert Penn Warren observed that for many in the South 'the negroes' were regarded as 'a dead and inarticulate mass in the commonwealth'.[136] These are Eliot's 'negroes'.'Women', 'jews', and 'negroes' are not interchangeably 'alien' in his work. They are, respectively, intimidating, sightless, and transparent; their deaths are respectively longed for, delighted in, and noted without emotion. To adapt a phrase of Hegel, ignoring these distinctions is to palm off the notion of the 'Other' as the night in which all cows are grey.[137]

A literary anti-Semitism

Anti-Semitism had certain uses for Eliot. In *After Strange Gods*, for example, the disparaging of 'free-thinking Jews' has tactical value, establishing Eliot's credentials as an intellectual with an audience that otherwise might be suspicious of him. Dismissing Jewish intellectuals allows the adjective to attract the opprobrium more usually directed at the noun.[138] One may find here, perhaps, an element of suppressed identification. Karl Miller has suggested that 'Eliot was his own Jew, that the Jew could serve him both as a type of the distressed human being and as a figure for some distressing part of his nature – wandering, free-thinking, heretical, frightful'.[139] I think this goes too far. At most the identification, which was never sympathetic, was not with Jews themselves but with certain supposed aspects of their condition. Thorstein Veblen proposed of 'the gifted Jew' that 'it is by loss of allegiance, or at the best by force of a divided allegiance, to the people of his origin, that he finds himself in the vanguard of modern inquiry'.[140] This was written in 1919, precisely the time at which Eliot might be taken to have reached a similar conclusion about the gifted American. 'A Song for Simeon' may be said to articulate through the Jewish Simeon just that longing for faith (and the difficulties in embracing it) that is characteristic of much of Eliot's post-*Ara Vos Prec* poetry. The modern Jew is one instance of the alienated artist; the New Testament Jew is one instance of the divided man of faith. Eliot may have glimpsed similarities between his own circumstances and the circumstances of some kinds of Jews. In 'A Song for Simeon', this recognition has a confessional quality. More typically, as in *After Strange Gods*, it is tacit and antagonistic. Eliot no more belonged in Virginia than did any free-thinking Jew whom he would have wished to exclude. But if Eliot himself thus spoke to his Virginian audience as an outsider, he was at least a 'Yankee' of distinguished parentage and education, unlike Jews of indeterminate origin and schooling. While his hostility toward Jews may thus contain an element of self-disgust, it is also the means by which that same self-disgust is kept in check. Perhaps the violence done to Jews in his poetry is prompted by a recoil from just this sense of shared circumstances. The violence is extreme. In 'Dirge' a dead 'jew' is assaulted; 'Gerontion' lists with relish the disfigurements of a squatting and leprous 'jew'. Jackson Lears has characterised Eliot as an anti-modernist Modernist 'resolving to search for faith even while accepting the knowledge which erodes it, resigning himself to the insoluble contradictions in his own psyche'.[141] This misses the violence with which Eliot wrestles with just these contradictions; excluding the 'free-thinking Jew', for example, was a device by which Eliot could refuse 'the knowledge which erodes' faith.

Anti-Semitism also provided the means by which Eliot was able to exploit further a characteristic tension in his work between the speculative, or elaborative, and the summarising, or apodictic. His prose typically is discursive, punctuated by epigrammatic judgments. There are occasions, however, when speculations that do not lead to any conclusion are interrupted by statements that admit of no challenge. In *After Strange Gods*, for example, Eliot posits an orthodoxy that he then labours, but fails, to define; he is able, however, to despatch Jews in an aside. It is a moment of relief in the lectures and a sign of their flawed nature. The speculative lapses into the digressive and the apodictic becomes the dogmatic. This tension between the elaborative and the summary also characterises much of Eliot's poetry up to *The Waste Land*. 'Portrait of a Lady', for example, is an instance of a Jamesian art of reflexive characterisation. The slighter 'Mr. Apollinax' and 'Cousin Nancy' are instances of a Theophrastan art of verbal caricature.[142] Consciousness may be simplified into automatism (Sweeney of the Quatrains) or divided into competing, incompatible perspectives (*The Waste Land*). 'Prufrock' combines the Jamesian with the Theophrastan. Its summary way with the 'women [who] come and go' is to be contrasted with its open-ended elaboration of an elusive and subtle mind, the poem's narrative voice. 'Prufrock' also protests against precisely such dismissive, bracketing judgments: '[t]he eyes that fix you in a formulated phrase'. It is a divided poem that is also divided against itself.

Anti-Semitism helped Eliot push this tension to its limits; 'Gerontion' is an extreme version of 'Prufrock'. A single mind divides; a representative Jew is captured in a few malign phrases. In this poem the 'speculative' is detached from a single, directing consciousness, while the 'summarising' fixes not one person or even a group, but an entire people. Jews can be summarised in a sentence, expelled with a verbal gesture. They represent the allure of certain knowledge and can be encompassed by hostile caricature. They may be pictured 'sprawling on a pin'. 'Burbank' is about both the elusiveness of Venice and the ready accessibility of Bleistein. While the city defeats representation, the 'jew' submits to the poet's libel. 'A Cooking Egg' both resists narrative logic and submits to the logic of anti-Semitism. While the poem cannot be reduced to a resolvable riddle, its hostility to Jews is instantly recognisable. Sir Alfred Mond is 'fix[ed] in a formulated phrase'. Likewise, the anti-Semitism of 'Sweeney Among the Nightingales'. Whatever its interpretive obscurities, we *do* know that the man with a golden grin is a Jew – one who conforms to that anti-Semitic caricature which pictures Jews' mouths as stuffed with gold fillings. There is a risk of losing the poem's anti-Semitism in its larger equivocations. To do so would be a failure in literary criticism.

Anti-Semitic discourse is semantically thick;[143] its 'Jew' is 'a conceptually overloaded entity'.[144] It can provide topics for a poet's imagination. Eliot's anti-Semitic poems wittily compress multiple anti-Semitic libels in a few phrases. This is their scandal, even though the poems are not merely scandalous.[145] They embrace anti-Semitism's contradictory imaginings of Jews as both powerful and feeble, plutocratic and indigent, international and ghettoised. These poems are charged with malevolent meaning and thereby conform to Eliot's description of Symbolism as 'the tendency of the word to mean as much as possible ... to mean as many things as possible'.[146] Anti-Semitic discourse comprises a stockroom of commonplaces and clichés about Jews, discovered and adopted anew by each generation of anti-Semites. Unlike, however, the many anti-Semites I quote below (who do not merit, by their utter unoriginality, individual attribution), Eliot did not merely take over but actually enlivened these fatigued topoi.[147] Indeed, he played variations on them with virtuosity comparable to the skill with which poets of the Latin Middle Ages adopted the topics of late Antiquity.[148] I have already examined one such topic: 'Jewish hands'. In the chapters that follow I examine others: 'the Jewish *femme fatale*', 'the leprosy of the Jews', and 'Jewish scepticism'. So while Eliot's Jews, in their ugly immutability, are an anti-Semite's, they are the creations of an anti-Semite of rare imaginative power. Critics who miss this underestimate Eliot. He doesn't just 'take over' the 'old conventions' of literary anti-Semitism;[149] he exploits these conventions to fresh and disturbing effect. Bleistein and Klein, for example, are not mere 'literary grotesques comparable to the portraits of Sweeney and Grishkin';[150] one should not seek to contrast the intricacy of Eliot's poetry with the vulgarity of its occasional anti-Semitism. The Jew-despising poems of *Ara Vos Prec* are themselves intricately anti-Semitic. Anti-Semitism need not obstruct or impede art. Very occasionally, as in Eliot's case, it is positively empowering.

Eliot's anti-Semitic poetry should be read as an assertion of the literary fitness of anti-Semitism. I take these poems to be among the most vigorous such assertions in the language since *The Merchant of Venice*. There have been others, mostly undistinguished save for a handful of novels, some of which equivocate in their anti-Semitism. The principal themes of these works were taken up by Eliot. The theme of Jewish wealth (*The Jew of Malta*, Trollope's *The Way We Live Now*) is alluded to in 'Burbank' (Sir Ferdinand Klein) and 'A Cooking Egg' (Sir Alfred Mond). The rivalry between a Jewish and a non-Jewish woman (Rebecca and Rowena for Ivanhoe) is mockingly inverted in 'Burbank' (Burbank and Sir Ferdinand Klein for Princess Volupine). The daughter's repudiation of her father's faith (*The Jew of Malta*, *The Merchant of Venice*, and, a variation on this theme, Maria Edgeworth's *Harrington*) is echoed by 'Rachel *née* Rabinovitch'. The sinister, predatory Jew (Defoe's *Roxana*, *Oliver Twist*; indeed a staple character of eighteenth- and nineteenth-century novels[151]) reappears, etiolated, in 'Gerontion'. 'Burbank' and 'Gerontion' both honour *The Merchant of Venice*, the one by its Venetian location ('On the Rialto once'), the other by the line 'the jew squats on the window sill' which alludes to Pope's 'ev'ry child hates Shylock, tho' his soul / Still sits at squat, and peeps not from its hole'.[152] These are instances of the engagement of Eliot's 'talent' with 'tradition'.

It was an engagement resisted by young poets indebted to his work: 'Job squats awkwardly upon his ashpit, / Scraping himself with blunted occam razors / He sharpened once to shave the Absolute';[153] 'The filthy Jew of Malta is spilling water from the hall-bucket'.[154] The first passage is from a poem by Auden, the second is from an effort by Tom Driberg. Auden's Biblical Jew and Driberg's Marlovian Jew represent each poet's attempt to remain loyal to the Eliotic precedent while also keeping faith with their repugnance at a poetry of Jew-baiting. When others sought to imitate that baiting they failed, as in these lines of Osbert Sitwell's: 'Mrs Freudenthal, in furs, / From Brioche dreams to mild surprise / Awakes';[155] and these lines of Edith Sitwell's: 'Lady Bamburgher airs / That foul plague-spot / Her romantic heart'.[156] Neither of these efforts has Eliot's venomous energy. After Eliot, literary references to Jews reverted to the clichéd or the honorific. Keith Douglas's 'he must navigate along the wild / cosmos, as the Jew wanders the world'[157] is an instance of the former; Auden's 'In Memory of Sigmund Freud', 'An important Jew who died in exile',[158] is the best instance I know of the latter. Eliot drew on, and exhausted (temporarily, at least), the poetic reserves of anti-Semitism.

This enterprise of Eliot's – the exploitation of anti-Semitic discourse – is an inseparable part of his greater literary undertaking. Exclude the anti-Semitic poems and one damages the integrity of *Ara Vos Prec*. Its silent Jews are part of that company of the mute that fills the book. The carnality of Klein's relation with Volupine is in keeping with the other sordid pairings and low venues in the poem's companion pieces. Eliot's doctrine of levels of consciousness,[159] separating the visionary from the unaware in his plays, had a specifically anti-Semitic application both in *Sweeney Agonistes* and in 'Burbank', 'Gerontion', and those others poems in which Jews are stolidly or malevolently dumb or otherwise insensate. Indeed, the sightlessness of these Jews is but one aspect of that preoccupation with sight evident in Eliot's poetry. The free-thinking Jews of Eliot's prose are important characters in those dramas of scepticism and affirm-ation, and of alienation and commitment, which underlie Eliot's cultural inquiries. One needs to have read *After Strange Gods* if one is to understand the place of both 'Tradition and the Individual Talent' and *Notes* in Eliot's work. One needs to have read *Sweeney Agonistes* if one is to gauge the extent of Eliot's descent into literary safety in his post-war plays. 'Gerontion' is the terminus at which the project represented by the early dramatic monologues ends and the further project represented by *The Waste Land* begins. And what is the reworking of anti-Semitic topoi, but one collective instance of that larger project of the reworking of the topoi of European literature that Eliot's œuvre may, in one aspect, be said to represent? Think, for example, of the great names that throng the poems of *Prufrock and other observations*; think, too, of the notes to *The Waste Land*; think of 'Ash Wednesday"'s way with the idealisations of medieval love poetry. Harold Bloom defines a topos as 'the place from which the voice of the dead breaks through'.[160] He means it metaphorically, but in 'A Song for Simeon' and 'Little Gidding' the dead do speak, as Eliot animates the topoi of the Jew acknowledging his obsolescence, and the poet receiving instruction from his master.

Christianity and anti-Semitism

When challenged with evidence of his anti-Semitism Eliot, overlook-ing that his anti-Semitic poems were written before his conversion, would protest that he was a Christian and therefore not an anti-Semite.[161] Eliot once said that he had *never* been an anti-Semite: 'It seems to me unfortunate that persons give that term such a broad and ill-defined definition.' He would respond, he said, to attacks 'if... responsible and sober'. Eliot added, 'it is a terrible slander on a man. And they do not know... that in the eyes of the Church, to be anti-Semitic is a sin.'[162]

Christian anti-Semitism emerged during the founding moments of Christianity itself. In John's Gospel, where the Jews are the opponents of Jesus[163] and the word 'jew' is a term of abuse,[164] Jesus addresses the

Pharisees, 'You are of your father the devil' (8:44). The Church Fathers built upon this new and potent form of Jew-hatred.[165] Modern anti-Semites draw much of their vocabulary from these Christian polemicists against the Jews. St John Chrysostom, for example, a master of anti-Jewish invective,[166] held the Jews to be a source of pollution and defilement; they were 'the pest of the universe'.[167] 'If the Jewish rites are holy and venerable', he reasoned, 'our way of life must be false.'[168] A patristic *adversus Judaeos* tradition flourished for several centuries.[169] Generations of anti-Semites have admired Luther's diatribe *Concerning the Jews and Their Lies*.[170] Many forms of persecution were either introduced or sponsored by Church institutions: the burning of the Talmud; forcible conversion; denigratory badges; petty, and not so petty, restrictions on Jewish communal life; public debates designed to humiliate Jewish men of learning; compulsory attendance at sermons. Indeed, there was substantial continuity between canonical and Nazi anti-Semitic measures prior to the implementation of the 'Final Solution'.[171] All this, and much else, derived from what Robert Wistrich has termed the ideological warfare waged by the Church against the Synagogue.[172]

Thus did the institutional defamation of Jews lead to, and justify, their institutional oppression. Individual clerics encouraged violence against Jews. When a fourth-century Christian mob, led by a bishop, burned certain Mesopotamian synagogues, St Ambrose defended their action.[173] The first medieval massacres of Jews were incited by clerical preaching, and the murderous bands were sometimes led by priests.[174] The massacres of the First Crusade were frightful. Dominican and Franciscan friars actively promoted anti-Jewish hatred among the laity of medieval Western Christendom;[175] they were responsible for a new and violent kind of Christian anti-Semitism, advocating Christian Europe's purging of its Jewish population. It is no surprise, then, that the political anti-Semitism of the nineteenth and twentieth centuries benefited from Christian support. In the United States Christian anti-Semitism was a primary cause of political discrimination against Jews.[176] The French Dominican, Hippolyte Gayraud, was an advocate in the nineteenth-century Christian Democratic movement of what he termed 'Christian anti-Semitism', declaring that 'a convinced Christian is by nature a practising anti-Semite'.[177] In late nineteenth-century Germany and Austria, the Protestant Church played a prominent part in anti-Semitic politics.[178] Practising Christians were directly involved in the Nazi extermination programme.[179] Indeed, Christian theologians have questioned Christianity's 'moral credib[ility]',[180] given its historical anti-Semitism. To Eliot's likely response that 'we must not confound the history of a Church with its spiritual meaning', one can give Eliot's own retort that 'a Church is to be judged by its intellectual fruits'.[181] Anti-Semitism is one of those fruits.

Eliot thus overlooked: the prevalence of anti-Semitism in the institutional history of the Christian Church; the provocation to Christian theology of Jewish survival;[182] assumptions that Judaism has been superseded by Christianity, and that Christian ethical values are superior to those of Judaism;[183] the injury to Jews caused by the Christian appropriation and reinterpretation of their scriptures and the misinterpretation of their history.[184] His self-defence was an implausible syllogism: Christians are not anti-Semites; I am a Christian; therefore I am not an anti-Semite. By identifying a practice as a vice one does not demonstrate thereby that one is free of it. Eliot elides the following statements: 'anti-Semitism is incompatible with a perfect Christian faith', and 'anti-Semitism is not possible in my Christian faith'. The denial by anti-Semites of their anti-Semitism is so routine that this denial has itself become one of the incidents of anti-Semitic discourse. They deny that they are anti-Semites instead of repudiating their anti-Semitism. 'No one literate enough to have heard the word', remarked Orwell, 'ever admits to being guilty of anti-Semitism'.[185]

ELIOT'S ANTI-SEMITISM, AND THE ANTI-SEMITISM OF HIS TIMES (AND OUR OWN)

Recognising that Eliot's anti-Semitism in its separate elements was unoriginal, can lead to the exculpatory judgment that it was typical of its time. Furthermore, given that anti-Semitism was 'in the air',[186] and that the literature of the period was unavoidably contaminated by it, is not a study of 'Burbank' by reference to its anti-Semitism the least illuminating way of proceeding – examining only what it shares with other works of the period, instead of what distinguishes it from them? William Empson, discussing the 'rejected passages of Jew-baiting' in the pre-Pound draft of *The Waste Land* commented: 'I am not inclined to pull a long face about this. A writer had better rise above the ideas of his time, but one should not take offence if he doesn't.'[187] Empson, not the object of the baiting, was altogether too brisk. His breezy shrug was inadequate to the provocation of 'Dirge'. He also assumed, without demonstration, that Eliot's anti-Semitism was no more than that of his time. Eliot simply failed to avoid the quotidian prejudices of the 1920s. This is a more critical lapse in judgment. Eliot's anti-Semitism was creative. It cannot be dismissed as mere repetition. Eliot did 'rise above' the anti-Semitism of his time, though not in the way Empson proposed. Eliot did so by putting that anti-Semitism to imaginative use. Indeed, as I seek to demonstrate in the following chapters, his poetry is one of anti-Semitism's few literary triumphs.

T. S. Matthews, who knew Eliot quite well, argued that because Eliot's times were anti-Semitic, his anti-Semitism should be forgiven. It was unavoidable. The culpable anti-Semites are those who choose to be hostile to Jews; those others, who merely 'reflect' the anti-Semitism of their milieu, should not be judged harshly.[188] Yet anti-Semitism is a social prejudice. As a group phenomenon it is not an appropriate case in which to plead moral safety in numbers. Widespread wickedness does not make individual evil less reprehensible. Writing an anti-Semitic poem does not reflect the anti-Semitism of the times; it enlarges it, adding to the sum of its instances. Eliot's work contributed to the anti-Semitism of his times.

The remarks of Matthews and Empson imply a distinction between 'timeless' and 'timebound' elements in Eliot's work. The appeal to the anti-Semitism of the times becomes one means by which this distinction is drawn, thereby detaching the permanent from the ephemeral, the valuable from the trivial, and ultimately the poetry from the anti-Semitism. This distinction, in any event inherently implausible, goes wrong when applied to Eliot's anti-Semitic poetry, which is made out of anti-Semitic materials. Ignore the anti-Semitism and the poetry itself disappears. Furthermore, anti-Semitism is no more to be restricted to the interwar period than is Christianity: indeed, anti-Semitism has the longer history. To assert that Eliot's poetry merely reflected the anti-Semitism of the times is as fatuous as asserting that his poetry merely reflected the Christianity of the times. Eliot's poetry engages creatively with both. In the prefatory paragraph to *The Waste Land*'s notes, a distinction is drawn: 'To another work of anthropology I am indebted in general, one which has *influenced* our generation profoundly; I mean *The Golden Bough*: I have *used* especially two volumes...' (my italics). Eliot knew better than to write that his poem was 'influenced' by Frazer. This would make too passive a thing of the creative process. *The Waste Land* is not a poem shaped by the influence of *The Golden Bough*; it is a poem composed by a man who has used that work for his artistic purposes. Eliot puts anthropology to work in *The Waste Land*; in 'Gerontion' he puts anti-Semitism to work.

There is a modern variant of the case made by Matthews and Empson. In its weak form it distinguishes between two ways of reading texts. The first reads a literary work as exemplifying discursive practices or ideologies; the second reads it as engaged in processes that render them problematical. The former is 'symptomatic', the latter 'critical' reading. The one considers a text in its 'documentary', the other in its 'work-like' aspect.[189] The assumption, common to deconstructionist endeavours but not limited to them, that literary works undo the arguments that they appear to articulate, is at the root of this line of reasoning.[190] Reading 'symptomatically' is, in the strong version of this case, a misreading. It mistakes subversion for endorsement. I dissent. Eliot's anti-Semitic poetry eludes the categories of both the 'symptomatic' and the 'critical'. It neither simply reproduces, nor cunningly undermines, anti-Semitism. What it does is to exploit anti-Semitism for its effects, and thus comprises a virtuoso display of what anti-Semitism can bring to the making of poems. This poetry is too inventive to be dismissed as merely reproductive of quotidian anti-Semitism. It is too faithful to that anti-Semitism to be praised as craftily or even inadvertently subversive of it. It composes creative variations on what has been described as the anti-Jewish polemic.[191]

With greater effort Empson and Matthews could have made a fuller case. Such a case would, by more detailed contextual study, contend that there is nothing in Eliot's work that is not found elsewhere in the anti-Semitism of the times. But demonstrating the close complicity of Eliot's work with the regularities of anti-Semitic discourse would defeat its larger purpose. Instead of proving that Eliot merely reflected anti-Semitic times, it would reveal him to be an anti-Semite. Eliot's work would become exemplary of anti-Semitism. The anti-Semitic context would then do more than just shed light on a poem such as 'Burbank'; it would explain it. Text would become continuous with context. The exposition of anti-Semitism would aid the elucidation of the poem; the exposition of the poem would aid the elucidation of anti-Semitism. If, as David Perkins has commented, 'historical contextualism tends to suppress critical intelligence',[192] it also suppresses *moral* intelligence, by partially relieving writers of responsibility for their work.

Anti-Semitism is not an universal sickness. Hostility to Jews has often been countered by vigorous, sometimes heroic interventions by others on their behalf. Of the examples that could be cited, those relating to the Holocaust are among the most striking. Thus one cannot assert unqualifiedly of any period that it was anti-Semitic. When Jews have been attacked, there have been others willing to defend them; when they have been calumniated, others have challenged their slanderers;[193] when, by a pervasive sentiment of exclusion, they have been kept at a distance, there have been those who have not flinched from welcoming them; when they have been demonised in novels and plays, there have been others who have striven either to represent them fairly or to keep them out when convention demanded a Jewish villain. In addition, there have always been many indifferent both to Jews and their antagonists. Anti-Semitism has rarely had an entirely free run: Jews have fought back, numerous non-Jews by their side. They have often won. Even discounting the massive counter-example of Joyce,[194] within the interwar literary culture of England there were many who were untouched by anti-Semitism, either neutral or in degrees philo-Semitic. E. M. Forster, for example, refused social contact with anti-Semites; for him, anti-Semitism was 'now [1939] the worst and most shocking of all things'.[195] John Middleton Murry condemned 'the subtle degradation of anti-Semitism'.[196] In 1939 Aldous Huxley arranged to get some Jewish children out of Germany and con-tributed to their education.[197] Even if one conceded that the dominant literary spirit was hostile to Jews – think of Belloc and Chesterton, Pound and Wyndham Lewis, Woolf,[198] Brooke,[199] Campbell,[200] Greene,[201] and (just as importantly) of minor writers such as Mary Butts[202] – it does not follow that anti-Semitism was of a strength to compel adherence.

Excusing anti-Semitism because it was typical of the times is often accompanied by the assertion that the anti-Semitism was itself not especially injurious. Of Eliot specifically, it is argued that his anti-Semitism should not be judged in the light of the Nazi variant. Eliot's anti-Semitism was representative, and representatively mild. Orwell, for example, commented that though one could find 'antisemitic remarks' in Eliot's 'early work', 'who didn't say such things at the time?'[203] 1934, he said, was the critical year; this was when the 'persecutions began'. It is as if anti-Semitism lost its innocence when Hitler came to power. He has 'paled the memory', Emmanuel Levinas has remarked, 'of the Jewish blood spilled before 1933–45'.[204] According to Orwell what would now 'be called' anti-Semitic was not so styled at the time. The Holocaust provokes the condemnation of work that does not deserve such censure if examined in the context of its first publication. Yet Eliot's anti-Semitism survived the Holocaust; he both affirmed it by the reprinting of his poems, and enlarged its scope by his remarks in *Notes* on 'culture contact' between Jews and Christians.

These are issues that call for nuanced judgment. Describing the anti-Semitism of 'Gerontion' as 'fascistic'[205] (as one Eliot critic has), demonstrates both the need for, and the difficulty in exercising, such judgment. Modern discussions of Eliot's anti-Semitism inevitably take place in the shadow of the death camps; 'anti-Semitic opinion can [now] scarcely be dissociated from the image of charnel houses', remarks Alain Finkielkraut.[206] Does this distort what one thinks about anti-Semitism in particular cases? Ricks argues correctly that it is wrong to 'mak[e] the murderous extremity of anti-Semitism synonymous with or coterminous with prejudice' (though he ignores the extent to which 'prejudice' enables 'murder').[207] The contention that the anti-Semitism of novels and poems is continuous with the anti-Semitism of legislative discrimination and social exclusion invites the further connection that both in turn are continuous with the anti-Semitism of systematic murder, a deeply unpalatable conclusion. Joseph Chiari, defending Eliot, insisted that 'one must not judge a few verbal irresponsibilities of sixty years ago by the scorching light of Auschwitz, Dachau or Belsen'.[208] What, then, was being done to Jews when Eliot's anti-Semitic poetry was first published? The record was a bloody one, full of recent disasters. Pogroms during the October Revolution and the ensuing civil war left 75,000 Jews dead.[209] In the months before Germany's defeat anti-Semitic organisations terrorised the Jewish communities of Berlin and Munich. Anti-Jewish riots swept Bavaria and a major pogrom occurred in Lemberg in 1919. When the Munich Soviet was crushed all foreign-born Jews were expelled.[210] These were rehearsals for that part of the Holocaust transacted outside the death camps. Any informed person of goodwill would have known enough then about Jewish ordeals to be aware of the capabilities of anti-Semitism.

Certainly, readers of *After Strange Gods* in 1934 would have had to struggle to distinguish its anti-Semitic proposals from those that were already being implemented in Germany.[211] Harry Levin has thus regretted 'those Virginia lectures, ill-timed in 1933 and ill-placed at the university of Thomas Jefferson'.[212] But the prevalence of anti-Semitism is such that there is never a good time to be unfair to Jews – one is always contributing to existing hostility. It has never been safe to be an anti-Semite – safe for Jews, that is. At any point in Eliot's productive lifetime a case can be made for the bad timing of these lectures. Further, Levin's argument half-suggests that such views are defensible in the abstract, and objectionable only by virtue of the occasion of their expression, which is self-evidently false. Lastly, poems and essays have lives beyond the moment of their publication and their authors are responsible for them, and the uses to which they may reasonably be put.

It is tempting to characterise Eliot's anti-Semitic poetry in terms of modern calamities. With hindsight one can make that poetry more horrible, or more prophetic than it is. In 'To T. S. Eliot', Emanuel Litvinoff adopts Eliot's language to place himself with those other Jews trapped and then murdered in Europe:

> I am not one accepted in your parish.
> Bleistein is my relative and I share
> the protozoic slime of Shylock, a page
> in Stürmer, and, underneath the cities,
> a billet somewhat lower than the rats.
> Blood in the sewers. Pieces of our flesh
> float with the ordure on the Vistula.[213]

The poet identifies himself with the persecuted; by implication he identifies Eliot with the persecutors. Bleistein and Shylock consort with the horror-Jews of Goebbels's Nazi rag. Litvinoff gives Eliot's insults an historical gloss (I return to the poem at the end of chapter 6). Many Jews indeed had a rat's fate. In June 1938 a British official reported from Berlin that 'Jews have been hunted like rats in their homes'.[214] During the slaughters of 1942 Rumanian soldiers would shout 'rats! rats!' as they fired at Jewish families hiding in haystacks or bushes.[215] In Lvov a few Jews survived the war by hiding in the city's sewers. Around their legs unseen rats would scuttle, beaten off with clubs and stones; elsewhere an army of rats fed on the corpses of Jews tracked down and shot; the sewers were cold and wet, and reeked of excrement; like the 'jew' in 'Gerontion' these men and women developed sores and rashes; on one occasion they almost drowned as rainwater threatened to flood their cell, thereby exposing them to the risk of Bleistein's fate.[216] What is one to make of Eliot's anti-Semitic poetry holding such images in one's mind? It cannot be claimed of them that they forecast a certain Jewish predicament in Occupied Europe; nor did they call for Jews to be driven to such desperate extremes. They were neither prescient nor programmatic. Their offence is not so much that they contributed to the terror that drove real Jews into real sewers but that they enact a parallel terror, one of scorn and contempt, against their own, fictional Jews. The poems themselves are persecutory; if they specifically also contributed to Nazi persecutions, then that contribution was oblique and is difficult to calculate.

Of Modernism and anti-Semitism, and their connections, one has to ask: what can the history of an infamy have to do with the examination of a major twentieth-century literary movement? The one study entails condemnation, the other, endorsement. Approaching anti-Semitism from the perspective of Modernism risks trivialising the horror in contemporary Jewish history. Interpreting Modernism from the perspective of anti-Semitism seems both perverse and reductive. Examining either one by reference to the other would seem to guarantee that justice is done to neither. There are thus books on Eliot that pretend that he had nothing to say about Jews. Conversely, there are studies of anti-Semitism in which he will be cited without any acknowledgment that he was a poet or that the quoted passage is itself poetry of a high and challenging order.[217] If the former refine anti-Semitism out of existence, the latter distil the poetry they study into an anti-Semitic essence. Both thereby miss numerous points, among which is the trite one that while poems do not cease to be so merely because they articulate anti-Semitic themes, equally there is nothing about poetic language that is especially resistant to anti-Semitism.

Indeed, poems can enhance anti-Semitism, making it more attractive by demonstrating its compatibility with artistic expression; Chaucer's 'Prioress's Tale', for example, dignifies the blood libel.[218] And while one is more likely to err when analysing the anti-Semitism of a poem or a novel than that of a speech or a pamphlet, consider the following. An eleventh-century Moslem poet composes a long poem calling for the assassination of leading Jews.[219] A medieval German poet writes: 'Woe to the cowardly Jews, deaf / and wicked ... / It would be well to forbid / their heretical Talmud, / a false and ignoble book'.[220] During the New York teacher's strike of 1968, leading to Black–Jewish conflict, this poem is broadcast by a local radio station: 'Hey, Jew boy, with that yarmulke on your head / You pale faced Jew boy – I wish you were dead'.[221] In the language of American jurisprudence, these are 'fighting words' likely to lead to 'imminent lawless action';[222] the broadcaster's conduct amounted to 'free speech plus'.[223] If not stone-throwers, these poets are word-throwers.[224] They seek to provoke physical injury. Anti-Semitism is ever thus spilling over from 'hate speech' into 'murderous act'.[225] In his study of French racism Tzvetan Todorov observes that discourses are also events: they make acts possible, and then they make it possible for these acts to be accepted.[226] I would go further and add that discourses can incite acts; to assert otherwise would be to ignore their perlocutionary[227] aspect. Poetry can move readers to hate. Indeed, in recognition of this Gavin Ewart has added to his poem, 'Pogroms', the following postscript: 'It is not, and was not, my intention in this poem to arouse anti-Semitic feeling'.[228] To hold that art can only promote the good was once received wisdom, but now it simply looks like sentimentality. Eliot played a part in the discrediting of this view, which does not survive a reading of his anti-Semitic poetry.

'As individuals', Eliot observed, 'we find that our development depends upon the people whom we meet in the course of our lives. (These people include the authors whose books we read, and characters in works of fiction and history).'[229] And elsewhere: 'A writer ... may be in his effect either beneficial or pernicious. I am not sure that I have not had some pernicious influence myself'.[230] What then, in such a context, of Eliot's anti-Semitic poems? Though not incitements, they have the capacity to harm, and probably have done harm. They are likely to injure four types of reader. There is the Jew who is rebuffed by them; 'You called me a name', protested Hyam Plutzik in his poem 'For T. S. E. Only'.[231] There is the anti-Semite, whose moral imagination is further blunted by the confirmations that they offer to him of his hatred; indeed, they might even make him think well of himself. There is the reader, hitherto resistant to anti-Semitism, who is persuaded by the poems to think ill of Jews; their 'eloquence may set fire to [his] reason'.[232] And there is the reader whose indifference to the poems' anti-Semitism makes him complicit in it. Take Denis Donoghue: 'That [Eliot] is still accused of anti-

Semitism seems to me absurd: the charge is as specious as if I accused him, citing his reference to "Apeneck Sweeney", of being prejudiced against the Irish'.[233] If the Irish Donoghue – this is the implication – can rise above the odd barb, why can't the Jews? He doesn't care about the anti-Semitism, and is irritated that others do.[234] Eliot's anti-Semitic poems are in fact comparable to those other works of 'group libel' that have provoked controversy. Some have been burned, others banned; pressure has been applied on their publishers to withdraw them; their authors have been harried and threatened. Invariably, they have been defended with the aesthetic alibi,[235] which proposes that admissible restrictions on freedom of expression are *in*admissible in the context of artistic expression. As Martin Jay puts it, 'What would be libellous or offensive in everyday life', and thus liable to proscription, 'is granted a special dispensation' if it is regarded as art.[236] Yet partly because 'art speech' can also be 'hate speech' the alibi is now under attack. I do not wish to defend it here. In its categoric version it is indefensible. However, this does not amount to an argument for suppression. I censure; I do not wish to censor. In any event Eliot's anti-Semitic poems are integral to his oeuvre, an œuvre which is to be valued and preserved. That means the *whole* œuvre, a necessary consequence of the case against the tendency to dismiss these poems as marginal. In addition, the opportunities that they offer for the study of anti-Semitism, and the study of the capacities of poetry, together probably outweigh the damage that they can do. One can teach anti-Semitism from such texts; one can also teach poetry. One reads them, appalled, and impressed.

CHAPTER 2

'Gerontion', criticism, and the limits of the dramatic monologue

'GERONTION' (I)

The Jewish landlord in 'Gerontion' lacks a name and is barely a noun on the page: in the pre-1963 editions of Eliot's poetry, the initial letter of 'jew' was printed in the lower case. Gerontion too lacks a certain name. The title means 'little old man'. One assumes it is the narrator's name, but it need not be. The poem is not the 'Song of Gerontion'. Like the 'jew', Gerontion does not get much beyond the generic. His lament lacks pain, his regret lacks pathos, his reminiscences are detached from any history that could give them coherence. He has 'no ghosts'. He also has no home. The 'jew' owns a property in which he cannot live; Gerontion lives in a property that he does not own. The poem meditates on a radical dispossession of self. It begins by reflecting upon an absence of tenure and ends by exposing an absence of identity. Though 'Gerontion' purports to be a dramatic monologue, this is a deception. It is not at home in the form; it is in a kind of exile. There is neither revelation nor development, the poem withholding such possibilities. Its continuities are buffeted by random interventions and unanswered questions. Consecutive but unrelated sentences press it toward its conclusion in chaos and storm.

Though the poem has seven stanzas of uneven length, it is best divided into five sections.[1] Midway between the earlier unitary poems and the later serial works, 'Gerontion' hovers on the brink of formal divisions. The first section locates a speaker. It is about places and sensations, the elemental and the tactile. It identifies the geography of a house and its inhabitants. While this is the poem's *mise-en-scène*, positioning actor and furniture, the second section does not begin the action. Instead it mixes theology with random, personal recollections, matching the momentous intervention of God in history, misunderstood or unwitnessed, with sinister, insignificant memories of acquaintances in familiar postures. The two are linked by the recalling of a ritual of consumption, ambiguously both devotional and trivialising. The third section is a reflection on the second: perplexity following upon a revelation that did not happen. Apophthegmic counters, the furniture of a mind, are arranged, rearranged, and disordered. This mental furniture is in similar disarray to the furniture of the house that the first section lays out. It is a poem that begins with a man with both mind and body in disarray. The residence does not quite amount to a home, the sententiousness doesn't quite amount to wisdom. The fourth section addresses an unidentified auditor in a spirit of uneasy explanation, offering equivocal self-justification. This half-dialogue – neither self-examination nor direct address – is obscure and anguished. It is as urgent as the previous section is ponderous, as personal as the previous section is discursive. It marks a return to the tactile only to negate it. Robbed of a secure place in which either to live or to think, deprived even of the capacity for animal existence, Gerontion disintegrates, dividing into his thoughts. The fifth section defies prose reduction, 'delirium' being the key. The last lines announce the dissolution of the poem's form as dramatic monologue. The poem that opens 'Here *I* am' ends, indifferently singular and plural, thus: '*Tenants* of the house, / *Thoughts* of a dry brain in a dry season'.

While the poem's title promises the Prufrockian dramatising of a consciousness, the poem itself denies that promise, beginning with the epigraph. The quotation from *Measure for Measure* denies that life is separable into two periods, 'youth' and 'age'. Neither is actually experienced. They indivisibly comprise a single dream. The epigraph puts into question the meaning to be given to the title – if there is no distinction to be drawn between youth and age, then why does it matter that 'Gerontion' means 'little *old* man'? The privileges that are claimed for age are not to be granted. Just as 'little' diminishes Gerontion, so the epigraph undermines any claim to sagacity. The contrast that one might expect therefore between the mature and the callow is not made. 'Little old man': the name divided against itself ('little' mocking 'old'), the epigraph subverting the adjective ('old'), the poem dissolving the noun ('man').

The opening stanza, confirming the refusal to contrast past with present, gives it another twist. The old man is being read to by a boy: Gerontion lacks the wisdom to teach. He confesses to his inglorious past. Though his present condition is squalid, it is without the pathos of decline. Lacking the means of dignity, he also lacks consolatory memories. There is no bitterness because there is no loss. The Jewish landlord has his place in this pseudo-lapsarian scenario, one of Symbolism's imaginary landscapes.[2] Barely human, he is at home in Gerontion's half-life. The poem is not a complaint, and the Jew is not its villain. This is not a poetry of melodrama; it lacks the necessary energy and optimism. Gerontion does not bemoan the fate of heroes exploited, fleeced by money-lenders or dispossessed by landlords. The poem does not mourn the decline of greatness, but its impossibility. While Gerontion – who has not seen action – has sufficient poetic gift to render the weary obstinacy of armed combat, he does not thereby live it. In an extraordinary imagining, it is the passivity of conflict that he represents. The elements, fire ('hot'), water ('rain'), and earth ('marsh'), would have stolidly immobilised him. He would have been fought at and to a standstill.

The poem is constantly misunderstanding what it does not see, and noticing the misperceptions of others. Its achievement is to articulate chaos without thereby giving it order. It is a poem that keeps faith with the negative. Gerontion insistently questions – the poem is punctuated by interrogatives – but never answers. And while he argues, he never reasons. It is a querulous poem. It is also a poem written by someone who has deliberately done considerable violence to his narrative gifts. The vexing domesticity of the poem's opening scene has its humorous side. As Gerontion frets, he creates a precisely realised image of the irascibility and incapacities of old age. But this novelistic moment is ended by language with an entirely different purpose. Portents are mistaken for spectacles; that is, events which have significance because they refer to other events are mistakenly taken to be significant in themselves. The desire for signs is unsatisfied because those who seek them are blind to their appearance. The 'Word' is demoted to 'word', the second such demotion effected by the substitution of the lower-case initial letter for the upper-case: 'jew' is less than 'Jew' and 'word' is less than 'Word'. There is no revelation here, only a muting and a concealment. The poem is restless. It does not alight anywhere for long, and wherever it does rest, it does not find peace.

There are no children in this poem except the boy who reads to Gerontion, and he is not the little old man's son. The boy, the woman, and the Jew are no more kin to Gerontion than the goat coughing at night in the field overhead. In place of the reproductive ties of family there is isolation, and dependency. Gerontion, in a state of alienation without independence, needs the boy to read to him, the woman to cook for him, and the Jew to house him. But Gerontion himself is 'dry', he cannot reciprocate. The repetition of words makes its own point about sterility. There will be no celebration in this poem of the fecundity of language: 'rain', 'fought', 'house', are all repeated within the first seven lines. Synonyms are word-partners, and this is a poem about the impossibility of partnerships – between men and other men, men and women, men and children, man and God, the present and the past. It is a poem that details severances. Gerontion's relation, or non-relation, with the Jew is merely one instance among many such instances.

The poem diminishes hope to mere expectation, knowledge to mere experience. It is, indeed, a poem in a continuous motion of retreat. It flinches in protest from what it represents: a squatting Jew, a goat, excrement. These 'merds' are, ambiguously, both the Jew's and the goat's, either the waste of the animal or the waste of the person squatting on the window sill, the poem thereby rehearsing through this ambiguity that anti-Semitic figure who associates Jews with goats;[3] Pound described the Jew as the 'usurer's goat', proving thereby the persistence of anti-Semitism's most primitive phantasms.[4] 'Merds' are turds, the close rhyme bringing the latter irresistibly to mind when reading the former. The poem shies away from the English and takes refuge in the French equivalent. Though the words are given the same definition by the *Shorter Oxford English Dictionary*, it is only 'turd' that is prefaced by 'Not now in polite use.'

'Gerontion' degrades human creativity. Just as the Jew is 'spawned' in an estaminet, so 'Unnatural vices / Are fathered by our heroism', and 'the refusal propagates a fear'. 'Fathering' becomes a sinister, destructive force, 'propagating' the means by which a denial leads to a recoil. But these words are used only in their metaphoric sense. The literal use is withheld – it is not '*fathered* in some estaminet'. The Jew is not conceived by parents and delivered in a hospital or a home, but 'spawned' in a low, public place, a café. Of course it is hard to imagine anyone being delivered in such a place – this is part of the general sense of geographical dislocation that the poem practices on the reader. In the order of Biblical creation, 'spawning' points away from the pinnacle towards the base, moving

back from the evening of the sixth, to the morning of the fifth, day.
The passage breathes hate, the sibilants hissing scorn:

> the jew squats on the window sill, the owner,
> Spawned in some estaminet of Antwerp,
> Blistered in Brussels, patched and peeled in London.

There is both revulsion and contempt here. The word these other
words intimate is 'spit'. It is Shylock's bitter complaint: 'You call me
misbeliever, cut-throat dog, / And spet upon my Jewish gaberdine /
... / You ... did void your rheum on my beard'. It is also Antonio's
triumphant, mocking response: 'I am as like to call thee so again, /
To spet on thee again, to spurn thee too' (I. iii. 125–6). Gerontion,
Antonio's brother in his dependency on a Jew, rehearses that abuse.
Spitting at the Jew in this opening stanza is one of the few moments
of passion in a poem that is animated by despair and exasperation.
Pound, whose anti-Semitism has an exhortatory edge that Eliot's
lacks, put it more excitedly, spitting not on the Jews themselves but
on their fawners: 'Let us be done with Jews and Jobbery, / Let us
SPIT on those who fawn on the JEWS for their money'.[5]

Gerontion's 'jew' is ugly in full measure. Spawned, blistered,
patched and peeled, he emerges as if from the swamp, diseased and
disfigured. Jews are swamp-life, breeding in uncontrollable numbers,
the alarm of generations of anti-Semites: 'The Russian Jews have
multiplied in Germany like frogs.'[6] Stock-exchanges are 'great leech-
ponds in which the cold, slimy [Jewish] leeches ... swim around by
the thousand'.[7] 'The Jew ... is a kind of perpetual discharge, a flow
that it is impossible to stop. The great reservoirs of Semiticism pour
forth incessantly their stinking hordes ... who let fall vermin wherever
they pass and create a constant danger to public health.'[8] 'The
Hebrew ... is a swamp that absorbs a great part of the water that
passes through it';[9] '[the Jew] sucks, he swells up like the leech. He
absorbs without giving anything in compensation';[10] 'Of all the
creatures who have befouled the earth, the Jew is the slimiest.'[11]
Maurras raged: 'we find in [Rousseau] in almost equal measure the
criminal, the savage and the lunatic. Madness, savagery and crime,
the adventurer, fed on Jew-inspired revolt ... This wild subhuman
thing, this life-form scarce emerged from the ... swamp.'[12] The
swamp is also the place where protozoa – simple organisms – live and
breed. This is Bleistein's element: 'A lustreless protrusive eye /
Stares from the protozoic slime'. Protozoa have two relevant characteristics:

they are mostly microscopic, single-celled organisms, found wherever there is enough moisture to support active life, and they are agents of disease. They are simple and they are dangerous. Again, then, the double charge: Bleistein, submersed in the swamp, is both infected and liable to be contagious; likewise Gerontion's landlord, Jew-spawn. In a broadcast, Pound talked of 'Jew slime'.[13] In Canto LXXIV he abuses at length 'the spawn of the gt. Meyer Anselm', the Rothschild banking family. Yet to use 'spawn' of a person is not always defamatory. Seamus Heaney uses the word to create a more complex, and grieving, effect: 'Fishermen at Ballyshannon / Netted an infant last night / Along with the salmon. / An illegitimate spawning, / A small one thrown back / To the waters'.[14] The infant is a 'spawning' because it has been washed up with other spawned life; because its claim to life has been regarded as lightly as if it were spawn; and because life originated in the waters. Eliot's Jew is spawn because, like spawn, Jews are indistinguishable from each other; because, like fish (and rats), Jews were said to breed in great numbers; and because he is not quite human. In Heaney's poem, the word mourns a death. In Eliot's poem, as in Pound's, it is a jeer.

Only ostensibly human, this 'jew' bears the scars of a body at war with itself. Blistering is a symptom of smallpox, an easily transmitted virus, associated with overcrowding, such as might be found in a ghetto. One might 'patch' an ulcer – a blister that has burst – to cover areas of skin that are otherwise denuded and eroded, or 'peeled'. The repulsiveness of Jews was a commonplace to anti-Semites, one of whom declared 'his almost physical sense of repulsion against the Jew and his skin'.[15] Jews, it was said, had 'loathsome skin and scalp diseases' and 'lupus, trachoma, favus, eczema, and scurvy' were supposed to afflict them.[16] 'The contemporary Kike', one anti-Semite observed, 'appears to be the confluence of every form of hideousness in the world'.[17] Eliot's Jew belongs to this number. He is a mosaic of pustular eruptions, greying scars, and raw, inflamed skin. According to Sander Gilman, it was traditional to regard 'the skin of the Jew [as] marked by disease as a sign of divine displeasure'.[18] Jews have an 'unsightly countenance'[19]; medieval wisdom held that their 'malodorous sores and unique diseases' gave Jews Satan's smell.[20] In anti-Semitic lore Jews bore the mark of an ancestral crime: 'I did not separate the idea of a Jew from that of a man with a swarthy head, dull eyes, flat nose, large mouth... God had printed a stamp of reprobation on their foreheads';[21] 'A curse was laid upon the Jewish people ... all European Jews have eczema of the seat, all Asiatic Jews mange upon their heads, all African Jews boils on their legs, and American Jews a disease of the eyes, as a result of which they are disfigured and stupid';[22] '[Jewish refugees are] the filthy, rickety jetsam of humanity, bearing on their evil faces the stigmata of every physical and moral degeneration';[23] 'the lower-class foreign Jews are ugly, obese and waddlers'.[24] There is the familiar association of vice with ugliness: 'O Lord ... you were setting me before my own eyes so that I could see how sordid I was, how deformed and squalid, how tainted with sores and ulcers.'[25] It is as if St Augustine here gazed upon himself only to see Eliot's 'jew'.

The 'jew' is an intruder. He hovers outside the house, making unwelcome proprietary claims over it. Such a Jew was a familiar type in anti-Semitism's gallery: '[the Jew is a] sucking vampire [knocking] at the narrow-windowed house of the German farmer';[26] 'the German people feel ... that there is no room for them and their very competent Jewish minority in the same house'.[27] Compare Eliot's other Jew, similarly intruding through a window into a house, the gold-grinning vulgarian of 'Sweeney Among the Nightingales'. The intruder brought the risk of disease: '[Eastern Jews] bring us all kinds of diseases ... We must ... prohibit ... [them from] spread[ing] their lice and their blemishes. We must establish solid barriers at the borders.'[28] Such fears prompted panic legislation. In 1854 the canton of Basel prohibited citizens from admitting Jews into their houses, on penalty of a fine.[29] In 1882 German regulations were introduced requiring the delousing of Eastern Jews before entering the country; later, train carriages that had transported these immigrants were ordered steamed after every trip.[30] Jews are to be feared, but they are also to be despised. They are dangerous, and yet they are also feeble and degenerate: 'Their physical strength, their muscular power, has diminished in each generation ... The Jew is, moreover, often misshapen; few races have so many men who are deformed, disabled, or hunch-backed'.[31] Eliot's anti-Semitic imagination also responded to a turn-of-the-century preoccupation with the threat posed by Jewish refugees to the nation's health.[32]

The 'jew' is on the window sill both because he has been denied any more secure resting place and because he himself may thus deny his tenant peaceable possession of his house. He crouches because he is weak; Bleistein's 'saggy bending of the knees' betrays a similarly impaired posture. The faulty posture of Jews, and in particular their weak feet, is an anti-Semitic theme that became, according to Sander Gilman, 'part of the ... discourse about Jewish difference in the latter half of the nineteenth century'.[33] Eliot's account of the physical characteristics of Jews exploits this discourse, and is also continuous with certain contemporaneous eugenicist anxieties.[34] This squatting Jew, in his inability to find any permanent place of rest, is also Eliot's gesture toward that most fatigued of cultural clichés, the Wandering Jew.[35] He gives the cliché a malignant twist in 'Gerontion' and a comic twist in 'Burbank'. 'Chicago Semite Viennese' suggests labels on a travelling salesman's suitcase. 'The Jews', said the anti-Semitic Voltaire, 'are the biggest tramps who have ever soiled the face of the earth.'[36] They are, said the anti-Semitic Bossuet, 'a monstrous people, having neither hearth nor home, without a country and of all countries ... We see before our eyes the remains of their shipwreck.'[37]

It gets worse. There is a sinister hint of leprosy in 'Gerontion'. In its tuberculoid form this wasting disease forms stain-like lesions with raised, reddish patches that become insensitive to stimulus as they spread. Leprosy also causes the progressive withering and ultimate loss of the sufferer's limbs. Lepers, such as this 'jew', in the extremity of their affliction, are forced to squat because their legs will not support them. Stigmatising Jews as lepers is an ancient, persistent calumny.[38] Tacitus claimed that Jews abstained from pork 'in memory of their tribulations, as they themselves were once infected with the [leprosy] to which this creature is subject'.[39] A medieval version alleged that Jews and lepers conspired together to poison wells.[40] Though in more modern times Jews and lepers were related by analogy as two similarly pariah peoples, the literal identification of Jews as lepers persisted. So while Maurras referred to 'the Jewish, anarchist, leprosy',[41] Drumont claimed that '[the Jew] is subject to all the maladies caused by the corruption of the blood: scrofula, scurvy, scabies, dysentery ... and hereditary leprosy'.[42] Marx associated leprosy, Jews, and syphilis, in his description of his rival, Lassalle: 'Lazarus the leper is the prototype of the Jews and of Lazarus-Lassalle. But in our Lazarus, the leprosy lies in the brain. His illness was originally a badly cured case of syphilis'.[43] Kipling provided a recent precedent with 'Gehazi', an execration of Rufus Isaacs published in 1915. It represents the Jewish politician as a leper. Kipling repeated the libel in 'The Burden of Jerusalem', referring to the Pharaonic Jews as a 'plaguey multitude'.[44] Lepers are weak but dangerous, and they form separate communities. They are thus analogous to the Jews of an anti-Semitic imagination. Such an imagination routinely turns analogy into identity: Jews *become* lepers. Eliot reworked the calumny, repeated so often that it became not just an accusation but the way in which Jews were routinely characterised, and he incorporated it into one of his finest poems.

'Gerontion', a condensed instance of all these anti-Semitic themes, economically renders them in the image of the squatting Jew, perched on a window sill, in a state of precarious quarantine ('mankind has put the Jewish race in quarantine' said Chateaubriand[45]), kept apart because he is unclean, unwelcome even in the house that he owns, wretched yet monied. These lines are a horror picture, drawn with loathing. One recoils from them.

SOME JEWISH CRITICS

Certain Jewish critics have been reluctant to acknowledge that 'Gerontion' represents one instance of vilification in a body of work insulting to Jews. For example, in his 1947 essay on 'Gerontion', Wolf Mankowitz notices the poem's anti-Semitism only to the extent of sanctioning it: '[Gerontion's] condition ... is passive, unresistant to decay and dominated by a rootless, cosmopolitan culture'.[46] 'Rootless cosmopolitan' has a specific anti-Semitic resonance. Mankowitz substitutes Eliot's highly charged, economical lines with some slack phrases of his own. He will not put any distance between himself and the poem, reading it immanently. His essay is a study of what the poem sees, not what it says; he is the poem's spokesman rather than its interpreter. Given the date of its publication, his passivity would be unremarkable were it not that his self-advertising Jewishness elsewhere, ingratiating to a different audience, makes it embarrassing ('I am a forty-two-year-old Russian-Jewish-English-Scorpio professional free-lance writer. Need I say more?'[47]). He refuses to acknowledge the insult, thereby condoning it and displaying a demeaning absence of resentment toward its author. There is a small history to be written of Jewish critics' insensibility to the anti-Semitism of anti-Semitic works of literature. Léon Blum advised his fellow Jews that 'since, after all, their lives are secure and their existence is on the whole tolerable, [they should] cheerfully ignore these little [anti-Semitic] affronts to their pride or their interests. They are of such small importance in the life of an individual...

Above all, no complaints!'[48] Mankowitz tacitly adopts Blum's slogan: no complaints!

Gabriel Pearson does notice the anti-Semitism of 'Gerontion', but insists that it is part of a larger strategy aimed at all its readers: 'Eliot murmurs "merds", and we are insulted and exult in the dexterity of the insult.'[49] When he comes to consider the poem's opening lines, Pearson writes on behalf of an undivided readership:

One can scarcely avoid an impression of inflicted retaliations. Here is 'the jew' placarded, as owner, on an appositional sill, being spattered, degraded and mutilated. Like a veritable Elder of Zion he is made to exemplify the squalor he is accused of causing. Yet the attack is at the same time deftly distanced. The indefiniteness of 'some' is furthered by the allusive knowingness of 'estaminet'. The reader finds himself divided between levels of aggression and disdain which may turn out to be an attack on him.[50]

I question in this passage 'The reader' and 'may'; I would substitute 'The Jewish reader' and 'does'. The poem does not offend against all. Its offence is selective, the greater because it is discriminatory. In a strong judgment, Pearson describes 'Burbank' as a 'hate poem',[51] but he refuses to acknowledge that the poem's hatred is directed against Jews.

I propose that this unwillingness of many Jewish critics to take offence, indeed their studious overlooking of the insult, had a number of distinct causes. First, there was Eliot's authority: his work was constitutive of the critical discipline, indeed, of the critic's vocation as a modern intellectual. Secondly, some Jews identified themselves with Eliot's career. Thirdly, many sought to rebut, by practical demonstration, the then prevalent view that Jewish literary critics were incapable of interpreting literary works indebted to a Christian culture. Fourthly, to the extent that the anti-Semitism was recognised, one might also posit a proud if only implicit claim of superiority to the insult. (Ignoring its presence was a way of overcoming it.) Fifthly, literary criticism was inhibited by the doctrine that the reading of poetry required the suspension of one's beliefs.

I can take the first two of these causes together. I noted in chapter 1 Eliot's dominance of the literary scene. Karl Shapiro, a Jewish poet of great distinction, observed that the 'Literary Situation' was 'largely Eliot's invention' and that Eliot himself was 'untouchable'. Eliot was 'Modern Literature incarnate'.[52] To reject Eliot was to reject modern literature. 'The Jewish intellectual of my generation', wrote Leslie Fiedler, 'cannot disown [Eliot] without disowning an integral part of himself. He has been a profounder influence on a good many of us than the Baal Shem Tov or the author of Job. We are not willing to resign from Western culture.'[53] (This oblique allusion to Heine marks the distance that some Jews believed they had travelled in a century: no longer required to convert, they merely had to submit to insults.) Elsewhere Fiedler proposed 'a special affinity ... between this expatriate High Church anti-Semite, for whom the entry of Jews into gentile culture was a nightmare ... and certain free-thinking Jews who for a little while threatened to replace WASPs like him as spokesmen for their country and its culture'.[54] Irving Howe has recalled that he 'fell crazily in love' with Eliot, and though 'I knew he was a reactionary [I] didn't really care'.[55] Howe has also tried to explain the poet's particular appeal to the young Jewish intellectuals of New York: 'Reading Eliot's poetry a half-century ago I felt so strongly ... attuned to its inner vibrations that I had little desire to be critical, especially of what might be passed over as a few incidental lines of bigotry. With a supreme hauteur, Eliot had made the journey from provincial St Louis to cosmopolitan London. The New York writers could not match his hauteur, but perhaps they could negotiate a somewhat similar journey from Brooklyn or the Bronx to Manhattan.'[56] Not only did these writers seek to parallel Eliot's trajectory, many adopted Eliot as a way of negotiating their own passage from their origins: 'Jewish intellectuals like the Trillings', argued Alfred Kazin, 'saw with the eyes of great twentieth-century masters, Eliot, Yeats, Mann, who were conservative and even aristocratic.'[57] Conceding Eliot's anti-Semitism often meant embracing it: 'I realized that there was this anti-Semitism, but I was willing to accept it. I thought, "He isn't saying too much I haven't already observed among the Jews and disliked" ... [I] thought it referred to the side of Judaism [I] had come to dislike in the first generation Jews who had to subordinate everything in order to make some kind of economic base for themselves ... Eliot was the major influence on my life.'[58] And Cynthia Ozick: 'the handful of insults in the poetry – I swallowed down without protest ... [Eliot] was poetry incarnate, and poetry was what one lived for.'[59] As in America, so in England. For example, one scans in vain *The Jewish Review*, a short-lived periodical of the 1930s, for any critical reference to Eliot, even though most issues contained articles on literary anti-Semitism.[60]

As for the third cause, it is well known that English faculties in America were once especially hostile to Jewish applicants.[61] The best known instance of such anti-Semitism is Lionel Trilling's experience at Columbia.[62] An earlier instance in which the Jewish Ludwig Lewisohn was barred from Columbia and every other English faculty to which he applied, had a more typical conclusion.[63] Karl Shapiro referred to 'the lofty anti-Semitism of English professors'.[64] Take Yale for example: 'The most popular rationalization for the attitude that Jews had no place in the Yale English department was the conviction that Jews lacked the cultural and religious background necessary for teaching English literature, much of which derived its meaning from the New Testament.'[65] It was doubted whether a Jew could give a proper account of Browning's 'Easter-Day', which begins 'How very hard it is to be / A Christian'. 'If I am interested in Judaism', remarked Geoffrey Hartman, 'it is both because it is part of myself, as I have realized, and because I felt that the academy had excluded it to a surprising degree'.[66] Wayne C. Booth has recalled 'the widespread claims of only a few decades ago that Jews should not be professors of English because they could not grasp the spirit of a predominantly Christian literature'.[67] This anti-Semitism complemented the reverence for Eliot that was another characteristic of many English departments. Asked 'What was the atmosphere at Yale in the late 1950s?', Harold Bloom replied, 'An Anglo-Catholic nightmare. Everyone was on their knees to Mr T. S. Eliot.'[68] Eliot, a Christian poet, was considered to be beyond the reach of non-Christian readers. Jews who studied English literature found that they were studying enemy texts: 'We had to read and study these [anti-Semitic] poems and we had a teacher ... who would say ... "Well, of course, only a committed Christian could really understand Eliot's poetry." Tough luck on the rest of us, I suppose ... I had been taught to love all this stuff that actually had a place for me in it as a villain.'[69] This is no overstatement. One Eliot admirer enthused: 'from reading Eliot, a boy can have a dawning sense of the tradition of Christian culture in Europe ... the Christian faith alone can make something positive out of the suffering of life'.[70] Alfred Kazin exclaimed: 'How we squirm and strain to get into Eliot's City of God ... though he has barred us from it in advance!'[71]

Browning's 'Filippo Baldinucci on the Privilege of Burial' helps identify the fourth cause. A community of Jews, looking for land for a cemetery, find a corner of a field. The owner sells it to them, but places a portrait of the Virgin overlooking the site. The Jews ask for the portrait to be moved to face the road, not the graves. They offer to pay a further sum, and the owner takes 100 ducats. But he cheats them, hiring an artist to paint a crucifixion scene in its place. The Jews accuse the owner of fraud. He defends himself: he promised to remove the Virgin, he didn't undertake to leave the place empty. The next day the rabbi's son visits the artist's shop to buy the picture. It is to have its 'place among my rank and file / Of Ledas and what not – To be judged / Just as a picture!'[72] Thus an affront to Jewish sensibilities is neutralised, demoted from an anti-Semitic provocation to mere art, and hung among examples of greater art. In such company its sting has been drawn. No longer defiling a graveyard, it simply decorates a living-room. It has ceased to be a vexation to Jews and has become instead an object of contemplation for a connoisseur. I read this poem as a parable for Jewish readers of Eliot. The Jew can demonstrate his superiority to the insult by refusing to be offended, treating the provocation as an instance of the aesthetic. He does not shift it physically from field to room, he moves it conceptually from insult to art. Indeed, he insists upon it as art. Browning's poem revises an incident in *Harrington*. The exemplary Mr Montenero buys a picture of a Jew being tortured. What is his reason? '"To destroy it",' said Mr Montenero. And deliberately he took the picture out of the frame and cut it to pieces, repeating "to destroy it, my dear, and every record of cruelty and intolerance. So perish all that can keep alive feelings of hatred and vengeance between Jews and Christians!"'[73] The difference in treatment of the two pictures is to be explained by the intervening emergence of an ideology of the aesthetic that both privileges art and renders it harmless in appropriate institutional contexts. But to ignore art's power to offend means failing to take it seriously. One does not describe either a howitzer or a work of modern literature, remarked Trilling, without estimating how much damage it can do.[74] Such an oversight should be related to that defensive reflex by which a person assumes (or pretends to assume) that an insult directed at him was not intended to offend: 'In reading [*After Strange Gods*] one must possess a sense of humour. The work cannot be taken too seriously. It starts off wrong by introducing the Hitler racial theory ... It has been commented on frequently adversely ... and I pass it by.'[75] What begins with humour ends in embarrassed silence.

As if the challenge of Eliot's anti-Semitic work was not hard

enough for Jews to meet, many of his admirers were themselves guilty
of the crudest anti-Semitism: '[On 'Gerontion':] the modern world
is now "owned" and enslaved by the only proliferating element in it,
the international money power. The inhuman and sub-human
quality of that power is suggested in the words "squats" and
"spawned"';[76] '[Eliot, Pound, Lewis, and Joyce] abominated the
bastard forms of internationalism, but became good Europeans';[77]
'The jew is international, the scum of Europe and its landlord.'[78] Or
they were blandly neutral, when neutrality was wrong: '"the jew",
Eliot's symbol (in lower case) for those in Western culture who are
not integrated in place (a particular national tradition) or time (a
particular historical tradition)';[79] 'the aura of social criticism which
invests ['Burbank'] owed something to the general mood of
1918–19';[80] 'this Jewish landlord is truly, like all Jews, cosmopolitan';[81] 'The question whether "Burbank with a Baedeker" was
anti-Semitic is obviously not a pressing one.'[82] There was also
considerable ignorance: 'there has been a continual forward movement, from Judaism to Christianity and through the different
Christian reforms, away from graven images'.[83] One could compile a
sottisier of such statements. Jewish critics were expected to take them
in their stride.

Now for the fifth cause. That the reading of poetry requires the
suspension of one's beliefs was, for a time, literary criticism's common
sense. I. A. Richards formulated the principle dogmatically: 'the
question of belief or disbelief, in the intellectual sense, never arises
when we are reading well. If unfortunately it does arise, either
through the poet's fault or our own, we have for the moment ceased
to be reading poetry and have become astronomers, or theologians,
or moralists.' Or Jews, Richards might have added.[84] In its
application to Eliot's anti-Semitic poetry, this principle is aporetic.
One cannot overlook the anti-Semitism without missing the poetry
itself. But to acknowledge its anti-Semitism is, according to Richards,
to cease to read it *as* poetry. Now, once this acknowledgment is made,
the 'question of belief' must arise. Thus engagement with the
poetry's anti-Semitism would be, for Richards, both necessary and
disastrous: ignore it, and one is blind to the poetry; see it, and what
one sees are not poems but something else. The key that unlocks the
door of the room in which the treasure is kept also works the lever that
drops the treasure out of the room. Hence the irresolvable alternation.
One is compelled to acknowledge the poems' anti-Semitism in order

to read them whole, yet equally compelled to suppress one's consciousness of that anti-Semitism in order to read them as poems. Mankowitz's essay makes 'Gerontion' a casualty of just this inhibiting principle. Eliot was more independent. Taking Richards's hint that 'the question of belief' might arise through the fault of the poet, he condemned Shelley's ideas as childish, feeble, and untenable. Poetry does not have to accord with the reader's beliefs; it does, however, have to espouse beliefs that have some merit. They must be worthy of respect.[85] This opened the way for critics offended by Eliot's anti-Semitism to follow his precedent-establishing rejection of Shelley. They did not take it.

It was then and it still is difficult to write about Eliot's anti-Semitic poetry. One risks distorting the work, even defaming the man. When Jewish, one risks even more. One puts in jeopardy one's credentials as a critic. One can seem a philistine.[86] The partisan of one's people, one ceases, it could be said, to represent the unprejudiced reader; guilty of misreading poetry as if it were propaganda, one overlooks the literariness of the texts. Less a critic than a vigilante, intruding oneself into one's criticism, one fails Eliot's own test, 'to discipline [one's] personal prejudices and cranks...in the common pursuit of true judgment'.[87] Eliot observed: 'The end of the enjoyment of poetry is a pure contemplation from which all the accidents of personal emotion are removed.'[88] All critics aspire to this condition, 'perfect critics' achieve it. Reject the doctrine from which it derives and one condemns oneself to 'imperfection'. This is an essentially Kantian formulation ('the delight which determines the judgement of taste is independent of all interest'[89]) and it was mocked by Nietzsche in its original form thus: 'If our aestheticians never weary of asserting in Kant's favour that, under the spell of beauty, one can *even* view undraped female statues "without interest" one may laugh a little at their expense'. 'Pygmalion', he added, 'was *not* necessarily an "unaesthetic man".'[90] To which I would add: Mrs Millin was likewise not necessarily an unaesthetic woman. Anger can inform and even improve aesthetic judgment. It is true, however, that such judgments are especially difficult to get right, as assessments of Eliot's work by certain Jewish critics have demonstrated. These assessments have an embattled, even querulous tone.[91] Jews are familiar with this hazard and have made a joke of it. Write an essay on the giraffe, a class is instructed; Cohen submits 'The giraffe and the Jewish question'. Everything refers back to Jews, in neurotic imitation of an obsessional anti-Semitism.[92]

Delmore Schwartz, haunted – indeed, 'obsessed'[93] – by Eliot's anti-Semitism, could have written such essays, but didn't. Instead he confined to conversations and unpublished lectures his discourses on, so to speak, giraffes and Jews. He would speculate with friends about the origins of Eliot's anti-Semitism, proposing fantastic causes. The subject was prominent in his lectures at Princeton in 1949. When challenged, he would reply, as if parodying the charge against Jews by professors of English, 'You couldn't know what I'm talking about because you're not a Jew.'[94] A Jew may not be able to read 'Easter-Day', but only a Jew can read 'Burbank'. Yet, of the four essays Schwartz published on Eliot, only one raised the subject of Eliot's anti-Semitism, and then perversely: 'What we get when we look through the seventeen bound volumes [of *Criterion*] is a kind of charity of the intellect, and this issues, one must remember, from one who maintained that excessive tolerance is to be deprecated.'[95] Better to have said nothing at all, one might think, than to have referred obliquely to the anti-Semitic passage in *After Strange Gods* in the context of complimenting Eliot. When Pound's *Guide to Kulchur* was published, Schwartz wrote promptly to the author, resigning as an admirer;[96] but when earlier on Eliot had published *After Strange Gods*, all Schwartz was capable of was the private and essentially childish gesture of copying out the anti-Semitic passage in his notebook, substituting 'Anglo-Catholics' for 'Jews'.[97]

If Schwartz was exemplary of what once was, then Harold Bloom is exemplary of what now obtains. The first major critic in the English tradition wilfully to assert rather than sublimate his Judaism, Harold Bloom has challenged the Christian direction of English literary studies.[98] He declares himself, in conscious opposition to Eliot's own earlier declaration of allegiances, as 'a Jewish Gnostic, an academic, but a party or sect of one',[99] and has reminisced, 'If one's cultural position was Jewish, Liberal and Romantic, one was likely to start out with a certain lack of affection for Eliot's predominance.'[100] His 'war' against 'the abominable Eliot',[101] is one consequence of this stance, and has led Bloom to underestimate him. Another consequence is his refusal to concede the uniformly Christian nature of Western literature. He does not read Shakespeare as a Christian poet, and regards Marlowe as a 'mad hermeticist who hates Christianity'.[102] He regrets that 'the malign influence of T. S. Eliot still lingers on in most contemporary accounts of literary tradition'.[103] His books on Yeats and Stevens maintain a running polemic against 'Eliot and his school',[104] 'the age of Eliot, Auden and the new criticism',[105] 'Eliot and his followers'.[106] His criticism makes inventive use of kabbalistic categories, and draws on Freud, Scholem, Buber, and Luria. In opposition to Eliot's theory of 'mutually benign relations between tradition and individual talent',[107] he sets up a relation of subversive, resentful violence.[108] Eliot and Bloom are at one only in their willingness to house the literary with the spiritual. Bloom's *Agon*, with its chapters on Blake, Emerson, Whitman, Hart Crane, and the cultural prospects of American Jewry, has a unity comparable to Eliot's *For Lancelot Andrewes*, with its essays on Baudelaire, Middleton, and Bramhall.

As the example of Bloom indicates, Eliot's authority is diminished. Though others have taken his place, no single individual dominates. Certainly, his career is no longer exemplary; Jewish intellectuals do not now model their careers on Eliot's. Passing, often glib, references to Eliot's anti-Semitism are common in literary criticism, and even in fiction;[109] once invisible or tacitly approved, it is now familiar, and routinely condemned. Modern literary studies have grown sensitive to anti-Semitism and to certain aspects of Jewish culture; the fascinated engagement of French intellectuals with Judaism in the 1970s and 1980s[110] has had its impact in America, and even in England. One notes, for example, the interest in techniques of Midrashic interpretation, and in the Hebrew Scriptures, a 'turn to the Judaic';[111] the regard of Derrida, himself of Jewish origin, for Jews such as Levinas and Jabès, and indeed, the very extravagance of his claim that 'the situation of the Jew becomes exemplary of the situation of the poet, the man of speech and of writing';[112] the willingness of critics such as Geoffrey Hartman to make Jewish traditions both an object of reflection and a source of their own criticism; the high standing of Walter Benjamin, especially that aspect of his work disclosed by Gershom Scholem; the early essays of George Steiner, and the examination of literary responses to the Holocaust; the innumerable studies of the figure of the Jew in literature. What is left, and what still protects Eliot, is the New Critical reluctance to engage with what poems actually assert, and the deconstructionist refusal to accept that, sometimes at least, poems mean what they say: I discuss this in chapter 3. For the rest, one may conclude that most of the constraints that formerly inhibited Jews from reading Eliot's anti-Semitic poetry have fallen away. Though it is hard to understand the force of the inhibitions, I do not believe that the Jews who were silenced by them behaved dishonourably.[113]

They are open to criticism, however, when they mobilise their Jewishness to defend Eliot's anti-Semitism. Jeffrey Perl has done just this in his recent book on Eliot, *Skepticism and Modern Enmity*. Arguing that Eliot 'was a skeptic, whose politics and baptism might be viewed ... as the gestures of a dadaist against an avant-garde establishment',[114] Perl is silent on his anti-Semitic poetry, regards *After Strange Gods* as taking 'refuge in *parodistic* extremes',[115] and misdescribes, by implication, a pre-war passage about Chamberlain's Munich settlement as a post-war passage about the Holocaust.[116] Perl's work is apologetic, endorsing what it represents as Eliot's general stance. Could this endorsement, Perl asks, lead some to think that he is thereby 'apologiz[ing] for tyranny'? Such people 'will perhaps want to know', he says, that he is 'Jewish in religion, of the American mainstream in politics, and ... no longer understand[s] what "classicism" means'.[117] This avowal of Jewishness amounts to the claim that Perl is an expert on anti-Semitism. If he can acquit Eliot of anti-Semitism, when he might be expected to be fierce in censure, then Eliot must be innocent of the prejudice. Perl's conclusions must also thereby be free of any special pleading: as a Jew he can hold no brief for the ostensible anti-Semitism of part of Eliot's work. We are invited to suppose by his declaration that he is as keen as the next Jew to condemn an anti-Semite. This is a posture that has become commonplace in a certain kind of apologetics.[118]

'GERONTION' (2)

Why does anti-Semitism not find fuller expression in the poem? The visceral hostility to the Jew demonstrated in the poem's opening lines should have produced something more than the lines on the Jewish landlord. One might reasonably anticipate, and a prior reading of 'Burbank' would encourage one to expect, that these lines would open out onto a wider statement about Jewish financial oppression. Such an account would be consistent with the poem's relentless generalising, its epigrammatic impulse, which issues in the puzzling certainties 'Unnatural vices are fathered by our heroism' and 'Virtues are forced upon us by our impudent crimes'. The poem could as easily have produced something of the order of 'the jew is underneath the lot'. After all, such an anti-Semitic statement could find a place in any digest of pseudo-wisdom. Why did it not?

It is because 'Gerontion' resists all consoling visions, including the consolations of anti-Semitism, which is a casualty of its relentless negativity. Its despair is articulated with force and conviction. The words 'After such knowledge, what forgiveness?' are as much a challenge as a lament. Cut off from Christian revelation ('We would see a sign'), Gerontion is lost in a maze of reflections on history, fear, and human folly. The poem refuses an organising principle. It embraces neither religion nor any of its secular alternatives. Gerontion has faith neither in the divine nor in history. He is equally without piety and optimism; he believes neither in God nor progress. History, a woman, tricks, bemuses, offers false consolations: 'Gives too late / What's not believed in'. History cannot be trusted; God cannot be found. The poem refuses the explanations of both liberalism and the Church. There is neither human progress nor spiritual salvation, neither utopia nor heaven, only corridors and passages that are like mazes without end, and meaningless rituals that imitate without enacting the drama of communion ('To be eaten, to be divided, to be drunk'). History's gifts impoverish; God's presence is withheld.

The poem does not posit any third means of revelation. Instead, it lays out the intellectual bric-à-brac of a disordered mind of genius. It mixes categories, leaping from the specificities of the domestic to the symbolism of the 'wrath-bearing tree' and the 'tiger', and from the description of persons (Silvero, Hakagawa) to the personification of concepts (History). Reminiscence and moralising are mingled, the one sinister, the other perverse. It dislocates space, imagining a house with a field overhead that is also a house that is 'under a windy knob'. It conjures the final vertiginous vision of an elemental whirling, shuddering, fracturing, running tempest, blanking out all sense of place, of fixity. It dislocates time, referring indifferently to 'a dry month', 'the juvescence of the year', 'depraved May', 'the new year'. It is a poem where the timing is always wrong, too late, or too early, and opportunities are lost or premature. It jumbles time with space to the greater confusion of each, giving History 'cunning passages' and 'contrived corridors'. It subverts causality, making actions unpredictable, as in 'Virtues / Are forced upon us by our impudent crimes'. Hence the impossibility of a more amplified anti-

Semitism. Even though its consolations are false, anti-Semitism does reduce chaos to order, offering a framework of ideas that purport to render the opaque transparent, giving meaning to experiences of deprivation, misery, and impotence. It is the object of the poem to deny meaning to those experiences.

Eliot's essay on Blake offers a clue to Gerontion's philosophising. Eliot regarded Blake's elaborate symbolic constructs as incoherent, eccentric, and formless. His 'supernatural territories ... illustrate' his 'crankiness'. He was too self-reliant. His philosophy was his own, like his visions and his technique. It was made up of odds and ends like home-made furniture. His gift of hallucinated vision should have been, but was not, controlled by a respect for impersonal reason. His genius should have been, but was not, framed by accepted and traditional ideas. Such a framework would have rescued his work from the confusion of thought, emotion, and vision into which it falls.[119] 'Gerontion', similarly eccentric in its amalgamating of the symbolic and the anecdotal, in its displacements and its perversities, is like one of Blake's didactic and symbolic works, but much shorter and without the scaffolding of preambular argument and multiple, speaking personifications. Blake and Gerontion, though similarly susceptible to bogus esotery, are distinct in the manner of their pondering. Blake's visions are windy, turgid dramas; Gerontion's fretful questioning, of a kind identified by Eliot as 'confusion of thought, emotion and vision',[120] is worked up to a pitch of measured hysteria. 'Gerontion', written out of a strong impression of Blake's presence, both adopts and rejects his idiom and vision. It too lacks a framework of accepted and traditional ideas. Its paradoxes mock those of Blake. Against his emancipating proverbs the poem sets epigrams that speak of fear, anxiety, and dread. Compare, for example, 'Unnatural vices / Are fathered by our heroism' with Blake's 'Sooner murder an infant in its cradle than nurse unacted desires' or 'The wrath of the lion is the wisdom of God'.[121] The first paralyses courage with the threat of evil consequences, the second releases it from unnatural constraints. The portentous 'tears are shaken from the wrath-bearing tree' reads like a parody of Blake.[122] The account that the poem gives of History – capricious, unreliable, and deceitful – is contrary to the inspirational optimism of, say, Blake's 'The French Revolution'. The tiger in 'Gerontion', directly identified as Christ in contrast to Blake's, does not liberate but annihilates in lines that turn the communion rite on its head: 'The tiger springs in the new year. Us he devours'. Energy destroys, it does not free. 'Gerontion' controverts Blake with its misshapen Jew, who mocks the divinity of the human form squatting on the window sill:

> And all must love the human form,
> In heathen, turk, or jew;
> Where Mercy, Love and Pity dwell
> There God is dwelling too.[123]

Here the lower case marks the poet's benevolent indifference to the differences between Heathen, Turk, Jew, and Gentile. It is Mercy, Love, and Pity that merit the upper case and confer grace on all possessors of the human form. Eliot's use of the lower case is contrary to this, discriminating against the Jew rather than including him within a larger circle.

Why doesn't Gerontion cry 'The Jews are our misfortune'? It is because he refuses the banal clarity of anti-Semitism. Scorning the Jew, he dismisses him. He does not dwell on him, dwelling in his property. His is an anti-Semitism of exclusion, not of explanation. Gerontion does not need Jews to explain his present condition, it is enough that they are a part of it. Hence 'We would see a sign', the cry of the Pharisees against Jesus, does not become the occasion of anti-Semitism in the poem:

Then certain of the scribes and of the Pharisees answered, saying, Master, we would see a sign from thee. But he answered and said unto them, An evil and adulterous generation seeketh after a sign.[124]

'Gerontion' refuses all explanations. It hesitates between premature conclusions and no conclusion at all: 'We have not reached conclusion.' The prospects for a more thoroughgoing anti-Semitism are frustrated by the essentially vacuous nature of the poem, passionate with nonsense, a parody of the sagacious, parading maxims useless as guides for conduct or belief. These maxims, indeed, advance the poem's dissociative work; as propositions severed from discourse,[125] that is to say statements that are detached from any one speaker's perspective, they help 'Gerontion' break with the dramatic monologue form, interrupting the continuity of what might otherwise simply be read as Gerontion's speech. They prevent the poem from being read as the utterance of a man, however little and old. The unremitting negativity of the poem aborts the anti-Semitism, leaving it undeveloped and lifeless. It is not repudiated by the poem; it is one of its victims. 'Gerontion' lacks the coherence of either personal statement or impersonal argument. While its themes are larger than any one man's experiences could encompass, they are dispersed through the poem without regard to any other organising principle. They do not make sense other than as the random thoughts of a disordered mind, yet this is an interpretation denied to the reader by the absence of a consistent first-person perspective in the poem. 'Gerontion' is what Eliot said of Webster's *Duchess of Malfi*: 'an interesting example of a very great literary and dramatic genius directed toward chaos'.[126] There is no vision in 'Gerontion', not even the bogus vision of anti-Semitism. The Jew squats on the margins of the poem, his presence explaining nothing.

'Gerontion' certainly is a strange sort of dramatic monologue: not a dramatised voice speaking to a silent auditor, but the poem itself addressing Blake, and its own form. Though the voice in the poem is of uncertain provenance, the voice of the poem is strong. Though the addressees in the poem are elusive, the poem's own poetic forebears are clearly flagged. It is the form that speaks, giving the poem unity, a single series of stanzas written below a one word title.

If this seems fanciful, then who is addressed in the line 'I would meet you...'? The insistent questioning that follows anticipates no response, and in a poem replete with names one knows only that none is the auditor. This passionate interrogation is not directed to Mr Silvero, or Fresca, or any of the others repudiated by name and gesture. By contrast with the emphatic presence of Blake in the preceding lines, these lines are directed into a void. They comprise a rich speech impoverished by lack of context: a voice haranguing a spectre. The 'I' and the 'you', so protrusively emphasised, are mere effects of language. They are hooks on which the poet hangs his poem, an exercise in rendering the negative. Ashen and sterile, 'Gerontion' registers loss in a number of keys. There is simple loss of proximity. There is defeat. There is, finally, the extinction of faculty – the loss of the senses. The poem retreats into self, and then retreats further, abandoning all personal pronouns. Gerontion disintegrates, the 'I' disappears, and the final lines of the poem are written in a tense and obscure third person that registers terror at what cannot be seen: white on white, the wind, shapes obscured by the ferocity of a storm at sea, the invisibility of the whole world when one is asleep.

THE BINDING OF ISAAC, AND THE DRAMATIC MONOLOGUE

The poem sets its face against the tradition of the dramatic monologue, achieving a break not only with Eliot's own earlier work, but also with the form's principal Victorian exponents, Tennyson and Browning. 'Prufrock' and 'The Portrait of a Lady' were innovative instances of dramatic monologue;[127] 'Gerontion' is an assault on the form, a counter-statement of it.[128] These three poems also help define the difference between Eliot's misogyny and his anti-Semitism, the first two being instances of the former, the third, an instance of the latter. As I have argued, the poet is engaged with women; he has no relation with Jews. Hence while his misogyny bears upon his exploration of the limits of the dramatic monologue, his anti-Semitism takes him beyond them. My point of departure for an examination of these propositions is the poem's own: 'Here I am.'

'Gerontion' begins by echoing an assertion of personality far greater than may be found in either Tennyson or Browning. 'Here I am' has a precise Scriptural resonance. These words punctuate the story of the binding of Isaac, the Akedah:

And it came to pass...that God did tempt Abraham, and said unto him, Abraham: and he said, Behold, *here I am.*[129]

'Here I am' may be glossed in three possible ways. The first is abject self-denial: I am ready to do what you wish. The second has taken the measure of that self-denial and recognised it to be special: Here *I* am, you may command me, but do not take for granted the obedience of anyone else. The third, observant of the nature of God's relation with Abraham, is ready to interpret the phrase thus: *I* am a man, with a man's affections and loyalties, and therefore unlike *You.* The second and third hint at self-assertion, and therefore open a space for dialogue. Though only a space to be filled later and by others, they question God's justice while acknowledging his authority. 'Gerontion', blind to God's presence and despairing of His mercy ('what forgiveness?'), begins with the same words, but with very different effect, the 'Here I am' spoken into a void.

As between reader and text, these same words demand a still further gloss. The story discloses an aspect of Abraham that sets him apart from everyone else, for he is willing to kill his son. Here I am, an exemplary (or hitherto exemplary) man and founder of a faith, willing to murder what is dearest to me, at the direction of a supernatural voice. I cannot be certain that the voice is God's (Kant argued that it wasn't[130]). Indeed that which I am ready to undertake will render my covenant with Him a nullity. I am to be denied the promise made to me; I will not found a people ('In the same day the Lord made a covenant with Abram, saying, Unto thy seed have I given this land'[131]). 'Here I am': the simplicity of this statement prefaces an action of incomprehensible and potentially destructive obedience. Of our possible responses, 'only horror is appropriate, humanly and morally'.[132] It is not something that we could do; it is not something that we can even understand.[133] Abraham becomes an object of perplexity. We thought we knew him, but we know now that we do not. He baffles us. It is in this way that Abraham meets Gerontion. Gerontion also announces himself with the simple certainty of 'Here I am'. The words, which fix a stable identity ('I') in time ('am') and place ('Here'), preface the unravelling of that identity, lost in time, unmoored in space. Abraham and Gerontion, though similarly old men, are otherwise opposites, save perhaps that, like the Abraham of Hegel's imagination, Gerontion is 'a stranger on earth, a stranger to the soil and to men alike'.[134] The Akedah and 'Gerontion', though antithetical texts, each mystify, their 'Here I am' representing in each case the moment of the text's escape from ready intelligibility.

The words are repeated twice in the Akedah. Abraham announces himself to God, and to his son, in the same way. He does not flinch from addressing Isaac thus, though he will kill him. I will not shrink from acknowledging that it is me, your father, who is about to do this thing to you. But it is to myself that I make this acknowledgment, not to you, whom I deceive for your sake, though I am ready to kill you for God's sake, and for the sake of my faith:

And Isaac spake unto Abraham his father, and said, My father: and he said, Here am I, my son.

The 'my father' poignantly affirms Isaac's innocence and depen-dence. On the third occasion Abraham, once more addressed, with arm outstretched and knife poised over Isaac, responds to a voice, 'Here am I'. Abraham thus, to the angel: even now, I am ready to do your further bidding. I volunteered myself when I did not know what God intended of me; I do so again, even though I am now aware how he tests me. Or: here I am, ready to be told that God no longer requires this sacrifice:

And the angel of the Lord called unto him out of heaven, and said Abraham, Abraham: and he said, Here am I.

These are the three critical moments: when God orders him to kill his son; when his son asks about the sacrificial lamb; and when the angel releases him from God's command. God addresses Abraham many times elsewhere, but it is only in this story, these three times, that Abraham responds thus. Given this, and given, too, the unnatural and extreme command, the phrase is highly charged.

The phrase is used only seven further times in the Hebrew Scriptures, in each case with the primary meaning of readiness to serve.[135] Isaac addresses Esau thus, then later Jacob addresses the blind Isaac, responding to his father's 'Here I am' with a lie. God addresses Jacob, and Moses, and Isaiah, who each respond: 'Here am I'. These are at critical moments of contact between father and son, and between man and God. Between generations it presages deceit: Isaac is twice deceived, once by his father, once by Jacob, his son. From man to God it can promise submission. But in every case the phrase assumes strong links and high stakes. It anticipates a demand from a being entitled to make the greatest demand. Travel some way and you have the form of the dramatic monologue: the acknowledgment of self, the drama of self-disclosure (submission) and pretence (deceit). 'Here I am' is the unacknowledged epigraph to that form. But one must travel the greatest possible distance from this sense of the phrase to arrive at the use in 'Gerontion'.[136] In this poem there is neither God nor family, neither revelation nor fiction. It is a repudiatory instance of the form, and therefore a fitting preface to that greater repudiatory instance, *The Waste Land*. By contrast, in 'East Coker', which has a less adversarial relation to the dramatic monologue, indeed which connects it in subtle and elusive ways to a poetry of confession, 'Here I am' becomes 'I am here / Or there, or elsewhere'.

Compare 'Gerontion' with 'Prufrock' and 'Hysteria', two misogynistic poems which represent the extremes of the dramatic monologue. 'Hysteria' is self-diagnosis without cure. It is the paradox of the man who acknowledges that his fears are illusory, and yet who is in terror of them. As self-consciousness without self-knowledge, it is suitable for someone else's lecture on hysteria. The narrator is concentrated into one, intense centre while the woman, the object of his attention, disintegrates into teeth, throat, breasts. The poem is

about the constricting of a single consciousness to bursting point
and, in the dismemberment of a woman, the breaking up of the
integrity of the external world. It marks an implosion and a
scattering, and derives its tension from its ability to render the verbal
equivalent of a centrifugal movement simultaneously with a centripetal movement. It also marks the narrator's double contest: with
himself, and with the woman who has caused his discomposure.
Hence the ambiguity of the title's referent: is it the narrator's hysteria
or that of the woman? Is it the condition of both, hysteria induced in
the one by exposure to the hysteria of the other?[137] It is a different
kind of dramatic monologue to 'Prufrock', in which it is the speaker
who lacks integrity, and where it is the external world that is present
in its plenitude. Prufrock is caught up in a motion of self-censure,
chastising a subject without a centre, identifying himself by what he
is not, or as parts of other objects. He lacks a thread to tie together his
multiple characteristics; for the anonymous narrator of 'Hysteria',
by contrast, that thread is a rope that chokes. The former has a name,
and a voice, but these are the deceptions of form, not the badges of
identity; the latter does not need a name because so inward is his
crisis that he has lost connection with the external world. In the crisis
that each poem dramatises, which stems from a bewildering
engagement with a woman or women, the 'I' of 'Hysteria' is a
nightmare, while the 'I' of 'Prufrock' is a chimera.

There is no such engagement in 'Gerontion', a poem of withdrawal. If 'Prufrock' and 'Hysteria' may be said to dramatise the
moments before a defeat, then 'Gerontion' marks the progress of a
retreat following defeat: 'I that was near your heart was removed
therefrom ... I have lost my passion ... I have lost my sight.' The
poem is articulated around a series of negatives: loss of faith,
intellectual inertia, and anti-Semitism (another negative). Gerontion
has turned his back on the poem's shadowy interlocutors. They do
not exist in a dramatic relation to him. Eliot disengages the dramatic
from the theatric in 'Gerontion': the monologue is not to be spoken
by a character.

With an inventive perversity, Eliot breaks up the form of the
dramatic monologue in the poems of *Ara Vos Prec*. 'Sweeney Erect'
limits the first-person to an opening invocation; unlike 'Hysteria', it
does not render the experience of hysteria, it observes hysteria being
observed and thus doubly distances itself from the emotion. The 'I'
of 'Whispers of Immortality' swerves from the discursive to the

surreal. The subjects of 'Le Directeur' and 'Lune de Miel' are mute, while the subject of 'Mélange Adultère de Tout' splinters into distinct personae. Both 'Dans le Restaurant' and 'Gerontion' lapse from dramatic monologue to third-person impersonality in their final stanzas. The single 'I' of 'The Hippopotamus' intrudes to deny the poem any simple allegorical sense, and to create a mystery: who is the witness who can claim to have seen 'the 'potamus take wing'? The title of 'Mr Eliot's Sunday Morning Service' promises self-revelation while the poem delivers a puzzle; its opening line eschews that short, autobiographical 'I' for the impersonal neologism 'Polyphiloprogenitive'.

But it is 'Gerontion' that represents the greatest challenge to the form. It is a negative imprint of Tennyson's 'Ulysses'.[138] While Gerontion is a 'little old man', Ulysses is a 'king'. The one has family, the other, none: wife and son for one, unrelated boy and woman merely adjacent to the other. While Ulysses has a kingdom to bequeath, Gerontion is not even master of his house. Ulysses 'cannot rest from travel'. Gerontion travels only in the sense that a dog circles a patch of ground without finding a place for itself. His restlessness is of a different order; it springs from alienation, not activity. Ulysses dispenses justice; Gerontion is a peeved defendant. Gerontion is not a soldier; he meets Ulysses' experience of 'the ringing plains of windy Troy' with 'A dull head among windy spaces'. Ulysses regrets his inertia; Gerontion finds virtue in it. Tennyson's object is to create character, while Eliot's is to dissolve it. The former dramatises a mind, the latter, its disintegration. And the key is in Ulysses' boast: 'I am become a name'. Gerontion, who can boast of nothing, can name others but not himself. The title of the poem, promising another 'Prufrock', delivers a preamble to *The Waste Land* in which the extinct form of the dramatic monologue survives as an ironic endnote: 'Tiresias, although a mere spectator'. Eliot criticised 'Ulysses', contrasting Tennyson's lack of narrative gift with Dante's account of Ulysses in the 'Inferno'.[139] This was unfair. Tennyson's Ulysses, having returned home, contemplates another journey. Dante's Ulysses does not reach Ithaca, and instead embarks on a journey into the Atlantic, where he perishes. The first is old; the second is still young. Tennyson asserts the claims of imperial adventure over age; Dante identifies the limits of the aspiring human spirit unaided by the Church. The unfairness is instructive. In his essay, as in 'Gerontion' itself, Eliot thrusts away an unwelcome and oppressive model with a

recklessness that disregards his own poetic practice: 'The very
greatest poets set before you real men talking, carry you on in real
events moving.'[140] This judgment disqualifies both Tennyson and
Eliot himself.

'Gerontion' is also a response to Browning's 'Rabbi Ben Ezra',[141]
a poem which is neither sermon nor dialogue, but something in
between the two. The rabbi begins: 'Grow old along with me!',
words too intimate to come from a pulpit. It is an invitation, not a
lesson, and it is from a friend not a stoic. It reaches out across the
chilly divide between preacher and congregation, establishing a
distinctive 'rabbinic' idiom. Ulysses-like, it welcomes old age: 'The
best is yet to be'. The poem celebrates wisdom, and therefore
endorses age, scepticism, adversity, and dissent. It rejects the ascetic's
distrust of the senses. It is an anti-'Gerontion', spoken by a Jew,
praising what that poem fears or scorns, repudiating what it
embraces. Browning's poem triumphs in the human exercise of
rational inquiry; Eliot's is ravaged by thought's destructive power.
Thought is dangerous, sinister, unpredictable. It lays siege to
Gerontion, the insistent 'Think ... Think ... Think' abstracting the
process of thought from any graspable subject matter, a demand that
cannot be fulfilled. The rabbi scorns the clod; Gerontion takes refuge
in sleep and in the insensate. He rejects the material, but is rejected
by the spiritual. He has enough faith to repudiate, but insufficient
faith to affirm. One world is abhorrent to him, the other is
inaccessible. While Gerontion shrinks from both flesh and the spirit,
the rabbi honours each. Browning's Jews are positively garrulous:
think of 'Jochanan Hakkodosh'[142] and 'Holy-Cross Day'.[143]

The epigraph to 'Holy-Cross Day' purports to be an entry in the
diary of the bishop's secretary celebrating the success of his master's
sermon to the Jews: 'What awakening, what striving with tears, what
working of a yeasty conscience!' Controverting this epigraph, the
poem's preface states: 'What the Jews really said ... was rather to this
effect ...' The note at the end of the poem laconically comments:
'Pope Gregory XVI abolished this bad business of the Sermon – R.
B.' Of the poem's three voices, the first is that of the bishop's
secretary, the second is that of the Jews, and the third is that of the
poet. The second exposes the first, while the third condemns it. Each
articulates certainties. In a hierarchy of truth there is the delusion of
the secretary, the steadfast opposition of the Jews, and the dismissive
censure of Browning himself. It is wrong for Jews to be persecuted;

Christians who force their religion on others do it a disservice; the capacity for self-delusion in support of faith is great. The irony is unambiguous. The first-person narration does not sacrifice truth to partial observation because it has the full endorsement of the poet. The Jews are expected to sit in silence while the Holy-Cross Day sermon does its work of conversion on them. Instead, they fidget, mock, and then recite under their breath a rival text – Ben Ezra's Song of Death. In this collective dramatic monologue, Jewish voices are heard, and the bishop's words go unreported. His hypocrisy is an object of derision. The enforced attendance is a tiresome diversion. It is not even an affront, just a bore. Christianity does not challenge these Jews; Christians persecute them. It is not a rival faith, merely a stronger enemy. From complaining, the Jews move to relating the history of their torments. And then – the Song of Death. It addresses Christ: if truly the Messiah, he should join with the Jews against tormentors who have repudiated his teachings. If the Jews withstood Christ then, they withstand Barabbas now. They will 'wrest Christ's name from the Devil's crew'.

Browning's poem shuts the bishop up and gives the Jews their platform. Eliot silences them again. His Jewish mouths are dumb, framing golden grins; the Jewish landlord is silent witness to Gerontion's eloquence; and Jewish dissenters are to be suppressed ('a spirit of excessive tolerance is to be deprecated'). It is the anti-Semite Gerontion, without the disguise of faith, who has the exclusive right of address. When anti-Semites do speak in Browning, they condemn themselves. 'Filippo Baldinucci on the Privilege of Burial',[144] for example, is narrated by an anti-Semite. The narrator repeats what he had been told as a child by his uncle, recalling how when younger he had won the older man's approval: 'His chuckle at my piece of news, / How cleverly I aimed my stone' at the Jews. But the old man warned the boy off: 'I fear we must not pelt the Jews!' And the story explains why: greater Jewish cunning will defeat the best efforts of the Gentiles. The uncle was a 'good old man' (not a 'little old man' like that other anti-Semite, Gerontion). Remembering him fondly, the narrator condemns him out of his own mouth. Gerontion is not similarly condemned. While Browning's poem exposes anti-Semitism, Eliot's poem gives it a home.

In 'Gerontion' the attack on 'the jew' and the attack on the form of the dramatic monologue are each a feature of the other. Anti-Semitism conspires with Modernism in the undermining of a poetic form; Modernism conspires with anti-Semitism in the libelling of the Jews.

Later Eliot would compose a poem that, in revisiting 'Gerontion', gives a voice to a Jew. 'A Song for Simeon' is a dramatic monologue in retreat from the formal challenges of its predecessor poem, 'Gerontion'; it is also exceptional in a poetry in which elsewhere Jews are dumb. The voice, however, is a disciplined one, and speaks lines prepared for it. The preposition in the title tells all. The song is *for*, not *of*, Simeon (contrast 'Prufrock'). Eliot gives the Jew lines that locate him, and by implication all Jews, wholly within the Christian drama. Incapable of denying its truth, but equally incapable of living that truth, Simeon welcomes death because his life is death. Published in 1928, shortly after Eliot's reception into the Anglican Church, the poem's source is a short passage in Luke. Simeon is told that 'he should not see death before he had seen the Lord's Christ', so he is brought to the temple where Joseph and Mary are having Jesus circumcised. He blesses them, and asks God for death, 'for mine eyes have seen thy salvation'.[145] The poem merits Alasdair MacIntyre's wider criticism: '[t]he attempt to speak *for* [Jews], even on behalf of that unfortunate fiction, the so-called Judeo-Christian tradition, is always deplorable'.[146]

Though the poem speaks in Simeon's voice it is not limited by his vision. Simeon is an old man awaiting death. He reviews his life, one of charity and observance, and anticipates the sufferings of his descendants, who will be persecuted for their Christian faith:

> Who shall remember my house, where shall live my children's children
> When the time of sorrow is come?

'The time of sorrow' is not the moment of the dispersion of the Jews but that of the trials of Christ, and of the early Christians. Jewish pain, save in this context, is not the poem's theme, and it therefore contemplates Simeon's dispossession with calmness. His house will become the house occupied by Gerontion. His children's children may find a ledge there to squat on. The Jews will be scattered, but it is the Christians who will suffer, and their suffering will re-enact the suffering of Christ. Simeon neither wants nor has any part in this. He belongs, in Helen Gardner's complacent phrase, 'to the world of the Old Covenant'.[147] He seeks the liberation of death, not new faith. He prays that the 'Infant' grant 'Israel's consolation', that is, herald the Messianic days. However, his own 'consolation' is to die, even though unredeemed. Addressing God in the lower case, Simeon acknowledges that others will address Him otherwise. 'Thee' is capitalised only this once in the poem, which Moody glosses as marking 'the difference between the saints' and Simeon's sense of Christ'.[148] This is true, though it matters more than Moody's explication allows. In a poetry which withholds the upper case from 'the jew', here is a poem in which a Jew withholds the upper case from God. This is the newly Christian nature of Eliot's verse, one which suffers wounds rather than inflicting them. Simeon does not know how to worship. Eliot allows him to condemn himself. His song is also his confession.

Simeon and Ahasuerus, the Wandering Jew, are opposing types, the pair together comprising the Jewish witness to the truth of Christianity. Simeon blesses the infant Jesus and is released into death; Ahasuerus curses the adult Jesus and is condemned to endless life. The death of the one, and the continued existence of the other, are similarly unregenerate. They are Jews for Christians. Eliot matches his Simeon with versions of Ahasuerus – Bleistein and the landlord of 'Gerontion'.

Simeon stands apart from Eliot's other Jews because he admits his handicap. Awareness of his inadequacy gives him a voice to articulate it:

> Not for me the martyrdom, the ecstasy of thought and prayer,
> Not for me the ultimate vision.

Simeon is in this respect a New Testament type of Moses, fated to see the Promised Land but not to enter it. Witness to its truth, but denied its redemptive power, the Jew stands solemnly, humbly, outside Christianity's gates. This posture of pious subordination makes anti-Semitism redundant. The poem is therefore another one of Eliot's triumphs over Jews: 'Let thy servant depart, / Having seen thy salvation'. At this moment Jews leave Eliot's poetry, humility and the full consciousness of subservience marking the occasion of their departure. Simeon, the witness to Christianity's superior truth, is a 'self-judging'[149] Jew who, by dying, does all that an anti-Semite could wish for.

'GERONTION' (3)

'A Song for Simeon' returns to Browning; 'Gerontion' breaks with him. At each point 'Gerontion' addresses, and attacks, the form of the dramatic monologue. If, as has been argued, 'Prufrock' is an interpretation of the form, then 'Gerontion' is a dismantling of it.[150] Eliot employs a technique of disruption. Consider Ricks's suggestion that 'the true tension of the dramatic monologue [is] the presence and the pressure of the silent interlocutor'. He proposes that 'the art of the dramatic monologue begins in an acute sense of the circumstances in which strong speech meets strong silence'.[151] Yet where is this in 'Gerontion', a joke at the expense of the form that it purports to represent?

The poem begins meditatively: crowded with possible interlocutors, it ignores them all. They are not addressed; they do not even constitute an audience. Gerontion does not meet their 'strong silence', he disregards their banal chatter. His vocal brooding cuts through the interference of a boy reciting, a woman sneezing, a goat coughing. The 'jew' is snubbed. In the section that follows, Mr Silvero and the others fare even worse. There is no sense of their presence. While the third section is a self-interrogation, the fourth conjures up an interlocutor only to confess the impossibility of connection: 'I would meet you upon this honestly'. Empson analysed 'honest' in *The Structure of Complex Words*. Among the relevant meanings that cluster around it are: I will tell you the truth; I will deal with you as a friend; I am a man, stripped to the essentials, and therefore honest; I am frank with myself, not self-deceiving. 'Honest' is a key word in the dramatic monologue. The relation between speaker and interlocutor is governed by degrees of disclosure and deception that makes the issue of honesty the poem's trial. As a claim, the word can be used dishonestly, but it is there in 'Gerontion' under false pretences. There is no friendship with an interlocutor; there is no truth-telling; there is no essential self-disclosure. This is not because there is enmity, or lying, or disguise. It is because there is no interlocutor; there is fantasy in place of truth or falsehood; there is contingency in place of essential man. Hence the final section, which leaves behind both auditor and interlocutor, truth and falsehood, substituting free-floating madness and fantasy, detached from any individual consciousness.

Eliot's assault on the form of the dramatic monologue is accomplished by the trivialisation of the Jew and the dissolution of Gerontion. Gerontion and the Jew are each alienated. It is their common condition. There are no ghosts for Gerontion; no natural parents for the Jew ('spawned'). Gerontion's homelessness is emphasised in the repetition of 'house' and the activity of the wind, representing 'a ceaseless randomness which cannot find an end and yet cannot die'.[152] The poem's elusive allusiveness makes metaphoric exiles of its readers. The inevitable failure in identifying the origin of quotations, recognised or remembered but not attributed, makes of these quotations echoes of unrecapturable voices. But one cannot thus argue that the anti-Semitism, the thrusting away of the Jew, becomes paradoxically an identification of the Jew as the type of the modern predicament. That would be too easy. The only claim that the Jew might make for sympathetic attention is his exilic condition: Eliot robs him of this tatter. 'Gerontion' strips the Jew bare of all residual human qualities. These paltry few are taken, and given to Gerontion. His self-dramatising interrogations, though they subside into randomness, at least have the dignity of speech. The Jew is voiceless. The pathos of Jewish history – exile, and deferred expectancy – is displaced onto Gerontion.

'Gerontion' is an anti-Semitic poem, and not just a poem about an anti-Semite. Ricks asks of this anti-Semitism: '[is it] to be held against Gerontion or "Gerontion"? Is it an earnest that the Jew is socially and spiritually rotten or that the dry brain which savours such gusto has rotted?'[153] He leaves the answer open. Allow that the poem is about Gerontion's anti-Semitism. Does that in itself prevent it from being anti-Semitic? This poem, which articulates a loathing of Jews, has as its subject a man who loathes Jews. It is an anti-Semitic dramatisation of an anti-Semite. It is an example of what it represents.[154] After quoting Gabriel Pearson's 'vivid exploration of the animus within the poem', which Ricks is careful to point out is 'not necessarily the same as the animus of the poem', he concludes:

the reader and the Jew do not exhaust the imaginable objects of attack: Gerontion, embittered and wily, is not immune from attack, ours or his. What his history gives may be 'What's not believed in'.[155]

He is right to unsettle the meaning of the poem. But to suggest that the anti-Semitism is thereby rendered less certain is an unwarranted further step. Unless he wishes to propose the general semantic instability of the poem (a deconstructive approach alien to his critical position), he must accept that a plurality of targets for the poem's animus does not make equivocal its hostility towards the Jews. It would be as absurd to suggest that the Jew is anything other than repellent as to suggest that the house is anything other than a tenement. Gerontion does not occupy a mansion, nor is his Jewish landlord a cultivated and handsome philanthropist. It cannot plausibly be argued that Gerontion's self-scepticism undermines 'his' account of the Jewish landlord. Those lines in the poem depend for their effect on a received notion of Jews. It is an effect that takes for granted a certain version of Jewish history. That notion, and that version, are real in the poem.

CHAPTER 3

'Sweeney Among the Nightingales', 'Burbank', and the poetics of anti-Semitism

PRELIMINARY

Notwithstanding my efforts to avoid reductive analyses, and my resolve to respect the literary nature of the texts examined in the preceding two chapters, there may be resistance to what I have so far argued. This resistance, which can be more than just a defensive reflex or the pain of wounded admiration, must now be considered. It is likely to derive from a tendency to elevate literature to an instance of 'Art', and a parallel tendency to diminish 'anti-Semitism' to mere rant. These tendencies have the effect of severing any relation between the two, because, so it is commonly believed, 'the artist never rants'.[1] This severance is bogus. There is no necessary incompatibility between the language and forms of poetry and the verbal thrusts of anti-Semitism. In this chapter I will try to show up some of literature's pretensions. My object is to prove that the study of the anti-Semitism of 'Sweeney Among the Nightingales' is the proper concern of literary criticism. I expect thereby to discredit literature's claims to immunity from anti-Semitism.

In discussions of the supposed anti-Semitism of certain of his poems, Eliot has been the beneficiary of a complex bundle of ideas about poetic truth. These ideas have placed a 'cordon sanitaire'[2] around poetry. They derive from the belief that while poetry has a different and less direct relation with the world to prose, it is also superior to prose. This is so because while poetry does not make statements about the world, it discloses essential truths about it (or, in the deconstructionist version, about language[3]). Poetic discourse is thus both non-propositional and benevolent. It informs without asserting, and what it discloses is enlightening. These ideas underlie the tenets of both Symbolism, which provided the context for the composition of Eliot's poetry, and the New Criticism, which provided

(and to an extent, continues to provide) the context for its reception
and study. Indeed, Eliot was an exemplary figure for the New Critics,
as de Man observed:

The perfect embodiment of the New Criticism remains, in many respects,
the personality and the ideology of T. S. Eliot, a combination of original
talent, traditional learning, verbal wit and moral earnestness, an Anglo-
American blend of intellectual gentility not so repressed as not to afford
tantalizing glimpses of darker psychic and political depths, but without
breaking the surface of an ambivalent decorum that has its own compla-
cencies and seductions.[4]

Eliot wrote out of Symbolism for New Criticism, which 'popu-
lariz[ed] ... the modernist idea of literature'[5] and was itself'anchored
in non-purposive Kantian-symbolist aesthetics'.[6] Purportedly a
theory of all poetry, it aided brilliantly the explication of certain
kinds of poetry, while ignoring or undervaluing other kinds. The
aesthetics of these schools of poetry and criticism did not emerge fresh
from a theoretical void. They were related to older views about the
constitutive properties of poetry, and of literature in general. They
persist as influences on many of those critics of Eliot who would
neither regard themselves as New Critics nor regard his poetry as
Symbolist.

In the following two chapters I define and then reject two
arguments about the relation between anti-Semitism and poetry.
Both insist that anti-Semitism negates poetry: where the poetic
prevails, the anti-Semitic is deemed absent. The first asserts that since
poetry cannot be propositional, it lapses into prose when it descends
to anti-Semitism. The second asserts that since poetry discloses
truths, it cannot articulate the wicked, false doctrine of anti-
Semitism. To the extent, then, that there is anti-Semitism in Eliot's
poetry, it damages it. It exists in the form of a number of blemishes,
or incidental 'ugly touches'. The ugliness of anti-Semitism disfigures
what would otherwise be the poetry's unblemished beauty. The
obscurity of Eliot's earlier poetry and the candidly Christian nature
of his later poetry together encourage these defences. The poetry up
to and including *The Waste Land* resists prose paraphrase, while the
poetry thereafter is too pious to be capable of fostering anything other
than virtue in its readers. Against the first argument I contend that
poetry can be propositional; it can present a 'CASE for the
prosecution' (Pound, Canto XLVI). Literary works may specifically

be written to dramatize and empower a set of beliefs.[7] Poems can affirm; in consequence, they can lie.[8] Against the second argument I contend that poetry may, but need not, disclose truths. Anti-Semitism, which is mired in ugliness and loathing, does not make poetry impossible. Indeed, not only can it provide the material for a poem, it can be a poet's inspiration. It can be a muse. I contend that, on occasion, it was Eliot's muse. 'We could make it a rule', the Jewish critic A. Tabachnick wrote, 'that if a work is art it is not anti-Semitic, even where the writer is an anti-Semite, and conversely, if a work is anti-Semitic it is not art, even if the author is a great writer'.[9] If there is such a rule, Eliot provided several exceptions to it.

POETRY AND THE PROPOSITIONAL

I begin with Cleanth Brooks's essay 'Irony as a Principle of Structure'.[10] He argues that metaphor, which dominates modern poetic technique, interferes with the direct statement of propositions by loading them with particulars. These particulars weigh down the general meaning; the abstract is freighted by concrete detail. But what exposes prose to the hazards of partialness and obscurity, defines poetry. Abstraction takes us out of poetry; metaphor keeps us within its borders. Poetry's metaphors are not mere illustrations of abstract statements, they are constitutive of the poem and are related to one another as an organic whole. Their connection is not one of mere contiguity, like the blossoms of a bouquet, but of interrelatedness, like the parts of a plant. They compose, they do not merely decorate. They do not ornament the poem's argument, they are its argument. It follows that particular images must be examined in relation to the sum of the poem's other images. As with the plant's stalk, leaf, or hidden roots, they derive their meaning from the whole poem, which is their context. This entails a re-evaluation of the meaning of ostensibly general statements in poetry. Take the apparently abstract 'Ripeness is all' in *King Lear*, and the apostrophic 'Never, never, never, never, never'. The reflective first, just as much as the protesting second, has to be understood as a dramatic utterance, spoken by a particular character at a particular moment in the play. The former is no more philosophical than the latter. Each is a component part of a complex, dramatic unity. This warping of statement by context is the province of irony, hence the essay's title.

Brooks admits to an overuse of the term 'irony': it is the best available to point to the effects achieved by drama in consequence of its organic nature. As with drama, so with poetry. Metaphor is to poetry what character is to drama: guarantor of the situation-specific nature of the language. Statements made in poems are to be read as if they were speeches in a drama.

There are two objections to this general argument. First, if every poem is to be read dramatically, poems that are dramatic monologues lose their generic distinctness. Secondly, while lyric poetry may be said to invite Brooks's special reading, to read philosophical poetry thus is to read it against its grain. Taken together these objections suggest that Brooks has overshot his target, mistaking one kind of poetry for poetry in general. Brooks neglects the differences between poems in pursuit of a unifying principle. He neglects the similarities in language uses in pursuit of a distinguishing principle. Against Brooks I adopt the following propositions. Poetry and prose cannot always be distinguished by reference to their use of metaphor. One way in which some poems differ from others is the manner in which the abstract is rendered. They can achieve a many-sided articulation of a philosophical problem that discursive prose cannot match. Poems that resist abstraction may yet thereby declare a general position in relation to the abstractions they resist. Poems that do not contain propositions may be otherwise referential. They can be propagandistic, inciting readers to action. They can make things happen.[11] They demand to be read in different ways and the demands that they make may be part of their challenge. Finally, one cannot escape the problem of poetry and politics – poetry and anti-Semitism – by arguing a super-strong case for the non-referential nature of poetry. The furthest that one can go is to insist upon the special difficulties of reading poetry in the same way as fly-sheet prose. I rely on Eliot's own critical observations as authority for certain of these propositions. I also rely on his poetry, large parts of which would be diminished to banality if read as 'dramatic' in Brooks's sense. I want to rescue that poetry from banality even at the price of asserting its anti-Semitism.

What is the effect of Brooks's theory on any argument about the anti-Semitism of part of Eliot's work? It makes it more difficult to assert of a poem: 'This is anti-Semitic'. It makes it very difficult to assert of its author: 'He is an anti-Semite'. It effects a severance both between poet and poem and between the voice of the poem and the voice in the poem. Reading a text dramatically creates a space in which to argue one of two alternative cases: first, that an opinion expressed within it is rejected by the text itself, or second, that the text makes no assertions more general than those that are relevant to the specific situation it addresses. The *first* case acknowledges that the text itself has an opinion, endorsing or rejecting other opinions expressed within it. The *second* denies precisely this: the text is merely the showcase for those opinions. The two cases are often confused. For example, it is often claimed of *The Merchant of Venice* that neither the anti-Semitism of the Venetians in the play, nor the play's own hostility to Shylock, is sufficient to indict the play of anti-Semitism. The play itself does not assert anything about Jews in general, only about the Jews on the stage during its performance; the statements about Jews in general are made by others on the stage who speak under the pressure of their own defined circumstances. While these characters may purport to make hostile claims about Jews as a whole, the play robs these animadversions of their generality, enclosing them in a context and ensuring that they are trapped in the specifics of their utterers' dramatic situation. So on this account the play hovers on the brink of, but does not collapse into, anti-Semitism. That is the *second* case. However, in its refusal to admit the abstractions of its characters (that is, their anti-Semitism), it may be said to repudiate those abstractions. And at this point one reverts to the *first* case, that is, the proposition that the play rejects the opinions that its characters voice, either because of the essential difference between what they say and what it is, or because as an aspect of its mode of existence, it ironises those opinions.

I reject both these accounts, and against them I contend that the shift from hostility to Shylock to hostility to Jews in general is achieved by the play, that such a shift is accordingly possible in any play, and therefore possible in any poem too (like Brooks, I assume the equivalence of play and poem). The refusal to admit of this possibility is one of the difficulties with Brooks's general argument. Wrongly, he refuses to recognise that a poem can endorse a speaker's 'dramatic utterance', thereby assuming the burden of a general position that would otherwise be a feature only of a subordinate part within it. Venetian anti-Semitism, endorsed by the play's own hostility to Shylock (by which I mean his given character and fate), amounts to the anti-Semitism of *The Merchant of Venice*. Shylock is 'a very Jew' (II, ii. 100); he has a 'Jewish heart' (IV, i. 80). The play is an anti-Semitic work of art.[12] There is no saving gap here, nor is there any equivalent such gap in 'Sweeney Among the Nightingales'.

Brooks would (by application of his general position), and Ricks does, tentatively but expressly, argue otherwise. The New Critics, in their founding distinction between poetic discourse where metaphor is constitutive, and non-poetic discourse in which metaphor is ornament or interference, do not address the problem posed by non-poetic discourses whose propositional impact is dependent upon metaphor. Concede that propaganda may rely upon metaphor to advance its propositions and the argument about the essentially metaphorical nature of poetic language, and hence its non-propositional status, wobbles. Eliot made the same point: 'Metaphor is not something applied externally for the adornment of style, it is the life of... language ... we are [completely] dependent upon metaphor for even the abstractest thinking'.[13] Take, for example, the misrepresentation of a nation's heterogeneous Jewish population as part of an international army of rats. This is both metaphor and misrepresentation, or misrepresentation by metaphor. Recommending the expulsion of these Jews thereby becomes a moderate proposal, given that rats are usually destroyed: 'Cannot we as easily shove the vermin across Turkey?'[14] This is propaganda reliant for its persuasive force upon a poetic effect. Similarly 'Sweeney Among the Nightingales' is a poem reliant for its aesthetic force upon an anti-Semitic effect. I want to test Brooks's case against this poem.

Ricks wears Brooks's clothes in his explication of the poem. Of the sinister effect achieved by the withholding of Rachel's married (or otherwise new) name, he comments:

> The effect is dramatic, in both senses of dramatic, and the line ... is beaded with the sweat of two equally horrible fears: the fear that the terrors, here in this sleazy dive, may be paranoid, and the fear that they may not be.[15]

'Dramatic', that is, in the sense of being arresting, and also in Brooks's sense. Ricks leaves the issue of the author's presence far behind: it is not Eliot's anti-Semitism. His interest is in whether the fear of Jews, not promoted by the poem but merely disclosed confessionally by the poem's narrator, is a response to a real threat. Rachel may be gentle and nondescript, or she might be bestially menacing. Ricks endorses a 'robustly demotic account of the dramatization of the narrator' in the poem, which proposes that '[h]e does not know what the hell is going on'.[16] There is, however, no reason to suppose the existence of a narrator. This is an unnecessary interpretive step, explaining nothing. It is a feint, the value of which is to enable the pleading of a special case about Eliot's anti-Semitism. The poem perplexes. By attributing that perplexity to a phantom narrator one escapes perplexity oneself. It becomes his perplexity rather than one's own. But the result is that at this moment of attribution, which is also the moment of escape, one has abandoned the poem.

'Sweeney Among the Nightingales' is enclosed by Agamemnon's agony. The epigraph quotes his cry when felled by his wife: 'Alas, I am struck deep by a mortal blow.' The concluding stanza returns to the scene of his murder, but this time the cry is silent, obscured by the sound of birds, his body dirtied by their waste. Within this frame the poem presents a sequence of low actions. Sweeney is slumped on a chair in a dive. Probably drunk, his arms hang by his sides, his legs gape. A caped woman slides off his lap onto the floor, tugging the tablecloth and knocking a cup over. This interior is at odds with the atmosphere outside. It is night. The air is thick with the portentous. Clouds obscure the moon, the stars are veiled, the sea stirs distantly. Sweeney has company. A waiter brings in exotic fruit. Another man, first met sprawling at the window sill, leaves the room and leans back into it through a window. Grinning, mouth framing gold fillings, he is a picture of sinister crassness. He is Jewish, as is the second, predatory woman in the scene. Her name is 'Rachel *née* Rabinovitch'. All we are told about her is that she 'Tears at the grapes with murderous paws'. That is enough. In this powerfully condensed sentence, which does much more than merely give a name and describe an action, Eliot concentrates three horrors – of Jews, of women, and of animals. A sense of danger is insinuated, associating the scene inside with the nocturnal disturbances outside. The two women and the man are, perhaps, plotting together. It is also possible that the man might be conspiring with just one of them, or even intriguing against both of them. They are all customers. Their host talks with someone else at the door. Nightingales sing near a convent, just as they did when Agamemnon was hacked to death by his wife Clytemnestra. Indifferent to time and culture, they celebrate their song, and defecate, thereby diminishing by their presence, and degrading by their evacuations the dead king's tragedy. 'Birds of the air will tell of murders past? / I am ashamed to hear such fooleries', remarks Machevill in *The Jew of Malta*,[17] a favourite play of Eliot's.

The poem's principal effect, of which the Agamemnon/Sweeney pairing is the chief cause, is of an extraordinary literary dissonance, yoking Greek tragedy with a fractured and experimental poetic melodrama, farcical and vicious in equal measure. The later, tamer Eliot of *The Confidential Clerk* and *The Elder Statesman* trod on safer ground, among more consonant harmonies designed to make classical and modern drama complementary.

It is as if the spaciousness of Aeschylean drama, the terrible significance of Agamemnon's death, has been emptied and replaced with something altogether meaner and more trivial. That space is filled with sordid, indecipherable detail. Tragedy has not put the quotidian in its place; the quotidian has instead intruded to rob tragedy of its pretensions. This is worse than Agamemnon dying as Icarus, in the corner of the picture. The birds do not just sing by him, as they would in Bruegel. They defecate on him. It is a spoiling, anticipatory variation on a theme that Auden later made his own. It is also an inverting of the Oresteian pattern. In Aeschylus's trilogy, the murder of Agamemnon was the second in a series of three deaths. In Eliot's poem, it inaugurates, and ends, an unrelated and less predetermined sequence, one of ambiguous acts, menacing silences, and lewd gestures. Agamemnon was first perpetrator and later victim, clearly one, and then clearly the other, in a mirroring play of guilty deed punished by guilty deed, the avenger assuming the burden of the crime avenged. Sweeney and the others are in the toils of no such logic. They are among neither the violators nor the violated, lacking both the knowledge of the former, and the innocence of the latter. In place of the *Oresteia*'s narrative simplicity, the poem substitutes murky uncertainties. It offers ambiguous but close detail (the fruit, the foliage) in order to avoid offering explanations, showing, so to speak, the trees because it cannot divine the wood, then returning to Agamemnon's story to disclose – by contrast and literally – the wood ('the bloody wood'). It dwells on contiguities because it cannot identify causalities. Why is Sweeney there? Are the two women in league? If so, against whom? What is their occupation? Whose 'gambit' does the man 'decline', and why? (The 'Therefore' of the seventh stanza establishes no obvious connection.) What is the host discussing, and with whom? Aeschylus tells you everything you need to know. Eliot, by contrast withholds the information that would make the poem's narrative intelligible. He shows Sweeney in a room with (amongst others) Jews – predatory women, sinister men.

The presence of these Jews is disquieting, because while their intentions cannot be guessed, their ill-will can be assumed. They are drawn from an anti-Semite's imagination. But he does not give any reason for their presence, nor does he identify the nature of the threat that they pose. It is therefore also a perplexed imagination.

Just as the *Oresteia* assumes Homeric mythology so is anti-Semitism taken for granted by 'Sweeney Among the Nightingales'. Yet while the former truly provides an explanatory context for the plays, the latter only purports to do so for the poem. Both Homeric mythology and anti-Semitism offer explanations intended to make sense of puzzling misfortunes in human life, the one by the intervention of the gods, the other by the intervention of the Jews. But while the former give meaning to the plays, the latter deny it to the poem, which hesitates before the larger claims of anti-Semitism. Jews are not malign Olympians who dispose of humankind by manipulative wizardry. The poem alludes to a world of squabbling gods and goddesses while refusing to endorse a darker world of conspiring Jews. Though offensive in its jibing at Rachel, the poem creates suspicion without delivering certainty. It will not reveal the Jew underneath the lot. It circumscribes anti-Semitism while adopting it. Jews are unpleasant. But though the women may be base and rapacious, and the men coarsely unappealing, they are not soldiers in a disciplined army at war with Christian civilisation. They are not rats. They are not even mysterious – the poem knows Rachel's real name. Fears are greater than realities. Olympian jealousies and rivalries may have dominated Greek life, thereby accounting for its direction, but positing an international Jewish conspiracy does not help to explain modern times. Eliot's anti-Semitism is at its closest, in this poem, to an aspect of Weininger's: '[the Jew] is non-moral, neither very good nor very bad, with nothing in him of either the angel or the devil'.[18]

When the anti-Semite feels at ease and unthreatened by Jews, he regards Jewish assimilation with contempt, mocking the efforts of those who try to conceal or abandon their Jewishness. In times of social dislocation and anxiety, the anti-Semite regards the same phenomenon as evidence of malign intentions. Anti-Semitism thereby passes back and forth between disdain and consternation, contempt and fear, snobbery and paranoia. In 'Sweeney Among the Nightingales', the most poised of Eliot's anti-Semitic poems, the account of Rachel and the grinning man are derived from the disdain, the contempt and the snobbery. Rachel does not fool Eliot; he knows what she is. He can fix her in a formulated phrase.

The anti-Semitism of the poem is akin here to that of de Man's wartime article 'The Jews in Contemporary Literature'.[19] The authors are similarly secure in their superiority to Jews. De Man complains that vulgar anti-Semitism, which regards post-war culture as degenerate because it is Judaised, condemns an entire literature. In such a context, a person who values modern literature could be taken to believe that it is indebted to the Jews, a myth to which Jews themselves have contributed. Though they have been important in the disordered and phoney life of Europe since 1920, literature obeys its own laws. The modern novel, for example, still follows Stendhal's definition of it as a mirror carried down an open road. Gide, Kafka, Hemingway, Lawrence, and others simply hold up this mirror to the interior life of their characters, thus continuing rather than breaking with past traditions. The same is true of recent poetry. Modern literature is not just a product of its times, and therefore the Jews, though now important, cannot take credit for it. Indeed, their insignificance in literature is surprising given that their detached intelligence is especially relevant to novel writing. Jewish writers have always been second rank, which is comforting. If even novelists have been able to protect themselves from Jewish influence, it is a sign that our civilisation is healthy. Segregating the Jews in a colony isolated from Europe – a solution to the Jewish problem – would thus have no damaging cultural consequences. We would lose some mediocrities, and literature would continue to develop according to its own laws.

De Man and the Eliot of 'Sweeney Among the Nightingales' may be taken to agree: repellent and untrustworthy though they may be, Jews do not matter as much as vulgar anti-Semites think. Putting the poem in the context of the article helps make this point. I should add that putting the article in the context of the poem helps make a second point. It demonstrates the folly of those, like Derrida,[20] who argue that de Man's opening repudiation of 'vulgar anti-Semitism' makes problematical (even if it doesn't altogether deny) the anti-Semitism of the rest of his article. Scoffing at vulgar anti-Semitism, and scoffing at the vulgarity of anti-Semitism are distinct activities. Anti-Semitism has always had rival versions – de Man picked the one that accented scorn for Jews over the one that accented fear of them. It was an arrogance made easy by the miserable conditions in which

Jews were then being forced to live. It is this, indeed, that makes the article especially squalid. It is triumphalist, celebrating the power-lessness of the Jews, at an historical moment of persecution and humiliation for them. De Man adds his own celebration to the sum of those other Fascist crowings over Jewish defeat.

'Sweeney Among the Nightingales' flirts with but refuses the notion of a Jewish conspiracy, and is thus to be compared to 'The Hollow Men', another poem that scorns conspiracies and the vanity of conspirators, successful or otherwise. Hollow men conspired with Brutus to assassinate Julius Caesar, and with Guy Fawkes to blow up Parliament. It is the vanity of the unregenerate to assume that they have the power to intervene in history and redeem it. It is the folly of one kind of anti-Semite to credit Jews with the power to intervene in history and possess it. Eliot's poetry is contemptuous of the claims of both. By a coincidence, that anti-Semitic fantasy of Jewish con-spiracy, *The Protocols of the Elders of Zion*, was published in England in February 1920, the same month and year as *Ara Vos Prec*.[21] Eliot's sinister Jews would have been instantly recognisable to readers of *The Times* and those other journals which gave credence to the genuine-ness of *The Protocols*.[22] It is 'Burbank', however, rather than 'Sweeney Among the Nightingales', that comes closest to their outlook. The pretension of Sir Ferdinand Klein matches Bleistein's grossness. He is the corruption at the top, Bleistein is the rottenness below. How does one explain Jewish power? How can one account for Sir Ferdinand's authority over Princess Volupine? 'The Jews vanquish', says Hegel, condensing to an epigram one of anti-Semitism's paradoxes, 'but they have not battled'.[23] It is out of this paradox – Jewish weakness, Jewish power – that conspiracy theories are born. Yet in Eliot's poetry, one might say, they are stillborn.

Attributing the anti-Semitism to a voice in the poem, and thereby neutralising it, ironically becomes the means by which the poem's own critique of a certain form of anti-Semitism is itself blanked out. Analysis of the poem's effects is falsely resolved into amateur psychology, and one considers: does the narrator witness the scene or imagine it? Is this an exterior or an interior landscape? Reality or fantasy? Ricks, reading for clues, discovers the answer in the poem's failure, when using 'née', to give the married name. It is fantasy; the poem is exonerated.[24] Yet the poem's title does not suggest the existence of a narrator nor does the poem itself use the first person. 'Sweeney Among the Nightingales' is not a dramatic monologue.

Title, form, and content are against the presence of a narrator. Entities are not to be multiplied beyond necessity: the interpretation of this poem does not require the postulate of a narrator – that redundant, extra entity.[25] Furthermore, the poem's Modernist edge disappears with his introduction. The complex spinning out of relations between the *Oresteia* and its own invented narrative vanishes. Instead, it is read as the outpourings of a deranged mind. Confession takes the place of literary experiment, and verisimilitude becomes the measure of its success. The narrator is mad, the poem is his discourse.[26] But the poem is not thereby so much explained as explained away. 'Sweeney Among the Nightingales' is less mediated, more demanding, than this, and protecting it from the charge of anti-Semitism thereby converts it from something extraordinary into something much duller. Insofar as this reading works, it does so at the price of making the poem banal.

Yet it is not a banal poem. It is an anti-Semitic, Modernist work of considerable complexity and interest. The anti-Semitism and the Modernism go together. Introducing the notion of a narrator entails the misreading of the poem as a puzzle concealing an answer signalled by clues. With ingenuity the answer will be discovered. This misses the point of the poem, which is precisely that there is no answer. The Jews comprise the clues to the question: what is the danger that the poem is attempting to understand? But the clues do not provide the answer, which the poem leaves suspended. Exegetical ingenuity is not a relevant talent to bring to this poem. It obstructs one's reading, distracting one from the text toward, amongst other things, Jewish conspiracy. (Anti-Semitism is to 'Sweeney Among the Nightingales' what the notes to *The Waste Land* are to the poem itself: bogus answers to the naïve question, 'what is going on?') This is where the anti-Semitism fits in. The poem suggests: though anti-Semites claim that the existence of Jews explains misery, identifying the Jew in the narrative of your suffering may not lead to a discovery of its cause. Sceptical of anti-Semitism's larger claims, the poem adopts a more limited version. It is the anti-Semitism of the club, not the platform. It accents the snobbery, not the fear. It meets Jews with scorn rather than hatred. The Jews do not conspire like Homeric gods against humankind. 'Sweeney Among the Nightingales' is thus the most poised of Eliot's anti-Semitic poems. It places Jews; but it also places anti-Semites. It draws on their overdrawn, poisonous anxieties to effect a connection with the universe of Greek tragedy (where the poem speaks, as Yeats incompletely appreciated, 'in the great manner'[27]). An unsettling poem, it invokes anti-Semitic anxieties in order to stoke its atmosphere of threat. Jewish menaces are invariably mysterious: 'many Jews toiled at that *obscure* conspiracy against Christendom, which some of them can never abandon' (Chesterton[28]). The poem is not a serious stab at arguing Jewish conspiracy; it does not adopt what has been termed the 'deadliest kind of anti-Semitism'.[29] It knows that this is a fiction, but exults in its artistic possibilities.

Indeed, the poem provides opportunities for anti-Semitism that pamphlet prose denies. Compare, for example, Pound and Eliot on 'Rabinovitch'. In wartime broadcasts from Italy, Ezra Pound would name Jews and 'servant[s] of Jewry', who were America's true enemies. On one such occasion he named Frances Perkins, to whose surname he appended, with a pseudo-revelatory flourish, '*née* Rabinovitch or something equally Oriental'.[30] Frances Perkins was a Roosevelt adviser, a New Deal administrator, and, for a period, Secretary of Labor. She was not Jewish, though she is said to have shared Roosevelt's openness to advice from Jews,[31] and Perkins was her maiden and not her married name. This phrase represents a small debt owed by Pound to Eliot, who was, in the matter of literary anti-Semitism, the better craftsman. Pound could not match the charged economy of Eliot's anti-Semitism.

'Sweeney Among the Nightingales' is exemplary in this regard. Just like 'Gerontion', it repudiates a Victorian precursor poem by a pointed anti-Semitism. The poem is Arnold's 'Rachel',[32] which celebrates the life of the great French actress, a 'Greek-soul'd artist … Sprung from the blood of Israel's race.' Born in a 'mean inn', her stage was the 'French Theatre'. She experienced, as we do, the contending influences of 'Germany, France, Christ, Moses, Athens, Rome', but her genius and glory were all her own. She was simply and superbly 'Rachel'. In Eliot's counter-poem, Rachel has not escaped the 'mean inn', her place of business. Her degraded gestures are antithetical to her namesake's sublime performances. Inescapably and wholly Semitic, yoked to her family name, she knows nothing of Athens and Rome, or Christ. She is instead a succinct reworking of five distinct anti-Semitic themes.

First, she is a product of those fantasies of feminine evil in *fin de siècle* culture described by Bram Dijkstra in *Idols of Perversity*. Rachel is a predatory Jewish woman (or 'Jewess', which evokes 'tigress'), like those other murderous Jewish women, Salome, the cause of John the Baptist's death, and Judith, who decapitated Holofernes. These two women figured prominently in the cultural imagination of the late nineteenth century. Salome was celebrated as an 'essentially Semitic type ... with the sensuous and soulless beauty of the tigress rather than the woman'.[33] Drumont described the actress Rachel as 'a little Bohemian tigress, a lascivious Jewess'.[34] Though farcically diminished, Rachel too is half-beast, possessing paws that tear rather than hands that caress or supplicate. Dijkstra has noted that in the art of that time, the 'bestial Jew' commonly was represented to be woman's closest degenerate companion in an otherwise civilised world. 'Salome and Judith were both Jewish women, as the intellectuals of the turn of the century did not tire of pointing out.' As such, Dijkstra observes, they 'combined the crimes of women with those of a "degenerate race"'.[35] Maurras wrote of a Semitic witch who 'did harm by evil magic, withdrew her spells and cast them again ... the thick smoke of her lair, the pernicious fever present in the heavy air added to the effect of the incantations which she chanted from the depth of her throat. She agitated men's hearts.'[36] Something of this atmosphere is intimated in Eliot's poem.

Secondly, and relatedly, Rachel is a whore; 'nightingale' is slang for 'prostitute'. Associating Jewish women with prostitution is a stock anti-Semitic practice; in late nineteenth-century France, for example, it was a commonplace. For Maupassant, the 'Beautiful Jewess' was an obligatory brothel 'type'. 'It is the Jewesses', asserted Drumont, 'who provide the largest contingent of prostitutes in all the great capitals.'[37] Pound connected Jews with prostitution and sexual excess.[38] The superior sensuality of Jewish women was a familiar literary theme: 'He thought of what Gallagher had said about rich Jewesses. Those dark Oriental eyes, he thought, how full they are of passion, of voluptuous longing!';[39] 'the mere term "Jewess" ... brings to my mind some vague, mysterious, exotically poetic image of all I love best in a woman. I find myself dreaming of Rebecca of York';[40] 'What voluptuous yet touching purity, love, sweetness, goodness, shone in that wondrous face that might have been gazing down from the minarets of Jerusalem.'[41] The Jewish prostitute is a degraded version of that theme – think of Baudelaire's 'affreuse Juive', vile but available to the poet, in contrast to his frigid beloved, 'reine des cruelles'.[42] Eliot degrades the theme still further by denying Rachel any allure. Hence the poem's seedy location by the

River Plate, attributable to the then topical anti-Semitic charge that Jews ran the White slave trade. South America was one of its centres. The anti-Semites ignored the small Jewish involvement, the unusualness of the phenomenon in Jewish history, the fact that Jewish traffickers dealt mainly in Jewish women, and the widespread and effective opposition to it from within Jewish communities. Anti-Semites regarded the trade as another instance of immutable Jewish vice. Their account owed much to the 'blood libel', that is, the canard that Jews abduct and murder Christian children at Passover; it bore little relation to the reality of commercial vice.[43]

Thirdly, Rachel is a creature from anti-Semitism's bestiary. For St Jerome Jewish prayers were as 'the grunting of a pig and the braying of an ass'. 'The Jews', preached St John Chrysostom, 'behave no better that pigs or goats in their gross lasciviousness and excessive gluttony.'[44] In the Middle Ages non-Jews who married or cohabited with Jews were prosecuted for bestiality.[45] In nineteenth-century France, once again, Jews were identified with vultures, crows, apes, monkeys, hyenas, jackals, foxes, wolves, dogs, goats, pigs, rats, snakes, crocodiles, toads, sharks, worms, locusts, fleas, spiders, slugs, and wasps.[46] A German anti-Semite of the same period expressed the view that Jews had 'the tenacity of a snake, the cunning of a fox, the look of a falcon, the memory of a dog, the diligence of an ant, and the sociability of a beaver'.[47] Browning drew from a similar bestiary with ironic effect in 'Holy-Cross Day', where Jews complain about being crammed into church for an Easter sermon: 'Higgledy piggledy, packed we lie, / Rats in a hamper, swine in a sty, / Wasps in a bottle, frogs in a sieve, / Worms in a carcass, fleas in a sleeve.'[48] Eliot's Jews vindicate the Pythagorean doctrine expounded in *The Merchant of Venice* '[t]hat souls of animals infuse themselves / Into the trunks of men' (IV. i. 132–3). Representing Rachel as an animal is another way in which Eliot relates the anti-Semitism of the poetry of *Ara Vos Prec* to its larger themes. With the rat-like Bleistein, the lupine Rachel belongs in the company of '[a]peneck Sweeney', the 'red-eyed scavengers', the reptilian 'silent vertebrate in brown', and the rankly feline Grishkin. As for 'Gerontion': the Jew squats, the goat coughs, companions in an animal realm. While Shylock at least is 'a creature that did bear the shape of man' (III. ii. 274), Rachel's paws ensure that no one can doubt her animal nature. Her 'desires', like Shylock's, '[a]re wolvish, bloody, starv'd and ravenous' (IV. i. 137–8). She is not the Swinburnian 'Lady of Pain' whose 'ravenous teeth...have smitten',[49] but a low Jewish woman whose paws tear.

Fourthly, Rachel is the Jewish daughter of a Jewish father. Her name is the clichéd sign of that relationship: 'what Moses does not obtain by subservience and flattery...his pretty daughter Rachel, prattling in French, conversant with romances and herself not averse to a little romancing, does.'[50] In Eliot's fictional social register, Rachel could have been '*née* Klein' (or '*née* Nathan', as she is named in the poem's French version, the translator correctly perceiving that any recognisably *Jewish* name would do[51]). She is the type of the convert: in the thirteenth-century collection of religious tales, *The Dialogue on Miracles*, the Jewish daughter who converts to Christianity against her father's wishes is named Rachel.[52] She is also related, as the daughter of Rabinovitch, to all those other, often faithless, literary daughters of Jewish fathers. She is sister to Shakespeare's Jessica and Marlowe's Abigail. She appears in Smollett's *Peregrine Pickle* and in numerous nineteenth-century novels and plays. Among the variations played on the theme, in 'Rebecca and Rowena', Thackeray's comic continuation of *Ivanhoe*, she repudiates her faith and marries the hero, while in an American novel of approximately the same period, her infatuation with a Gentile debtor of her father leads to her death.[53] She represents a theme that was all but played out by the time Eliot came to write his 'Sweeney' poem, in part because modern anti-Semitism denied just that possibility of redemption through conversion on which the theme was predicated. Still, it lingered on at the margins of James's *The Tragic Muse*, and in an enfeebled state in Waugh's *Decline and Fall*. It had become a literary cliché, fit only for trivial 'romances' such as Glossop's *The Jewess of Hull*. Lessing provided an early challenge to this theme, by writing a play about the adopted daughter of a Jew who grieves when she learns that he is not her natural father and that she was born a Christian (*Nathan the Wise*); George Eliot challenged it by writing a novel about a son who returns to the faith of his Jewish mother (*Daniel Deronda*). Eliot evoked the theme in a phrase, but *he* challenged it by making his Jewish daughter odious.[54]

Fifthly, Rachel attempts to deny her Jewishness by repudiating her surname. Eliot restores it, thereby enacting the anti-Semitic practice of revealing the Jewish origins of men and women who, for the worst of attributed reasons, are thought to deny those origins. 'Jews', remarked Santayana, 'are ashamed of their race.'[55] They often concealed their names, anti-Semites said, the better to deceive and subvert. It was once the practice to 'unmask' revolutionists: 'The real name of Chernov ... is Feldman. The real name of Steklov ... is Nahinkes, German Jew ... As for Lenin, everyone knows that his name is Zedeblum';[56] in 1920, a book listed the 'pseudonyms', 'real names', and 'race' of the Bolshevik leaders, most being 'revealed' as Jewish.[57] These remarks of Céline are merely a fantasy version of an anti-Semitic commonplace: 'The Jews, you know, they're all camouflaged, disguised, chameleon-like, they change names like they cross frontiers ... anything at all ... that throws people off, that sounds deceptive.'[58] Part of the poise of 'Sweeney Among the Nightingales' derives from the poem's assurance that it has not been 'thrown off' by the Jewish Rachel. When Jews were not conspiring together, they were attempting integration. This too should not be permitted. Jews should not be allowed 'to pretend to be Christians', as the Prussian Friedrich Wilhelm III put it, rejecting a petition from a Jew for permission to change his name; 'for some time', the king complained, 'the Jews have been adopting names which mean that they can no longer be recognised as Jews'.[59] Liberated from the gates of their legal ghettos, Jews were to be confined in a ghetto of names. In 1922 Hilaire Belloc suggested that one of the causes of anti-Semitism was the Jewish 'assumption of false names and the pretence of non-Jewish origin in individuals'.[60] In a letter to Pound, Eliot praised Louis Zukofsky for not concealing his origins: 'his verse is highly intelligent and honourably jewish';[61] by 'honourably', Eliot means 'openly'. Rooting out the Jew behind the Anglicised name was a party game for the Jew-conscious; thus Eliot wrote to Pound, 'Burnham is a Jew merchant, named Lawson (sc. Levisohn?)'.[62] Others have played a similar game: 'Viscount Beaconsfield – an Israelite by birth (né Disraeli)'.[63] Likewise, Christopher Hitchens can't resist mocking Ralph Lauren's phoney 'Edwardianism of dress' by unmasking his phoney surname: 'Ralph Lauren, née Lipschitz'.[64] Lauren, a purveyor of Anglophilic snobbery, is put in his place by a superior snobbery.

Eliot's anti-Semitism was thus compact. 'Rachel née Rabinovitch tears at the grapes with murderous paws' is a line derived from a cluster of literary and anti-Semitic clichés: conventions exhausted through overexposure, and abuse staled by repetition. What un-promising material! With great virtuosity, Eliot turns that material into art. He compresses it into a single, powerfully charged sentence, and thereby restores its resonance and its menace. The conventions acquire new life, the abuse, a sharper edge. Our sense of this poet's vocation has to be enlarged to take in his aesthetic commitment to anti-Semitism.

ANTI-SEMITISM AND THE NON-PROPOSITIONAL

If I have been wrong so far, and poetry does by its supposed 'statement-denying dynamic'[65] refuse the propositional, does this make the phrase 'anti-Semitic poetry' oxymoronic? Is the tension between the two such that either poetry refines anti-Semitism into something pure, or anti-Semitism degrades poetry to the level at which it is no longer poetry, so that one has only to ask: does anti-Semitism cease to be anti-Semitic, or poetry cease to be poetic, when attempts are made to write anti-Semitic poetry? Until now I have treated anti-Semitism as if it were simply a series of false and wicked propositions about Jews. I have assumed that to be anti-Semitic, poetry must thereby be propositional. I have disputed the contention that poetry thereupon ceases to be truly poetic and becomes something else, posing as poetry. I have argued that, to the extent that anti-Semitism can be characterised as propositional, it is not inaccessible to poetry. I now approach the problem from the opposite end and consider the degree to which poetry can suit an anti-Semitism that precisely is *not* propositional. I develop my case by reference to Symbolist poetry, partly because I take Eliot's poetry to be explicable by reference to Symbolism, and partly because poetry of this kind is the least susceptible to such an argument. Indeed, one might suppose that its esoteries, its intangibilities, and its rarefied and personal visions, would make it invulnerable to the conformist vulgarities of anti-Semitism. As Mallarmé put it: 'Le sens trop précis rature / Ta vague littérature'.[66] To be sure, poetic language in general would seem to sit uneasily with anti-Semitism. Too generative of ambiguity, designed to be read with too heightened a sense of nuance, and of the plurality of meanings, surely (someone might insist) poetry demands to be set apart from the flat statements of the bigot? Isn't the language of anti-Semitism 'heavily dependent on clichés', while the poet's task precisely is to 'renounce the comforts of cliché'?[67] Doesn't anti-Semitism speak solely in the more limited language of prose, and in particularly debased forms of prose at that?

Is it not articulated either in the clotted, polysyllabic prose of 'scholarship', or in the telegraphic sentences of the political agitator, harsh and direct? To which one answers: yes, it is true that to study anti-Semitism is to immerse oneself in stultifying treatises, and slogans one step away from assaults. But such lumpen texts do not represent the limit of one's research – poems have to be studied too. To think otherwise would be to misunderstand the elastic scope of anti-Semitism. Anti-Semitism is not limited to a series of opinions. It derives from corrupt imaginations that neglect truth; it is a 'passion'.[68] It lives in fiction; it is, in Maurice Blanchot's phrase, a 'portrait-accusation'.[69] It comprises a parcel of descriptions of 'Jews' that are adverse, and hostile, but also incoherent and contradictory. The descriptions of 'Jews' in Eliot's Symbolist poetry are pulled out of that parcel.

The following, from an article written in 1898 by J. K. Huysmans, has the force of a disagreeable revelation for Eliot's readers. It discloses his affinity with an aspect of Symbolism that is unpleasant and not wholly contingent. Here are the Jews of a Symbolist:

They were hideous with their skulls covered with astrakhans, their glassy eyes bulging as if on stalks, their mouths like unbandaged wounds, their beards like dirty yellow vegetation, their cheeks puffed-out and crimson, like the raw backsides of monkeys. They stank like animals; all the horror of immiscible tribes was there ... a detailed map of all the vices; they seemed to me to represent, in their features, in the lines of their faces, the folds and crevasses of innumerable bankruptcies, a whole chart of the geography of greed and money-making.[70]

Huysmans's novel *A Rebours* is one of Symbolism's principal texts. Mallarmé dedicated one of his most opaque texts to its protagonist, des Esseintes.[71] Huysmans has a place both in Arthur Symons's *The Symbolist Movement in Literature* (1899), and in Edmund Wilson's *Axel's Castle* (1931). While Symons's book introduced Symbolism to Eliot, Wilson's book introduced Eliot to a reading public perplexed by Modernism and its relation to Symbolism. Huysmans continues to figure both in studies of Symbolism and anti-Semitism.[72] He gave public support to organised anti-Semitism: 'I am an anti-Semite, because I am convinced that it is the Jews who have turned France into the sad country, agitated by the lowest passions, the sad country without God, which we now see.'[73] His Symbolism and his anti-Semitism make common cause in the passage quoted above. In the dramatising of an extreme emotion, in the exotic, abundant, and vertiginous use of metaphor, in the visionary pose that it strikes, and in its combination of fantasy and revelation, it is a Symbolist prose poem masquerading as a piece of reportage. When Symons said of Huysmans that he has 'a brain all eye, a brain which sees even ideas as if they had a superficies', that he 'cares only to give you the thing seen, exactly as he sees it, with all his love or hate, and with all the exaggeration which that feeling brings into it', and that 'no one has ever invented such barbarous and exact metaphors for the rendering of visual sensations',[74] he could have had (though he did not have) this passage in mind.

This illustration of the Symbolist possibilities of anti-Semitism, and the anti-Semitic possibilities of Symbolism, helps to make my general argument, which is that while Eliot's poetry is Symbolist, and its anti-Semitism is of this kind, the anti-Semitism also represents a crisis in its Symbolism. Anti-Semitism marks the site of the poet's struggle against the non-propositional nature of his poetry. It represents the point at which he engages with the world, and with a kind of human experience that is social and collective, rather than hieratically personal. The anti-Semitism is therefore both an effect of the poetry's Symbolism and an effect of its struggle against it.

Though in 'From Poe to Valéry', Eliot avoided acknowledging his own debt to the Symbolist tradition at the point where one would most expect it,[75] his other assessments were not so disengaged. Edmund Gosse's belief that late nineteenth-century French poetry had no influence on 'English metrical writers' showed, Eliot had said, that he was 'completely out of touch with modern poetry'.[76] Even as late as 1946, when praising 'the tradition which starts with Baudelaire, and culminates in Paul Valéry', he remarked that without it his own poetry 'would hardly be conceivable'.[77] Certainly Eliot's indebtedness to French Symbolism has been a critical commonplace since *Axel's Castle*. Donald Davie endorsed and built upon this commonplace in 'Pound and Eliot: A Distinction'. From his early Laforguian exercises to the paraphrase in translation of Mallarmé in 'Little Gidding', Eliot remains, for Davie, the one poet writing in English 'centrally in the symboliste tradition'.[78] Wilson, in typically brisk fashion, lists its characteristics. There is the Symbolist poet's desire to approximate the condition of music. There is a blurring of the distinctions between the real world and the imaginary world, and between the perceptions of the different senses. There is an attempt to communicate unique personal feelings. The poet chooses arbitrary symbols to stand for special ideas of his own and the symbols are, Wilson says, a 'disguise' for these ideas, not tokens of them.[79] By contrast with Dante, whose symbolism is 'conventional, logical and definite',[80] the symbolism of Mallarmé is vague and suggestive, obliquely allusive rather than direct and specific.

Davie, who combines an exposition of Symbolism with a Symbolist account of Eliot's poetry, emphasises the musical, anti-propositional, and reflexive, aspects of the tradition. This is an advance on Wilson's account of Symbolism, which has a *fin de siècle* quality. Davie recognises that these aspects appeal to the Symbolist poet because they allow for a poetry that is not merely non-propositional, but non-referential. He thus scorns the hunt for meaning in 'A Cooking Egg', an especially difficult puzzle poem for Eliot critics.[81] The mind's capacity to make connections that cannot be made in the external world is Symbolism's revelation. It represents a yoking together of disparates, which exceeds metaphor. Symbolism is the poetry that is produced when metaphor is rejected as inadequate. It is poetry beyond metaphor, without anchorage in reality; in I. A. Richards's terms, 'vehicles' cut loose from their 'tenors'.[82] Kermode, in his exposition of the aesthetics of Symons and Pater, explains it thus: 'the work ... must not *mean* but *be*. The art that most perfectly achieves this state is music; in poetry there are difficulties of the sort that start barren arguments about the status of the poet's thought extracted and discursively considered ... [music is] the one art divinely void of meaning.'[83] The Paterian critic would argue that it is as absurd to postulate anti-Semitic Symbolist poetry as to postulate anti-Semitic music. Except that it is easy to imagine such music, which could take themes associated with Judaism in order to mock or silence them. One cannot wholly escape 'meaning', even in music.[84]

The Symbolist assimilation of poetry to music helped one Jewish critic, Harold Rosenberg, to avoid taking personally the insults of 'Gerontion' and 'Sweeney Among the Nightingales':

Why should I resent Eliot's poem for its Jewish landlord repulsive to the aristocrat who lost his property? Alas, says, Eliot, in the modern world there is no entailed real estate, no integrated culture, no 'roots', no high ritual, nothing but capitalism, Jews, and progress, tsk, tsk. I take this music as I do that of a Hungarian string trio in a restaurant with atmosphere (the very restaurant of 'Rachel *née* Rabinovitch'). So aristocratic, dancers in genuine ermine. What if the waiter is a White Guardist and an ex-pogromchick?

Another chilled vodka, please! It is quite a different thing when Eliot puts down his harmonica, mistakes himself for the dispossessed Prince Romanoff, and proposes communities with NO JEWS signs on them.[85]

This is to degrade the music of poetry to mere background ambience. The flippancy of tone masks an argument in a state of some desperation. There is no difference between the propositions Rosenberg derives from 'Gerontion' and from *After Strange Gods*. Yet the first is acceptable to him, while the second is not. The distinction between prose and poetry has rarely looked so threadbare.

It is easy to characterise anti-Semitic discourse in Symbolist terms. Anti-Semitism blurs the distinction between the real world and an imaginary one. It too, when covert, may be vague and suggestive. Like Symbolism, anti-Semitism also posits arrangements that do not correspond to any that obtain in the real world. And while none of this should be taken as contending either that anti-Semitism is inadvertently Symbolist, or that Symbolism is potentially anti-Semitic,[86] there is sufficient congruence between the two to make for the possibility of anti-Semitic, Symbolist poetry. This is a possibility that distinctions between the literary and the non-literary, the fictional and the mythic, cannot frustrate.

Frank Kermode has argued that '[f]ictions can degenerate into myths whenever they are not consciously held to be fictive. In this sense anti-Semitism is a degenerate fiction, a myth; and *Lear* is a fiction.'[87] This is too categoric. Anti-Semitism does not consist solely of lies. It is also bulky with descriptions, which is why it cannot be defeated by counter-proofs and refutations alone. It is a way of imagining Jews, a pernicious, elaborate fiction, and not just a series of theorems about the Jewish people. Furthermore, Kermode's distinction depends either on imputing a reflexive consciousness to the work, which is fanciful, or on making the sincerity of the author determinative, which is futile. If it depends on the first, it imports the pathetic fallacy into literary criticism: if on the second, it imports a variety of the intentional fallacy especially difficult to defend. Kermode is also too easy on himself. Since there is nothing in *Lear* to relate it to the genocidal anti-Semitism of Buchenwald, the myth/fiction distinction seems manifestly just. But what if, instead of *Lear*, 'Burbank' had been Kermode's example? Is it myth as fiction? What does it mean to ask of that poem: does it consciously hold anti-Semitism to be fictive? It does not ironise, it embraces, anti-Semitism. Kermode's argument does not admit of the possibility of anti-Semitism being anything other than a degenerate fiction, that is, ontologically non-literary. Yet while 'Burbank' is 'consciously' a poem, that is, one which owns its formal properties, it does not consciously hold its anti-Semitism to be fictive. If anti-Semitism is a degenerate fiction, and 'Burbank', as a poem, is a fiction, how does one understand the anti-Semitism of 'Burbank'? The answer is that one cannot. Either Kermode's distinction has to go, or the poem.

But if Kermode's general argument does not work, and it is true that Symbolism may accommodate anti-Semitism – as Eliot's anti-Semitic Symbolist poetry suggests – it is equally true that there are tendencies in anti-Semitic discourse that pull away from the Symbolist toward the unequivocally assertive, thus moving not so much from the Mallarméan to the Dantean (to adopt Wilson's distinction), as from the Mallarméan to the comic-strip caricatural. Eliot's poetry suggests this, too. It is this tension between accommodation and rejection that I now want to consider.

It can be approached by an examination of the notion of the 'symbolic': 'in 1918 or 1919 such a reference to the Jew as a *symbol* of capitalist–industrialist exploitation was hardly more prejudicial than it would be today to refer to the Scot as cheese-paring'[88] (my italics). This remark of Spender's is plainly unsatisfactory: identifying the Jew with the evil of the modern world is to focus upon him an animus far greater than anything likely to be directed at supposed skinflints. (The 'Jew joke', remarked Orwell, is 'always somewhat more ill-natured than the "Scotch" joke'.[89]) More importantly, however, Spender also neglects to place this 'symbolic' Jew in the context of the Symbolism of the poem. For him Bleistein is symbolic in the sense that he is a token for something else. To borrow Wilson's characterisation of Dante's symbolism, 'Bleistein' is a conventional, logical and definite symbol. This Jew stands for 'capitalist–industrialist exploitation' and, by implication, nothing else. The relative innocence of the poem's anti-Semitism is held to lie exactly in this supposedly thin and unremarkable rendering of a typical Jew. Spender imagines Bleistein to possess the flat fixity of an anti-Semitic caricature in a broadsheet. In its propagandistic edge of incitement, it is the polar opposite to the diffuse evocations – the semantic 'blur' – finessed by a Symbolist poetry which is, in this sense, like all other kinds of poetry, only more so. Symbolism has therefore been treated as paradigmatically poetic, and invoked by those like Brooks and Sartre who argue a strong case for distinguishing prose from poetry.[90]

I have three comments to make on this.

First, this 'jew' is much more than the cipher of Spender's reading. 'Burbank' adopts the anti-Semite's doctrines of the unity and wickedness of the Jewish people, and the trans-historical struggle between Jews and Gentiles. The title, and the poem's characters, together amount to an acknowledgment of the truth of those doctrines by the related pair Bleistein and Klein, and the opposing pair Burbank and Bleistein. The poem itself rehearses some major themes of anti-Semitism in the space of its eight stanzas. It is densely packed, both complex and succinct. Oblique, ironical, and allusive, the poem is also occasionally direct, and sometimes prosaically flat. A bravura piece, it has to be explicated with patience. It takes time to do justice to the multiple injustices that 'Burbank' does to Jews.

Secondly, achieving these complicated effects is just what Symbolism is good at. In 'Burbank' Eliot achieves in a twenty-four line poem what prosy anti-Semites cannot cram into two-volume treatises. His Symbolism is both a technique of compression and a method of reconciling contradictory meanings. Anti-Semitism's confusions become the suggestiveness of 'Burbank'. Defending the range of allusions in 'Burbank', I. A. Richards wrote: 'These things come in ... for the sake of the emotional aura which they bring and the attitudes they incite. Allusion in Mr Eliot's hands is a technical device for compression. *The Waste Land* is the equivalent in content to an epic. Without this device twelve books would have been needed.'[91] 'Burbank', if not quite an epic, is still a match to any Jew-hating treatise in the pregnant fullness of its anti-Semitism.

Thirdly, the poem's Symbolism actually encompasses both the Dantean and the Mallarméan, and shuttles back and forth between the starkly categoric and the allusively suggestive. There is the anti-Semitism of 'The jew is underneath the lot', which is conventionally symbolic, and the anti-Semitism of 'A saggy bending of the knee', which echoes other such sneers and caricatures ('the Jew with crooked heel, / crooked nose and baggy slacks'[92]). But there is also the anti-Semitism of 'A lustreless protrusive eye / Stares from the protozoic slime', which evokes reptilian associations without explicitly making them, and the anti-Semitism of 'Who clipped the lion's wings', which insinuates an answer without expressly articulating it.

The title 'Burbank with a Baedeker: Bleistein with a Cigar' is a Baedeker to the poem, presenting a contrast, and by implication inviting a choice. It also invokes an anti-Semitic cliché. The American carries with him a Baedeker; the Jew has a cigar. Their needs are expressed in these artefacts: for the one, a textbook of permanent treasures; for the other, an instrument of ephemeral pleasure. The cigar offers immediate gratification and is the symbol of both plutocrat and father: both witnesses to and beneficiaries of the labour of others. The contrast has the attenuated force of cliché. It thus immediately suggested itself to the anti-Semitic Rupert Brooke, when describing two kinds of American. There is 'the tall, thin type of American, with pale blue eyes of an idealistic, disappointed expression' and by contrast, there is the 'small, bumptious, eager, brown-faced man, with a cigar raking at an irritating angle from the corner of his mouth'.[93] In his survey of London's East End, Walter Besant described a Jewish shop proprietor with 'a large cigar... between his lips; it is a sign and a symbol'.[94] 'The smell of the cheap cigar puts the final touch', remarked Wyndham Lewis, to anti-Semitism's picture of the Jew;[95] even by the end of World War II, it was still supposed that Jews 'wear gold watches, [and] smoke cigars'.[96]

The first three stanzas of the poem are about Burbank, the second three are about Bleistein, the seventh stanza introduces Sir Ferdinand Klein, and the last stanza returns to Burbank. The poem opens with an account, in the idiom of a detective's report, of Burbank and Princess Volupine's rendezvous in a 'small hotel'. It then shifts idiom when observing what happens thereafter to each. The middle stanzas savage Bleistein, concluding with lines that obtrude from the poem like a fist. Sir Ferdinand Klein is 'entertained' by the Princess. Klein and Bleistein are a complementary pair: the one effortlessly philistine, the other bogusly aristocratic, and both Jewish. The poem concludes with Burbank in meditative pose, brooding on Venice and other mysteries. 'Burbank' may be read as a Symbolist rendering of a Jamesian theme. It is constructed out of two kinds of engagement with Venice. There are the meetings of Burbank and Klein with Princess Volupine. There are also the encounters of Burbank and Bleistein with the culture and history of Venice.

The undiscriminating nature of the Princess's attentions allows for two possible inferences. It is prostituted Venice, either extending hospitality to Jew and Gentile alike, or else submitting to a specifically Jewish pimping. The courtesan's degraded impartiality toward her clients is a parodic, anticipatory version of *The Waste Land*'s embracing of 'Gentile or Jew'. It may also be read as postulating one part of the two-part, and typically contradictory anti-Semitic sexual fantasy of Jewish women as prostitutes (Rachel *née* Rabinovitch) and Jewish men either as pimps who exploit non-Jewish women or as 'pleasure-loving ... businessmen [who] pursue Gentile girls'.[97] Either way, however, Princess Volupine is to be contrasted both with Burbank's republican lack of title, and with Sir Ferdinand Klein's newly acquired handle. The pairings tell their own story of defeat: the republican seduced by the aristocratic; the aristocratic subordinated to the plutocratic. Burbank submits to the Princess just as she herself ministers to Sir Ferdinand. Venice was once both republican and independent, but can only re-establish contact with its past through its tourists, representing aspects of that past. In that sense both Burbank and Klein become part of the texture of the poem's evocation of Venice. They represent ways of imagining both its civic decline and its waning power as a literary subject. Venice has lost a double independence. Assimilated into Italy, the city also has been absorbed into the many literary treatments of it. It has lost its distinctness. Visit Venice and you visit Italy; write about Venice and you write about Browning, or Gautier, or Shakespeare, or James, writing about Venice. 'Burbank' makes both points. The impossibility of getting to the essential Venice – the absence of an 'essential' Venice – is a frustration relieved only by the poem's ready ability to get to the essential Jew. An anti-Mosaic mosaic, 'Burbank' is also a compressed Baedeker to literary Venice.

The poem does not damn Klein and Bleistein in order to praise Burbank. His brooding is as debased as his romance. Each is as trivial as the other, while both are conducted in obscurity. His rendezvous with Princess Volupine takes place in the secrecy of an hotel; his reflections on Venice are hidden in mysteries. This 'meditation' is impossibly complex and obscure. As a subject for reflection, 'Time's ruins' is demanding enough. Taken together with (all) 'seven laws', a satiric purpose becomes evident. The sterility of Burbank's engagements is rendered by a text of exceptional literary pregnancy. For example, the first stanza's 'They were together and she fell' alludes to Tennyson's 'The Sisters',[98] a violent revenge poem. It is a dramatic monologue, spoken by one sister of another. The poem is about the shame of seduction, and the extremities of disgrace and revenge. It is about madness and loyalty, and it has a single voice of commanding individuality. In each particular, the poem reverses 'Burbank'. The banalities of clichéd thought and clichéd sex, not passion, is its theme. The brief, trite exchange between Burbank and Princess Volupine is matched by the ponderous banality of Burbank's subsequent musings. Burbank is equally incapable of sin and meditation. Just as he does not truly 'fall' following his encounter with the Princess, so his brooding on Venice's decline does not elevate him.

When Bleistein appears, he assumes the representative form of the anti-Semite's Jew. The poem stays outside him. We share what Burbank thinks; he is our fellow. Bleistein is merely part of what we see; he has no 'inner life'.[99] Inside Venice, the poem surveys the city, describing its residents, sketching its place in literature. It speaks of Venice by gathering texts that take it as their subject. Then: 'Chicago Semite Viennese'. The cities of 'Burbank' cities have different lives. While Venice is unnamed and thus elusive, 'Chicago' is a bare noun and 'Viennese' a self-explanatory adjective. The second is alien in its lack of feature, the third has the fatigued presence of a cliché. 'Viennese' invokes a conventional, xenophobic sense of the city: promiscuous, decadent, heretical, Jewish. The poem blurs the distinction between what Venice is, and how it has been imagined. The city is evoked by fragments of other evocations of Venice.

Bleistein's perspective on it is subaqueous, where the most primitive forms of life are first quickened: 'A lustreless protrusive eye / Stares from the protozoic slime / At a perspective of Canaletto.' Bleistein 'stares' because he does not understand. Jews lack an aesthetic sense. They can neither create nor appreciate art. They are either bogus artists or traders in the art of others. They are fakers or dealers. This rehearses a familiar anti-Semitic jibe. Maurras, for example, claimed that no Jew could understand Racine's 'Dans l'Orient désert, quel devint mon ennui'.[100] These views have their origins in eighteenth-century aesthetics, as Sander Gilman explains: 'The sense of the beautiful became one of the major touchstones distinguishing between the civilized and the barbaric. And the Jews were among the barbarians.' A Jewish critic of the time complained of the denial to Jews of 'any sense of the beautiful, good, [or] noble'.[101] A modified version of this libel allowed Jews an aesthetic sense, and thus a measure of creativity, but deriving only from Jewish tradition.

Consider this remark of Eliot's:

The poetry of Isaac Rosenberg... does not only owe its distinction to its being Hebraic: but because it is Hebraic it is a contribution to English literature. For a Jewish poet to be able to write like a Jew, in western Europe and in a western European language, is almost a miracle.[102]

The two versions of the libel I have just described are thus represented by Bleistein and Rosenberg respectively. Eliot's eccentric praise of the Jewish poet is consistent with his larger deprecations. 'That a Jew can do this!' registers the surprise of the anti-Semite. What is it to write like a Jew? Richard Wagner explains: 'The Jew speaks the language of the country in which he has lived from generation to generation, but he always speaks it as a foreigner.'[103] A Jew cannot compose German music; when he purports to do so, he deceives. The Jewish composer could only compose music as a Jew by drawing on the 'ceremonial music' of the synagogue service, a 'nonsensical gurgling, yodelling and cackling'. These 'rhythms ... dominate his musical imagination';[104] they are irresistible. So while the talented Jewish composer is disqualified by his race from composing German music, he is disqualified by his talent from composing Jewish music. Rosenberg was luckier. He was able, by 'almost a miracle', to write in English 'like a Jew'. The difference between Eliot's anti-Semitism and Wagner's is defined, on this point, by the possibility of this 'miracle'.

The poem's sixth stanza presents a landscape drawn by an anti-Semite. 'Piles' can be great fortunes or ancient, lofty buildings. They can be supporting timber posts for bridges, or driven into river beds or marshes. A 'pile', furthermore, can be the reverse side of a coin, or downy, short hair such as a rat has. 'Burbank' draws on all these meanings. 'Piles' evokes the buildings and the timber posts, the fortunes and more particularly the coins, and the rats. These rats are related obscurely to the wealth, both at its source as well as being the cause of its undoing. They are so closely to be identified with what they destroy that, by the synecdoche 'piles', they become it. 'The jew is underneath the lot' is to be glossed as *first*: Bleistein's subaqueous perspective, 'star[ing] from the protozoic slime', is beneath even that of a rat, Jews being lower than vermin; and *secondly*: the world, which is rotten but perplexing, is to be explained by reference to the Jews, their influence and power. This is a common enough anti-Semitic trope: '[the Jewish people are] indestructible and humiliated, the enemy of mankind and its eternal slave'.[105] The Jews are 'underneath' both in the sense of being the most worthless, and in the sense of being the most significant, as when one asks, 'what's at the bottom of all this?' (As in: 'The Jews here are at the bottom of most of our troubles and will someday suffer for it';[106] '[Jews] are always to be found at the bottom of every new villainy';[107] '[the] subterranean and invisible influence [of the Jews]'.[108]) Jews, asserts Eliot, will make money out of anything, even rats' pelts; in the early twentieth century the American fur industry had a predominantly Jewish character.[109] Jews become, in the poem's extravagant spasm of disgust, furry rats themselves.

Identifying Jews with rats is an anti-Semitic commonplace, and entails a recommendation: expel them, or exterminate them! Thus: 'If you want to avoid the bubonic plague, send the yids to Panama';[110] 'this usurious vermin' should be exterminated 'like trichinae and bacilli';[111] 'For us, the Jews are only a passing pest and a cholera.'[112] '[Rothschild] belong[s] to the rodent order; he looks like a rat, a colossal Leviathan of a rat';[113] 'the Jerusalem of filth, stinking of rats, in which Jews, covered in muck, scramble for pieces of gold';[114] 'this poisoned rat [Reinach] behind the woodwork';[115] '[a fictional Jew:] a dirty, greasy rat [with] a strange power over women';[116] '[Jewish refugees to Australia:] weedy East Europeans ... slinking, rat-faced men';[117] '[Jewish refugees to England:] the unwashed verminous alien';[118] '[Jewish immigrants] live like rats in a hole – I cannot find words bad enough for them.'[119] Pound fulminated against 'importations ancient and modern from the sewers of Pal'stine'.[120] 'Freud, Bergson', he wrote, were 'crawlin' in through all the crevices.'[121] American 'sovereignty', he insisted, had been 'handed over to VERMIN';[122] elsewhere he wrote of 'usury vermin'.[123] In a short, typically apodictic piece written in 1939, Pound declared: 'We want an European religion. Christianity is verminous with semitic infections.'[124] Anti-Semitism's most poisonous invective hisses in 'Burbank'.

However, such is its formal poise that though not a monologue it seems to call for an actor's delivery. With 'this or such was Bleistein's way' one imagines a pose being struck. 'Money in furs' is another histrionic moment: one imagines the sentence lispingly spoken, with satirical relish. It evokes a raconteur's mimicry. The lines 'She entertains Sir Ferdinand / Klein' offers another opportunity for comedy, the enjambment allowing for a comedian's sense of timing, the drop to Klein deferred by a pause that promises something significant but delivers something small (something klein). Add

Burbank's musings and it becomes clear that this is a poem to read aloud, in different voices.

Klein shares his forename with Ferdinand of Aragon, who expelled the Jews from Spain. Giving Klein that name, like linking Bleistein with anti-Semitic Vienna (indeed, 'the most anti-Semitic city in Europe'[125]), is one of the poem's jokes on the Jews. It associates them with their persecutors. He is not the only 'little' Jew in Eliot's poetry. Lady Kleinwurm ('little worm') and 'little Ben Levin the tailor' figure in the pre-Pound version of *The Waste Land*.[126] Anti-Semites refer to Jews as 'little' when they have the confidence to mock: 'this little Jew [Hore-Belisha] who was inflated to become Minister of War in time of grave national emergency';[127] 'There were thousands of little chairs and almost as many little Jews; and there was music in an open rotunda, over which the little Jews wagged their big noses';[128] 'And when the little sheenies die / Their souls will go to hell';[129] 'undersized Semites';[130] 'The Jews…fell into both littleness and arrogance: into the littleness of being content with anything, with small gains and private safety; and into arrogance in proclaiming that, in their littleness they possessed the highest good';[131] '[of Disraeli:] a little great man'.[132] In a characteristic anti-Semitic trope, contempt is allied to fear: 'the small may bring down the great by using suitable weapons'.[133] The poem clips Klein's wings by the mocking pause between the grandeur of his title and forename and littleness of his surname.[134] And then a new sentence, and a question: 'Who clipp'd the lion's wings / And flea'd his rump and pared his claws?' If the poem has an answer to Burbank's question it is Klein. Change the punctuation from a full stop to a comma and the culprit is disclosed: 'Klein, who clipp'd the lion's wings …' Clipping, fleaing and paring: do these emasculate or simply manicure? Has Klein subdued the lion or is he merely its ignoble personal servant? Clipping and paring could render Venice, the winged lion, powerless; fleaing it would perform a necessary but menial service. The first is a threat, while the second is a propitiatory, servile gesture. The poem is divided between the two. Klein is both domesticator and domestic, or in a stronger version both degrader and degraded. In the first role he is savaged, in the second he is derided. 'Burbank', unwilling to choose between the two, adopts both by its own act of emasculation. This points to the incoherence of anti-Semitism: the dual gesture of defeat and scorn. Either Jews are omnipotent or they are contemptible. If the first, their dominance cannot be combated. If the second, their existence cannot provide an explanation for the injuries for which the anti-Semite would hold them responsible. The anti-Semite always seeks to have it both ways, yoking together in his account of the Jew the most disagreeable though contradictory characteristics. While the poem hovers over this dilemma by its punctuation, it favours scorn over defeat. Hence the full stop. The anti-Semitism of 'Burbank' is defined by that period.

Ricks writes of 'Burbank': 'the effect of the article, "The Jew", is to disparage all Jews... while nevertheless leaving open a bolt-hole for the disingenuous reply that a particular Jew only is meant.'[135] The criticism of the poem's anti-Semitism becomes a criticism of the poem; 'Burbank' has failed to dramatise the prejudice and therefore has fallen victim to it. Good poems cannot be anti-Semitic. Ricks's critical practice here submits to the slogan: 'Dramatise or condemn!' He dramatises 'Gerontion' and 'Sweeney Among the Nightingales', and condemns 'Burbank'. What Brooks was able to do with 'Ripeness is all',[136] Ricks is unwilling to do with 'The jew is underneath the lot'. He is right. Indeed, it is this refusal that makes his analysis of the poem superior to the analyses of certain other critics. For example, Ronald Bush proposes, and James Longenbach agrees, that it is not Eliot speaking in the poem but 'an [Henry] Adams-like compatriot'. Bush adds that we do not 'see' Bleistein 'through the lens of an objective narrator but through Burbank's refined yet debilitating sensibility'.[137] That is, Burbank is an anti-Semite. If this is what he 'sees', he must hate Jews. Bush is too nonchalant about the poem's anti-Semitism to make this point expressly; it is there by implication of his argument only. Longenbach goes slightly further. He argues generally of the poems of *Ara Vos Prec* that their 'layer of self-consciousness does not always save [Eliot] from the implications of the anti-Semitism or anti-feminism of the poems' personae'.[138] Not always? Against these evasions and half-readings it is my case that Eliot manipulates anti-Semitism in 'Burbank'. But to what purpose?

It could be argued that 'Burbank' economically rehearses, and subverts, the clichés associated with the innocent abroad and the malign philistinism of Jews. Such an argument would go as follows. While the poem's anti-Semitism is harsh, hysterical, and concise, it is also uncertain. 'The jew is underneath the lot' refers neither to Bleistein nor Klein. Dislocated from the poem's narrative, this line perplexes by positing the dominance of Jews while also representing them in a state of degradation and squalor. Its slogan-like simplicity jars, a dissonance that derives from a sharp division in the poem's tone – a street shout, against the library murmur of Burbank's musings. And the street shout doesn't quite work as a shout. It is alienated in its context and so compressed that it articulates more than a slogan could convey. What would otherwise come close to an incitement, instead becomes part of the puzzle. 'Burbank' puts anti-Semitic discourse on display, and thereby unmasks it. 'Naturally scorning [such a] credulous view of the world', the poem presents anti-Semitism as a 'visible object'.[139] Looked at in this way, it is susceptible to a deconstructionist analysis: 'To deconstruct a poem is to indicate the precise location of its figuration of doubt, its uncertain notice of that limit where persuasion yields to a dance or interplay of tropes.'[140] What would otherwise have been read as the central proposition of the poem's anti-Semitism instead has been disclosed as 'its figuration of doubt', unmoored from reference and divided within itself. One could say that Eliot has kept the arguments open and the poetic object closed.[141] One learns about anti-Semitism when one reads 'Burbank'. The poem purports to assent to it, while in fact undermining it by the play of its language, which cannot be straitjacketed by the rigidities of anti-Semitic discourse. The poem makes its readers work; it does not work on its readers. It is not manipulative; it is resistant to manipulation. To describe it in language borrowed from an account of another poem, also read as univocally political, 'it confounds the clarity' of anti-Semitism.[142] Jerome McGann, advancing a sophisticated version of this argument in relation to a work most resistant to it, Pound's *Cantos*, thus asserts that 'poetry may not be "totalitarian" even when its ideology is'. Certain lines in the *Cantos* 'open to critical thought those ideologies to which the poetry has committed itself'. This is something that 'poetry always does'.[143]

This is an argument one can respect, though I reject it. In 'Sweeney Among the Nightingales', anti-Semitism is indeed interrogated. Some of its claims look weaker after a reading of the poem. In *The Rock*, anti-Semitism of a certain kind is repudiated expressly. But in 'Burbank' it is equally expressly endorsed. This can only be denied if one holds that every ostensibly anti-Semitic poem must, as a principle of its poetic being, undermine anti-Semitism's dogmas. To adopt this position is to ignore the differences between poems. Some will query anti-Semitism, others may endorse it. They cannot avoid its contradictions, so even those poems that promote anti-Semitism to that extent 'expose' them. Yet the contradictions that they expose are evident in every anti-Semitic pamphlet pushed through a door, and in every anti-Semitic speech delivered at a rally. When one witnesses the collapse of a process of reasoning in an anti-Semitic poem, it is not the operation of literary language at work but the pressures of anti-Semitism's own irrationality. Identifying 'illogic' in an anti-Semitic passage is not in itself evidence that its author is 'ill at ease with his prejudice'.[144] On balance, therefore, the above interpretation is too generous, conforming with the worst aspect of deconstruction, 'its dreary and repetitious discovery of tiresomely familiar "inherent strains and contradictions"'.[145] While the anti-Semitism of 'Burbank' is elusive, it is also capturable. Though the poem subjects anti-Semitism to intense pressure, it holds up. This exemplary modern poem, thus 'full of gaps and full of lights, filled with absences and overnourishing signs, without foresight or stability of intention, and ... so opposed to the social function of language',[146] yet finds a place for anti-Semitism. Indeed, anti-Semitism is embraced as an opportunity for a modern poem; it also represents a moment of recoil from that indeterminacy of meaning which is modern poetry's regime. 'The task', wrote Eliot of Kipling's poetry, 'is the opposite of that with which we are ordinarily faced when attempting to defend contemporary verse. We expect to have to defend a poet against the charge of obscurity: we have to defend Kipling against the charge of excessive lucidity.'[147] The anti-Semitism of 'Burbank' is precisely of this excessively lucid kind; it is both the occasion for the poem, and an anomalous element within it. It is a challenge both to our understanding of the nature of modern poetry and of the aesthetics in which that poetry has been cultivated.

Let me return to the impact of a first reading of 'Burbank'. The anti-Semitism is unmistakable. It reaches out like a clear signal to the reader, bemused by everything else in the poem. There is the music hall, open-palmed gesture of Bleistein, his fat cigar and subhuman, dead eyes; there is the manipulative, corrosive sophistication of Klein; there is the destructive philistinism of them both, and their parasitic homelessness; and there are the rats that spread plague, noiselessly and invisibly destroying what they infest. The poem demands a careful reading, one that takes us some distance from our first impressions. But to forget those impressions is an error. 'Burbank' does not ironise anti-Semitism – it is not a love mas-

querading as a hate. When the world becomes too variously complex
to grasp, simplifications seem to become necessary. Anti-Semitism is
the great simplifier. It offers coherence and comfort. In the words of
Eliot's mentor, Charles Maurras: 'Everything seems impossible, or
frightfully difficult, without the providential arrival of anti-Semitism,
through which all things fall into place and are simplified.'[148]

Eliot's own account of the place of 'subject-matter' in a Symbolist
poem is germane. He proposes that 'it is important as *means*: the *end*
is the poem. The subject exists for the poem, not the poem for the
subject.'[149] If this was right, one might say of 'Burbank' that anti-
Semitism is its means. It enables a Symbolist poem to be written, with
nothing in view but itself.[150] But Eliot is wrong, and so it would be
wrong to leave the problem at this point. He postulates a mistakenly
complete distinction between 'poem' and 'subject', and a false
antithesis between Symbolist and non-Symbolist poetry. Insofar as
the two entities can be abstracted, it is perhaps better to argue that
the relation between 'subject' and 'poem' is dialectical, that is to say,
reciprocally shaping. Specifically, anti-Semitism is not just one topic
amongst others that the Symbolist freely may choose without that
choice having implications for his poetry. When a poet chooses this
'subject matter', he discloses his relation to Symbolism. The 'means'
corrupt the 'end', thereby ensuring that the complicated, corrupting
anti-Semitism of some of Eliot's earlier poetry produces a complicated, corrupt Symbolism. An account of the Symbolism of Eliot's
poetry that is not also an account of its occasional anti-Semitism is
thus incomplete. The anti-Semitism is evidence of a Symbolism in
crisis. Its appearance represents the moment at which the impressions
of a sensitive, self-dramatising poet have become the prejudices of a
vicious group. The intuitive has become the programmatic, and the
vague and suggestive, a fantasy of half-glimpsed conspiracies.
Symbolist obliquity promotes anti-Semitic obloquy.

This is similar to Gabriel Pearson's argument in 'Eliot: An
American Use of Symbolism'.[151] He maintains that for Eliot,
Symbolism was both his patrimony and his predicament, and that
this predicament in turn became a central issue of his poetry. Eliot's
poetry does not celebrate but struggles against the 'self-substantive
verbal universe' that it creates. It is marked by 'the intolerable
wrestle / With words and meanings', a contest that can lead to the
extreme conclusion that 'The poetry does not matter'.[152] For
Symbolism, the referential aspect of language is something to

overcome, an obstacle to the realisation of the ideal poem.[153] Hence the privileging of music as the model art form. For Eliot, by contrast, this dimension of language in poetry is both inevitable and necessary. He rejects the goal of 'pure poetry', because 'poetry is only poetry so long as it preserves some "impurity" in this sense: that is to say, so long as the subject matter is valued for its own sake'.[154] Pearson asks: what poetry can a Symbolist write if he acknowledges that words 'are [also] ... social deposits and repositories of social acts'?[155]

To which one answers: anti-Semitic poetry, and Christian poetry. Each reaches out to relate words to forms of existence outside language. In its barbarisms, anti-Semitism degrades 'the word'; Christianity is the triumph of 'the word' become Word. The language of anti-Semitism is abandoned for soundless violence. The language of Christianity is transcended by voiceless prayer. Anti-Semitism is realised in the infliction of humiliations, Christianity in the rituals of worship. Acts of persecution, acts of reverence – anti-Semitism and Christianity are each integrally gestural as well as linguistic. Pearson correctly identifies the Christian resolution to Eliot's dilemma: 'Eliot took the logic of Symbolism to an extreme and then attempted to return it to experience by connecting the word with the Word.'[156] But there is also the anti-Semitic resolution. Pearson's case for the affinity of Symbolism with anti-Semitism is an external affair, to be described in political terms as a 'resistance against the debasements of bourgeois democratic mass society'. This gives Symbolism an ideological dimension, allowing him to identify the anti-Semitism in Eliot's work as central to it because it is central in 'Gerontion', which is itself 'central to Eliot's poetic practice'.[157] This is worth saying, though too contingent to Eliot's poetics to be helpful in the present context. I propose instead the following as Eliot's anti-Semitic resolution.

It is to return Symbolism to experience by connecting 'the word' with 'the jew'. In opposition to the upper-case 'Word', there is the lower-case 'jew'. The word reaches upwards to one and downwards to the other. 'The jew' is the lowest, to be found in places beneath the reach even of wharf rats, in the protozoic slime. Christianity and anti-Semitism themselves represent two possible extremes of experience. The Christian wishes to become that which he worships; the anti-Semite wishes to crush that which he fears and despises. The ambition of the first is effacement of the (sinning) Self; the ambition of the second is erasure of the (Jewish) Other. Christianity and 'the jew' are thus in polar contrast in Eliot's poetry. Eliot insisted, it will be recalled, on the impossibility of a Christian anti-Semitism.[158] This self-serving and erroneous claim becomes intelligible in the context of what I have just been describing. Such a combination would make his poetics incoherent, pulling his poetry in opposite directions. What can a poetry of the 'Word' have to do with the 'jew'?

CHAPTER 4

'*Dirge*', '*A Cooking Egg*', The Waste Land, *and the aesthetics of ugliness*

THE UGLY AS A PROBLEM AND AS A PROJECT

'Beauty is difficult' (Canto LXXIV), remarked Pound in a work which explores the limits of the beautiful in order to transgress them. 'The poets loved by Ezra Pound are tired of Beauty', wrote John Butler Yeats to his son, 'since they have met it so often … I am tired of Beauty my wife, says the poet, but here is that enchanting mistress Ugliness.'[1] In 'The Serious Artist', Pound praised the 'cult of ugliness' as 'diagnosis'.[2] Wyndham Lewis derided, while also reflecting in his own work, the fashionable modernity of the ugly: 'It did not take [Picasso] long to see that "beauty" was the last thing his contemporaries demanded of the artist. And since then he has never looked back – a long succession of novel brands of idiocy, acromegalic sluggishness, hysteria and abortion have continually poured from his brush.'[3] C. K. Stead has observed: 'With the establishment of Eliot as a major critic and poet, "Truth" was out as a simple test of poetic merit; so was "Beauty".'[4] So much for Modernism; now for the Jews. At the end of Richard Sheridan's *The Duenna*, the duped Jew is abused: 'Dare such a thing as you pretend to talk of beauty? A walking rouleau! – a body that seems to owe all its consequences to the dropsy! – a pair of eyes like two dead beetles in a wad of brown dough? – a beard like an artichoke, with dry shrivelled jaws that would disgrace the mummy of a monkey!'[5] According to Sander Gilman, it was a 'commonplace in the anthropological literature' of the late nineteenth and early twentieth century, that Jews 'could never be truly beautiful'.[6] 'Anti-Semitism', Phillipe Lacoue-Labarthe suggests, 'is primarily, fundamentally, an aestheticism. (In his essence, the "Jew" is a caricature: ugliness itself.)'[7] According to Hegel, 'With the Jews, the state of independence was to be a state of total passivity, of total ugliness.'[8] Indeed, one commentator has remarked that for Hegel 'Judaism is ... the fulfilment of ugliness as Hellenism was the fulfilment of beauty.'[9] 'Let us remember', says Poliakov, '[the] equation between Judaism and ugliness.'[10]

As for Eliot, note the shift between an extract from an essay he published in 1920, in *The Sacred Wood*:

The contemplation of the *horrid* or *sordid* or *disgusting*, by an artist, is the necessary and negative aspect of the impulse toward the pursuit of beauty. But not all succeed as did Dante in expressing the complete scale from negative to positive. *The negative is the more importunate.*[11]

and this, part of a lecture he gave in 1933 and published later that year in *The Use of Poetry*:

It is an advantage to mankind in general to live in a beautiful world; that no one can doubt. But for the poet is it so important? We mean all sorts of things, I know, by Beauty. But the essential advantage for a poet is not to have a beautiful world with which to deal: it is *to be able to see beneath both beauty and ugliness*; to see the boredom, and the horror, and the glory.[12]

These two passages may be read as variations on this passage of Emerson:

Art lives and thrills in new use and combining of contrasts, and mining into the dark evermore for blacker pits of night. What would a painter do, or what would poet or saint, but for crucifixions and hells? And evermore in the world is this marvellous balance of *beauty* and *disgust, magnificence* and *rats*.[13]

Against Emerson's rapt contemplation of 'balance', Eliot substitutes first an imbalance (the greater importunity of 'the negative'), and then an aesthetics that repudiates beauty and its opposite in favour of what lies beneath both. The first passage is contemporaneous with *Ara Vos Prec*; the second follows by a few years the publication of 'The Hollow Men' and 'Ash Wednesday'. The 'importunate negative' may be taken as a gloss on the Quatrain poems and parts of *The Waste Land*. The vision of 'the boredom, the horror and the glory' may be taken as a gloss on the later poetry, and on other parts of *The Waste Land*, the deleted epigraph of which is Conrad's 'The horror! The horror!' It is *The Waste Land* and *Sweeney Agonistes* that are in this context the transitional texts, written by Eliot in his journey from the aesthetic represented by the first passage to the aesthetic represented by the second. Hence the suppressed anti-Semitism of the former and the marginal anti-Semitism of the latter. There is a considerable gap between an art of 'the horrid or sordid or disgusting' and an art of 'the boredom, and the horror and the glory'. The two passages quoted point toward two distinct aesthetics; only the first is consistent with anti-Semitic poetry. Passing from one to the other, Eliot dropped anti-Semitism. An aspect of 'the negative', it no longer importuned him. *The Waste Land* erases just those distinctions upon which anti-Semites most insist: between Gentile and Jew, and between Athens and Jerusalem. 'Wavering between the profit and the loss', and 'the blind eye', carry no anti-Semitic charge in 'Ash Wednesday'. In 'East Coker' one may imagine the anti-Semites accompanying '[t]he captains, merchant bankers, eminent men of letters', and others, 'into the dark, / The vacant interstellar spaces'. There is no room for anti-Semitism in the *Four Quartets*.

The poems of *Ara Vos Prec* thus represent a distinct moment in Eliot's career as a poet. They are the fruits of his anti-Semitic period. They are not merely transitional texts.[14] It was in *Ara Vos Prec* that 'Gerontion', 'Burbank', 'Sweeney Among the Nightingales', and 'A Cooking Egg', were published together for the first time. Eliot's newly displayed anti-Semitism, dominating the collection, should have shocked reviewers. It did not. They were not wholly blind, however, to the differences between this volume and the earlier *Prufrock and other observations*. One complained, for example, that Eliot 'ha[d] forgotten...his sense of beauty'.[15] This question of 'beauty' was raised repeatedly by Eliot's early critics and reviewers, especially in relation to *Ara Vos Prec*. They were right to do so. The poems of *Prufrock and other observations* take ugly scenes as their subject; the poems of *Ara Vos Prec* are themselves ugly. The former have thus been justly praised as 'paradoxically render[ing] ugly things beautiful or beautifully';[16] in the latter, by contrast, critics have found 'scorn' and 'contempt',[17] and a poetry of 'execrable taste'[18] that is 'more nasty than witty'.[19] These poems make beauty difficult.

The opening question for this chapter is: given that anti-Semitism is both wicked and false, can poetry survive it? Let me start with a disagreement between Christopher Ricks and George Steiner. Ricks opens his chapter on anti-Semitism in *T. S. Eliot and Prejudice* with a letter by Steiner to the *Listener*:

The obstinate puzzle is that Eliot's uglier touches tend to occur at the heart of very good poetry (which is not the case with Pound). One thinks of the notorious...[20]

... and the letter continues with Steiner listing those lines and phrases that go to make the case against Eliot. In a sequence of rapid-fire judgments on the letter, Ricks: praises Steiner's courage in making this point; says that Pound should be thanked because the poetry in the *Cantos* would not suffer if the anti-Semitic passages were deleted; and picks Steiner up on 'puzzle', the wrong word because it suggests the possibility of a solution. These three assessments are of a piece, stemming from a view of the nature of art that the two critics share by implication. A poetry of anti-Semitism violates deeply held convictions about the purpose of art and the mission of the artist. While Steiner is brave to notice the breach, Ricks considers him mistaken in suggesting that it can be repaired. Pound deserves gratitude for not causing a similar breach. This last point is absurd. Our pleasure that the anti-Semitic passages are erasable without damage to the *Cantos* does not put us in Pound's debt. One might as much thank a criminal for bungling his crime. Ricks treats a happy failure as a moral triumph.

He drops the argument with Steiner: it points the wrong way, away from Eliot and toward the root of his own critical approach. He settles instead into a textual explication so detailed that it frustrates the reaching of any settled conclusion on Eliot's anti-Semitism. He works to unsettle our prejudices about Eliot's prejudices by redeeming individual texts from blanket dismissal, striving to present them instead as 'diverse and elusive'.[21] He rescues one text from a prejudiced reading that assumes anti-Semitism, equivocates over another, and regretfully concedes a third. Yet his analysis fails to achieve its ambition of rendering the diversity of the texts. This is because what he intends by 'diversity' is mere distance from anti-Semitism. He does not grasp the diversity within anti-Semitism. And what he intends by 'elusiveness' is merely the ability of the poems to evade the charge of anti-Semitism. Ricks ignores the complexity of anti-Semitism and thus the options within it for the poet.

The 'puzzle' posed by the Steiner letter is simple to express but difficult to answer. How can the 'ugly', as in 'uglier touches', be intimate with 'very good poetry' without being transformed by it into something benign? By 'ugly', Steiner and Ricks understand 'evil'. This is a condensed version of the proposition that the poetry's uglification of Jews – its anti-Semitism – is wicked, and I follow them here. The issue they raise opens out onto a venerable problem in aesthetics, though it goes deeper than merely the challenge to art of the unbeautiful. Steiner is happy to raise this large question about Eliot's poems without attempting an answer. Ricks shrinks from it altogether. The one escapes from the texts too soon, while the other locks himself into a tight dance on their punctuation, their individual words, and their separate lines. Steiner uses the quotations as slogans; Ricks pores over them as mysteries. The result is that what Steiner raises too elliptically in a letter, Ricks fails to answer discursively in a book. The puzzle becomes less intractable when the aesthetic limiting art to the beautiful and/or the good and/or the true is abandoned. Indeed, if one could assert that art is not flawed by wickedness but instead can cohabit happily with it (as it can with common cruelty and other ordinary vices), the puzzle would disappear altogether. But neither Steiner nor Ricks is able to make this assertion because for them art redeems. (In the chapter on anti-Semitism, Ricks says: '[Eliot's] art is redemptive'.[22]) It inspires, rather than incites, and it certainly does not foment hate. The force of Steiner's surprise, the 'puzzle' itself, is a knot made up from diverse but related strands of aesthetic speculation, such as the following four.

First, there is the (once patent, but now more usually implied) association of artistic with divine creation, which carries with it, without strictly entailing, certain notions of the artist's benevolence, wisdom and insight, and the artist's presence in his or her work. The ancient derivation of aesthetics in cosmology (for example, the Pythagorean doctrine of the sphere's beauty[23]) is one source of this conception of the artist. The artist is God, and the work is his or her world. Poetry does not imitate nature; it is poetry's composition that imitates the creating, naming Godhead. Thus, Cowley's muse 'speak'st ... in the same style as He'.[24] For Shaftesbury, the poet is 'a second maker';[25] for Herder, he is a 'second creator';[26] for Kandinsky, 'the creation of works of art is the creation of the world'.[27] Some sense of the difficulty that Eliot's work causes these notions, and the association from which they derive, may be caught both in Frank Kermode's description of *The Waste Land* as a work of 'decreation',[28] and, by contrast, in the way in which some have tried to read that poem in spiritual terms. The poem is thus taken too far from or brought too close to God.[29] It falls on one side or the other of artistic creation, thereby repudiating the analogy between God's work and that of the poet. It is a work which defies that analogy. Whether nihilistic or confessional, it refuses to create a world.

Secondly, there is the conviction that art has an ethical dimension.

One aspect of this conviction is the belief that the poet is a superior human being because, by the fruits of his creativity, he enhances freely the quality of human life. The writing of poetry is thus an act of supererogatory goodness for which the poet should be honoured.[30] The particular sense in which Eliot's early work offends against a belief in the ethical nature of poetry is in its alienation from its subjects, Jews amongst them. Take, for example, Shelley's affirmation: 'The great instrument of moral good is the imagination; and poetry administers to the effect by acting upon the cause.' The ethical faculty is one of identification, a quality of the imagination: '[a] man, to be greatly good, must imagine intensely and comprehensively; he must put himself in the place of another and of many others; the pains and pleasures of his species must become his own.'[31] The poet of 'Burbank' does not make the pain of the persecuted his own, but makes his own contribution to that pain. The poem adds to their suffering. It is wounding, not healing, an exercise in hostility, not empathy. It is an imaginative study in the withholding of imaginative sympathy. It counters that Romantic practice of bemoaning the departure of one's imaginative faculties. In contrast to the Coleridge of 'Dejection: An Ode', the poet of 'Burbank' exults in his 'viper thoughts'.[32] The poem has been defended thus: '[t]he period between the wars ... closes with ... an anti-Semitism grown cruel and murderous in a way unimaginable to the conceiver of Bleistein twenty years earlier'.[33] This is intended to excuse, 'unimaginable' meaning 'unanticipatible'. The word is right, the intended meaning, wrong. What 'Burbank' demonstrates is that a defeat of the imagination does not always entail a defeat for art. It does not help one to be 'greatly good'; it invites one to be unconcerned about the torments of others. It gives the reader a 'moral holiday',[34] making art out of the suffering of others, not by realising it, but by ignoring its reality. Shelley's argument has been adopted by the liberal Richard Rorty. Poets speak for 'victims of cruelty, people who are suffering'.[35] Literature helps us to be better liberals by enlarging the scope of our imaginative range. Eliot's illiberal Quatrains (antagonistic to a 'society ... worm-eaten with Liberalism'[36]) contrive to reduce it.

Thirdly, there is that tradition of English cultural criticism which argued for the redemptive qualities of poetry as a substitute for religion, or as a means of education. It is represented in Arnold's work (see, for example, 'The Study of Poetry'[37]), and in the work of

I. A. Richards. Of the nostrum 'poetry is capable of saving us', Eliot once remarked: 'There is of course a locution in which we say of someone "he is not one of us"; it is possible that the "us" of [this nostrum] represents an equally limited and select number.'[38] Eliot fastidiously excluded himself from this number; poetry could not, at any rate, save *him*. Quoting Richards's *Science and Poetry* ('We shall ... be thrown back, as Matthew Arnold foresaw, upon poetry. Poetry is capable of saving us'), Eliot commented:

I should have felt completely at a loss in this passage, had not Matthew Arnold turned up ... I am sure ... that salvation by poetry is not quite the same thing for Mr. Richards as it was for Arnold; but so far as I am concerned these are merely different shades of blue.[39]

Richards's Arnoldian perspective led him to discover in Eliot's poetry a redemptive quality it does not have: 'some readers find in his poetry not only a clearer, fuller realization of their plight ... than they find elsewhere, but also through the very energies set free in that realization a return of the saving passion.'[40] It is against this aesthetic of the 'saving passion' that Eliot wrote when he asserted in his 1928 Preface to *The Sacred Wood* that 'Poetry is a superior amusement ... and no more is it religion or an equivalent of religion, except by some monstrous abuse of words.'[41] This was a liberating moment in the history of English literary criticism, freeing poetry from the burden of Arnoldian expectation and creating a space for the reception of Eliot's own poetry. Eliot took issue with this aesthetic once again in the final chapter of *The Use of Poetry*. His strategy throughout was twofold. First, he demoted poetry: 'a superior amusement'. Secondly, he insisted upon its diversity: 'A perfectly satisfactory theory which applied to all poetry would do so only at the cost of being voided of all content.'[42] This opened up the possibility of a poetry of scorn and deflation. It made room for the Quatrains. It also allowed for *The Waste Land* and 'Ash Wednesday', poems respectively of despair and devotion. Of course, objections to Eliot's anti-Semitic poetry can stem from this rejected aesthetic. But they may derive equally from an objection to works of defamation. One need not assert the constitutive benevolence of poetry to find hate poems offensive.

Fourthly, there is the doctrine presented in Murray Krieger's *Theory of Criticism*, but of considerable pedigree. Krieger contends that poetry is to be prized because it 'break[s] free of the limiting blinders' of discursive language, which by contrast dwells among 'dead universals'.[43] Poetry can be 'a microcosm of the particularizations that existence offers'; discursive ('normal') language is forced to ignore these particularisations in consequence of its 'generic' nature. This redemptive nominalism gives literature a 'cognitive function', disclosing a 'social role for poetry' that is 'profound'. 'We still generally assume', remarked Donald Davie, 'that it is the poet's duty to exclude abstractions in favour of concretions.'[44] There is an Arnoldian dimension to this, too:

The grand power of poetry is its interpretative power ... the power of so dealing with things as to awaken in us a wonderfully full, new, and intimate sense of them, and of our relations with them. ... we feel ourselves to be in contact with the essential nature of those objects ... The interpretations of science do not give us this intimate sense of objects [45]

Poetry is revelatory, giving us access to essences otherwise hidden. Describing this as poetry's 'fidelity to experience'[46] is thus too weak. It is a capacity of poetry to be described, in a more Symbolist mode, as noumenal. Now, one has only to place the 'jew' of 'Gerontion' in the context of such a passage to grasp the nature of that poem's provocation to this doctrine. Here is a poem that animates the 'dead universal' of the anti-Semite's version of the Jew, disclosing a social role for poetry that so far from freeing humanity to gaze direct upon the 'existential' reality of 'the outward world', actually mires it deeper in that pernicious false consciousness which is anti-Semitism.

Critics have been reluctant to acknowledge the radical nature of Eliot's achievement. One such critic has gushed of Eliot's early poetry that '[its] whole world is touched with pity'.[47] Another declared that Eliot 'seemed himself at one with the rejected'.[48] These perverse pieties indicate what is expected of poetry, and how blind to Eliot's work such an expectation can be. Steiner's discomfort, by contrast, derives from a clear-sighted view of the incompatibility of that work with those expectations, allied to an unwillingness to reject either the work or the expectations. Re-rehearsing his puzzlement in correspondence after publication of Ricks's T. S. Eliot and Prejudice,[49] Steiner affirms his elevated notion of the poet. He is therefore 'deeply perplexed by certain passages in the poetry and prose of a great master of sensibility, language and cultural argument'. 'Poets', he insists, 'should be most alert to the articulation of inhumanity within human speech.' And yet Eliot was not alert. In the choice that innovative art compels between modifying our sense of art's possibilities and rejecting that work's aesthetic credentials, Steiner elects for neither, acknowledging the quality of Eliot's work, while adhering to criteria that cannot accommodate it. It is a troubling, inconclusive enlargement of art's capabilities for Steiner to propose that 'in Eliot, the Jew-despising passages come in the midst of very great poetry and are thoroughly integrated with it'. The final clause represents the key concession, given the availability of the easier route of arguing that that poetry is flawed by anti-Semitism. Steiner's letter suffers from a theoretical cramp. Forced to admit an exception to his rule, the rule is left discomfited, with no other rule to replace it. Robert Lowell was similarly perplexed:

in Eliot, the Jew spelled with a small 'j' in 'Gerontion', is that anti-Semitism or not? Eliot's not anti-Semitic in any sense, but there's certainly a dislike of Jews in those early poems. Does he gain in the fierceness of writing his Jew with a small 'j'? He says you write what you have to write and in criticism you can say what you think you should believe in. Very ugly emotions perhaps make a poem.[50]

Steiner is right to recognise that the line 'The jew is underneath the lot' cannot be dismissed as a 'serious blemish on a beautiful poem', to borrow Eliot's words in another context.[51] Nor is it mere 'dross'.[52] It has a more intimate relation with the poem than such a criticism would allow. The problem seems to resist resolution.

The answer does not lie in any celebration of the evil in art. The thrill at the risks literature takes is a resonantly Romantic critical theme that has maintained its appeal. Blake provides a typically extreme text: 'The poet is independent and wicked; the philosopher is dependent and good. Poetry is to excuse vice, and show its reason and necessary purgation.'[53] There are endorsements of this creed from the university: 'It is of the essence of imaginative culture that it transcends the limits both of the naturally possible and the morally acceptable';[54] and from the avant-garde: 'the story of writing always begins with hell... Our wickedness is one of vertiginous themes that opens the space of writing.'[55] But Eliot's anti-Semitic poems do not represent a liberating eruption of evil. While they are cruel in places, they are not demonic. Though exercises in the refutation of Shelley's poetic prescriptions, they cannot be elevated into examples of Blakean immorality. Rhapsodisers of the potential for evil in literature identify goodness with restraint, and vice with the unconventional: 'submission and obedience ... are on the side of Good'.[56] But this is not anti-Semitism, which is the panic of conformism, which does not free but imprisons, and which is indeed the malevolence of the confined unable truly to emancipate themselves. Anti-Semites are not fearless thinkers; they are scoundrels.[57] Their apocalypses are murderous but bogus, their armageddons are staged. Anti-Semitism is an amalgam of ordinary vices, aggravated by history and compounded by anxieties of religion and nation. It is not 'transgressive'; if only the pervasive, tacit anti-Semitism of our time and place *did* shock. In contrast to the transgressive *Satanic Verses*, or Salman Rushdie's gloss on it, Eliot's anti-Semitic poems do not 'dissent ... from imposed orthodoxies of all types, from the view that the world is quite clearly This and not That'.[58] On the contrary. They endorse a received and disparaging view of Jews, a view that Jews are very precisely 'This' and not 'That'.

These poems, which make Jews ugly, partly derive from just those Modernist animadversions against beauty quoted at the beginning of this chapter. They challenge received theories of the place of the ugly in art. I know of six such theories. The first finds a place for untransformed ugliness in art. This has an ancient derivation.[59] Since both imitation and the pleasure in imitation is innate in human beings, an imitation is often agreeable though the thing imitated is disagreeable. Indeed, when the principle of imitation is made the end of art, as Hegel pointed out, 'objective beauty itself disappears', the only question being the 'correctness of the imitation'.[60] The second theory proposes that the ugly in nature, when rendered in art, elevates the reader. It has thus been argued of Eliot's poetry that by 'describing ugliness and horror ... [it] thereby lifts from us their burden'.[61] The third theory proposes that art can transform the ugly into the beautiful: 'The horrible, artistically expressed, becomes beauty.'[62] The artist may be able to educate his audience to recognise the 'essential' beauty within the ugly, a claim made for Eliot's work: 'See how deformity / Under attentive eyes / Bears perfection within it.'[63] The fourth theory acknowledges a place for the ugly in the context of art's inclusiveness: 'What we call ugly is part of the great whole which escapes us and which harmonizes, if not with man, then with the entire creation';[64] 'A picture may be beautiful when it has touches of black in appropriate places; in the same way the whole universe is beautiful, if one could see it as a whole, even with its sinners, though their ugliness is disgusting when they are viewed in themselves.'[65] The ugly has to be accepted as an element in the natural order. The fifth theory makes the representation of the ugly in art genre-specific. Nietzsche, for example, proposed that it is 'the tragic myth that... convince[s] us that even the ugly and disharmonious are part of an aesthetic game'.[66] Of course, Nietzsche made substantial claims for tragedy; there are other, tamer versions of the argument that the 'ugly' is appropriate to some, but not all, kinds of art. The sixth theory holds that ugliness in art is the badge of its failure: 'the ugly is unsuccessful expression'.[67]

None of these theories addresses Steiner's objection to Eliot's poetry. The first is derived from an inadequate psychology, while the fourth is unable to account for works in which the ugly is *excluded* from the given natural order. The second, third, and sixth devalue Eliot's anti-Semitic poetry. The fifth fails because it depends on the unsustainable premiss that anti-Semitism has a given place within a specific genre or genres. Eliot does not make anti-Semitism beautiful, he exploits its ugliness. With great force and dexterity, he taps its poetic resources.

Each of these theories assumes the natural ugliness of the represented entity. In Eliot's case, however, it is the anti-Semitism that makes Jews ugly, and is ugly itself. A comparable aesthetic commitment to ugliness is constitutive both of satire and the grotesque.

The Jews of Eliot's anti-Semitic imagination lack, however, that dimension of supernatural horror which, as Wolfgang Kayser has shown, is an element of the grotesque. Though Rachel is an instance of that commingling of human and animal traits typical of the sub-genre of the 'realistic' grotesque, the effect in this case is to degrade her and not to remove her into a realm that is fantastic and unsettling. Eliot's anti-Semitic poems are not, in Kayser's 'final interpretation' of the grotesque, 'attempt[s] to invoke and subdue the demonic aspects of the world'.[68] The poems' Jews are not that menacing.

Satire's object is to unmask the ugliness beneath the appearance of beauty. It therefore confirms art's moral purpose: '[it] is ethical art par excellence. The ethical will to admonish, educate, and change is always aggressive... [it] seeks to destroy evil, in order that the good can unfold.'[69] Even the notionally 'non-ethical satire' of Wyndham Lewis, purportedly savaging stupidity and not vice, has a significant moral charge, privileging the 'free-man' over the 'machine-like

human' 'type' in its 'Massacre of the Insignificants'.[70] Hugh
Kenner, anxious to conceal the ethically problematical nature of the
Quatrains, describes them as 'satires'.[71] They are not, though they
do stand in a certain relation to satire. They draw upon its capacities
for ethically sanctioned belligerence. Anti-Semitism is invective that
often poses as satire. Santayana, for example, misrepresented his own
anti-Semitism as satirical: 'I see that my expressions about the Jews,
if taken for exact history or philosophical criticism, are unfair. But
they were meant for free satire, and I don't like to yield to the
pretension that free satire must be excluded from literature.'[72]
Santayana overrated himself in this respect: when he wrote about
Jews, he did not satirise, he merely sneered.

So far in this chapter Eliot's 'ugly touches' have escaped aesthetic
embrace. His anti-Semitic poetry does not transform the ugly; it is
not a celebration of the poet's ability to embrace the world in its
multifarious variety; it is not a rhapsodic purgation of evil. Eliot
wrote to his brother regarding the reception of *Ara Vos Prec*: 'even
here I am considered by the ordinary newspaper critic as a wit or a
satirist, and in America I suppose I shall be thought merely
disgusting.'[73] He rejects in advance the defence of satire others will
make for these poems. He dismisses that primitive reaction to the
poems which finds them 'merely disgusting', notwithstanding his
own defence in the same year of a poetry written in 'contemplation
of the horrid or sordid or disgusting'. Making due allowance for the
informality of the occasion of these remarks, they disclose an Eliot
uncertain how to characterise these poems. The best that he can do
is to describe two of them ('Burbank' and 'Sweeney Among the
Nightingales') as 'intensely serious'.[74]

'DIRGE', AN UGLY POEM

Poe asked, 'When is death most poetical?', and answered, 'When it
most closely allies itself to Beauty.' 'The death of a beautiful woman'
he wrote, 'is, unquestionably, the most poetical topic in the world.'[75]
It follows that the death of an ugly Jew is the *least* poetical topic in the
world, and the very enemy of Beauty. This is the topic of 'Dirge', an
'ugly touch' that cannot be dismissed as bad poetry. With a gleeful
cruelty it conceives of Bleistein's corpse decaying on an ocean bed
'lower than the wharf rats dive'. Crabs pick at his eyelids; Grave's
Disease lives in his dead eyes; the flesh of his nose has a lacy thinness;

'bones peep through' his 'ragged toes'; the currents lay bare his gold teeth. Empson admired the poem in each of its two versions, praising them as 'exultantly rancorous parodies'. They were, he said, 'plainly among the major impulses behind' *The Waste Land*. 'The rejected passages of Jew-baiting', he concluded, are 'deeply involved in the final poetry.'[76]

'Dirge' is an Emersonian poem of 'disgust' and 'rats', but without any corresponding Emersonian 'balance' of 'beauty' and 'magnificence'. Bleistein's face is a Jewish physiognomy out of an anti-Semite's album – protruding eyes, prominent nose, gold-filled teeth. As a picture or caricature, this face has appeared on innumerable occasions in leaflets and newspapers, on posters, and as illustrations in books. Hostile descriptions of such faces incorporate these features in their inventories of Jewish traits. Eliot's specific contribution is to incorporate a retaliatory element in the account. Thinking of Rachel, we may say that the crabs tear at Bleistein with murderous claws. The poem does not just communicate an anti-Semitic message. It enacts that happiest of anti-Semitic diversions, the humiliating of a Jew.

The poem surveys a body in its differential decomposition, passing from limbs to face, and from face to eyes, Grave's Disease its mock diagnosis. It is a repudiation of art's 'business' (as conceived by Hegel), which is 'to expunge the difference between the spiritual and the purely natural, and to make the external bodily presence into a shape, beautiful, through and through developed, ensouled and spiritually living'.[77] The ugliness of Bleistein in this poem, and his lack of aesthetic sense in 'Burbank', together comprise the two parts of a single anti-Semitic truism, given most succinct expression by Richard Wagner: 'a race whose general appearance we cannot consider suitable for aesthetic purposes is by the same token incapable of any artistic presentation.'[78]

Bleistein has become food for the sea creatures. This is horrible in itself. With the corpse's popping eyes, the principal symptom of Grave's Disease, we have already entered the realm of the gratuitous. Sufferers of the disease have a fearsome, startling appearance. They are wild-eyed and appear demented. The hideousness of their demeanour would be aggravated if their eyelids were torn away, for example by crabs. It is the peculiar horror of 'Dirge' that it celebrates the putrefying of Bleistein, achieved furthermore not by natural process but by animal ravaging. One recoils not just from the unsightliness of this unsighted Jew. One also recoils from the bestial

devouring of the exposed dead. It is loathsome. Julia Kristeva glosses
the primal horror of an exposed corpse thus: 'A decaying body,
lifeless... blurred between the inanimate and the inorganic, a
transitional swarming... the corpse represents fundamental pollution. A body without soul, a non-body, disquieting matter, it is to be
excluded from God's territory... it must not be displayed but
immediately buried so as not to pollute the divine earth.'[79] Eliot
'excludes' Bleistein's body, just as he excludes the 'jew' in 'Gerontion'. He also defiles that body while ensuring that it may not itself
defile. The rotting body does not endanger others. Drumont worked,
so he claimed, to purify France of 'Jewish miasmas',[80] the noxious or
infectious exhalations from putrescent organic matter. What
Drumont laboured all his life to achieve, Eliot manages in a line.
True to his poetry of contempt, Eliot ensures that Bleistein cannot be
imagined as a threat.

In its refusal of compassion or even common respect for the dead,
the poem denies that dread of an unburied, unconsecrated, corpse,
paradigmatically expressed by Antigone. In Sophocles' play, she
protests at Creon's order which condemns her brother Polynices, 'not
to be buried, not to be mourned; / To be left unburied, unwept, a
feast of flesh / For keen-eyed carrion birds'. Antigone's impassioned
advocacy of Polynices' cause is to be contrasted with Eliot's sardonic
repudiation of any relation with the dead Jew. One may think of
'Dirge' as a poem written by a debased Creon, a Theban king
become anti-Semitic demagogue. 'Dirge' takes a delight in the
rotting of the corpse; Creon shares Antigone's horror. The poem
merely evokes that horror in order to achieve the effect of a violation.
It is a poem whose purpose is to shock and repel. The recoil from
imagined infection in 'Gerontion' is matched by the recoil from the
imagined violation of the dead in 'Dirge'. Each is multiply ugly,
rendering physical ugliness as the sign of a body's disease and
dishonour.

Polynices forfeited the right to a grave when he turned against
Thebes: repudiating the city, he lost its protection when dead. The
Latin poet Publilius remarked that 'the man without a country is a
corpse without a grave';[81] Eliot's anti-Semitic poetry may be said to
concur. The Bleistein of 'Dirge' has no terrestrial grave because he
has no country. In gloating over the circumstances of his decomposition, the poet also celebrates the condition of Jews as stateless
transients during extended periods of Europe's history. This Bleistein

is a Jew from a medieval sermon. He has 'become the opprobrium of the universe, wandering, fugitive, scorned, without altar, without land'.[82] Eliot's Jews are fixed by their lack of rootedness. They are 'placed' by the poems' refusal to grant them homes. They have neither soul nor domicile. They are composed of gestures, and have to make do with temporary addresses. Though they are alien, they are not from any other specific place, which makes their strangeness more disturbing. They are nowhere at home, strangers wherever they live. They refuse the ties of nation. 'The very first lesson' learnt by Jewish converts, Tacitus says, is to 'shed all feelings of patriotism'.[83] 'The fatherland of the Jews', says Schopenhauer, 'is other Jews.'[84]

Bleistein's 'lustreless protrusive eye' in 'Burbank', his 'dead jew's eyes' in 'Dirge', and the 'heavy eyes' of the Jew in 'Sweeney Among the Nightingales', parody Shylock's celebrated protest 'Hath not a Jew eyes!' The protest is itself an anti-Semitic joke because Jews in medieval caricatures frequently had oversized heads and bulging eyes.[85] These eyes are ugly, and the ugliness indicates a spiritual incapacity. The blindness of the Jews was a theological condition. Anti-Semites of a Christian disposition railed: 'I feel pity and horror for [the Jews], and I pray God with the Church that he remove from their eyes the veil which prevents them from seeing that Jesus Christ has come';[86] 'Yea what art thou, blind unconverted Jew';[87] 'the obstinate, blind dogs';[88] 'Jews are always born blind.'[89] By contrast, in literary tradition, Jewish eyes startled, intimidated, were magnetically bright, and were always worthy of comment: 'the dark mongoloid eye ... the Evil Eye';[90] '[Fagin's] eyes glistened as he raised the lid';[91] 'intent eyes – eyes gleaming with suspicion, with pride, with clarity, with cupidity, with comprehension ... hawk's eyes';[92] 'His countenance was strongly marked, and his eyes were large, black, and sparkling: yet there was something in his look which ... inspired me with a secret awe, not to say horror';[93] '[Svengali was] of Jewish aspect, well-featured but sinister ... [with] bold, brilliant black eyes';[94] 'he wou'd turn and give a Look at me, like the Devil; I thought I never saw any thing so frightful in my Life.'[95] Eliot reinstates the theological blindness of Jews, and denies the literary magnetism of their gaze. Insensate, their eyes are lights that have been extinguished.

'Dirge' also parodies some famous lines from *The Tempest*: 'Full fathom five your Bleistein lies / Under the flatfish and the squids'. It mocks Bleistein's corpse, while also mocking Ariel's song. 'Dirge' indeed is a lyric that is founded upon derision. This is an additional form of ugliness, an additional violation. It is more than the harmless Dadaist impulse to tease a masterwork banalised by over-exposure. 'Dirge' does not paint a moustache on *The Tempest*. Eliot's poetry, remarked Harold Rosenberg, 'contained a good dose of Dada'.[96] This is too kind a judgment on the disfigurement by 'Dirge' of Shakespeare's poetry. Ariel's song dissipates the horror of decomposition on an unconsecrated seabed. It consoles Ferdinand, who believes that his father has drowned. The song offers a vision of the transforming powers of the sea. Ariel masks the macabre; 'Dirge' unmasks it, making it more frightful by rendering it in similarly lyrical language. Like a threat uttered sympathetically, or a violent gesture accompanied by a smile, though the title promises something compassionate, it delivers a brutal anti-requiem.

While Ariel's sea works magic, the sea of 'Dirge' is rapacious. Alonso and Bleistein both cheat it, but in different ways. Though the sea fails to change either man, it is only Alonso who is saved from drowning. Bleistein, though truly the sea's victim, is not transmuted into something finer. The sea violates him without reforming him. He is immune to its purificatory powers, and resists its baptismal cleansing. He may be imagined as a 'hydrophobic' Jew, in Wilhelm Marr's phrase, who 'sh[ies] away from a few drops of water'.[97] Indeed, it is not a baptism that is celebrated, but a death. Luther's declaration is the relevant precedent: 'If I find a Jew to baptize, I shall lead him to the Elbe bridge, hang a stone around his neck, and push him into the water.'[98] Alonso's 'sea-change' turns him into 'something rich and strange'. Bleistein, by contrast, is '*still* expensive, rich and strange'. In this way it can be said that 'Dirge' changes Ariel's song, by reductive parody, into something poor and familiar – an anti-Semite's song. Bleistein remains the immutable Jew, as irreducibly alien on the seabed as in any terrestrial city. Underwater, he simply exchanges one form of display for another. (Jewish ostentation is another resonating theme of anti-Semitism's: Mein-ecke, for example, commented silkily of German Jews in the 1880s that 'they were inclined to enjoy indiscreetly the favourable economic situation … smiling on them'.[99]) Hence the poem's rendering of the decomposing nostrils as lace, and the substituting of one form of vagrancy for another; not toes peeping through ragged shoes, but bones through ragged toes. The Jew is in death as he is in life: both plutocrat and pauper, flashy (hence the 'lace') and indigent (hence the 'ragged').

Walking along the beach, Stephen Dedalus sees the body of a drowned man being reclaimed, and these thoughts pass through his mind:

Five fathoms out there. Full fathom five thy father lies. At one he said. Found drowned. High water at Dublin bar. Driving before it a loose drift of rubble, fanshoals of fishes, silly shells. A corpse rising saltwhite from the undertow, bobbing landward, a pace a pace a porpoise. There he is. Hook it quick. Sunk though he be beneath the watery floor. We have him. Easy now.

Bag of corpsegas sopping in foul brine. A quiver of minnows, fat of a spongy titbit, flash through the slits of his buttoned trouserfly. God becomes man becomes fish becomes barnacle goose becomes featherbed mountain. Dead breaths I living breathe, tread dead dust, devour a urinous offal from all dead. Hauled stark over the gunwale he breathes upward the stench of his green grave, his leprous nosehole snoring to the sun.

A seachange this, brown eyes saltblue. Seadeath, mildest of all deaths known to man. Old Father Ocean.[100]

The reference to Ariel's song is Shakespearean embroidery, part of the texture of Stephen's experience of the scene. The allusion is not to *The Tempest* itself, but to a contextless, well-known quotation. It has its proper place in the internal monologue as one of a number of associations, without priority. It does not pretend to make sense of the spectacle, or to give the dead man dignity. It does not diminish the horror; it does not make it worse. It does not explain the scene, it is part of it, because it figures momentarily in Stephen's consciousness, which itself is part of the scene. Of course, if this were not so, if the song stood as an epigraph to the event, the effect would be kitsch, the false domestication of a work of art in an attempt to give significance to the banal. Resisting this, Joyce submerges Ariel's song, while Eliot, facing the same risk, defaces it. Both address this question: given the unavoidability of the song, how does one incorporate it in an account of a drowned man? Joyce mixes it up in a jumble of associations, frankly acknowledging its enfeebled condition as a sort of verbal *Mona Lisa*, familiar beyond its dramatic context, known to many who do not know *The Tempest*. Joyce accepts that, finding a place for the song in its present state of overexposure. Eliot does something new with it, deforming the text to make it fit the violence of his literary rendering of a dead Jew's corpse. 'Dirge' savages both Ariel's song and the 'poetical' sea, redeeming them from staleness, recovering them for its own poetry of contempt and loathing. In disfiguring Bleistein, it disfigures elements of classical and English literary culture. The violation of Bleistein's body in the poem enacts the violation by the poem of its sources. Those sources live on as literary clichés. 'Dirge' does not restore their brilliance, it attacks them. So Eliot can say, with Rimbaud: 'Un soir, j'ai assis la Beauté sur mes genoux. – Et je l'ai trouvée amère. – Et je l'ai injuriée.'[101] To adopt a phrase of Arthur Danto's, the object of his aesthetics is not the transfiguration of the commonplace[102] but the disfiguration of the beautiful.

Returned to the sea, the drowned man takes his place in Joyce's subversive series – the theological tailing off into the playful – as in the sequence God to man to fish (or, with Christ, God as man as fish) to feathers to featherbed mountains. Like Bleistein, he is also food for the fish, he too suffers the leper's fate, he rots, and exhales foul odours. His 'leprous nosehole', however, is far from the language of anti-Semitism. Joyce's phrase is innocent of the innuendoes of 'Gerontion'. 'Dirge' does not gaze at the hideous in order to subordinate it to its art. The ugliness of the poem cannot be defended as a case of the artist exercising his right to render in his art that from which others flinch. Though the poem pretends surgical detachment in its precise reference to medical disorder, and careful notation of the detail of decomposition, it cannot truly claim it. Eliot is not like the artist in the operating theatre, or the novelist during the plague. He is neither Rembrandt nor Defoe. This poem reverses the great affirmation of the humanist, 'I am a man, and reckon nothing human alien to me', appropriately rejected by the anti-Semitic Santayana: 'If the humanist could really live up to his ancient maxim, "Humana nil a me alienum puto", he would sink into moral anarchy and artistic impotence.'[103] The denial of this maxim is one way in which Eliot defeats 'artistic impotence'. 'Dirge' says: that which is human *is* alien to me. At any rate, that which is human, but Jewish, is alien. Compare Joyce in a Jewish cemetery:

Corpses of Jews lie about me rotting in the mould of their holy field. Here is the tomb of her people, black stone, silence without hope ... Pimply Meissel brought me here. He is beyond those trees standing with covered head at the grave of his suicide wife, wondering how the woman who slept in his bed has come to this end ... The tomb of her people and hers: black stone, silence without hope: and all is ready. Do not die![104]

This is from *Giacomo Joyce*, a short prose work that relates Joyce's passion for a young Jewish woman. These are lines of respect for the Jewish dead; their bodies are uncovered to mark the writer's imaginative intimacy with them. Meissel mourns the death that ended his marriage; Joyce fears the death that will likewise rob him of the object of his infatuation: 'Do not die!' 'Dirge' reverses that injunction; it is a poem that celebrates the death of a Jew. As Sartre observes: 'A destroyer in function, a sadist with a pure heart, the anti-Semite is, in the very depths of his heart, a criminal. What he wishes, what he prepares for, is the death of the Jew.'[105] Two corpses: Antigone mourns Polynices, while the poet who wrote 'Dirge' may be imagined exclaiming 'Bleistein is not my brother'. Indeed, the substitution of Bleistein's name for the 'father' of the original text has the effect of severing the Jew from all family relations, thereby taking him outside, in a telling cliché, the 'family of man'. This poem, and the Quatrain poems written across the same period, are a sour celebration of the isolation of the artist, and thus represents the terminal point of a Romantic, and latterly, Symbolist, tradition.

Anti-Semitism is constituted by its multiple misrepresentations of Jewish history, Judaism, and Jews: collectively, the object of its animus. It preys upon Jewish history, taking its themes to pervert them. Those themes are homelessness, social solidarity, and aspects of intellectual freedom and material prosperity. Each is given a twist by anti-Semitism. The calamity of exile is substituted by the stigma of rootlessness, the virtue of communal self-help becomes the monster of international conspiracy, dissent is treated as subversion, and the wealth of a few is expanded into the parasitic affluence or indigence of all. The destructive dependence of 'Dirge' on Ariel's song is thus imitative of anti-Semitism, which is parasitic upon that which it travesties. It cannot be grasped without a separate sense of its target. Eliot gives an anti-Semitic twist to texts that are either untouched by anti-Semitism or, as with *Ulysses*, actively resist it. He visits Jews upon them like a malignancy. Passages from *The Tempest* and *Ulysses* undergo a sea-change in 'Dirge', rotting into anti-Semitism. They are made ugly. The poem finds a small place for itself between the interstices of these other works, its repulsion of their complexly benign impulses itself repulsive. But 'Dirge' also reaches beyond its travesty of *The Tempest* and its dialogue with *Ulysses* to offend against *Antigone*. It squats in ugly opposition to Sophocles' drama, which places reverence for the dead in the balance against the imperatives of citizenship. The Jew, a threat to the modern polis, is driven off the earth, his body exposed and degraded. There is no Antigone to lament him. In rejecting Jews, and thereby setting its face against *Antigone*, and also *The Tempest*, and *Ulysses*, the poem rejects its own sources of inspiration. In disfiguring Bleistein, it disfigures elements of classical and English literary culture. It is, in a sense, 'anti-art', a destructive parody of more powerful, predecessor works. Self-mocking and technically accomplished, it is exemplarily modern.[106]

'Dirge', which is both disgusting and offensive, risks losing the honorific title of 'art'. Schopenhauer puts the received view: '[the] disgusting or offensive ... disturbs purely aesthetic contemplation ... it rouses the will by holding before it objects that are abhorrent. It has therefore always been recognised as absolutely inadmissible in art.'[107] Excluding 'Dirge' from the category of the aesthetic is appealing, not least because such an exclusion matches the poem's own exclusion of Bleistein, and the poet's exclusion of the poem from *The Waste Land*. But if it isn't art, how is it to be characterised? It is a poem, which is a literary form and thus eligible to be considered as an instance of art. What is more, it has a relation to already existing works of art, indeed, to that heterogeneous assembly of texts termed the literary canon. This relation can be characterised as a stance of belligerence. 'Dirge' is only one instance of Eliot's posture of aggression, which is evident in the following passage from his essay on Phillip Massinger:

> Immature poets imitate; mature poets *steal*; bad poets *deface* what they take, and good poets make it into something better, or at least something different. The good poet welds his *theft* into a whole of feeling which is unique, utterly different from that from which it was *torn*; the bad poet throws it into something which has no cohesion. A good poet will usually *borrow* from authors remote in time, or alien in language, or diverse in interest.[108]

Supporting this series of contrasts – mature poets against immature poets, and good poets against bad poets – are correspondingly contrasting terms of violent appropriation and of deference and passivity. The poets of whom Eliot approves steal and tear; the others imitate. It is a startling, provocative account of poetic creation, itself 'stolen' from Emerson![109] It is full of disrespect for the integrity of existing literary works. They are to be quarried, not replicated. But Eliot fails to maintain the momentum of his argument. He slides into pieties about the uniqueness of successful poems. He also fights shy of 'deface', a term that he allocates inappropriately to the bad poet, just as he misallocates 'borrows' to the good poet. Bad poets cannot get close enough to antecedent works to deface them; good poets cannot *both* 'steal' *and* 'borrow'. The terms need to be switched. Good poets deface, on occasion; bad poets feebly borrow. In *The Waste Land*, Eliot defaces works by, among others, Spenser and Marvell. 'Prothalamion' and 'To his Coy Mistress' are distorted and mutilated. The Massinger essay retreats before the implications of its own radicalism and the point of retreat is marked by the application of 'deface' to bad and not good poets.

There is a related denial, similarly unargued, of the radical nature of the modern poet's aesthetic in *After Strange Gods*. Eliot writes with self-revealing loathing about a short story by Hardy, 'Barbara of the House of Grebe'.[110] Barbara loves Edmond, from whom she has been separated by her family. When in Italy, he commissions a bust of himself that he sends to her. He is then horribly injured. On his return, Barbara recoils from him. He dies rejected; she marries someone else. Infatuated with the bust, she visits it each night until a sculptor employed by her husband disfigures it to match Edmond's disfigured face. She is exposed to it repeatedly until her love turns to loathing. She sickens and dies. After her death a sermon is preached on the folly of sensuous love. One can ignore this moralistic gloss. It is a story that celebrates the power of the artist, both to charm and to terrify. Its heroes are the two sculptors. Each is creative, even though the second preys upon the work of the first. Eliot is the student of them both, a proposition confirmed by the violence of his hostility to the second one. The second sculptor disfigures a statue to create a new statue of a disfigured man.

In 'Dirge', Eliot disfigures Shakespeare's poem to create a new poem about a Jew who is disfigured. This poem, and the greater poem of which it was once part, are examples of the impulse to deface in Eliot's work; a deliberate disfigurement of the work of others, dislocating their language into his meaning (to adapt his own violent words[111]). Maud Ellmann has written well about this aspect of *The Waste Land*. It is a poem that 'desecrates tradition' and 'uses nostalgia to conceal its vandalism'. The line 'April is the cruellest month', she says, 'blasphemes against the first lines of *The Canterbury Tales*, which presents April's showers as sweet.' 'O keep the Dog far hence' is 'purloined from Webster'. Eliot practises a 'verbal kleptomania', challenging the convention 'that literary texts are private property'. The poem as a whole displays an anxiety 'about originality and theft'.[112] Rightly, Ellmann runs the thefts and the defacements together, implying a connection that Eliot is at pains to deny. The defacement and the anti-Semitism make common cause in Eliot's work. What, after all, is 'The jew is underneath the lot' if not a slogan of the kind one might expect to find chalked on a wall? The line defaces the poem, which in turn defaces Browning's poetry of Venice, and Shakespeare's, and Byron's, and Shelley's, and Gautier's, that is to say poetry that 'Burbank' invokes in order to deride.

Dada's lesson, which Eliot refused to grant in his criticism, while improving upon in his poetry, is that defacing has its own artistic possibilities. 'Dirge' represents a spoliation of art. It is a savage and parasitic poem that parodies an 'original', and is thus as dependant on the labour of others (*The Tempest*) as is the anti-Semite's Jew upon his Gentile hosts. 'Dirge' is parasitic upon and yet destructive of the beauty and riches of other texts. It violates art's parameters in the name of art. The anti-Semitism of 'Dirge' completes the extraordinary hierarchy of aesthetic and ethical violations in the poem. It defaces Ariel's song; it assaults its Jewish subject; it affronts or excites its readers. Anti-Semitism thus does not disfigure Eliot's poetry; Eliot's anti-Semitic poetry disfigures the poetry on which it preys.

'Dirge' is a deeply distasteful work, whatever one's enthusiasm for its formal belligerence. Pound's '?? doubtful'[113] against Eliot's manuscript gets nowhere near its true 'doubtfulness' (and that is assuming that Pound was not just querying the poem's place in the larger work). The poem is distasteful principally because it combines sophistication and viciousness, its effects artful and repulsive, bewildering in the way it gloats in tranquillity over the dead Jew, his body still house to disease and subject to humiliation.

In 'Disgust and Other Forms of Aversion',[114] an essay in anti-aesthetics, David Pole lists things that disgust us: the semi-liquid and the viscous; slugs, lice, and the like; excrement and dirt; monsters and freaks, deformities and mutilations; vegetable and animal decay. If one wanted illustrative material across this range of instances, Eliot could help. The landlord is disfigured, possibly mutilated, in 'Gerontion'. Bleistein is immersed in slime in 'Burbank', and is associated with rats, carriers of disease who breed out of dirt. In 'Dirge', his body is diseased and violated, its decay accelerated by the crabs' feasting, a culinary inversion that intensifies the disgusting nature of the account. That which should be eaten instead becomes the consumer – crab eats man. The scene would be even more loathsome to a Jew, because the crab is food forbidden by the rules of kashrut.

Disgust causes one to recoil, says Pole. We retreat from that which disgusts us; our impulse is to remove it, to expel it. It is an impulse born of horror, a particularly potent kind of fear. (Wyndham Lewis wrote that Jews were 'objects of dislike, and even of horror'.[115]) It can leave one helpless; it can, indeed, be paralysing. The feeling of disgust is baffling, unmanageable. Of the objects of one's disgust, one can only say that one would rather not have known of their existence. Disgust can induce panic; invariably it will prompt revulsion. One retreats from the object that causes disgust, and yet one cannot escape one's consciousness of it. 'Burbank' and 'Dirge' dramatise this especially disagreeable experience in their accounts of the noxious Bleistein, who is both remote ('Lower than the wharf rats dive') and yet pervades everything ('The jew is underneath the lot'). How can one deal with such a figure? At best, by gestures of exclusion. Pushed out of view, the Jew reappears 'outside the window, leaning in'. Jews are not so much marginal in Eliot's work as marginalised by it.

The object of disgust is likely to disturb our scheme of known distinctions. It is liable to be anomalous. 'Dirt' is at the bottom of such anomalies. Mary Douglas defines dirt in *Purity and Danger* as 'matter out of place', which entails both the existence and the breach of 'a set of ordered relations'. The word is an 'omnibus compendium' comprising a miscellany of what we reject. It is thus a 'residual category'.[116] This helps clarify the relation between 'the jew squats on the window sill' and lines that follow, 'The goat coughs at night in the field overhead; / Rocks, moss, stonecrop, iron, merds'. The rocks and the moss, the stonecrop, the iron and the merds, comprise the landscape's waste, everything that civilisation rejects. Rocks unbroken for human use, moss weed-like and drifting, stone-crop wild and clinging to rock, and iron, lowest in the Ovidian order, appropriate to either primitive or degraded societies, each stand in a metaphoric relation with the Jew. Both the Jew, and this collection of rubble, weed, and excrement, comprise precisely those 'rejected elements of ordered systems'. Within the logic of the poem they amount to a single list. The Jew is to be driven from houses and off land onto ocean beds, always outside normal habitations. 'Gerontion' insinuates the analogy between the merds that are expelled from the human body and the Jews that are expelled from the social body. The Jew, Drumont declared, was 'not made for civilisation'.[117] Kipling saw Jews 'slink about the rubbish heaps in [their] quarter'.[118] The modern Jew is both literally and meta-phorically unclean: 'the verminous uncleanness of the Jewish masses is all of a piece with the spiritual uncleanness of the mentality of the race.'[119] In 'Sweeney Among the Nightingales', another poem that associates the excremental with the Jewish, birds defecate on Agamemnon while elsewhere Jews consort sinisterly with each other.

This is one of anti-Semitism's most dangerous themes; Eliot implicates himself in the practice of associating Jews with waste. Jews lived in waste, consumed waste, were comparable to waste, or, in the vilest formulation (not Eliot's), simply *were* waste. Drumont wrote: 'Now that [the Jews] are our masters, they vomit on us all the excrement swallowed by Ezekiel.'[120] In response to immigration from Eastern Europe, an English newspaper condemned 'Foreign Jews... [who] either do not know how to use the latrine, water and other sanitary accommodation provided, or prefer their own semi-barbarous habits and use the floor of their rooms and passages to deposit their filth.'[121] Wyndham Lewis noted the anti-Semite's propensity to denounce Jews as 'human garbage'.[122] It was suggested that a notice be placed at the mouth of the Thames, 'no rubbish to be shot here'.[123] The squatting Jew, his posture defecatory, becomes what he expels, just as his own motion enacts what must be done to him in a characteristic anti-Semitic elision. An anti-Semite proposed that 'all social excrement, especially the Jews'[124] should be expelled from France. The Camelots du Roi pursued Léon Blum with the slogan 'A bas le détritus humain'.[125] Marx abused Feuerbach for conceiving of 'practice... only in its dirty-judaical manifestation'.[126] The American Black separatist Louis Farrakhan echoes Marx in his abuse of Judaism as a 'dirty religion'.[127] Stephen Wilson, in his magisterial survey of late nineteenth-century French anti-Semitism, concludes that '[t]he polluting, threatening quality of the Jew lies in the fact he is hard to define; he is ambiguous, marginal, in-terstitial'.[128]

'Uncleanness or dirt is that which must not be included if a pattern is to be maintained' says Mary Douglas.[129] The 'pattern' here is Eliot's cultural map, the 'dirt' is the Jew, and 'dirty Jew' is the figure of speech that haunts Eliot's anti-Semitic poems. It is the figure that is underneath the lot, at the bottom of all those other anti-Semitic themes I have identified. These poems tap anti-Semitism's stale and debased imagination. They draw on its lexicon. Its clichéd phrases of abuse are summarised by and derived from that other, most degraded and handiest of insults, 'dirty Jew'. It is a form of address that was commonplace in 'late nineteenth-century France, the adjective going with the noun without deliberate thought'. It was a 'cliché that Jews attempted fruitlessly to counter'.[130] The phrase remains in use today, though many readers of Eliot may come across it only through his poetry. Eliot took the gibe, 'dirty Jew' – a vicious, everyday expression – and made poetry out of it.

Eliot once praised Dostoievsky for possessing the gift of 'utilizing his weaknesses'.[131] Perhaps he too had that gift. While I cannot celebrate the poetry flowing from that 'weakness', which is the poet's anti-Semitism, these poems do have substantial merit. More than merely well-crafted, they display Eliot's mastery over a heterogeneous mass of material. Triumphs of form, they are poems that a reader schooled in Eliot's literary criticism would be likely to value. There is, however, a difficulty in reconciling them with the aims of art, which requires both artist and reader not to recoil, the first for the purpose of composition, the second for the purpose of reception. Eliot solves this aesthetic problem by a combination of means.

Principally, readers are encouraged to stay with his anti-Semitic poetry because in each poem the object of disgust, the Jew, is invoked in order to be expelled, thereby giving a satisfaction analogous to that offered by melodrama. Exposure to the ugliness of the offender is the price to pay for the pleasure of being present at the scene of punishment. This punishment is severe: Bleistein is punished for Rachel's offence. Crabs tear at his eyelids in retribution for Rachel's own tearing with murderous paws, one Jew paying the penalty for another's crime. There is an element of kitsch in this, an element of pleasurable horror, converting the disgusting into the harmlessly scary, modifying recoil into mere frisson – the domestication of the appalling. Of course, there is also the virtuosity of the exercise: a demonstration of the poet's innovating range, as, for example, for Leavis, for whom Eliot's poetry eschews the notion of 'the intrinsically poetical'.[132]

In addition, Eliot exploits two ostensibly antithetical effects. The first is the revelatory – as if to declare, 'This is what Jews are truly like!' – where the recoil in disgust is balanced by fascination at the disclosure. The second, conversely, is to this effect: I will tell you something amazing from which you will conclude that you knew it all along. The combination of the sensational and the obvious works on many literary levels: tabloid journalism, for example, exposes behaviour regarded as typical of the subject's class. It uncovers a very familiar body: the pederastic vicar, the drug-taking celebrity, the hypocritically affluent socialist. The revelations have the paradoxical effect of confirming rather than disturbing conventional wisdom. They tell us what we already know. These stratagems, taken together, ensure that the artist who creates is liberated from the man who recoils. 'Towards Meyerbeer my position is a peculiar one', remarked Richard Wagner. 'I do not hate him, but he *disgusts* me beyond measure';[133] 'The Jew', said Henry Adams, 'makes me creep.'[134] Eliot may be taken to concur.

'DIRGE' IN CONTEXT: 'A COOKING EGG' AND
THE WASTE LAND

It might be objected: so much argument to derive from a single, suppressed poem! 'Dirge', after all, was rejected by Pound and then by Eliot. We might never have known of it had it not been recovered by Eliot's widow. Is not the poem separate from the rest of the work, distanced from it by more than just contingencies of publication? To which I answer, no, it is not. It is another variation on an Eliotic theme – the death of a Jew; it is another instance of a practice – the exploitation of anti-Semitic discourse; it is an addition to a series – another one of Eliot's anti-Semitic poems. And I ground my answer by considering the deaths of the Jewish Sir Alfred Mond in 'A Cooking Egg', and the Semitic Phlebas the Phoenician in *The Waste Land*.

By its simplicity of language and its obscurity of meaning, by the studied flippancy of its tone and the solemnity of its subject matter, by its swerves from the domestic to the paradisal, and from mountains to tea rooms, 'A Cooking Egg' is typically, even generically, Eliotic. It is written as if in answer to the question, 'what is a poem by T. S. Eliot like?' To which one might respond, 'It is like a cooking egg.' It cannot be consumed raw; it has to be cooked, that is, interpreted. The title to the poem would thus also serve as the title to the poetic œuvre. It is a 'five-fingered exercise', a practical joke at the expense of exegetes. It is also a sophisticated poem of naïve self-display, worthy of a deferential heir to Browning. The speaker plans to be on intimate terms with the great; he has a sensibility that deplores the viciousness of modern bourgeois life. Yet this familiarity with the great will be achieved only in death when all are equal, and his regrets cannot distinguish between the trivial and the momentous:

> But where is the penny world I bought
> To eat with Pipit behind the screen?
> ...
> Where are the eagles and the trumpets?

The bathos of the first regret makes banal what would otherwise be the pathos of the second. Hence the slightly absurd snobbishness in the name dropping that undoes itself in a parade of famous personalities whom the speaker can never know, and the exaggerated scorn by which the unnamed are invoked: red-eyed scavengers, weeping multitudes.

The epigraph promises something confessional, and, for once in an *Ara Vos Prec* poem, it delivers. It is the closest the Quatrain poems get to the conventional, dramatic monologue – one voice revealing itself in its self-deceptions – and in this sense it is the least interesting poem in the collection.

The poem's anti-Semitism lies in a pairing and a contrast: Mond *with* the scavengers, and *against* Sir Philip Sidney. The contrasts flow from that initial, emblematic opposition: the egotism of accumulation against the altruism of heroism, capital versus chivalry, the merchant and the soldier, Jews and Gentiles. 'I want to put every money-lender to death', wrote Henry Adams, '[t]hen perhaps men of our kind might have some chance of being honorably killed in battle and eaten by our enemies.'[135] As Eliot put it in *The Idea of a Christian Society*, without Adams's ironic overstatement: 'a people feels... more dignified if its hero is the statesman however unscrupulous, or the warrior however brutal, rather than the financier.'[136] Mond is alone, passive, and in comfort ('lapt'); the heroes are in assembly, to be imagined engaged in vigorous debate or combat. While they fight, he trades. The contrast with Sidney removes the capacity for heroic conduct, and thus honour, from Mond; by implication it denies both to Jews as a whole. 'A Cooking Egg' draws on an anti-Semitic tradition that characterised Jews as dishonourable and money-grubbing, and as foreign and unpatriotic. Sidney died a patriot in battle; Mond did rather well out of his war. (Eliot was too cautious, however, to make the contrast anything more than tacit.[137]) Many tried to put Mond, and others identified as of his class, on the defensive. During the Great War another Jewish financier of foreign origin, Sir Ernest Cassell, was threatened by a campaign to strip him of his titles and citizenship.[138] Giving Jews knighthoods often provoked parodic exaggerations: 'Samuello-von-Isaac-von-Meyer de Stuart de Plantagenet de William the Conqueror.'[139] For a Jew unfit for combat and lacking a true relation with land, to receive the chivalric honour of a title was absurd. Pound mocked 'Lord Goldsmid, the flower of Chivalry'.[140]

And the red-eyed scavengers? Tramps get red eyes from too much raw spirit, and from lives lived rough, sleep-disturbed and humiliated by disregard. They are also red-eyed with a kind of lethargic menace, and their stare can alarm passers-by with its unfocused malevolence. They are scavengers because they subsist by collecting things discarded by others. They live on refuse; they take what the rest of us reject. These men and women are kin to those glimpsed by the poet '[g]athering fuel in vacant lots' ('Preludes'). Scavengers become hordes when they begin to threaten what we value, and then the menace they represent taps deeper, cultural anxieties: 'Who are these hooded hordes swarming / Over endless plains…' (*The Waste Land*). This portentous questioning is satirically prefigured by the hordes from… Golders Green and Kentish Town, two London suburbs known for their respectability. It is comic to imagine scavengers from such dull, middle-class places. These scavengers could be Jewish, but not necessarily, and not just. Golders Green after the war was already an area where Jews were settling; furthermore, there is a precedent in 'Burbank' for the pairing of low and elevated Jews – Mond and the scavengers meet Klein and Bleistein. It is part, however, of the relaxed nature of the poem's anti-Semitism that this is left open, as a connection that the reader might but is not compelled to make.

Though 'A Cooking Egg' is anti-Semitic, at first glance it seems to lack the energetic ill-will of Eliot's other Jew-hating poems – of 'Burbank', for example, in which the globally impressive 'Mond' is reduced to the little 'Klein'. Mond and Sidney dwell together, both at repose in an afterworld alien to any Christian imagination. And any stable contrast between the two, of the kind identified above, does not survive the stanzas that follow in which Lucretia Borgia, Madame Blavatsky, and Piccarda de Donati appear in miscellaneous procession. This has the effect of converting a binarism, Gentile and Jew, into the first two terms in a greater and more open-ended series of historical figures, exemplifying Honour, Capital, Society, and then, as if in mockery of these hypostatics, Pipit, pure accident. Furthermore, it is difficult to maintain a satirical distance from theosophy, with its claim to have unlocked the secrets of the universe,[141] while at the same time adopting anti-Semitism, with its similarly inflated claim to hold the key to the mysteries of modern existence.

On the face of it, Mond and the Bleistein of 'Dirge' have quite different fates. One is in Heaven, the other in a watery Hell; one in comfort, the other ravaged by sea creatures; Mond, so far from being excluded from human society, will rest cosily with the poet. The poems mark two extremes: the one, an anti-Semitic violence of pornographic intensity; the other, a playful toying with an anti-Semitic trope. But they are both anti-Semitic, and in one respect, 'A Cooking Egg' goes further than 'Dirge'. It locates a Jew, vigorously alive and prominent in English society, in Heaven. *It thus imagines him to be dead.* Eliot could have chosen, if he had wished, another financier, one who was already dead. All the others in the poem were dead when the poem was published; Madame Blavatsky, the most recently deceased, died in May 1891.[142] In such a context to conceive of someone as dead is to wish him dead. It is this, as much as anything else, that roots 'A Cooking Egg' in a tradition of anti-Semitic poetry and makes it a companion piece to 'Dirge'.

And now for Phlebas, and another death. Eliot inaugurated his literary career with lines about undrownable women and drowned men; towards its end, he wrote a play in which an apparently undrownable woman drowns. Thus 'Prufrock': 'We have lingered in the chambers of the sea / By sea-girls wreathed with seaweed red and brown / Till human voices wake us, and we drown'; and *The Family Reunion*: '[Harry:] You would never imagine anyone could sink so quickly / I had always supposed ... / ... / That she would be unkillable.'[143] Drowning is a theme in Eliot's poetry; in *The Waste Land* it provides a title, 'Death by Water'. The death is that of Phlebas the Phoenician, who is present in each of the poem's five sections. In the first, Madame Sosostris produces 'the drowned Phoenician sailor' from her 'wicked pack of cards'. The first and second sections allude to him with the line 'Those are pearls that were his eyes'. In the third, as in the first, Phlebas is invoked by reference to places: Phoenician Carthage, and Mylae, where a naval battle of the first Punic War was fought. Then 'Death by Water', which is a version of the final stanza of an *Ara Vos Prec* poem, 'Dans le Restaurant'. In the fifth section, the line 'He who was living is now dead' may be taken to refer to Phlebas, among others. The poem warns: 'Fear death by water.'

The Phoenicians were sailors and traders. They settled in Spain and established colonies on the northern coast of Africa, Carthage among their number. The religion, art, and language of the Greeks all reflected Phoenician influence.[144] Carthage survived its Phoenician founders to rival Rome, fighting the Punic Wars to its ultimate destruction. Centuries later, rebuilt, it again confronted Rome, this time triumphantly: 'Rome and its inhabitants', writes Gibbon, 'were delivered to the licentiousness of the Vandals and Moors, whose blind passions revenged the injuries of Carthage.'[145] It was the city where Aeneas's journey almost ended, and St Augustine's began. Each left to answer their callings: to found Rome, to become a Doctor of the Church. It was a Semitic city; it would not have escaped the poet of 'Burbank' that Henry Adams likens Chicago to the 'Semitic Carthage' in his autobiography.[146] The English merchant seafarers were taken to be a modern Phoenician nation by both their admirers and their enemies.[147] H. G. Wells considered the Phoenicians at length in *A Short History of the World* (1922). Unlike the 'little Semitic people, the Hebrews', the Phoenicians were 'sea Semites', vigorous and inventive. The contest between Carthage and Rome, he argued, was the inaugural instance of a struggle between Semite and Aryan that is trans-historical and 'continues to this day'; further, it is a 'rivalry' that 'merge[d] itself later on in the conflict between Gentile and Jew'.[148] (This was a common enough and quite long established view. Michelet, for example, regarded the Punic Wars as a 'struggle... to settle which of the two races, the Indo-Germanic or the Semitic, was to rule the world';[149] 'I am ever as deeply aware of the gulf between pure German and pure Jewish blood as a Teuton would be aware of the gulf between him and a Phoenician',[150] remarked a German anti-Semite.) In *Ulysses*, also published in 1922, Joyce concurred with Wells's insistence on the continuity of Phoenician and Jew in a larger 'Semite', but where Wells thereafter saw struggle and polarity, Joyce celebrated fusion: 'Jewgreek is greekjew'.[151] For Joyce, the Phoenician origin of the *Odyssey* meant that a Semite was a credible Ulysses. He was taken with the thesis that Homer had relied on Phoenician records of voyages,[152] and he also believed that 'this adventurous people, who had a monopoly of the sea', had colonised Ireland.[153] Eliot may be taken to answer Wells's 'Aryan and Semite' and Joyce's 'Jewgreek' with 'Gentile or Jew', denying the determinative contest of the one and the creative combination of the other, submitting both to the erasure of the sea, their struggles and syntheses as if traced on water.

Only a few lines of 'Death by Water' survived Pound's editing; related poems, principally 'Dirge', were scored through. Suppose that Eliot had not accepted these deletions, in particular preserving 'Dirge' in his larger work. What then? The effect would have been to lock Phlebas into a relation with Bleistein. Bleistein is an ugly Jew; Phlebas is a handsome Phoenician. Bleistein is 'expensive rich and strange'; Phlebas is a trader and sailor, and sailors are honoured in the original 'Death by Water' as 'clean and dignified'. Bleistein is outside the human race; in the first draft of 'Death by Water', the poet addresses the dead man as 'brother'.[154] Yoked together, Bleistein and Phlebas are each unambiguously singular; exclude Bleistein, and Phlebas expands into ambiguity. By deleting 'Dirge', 'Death by Water' was liberated. Freed from the play of opposites, the lines about a drowned Phoenician resonate more generously in the poem, its themes of city and empire, of trade and war, of the secular and the spiritual, and of quest, so thoroughly implicated in that short fourth section, 'Death by Water'.[155] Retaining the anti-Semitic 'Dirge' would thus have had a cramping effect on *The Waste Land*. Keeping it out was a vindication of the aesthetic judgment implicit in Eliot's work that anti-Semitism must be enabling in poetry, and when not, is absolutely to be prohibited.

Phlebas first appears in 'Dans le Restaurant', a poem of three stanzas. In the first two stanzas, the poet sits in a restaurant, pestered by a broken-down old waiter who tells a tale from his childhood. He was seven years old, caught in a shower, sheltering by willow trees with an even younger girl. It was a delicious moment; but then a dog appeared, pawing at them, and the little boy ran off. 'C'est dommage', sighs the old man. The poet reacts with surprise and disgust. The waiter is a 'vieux lubrique', and his story implausible. But worse, if the story happens to be true, this man must suffer just like the poet: 'Mais alors, tu as ton vautour!' This is too much. The poet will not acknowledge the pain of another – the waiter is dismissed, insultingly, with ten sous for a bath. It is a moment of alienation: 'De quel droit payes-tu des éxperiences comme moi?' And it is followed by another, less troubling, such moment. The poet contemplates the corpse of Phlebas, the waiter as remote to him in life and station as the seaman is in death and location. The waiter, once a child, is now decrepit; Phlebas, once handsome and tall, is now dead. When buttonholed by the waiter, the poet responds with exasperated scorn; untouched by Phlebas, the poet is free to regard his fate with a calm indifference: 'c'était un sort pénible.'

'Death by Water' makes some changes. The glib 'sort pénible' goes, and Eliot adds 'Gentile or Jew', spelling out and thereby giving emphasis to the airily inclusive 'figurez-vous' of 'Dans le Restaurant'. This Pauline phrase, refusing the distinction between Jews and others made by the Jews themselves (part of their supposed unregeneracy), has special significance in a poem that seeks to blur distinctions between Jews and Gentiles, indeed between men and other men, and women and other women, and even between men and women:

> Tiresias, although a mere spectator and not indeed a 'character', is yet the most important personage in the poem, uniting all the rest. Just as the one-eyed merchant, seller of currants, melts into the Phoenician sailor, and the latter is not wholly distinct from Ferdinand Prince of Naples, so all the women are one woman, and the two sexes meet in Tiresias.

This blurring, or 'melt[ing]', makes anti-Semitism difficult, since it depends on maintaining distinctions between Jews and Gentiles, Bleisteins and Burbanks. 'Melting' is implicit in 'Gentile or Jew', the addressee indifferently Jewish or Gentile. In 'Dans le Restaurant' the phrase merely would have compromised the anti-Semitic complexities of *Ara Vos Prec*; in *The Waste Land*, it lets in fresh complexities.

It signifies an abandonment, not a refutation, of anti-Semitism. That larger use was left to Joyce:

> – Mark my words, Mr Dedalus, he said. England is in the hands of the jews. In all the highest places: her finance, her press. And they are the signs of a nation's decay. Wherever they gather they eat up the nation's vital strength. I have seen it coming these years. As sure as we are standing here the jew merchants are already at their work of destruction. Old England is dying.
> ...
> – A merchant, Stephen said, is one who buys cheap and sells dear, jew or gentile, is he not?[156]

Eliot may be taken to agree. Gentiles as well as Jews 'turn the wheel and look to windward'. But 'Death by Water' is to be distinguished from this passage in *Ulysses*. Stephen Dedalus seeks to controvert Mr

Deasy's account of English decline. It is all the fault of the Jews, the anti-Semite declares. *The Waste Land*'s more powerful and inclusive vision of decay, by contrast, does not derive from any anti-Semitic perspective. It is not the Jews 'at their work of destruction' who have laid waste the lives and landscapes that the poem surveys. The admonitory last lines of 'Death by Water' thus do not challenge that vision, they intensify it. Death does not offer the prospect of resurrection, only the certainty of decomposition, and Gentile or Jew, that is all that a man may expect. These gentle, elegiac lines articulate a dismal materialism. In our bodies, our limbs and internal organs, we are neither Gentile nor Jew but merely mortal and therefore liable to die. 'Once handsome and tall', we too may find our bones being 'picked ... in whispers'. Without Bleistein to define him, Phlebas becomes everyman, his fate a warning to every other man. I believe that by 1922 anti-Semitism had become a restraint on Eliot's imagination. When Eliot suppressed 'Dirge' he excluded from his œuvre an anti-Semitic poem of exceptional force. But he also, with Pound's help, thereby clarified the nature of his greatest poem, *The Waste Land*.

Let me recap. While the transformation of the ugly into the beautiful may be one of art's functions, the transformation of the beautiful into the ugly has no name: 'if there is any causal connection at all between the beautiful and the ugly, it is from the ugly as cause to the beautiful as effect, and not the other way around.'[157] In his anti-Semitic poetry, Eliot inverts this rule, just as he substitutes for a related definition of art as 'Beauty plus pity' his own definition of 'Ugliness plus contempt'.[158] Eliot's anti-Semitic poems are ugly, both in Steiner's moral sense, and in the simple sense of repellently rendering the neutral as ugly. They thus represent a challenge within art to aesthetics, and Eliot thereby emerges as a more radical, iconoclastic figure than his present reputation allows. He compels us either to accept that art is capable of 'Gerontion', 'Sweeney Among the Nightingales', 'Burbank', 'A Cooking Egg', and 'Dirge', or else surrender our claim to understand its protean varieties.

CHAPTER 5

Free-thinking Jews, persecuted Jews, and the anti-Semitism of Eliot's prose

PRELIMINARY

This is Eliot on Marx: 'I never expected that Hegel, having been inverted by a Jewish economist for his own purposes, should come back again into favour.'[1] Though born to Jewish parents, Marx was baptised at six, and was brought up outside Judaism. He did not consider himself to be a Jew and was indifferent, when not hostile, to all things Jewish.[2] Describing Marx as a 'Jewish economist', when he was less than a Jew and more than an economist, is insulting. Eliot's remark wraps a sneer at Marx inside a sneer at Jews in general. Marx the Jew was not original; he merely turned Hegel on his head. As with Marx, so with all Jews: they lack true creativity. Pound put it less obliquely: 'Marx was a Jew ... [he] invented very little.'[3] Eliot identifies Marx as a Jew to discredit him, a familiar enough anti-Semitic thrust.[4]

And on Disraeli: 'Disraeli also deserves a pass degree [in Christianity], though churchmanship is the one point on which I feel more sympathy with Mr. Gladstone.'[5] Edmund Wilson imagined Eliot pausing after the 'also': 'One free-thinking Jew is all right if he is working for the interests of the Tories.'[6] The thought is a crude one; Wilson may have overstated the objection to this obscure comment. I think that Eliot intended an allusion to the religion of Disraeli's family and not just to what Robert Blake refers to as his 'eccentricity' in religious matters.[7] The remark was sly, and faintly mocking.

As for Kipling: 'I am not aware that he cherished any particularly anti-Semitic feelings.' Kipling's anti-Semitic poem, 'The Waster, 1930', insinuates the common complaint that Jews are especially vigorous in complaining of slights, and that one therefore has to be covert when writing about them. When 'Jew' is the expected word,

Kipling substitutes 'etc.'.[8] He relies on a reflex of identification, intimating that a more candid and open hostility to Jews is not permitted. This self-pity – I have been silenced by the Jews and their friends! – is a commonplace of anti-Semitic discourse: a British Fascist cartoon of 1937 depicted stereotypical Jews standing outside business premises marked 'shop owned by gentleman whose race must not be mentioned'. Anti-Semitism is the garrulous prejudice that yet dares not speak its name.[9]

This is Eliot on a contemporary: 'there is the hard Semitic bitterness of Mr Bodenheim, who has not all the qualities of a poet, but some of them in an exceptionally high degree.'[10] The judgment is adverse, at least in relation to the 'bitterness', though difficult to fathom. It is as if the quality of Jewishness *had* to be the explanation for what was disagreeable in the poetry of an empirical Jew. Eliot was highly conscious of the Jewishness of Jews; Marianne Moore, who by contrast was not, was thus able to write at much greater length about Bodenheim without once referring to the fact that he was Jewish.[11] The Schiffs, for example, were according to Eliot 'very nice Jews'.[12] That is probably not how they would have wished to have been described. Again, in private letters: 'I have a small Jewish messenger boy named Joseph'; 'I had some correspondence with a Jewish lady in Whitechapel.'[13] The 'precocious youth' told Eliot how he would spend a fortune; the subject of Eliot's correspondence was 'old clothes'.

And lastly, here is Eliot on Freud, an object of scorn in both poetry and prose. Psychoanalysis is quackery: 'To explore the womb, or tomb, or dreams; all these are usual / Pastimes and drugs, and features of the press: / And always will be, some of them especially / When there is distress of nations and perplexity / Whether on the shores of Asia or in the Edgware Road'.[14] It is alien: 'some alien or half-formed science, as of psychology'.[15] It is fashionable: 'we have read books from Vienna...we have a curious Freudian-social-mystical-rationalistic-higher-critical interpretation of the Classics and what used to be called the Scriptures.'[16] It is absurd: 'Let us imagine (if we can imagine such persons agreeing to that extent) the fatuity of an encyclical letter produced by the joint efforts of... Dr Freud, Dr Jung and Dr Adler.'[17] It is a 'parvenu science'.[18] Eliot's hostility to Freud and psychoanalysis on occasion skirted anti-Semitic themes. 'Parvenu': Sir Ferdinand Klein would feel this insult's sting.

So far, so trivial. These observations by Eliot, offensive though they are, do not bear on my theme in this chapter. If one seeks a distinct 'prose' anti-Semitism, it is not to be found in this miscellany of insults, insensitivities, and condescensions.

FREE-THINKING JEWS

There is missing from Eliot's poetry of anti-Semitism any characterisation of the sceptical and unattached intellectual of Jewish origin, that is, the 'free-thinking Jew'. It is the omitted theme from what is otherwise an anti-Semitism of considerable range. By contrast, this is precisely the theme that Eliot's prose exploits. One finds here an hostility toward a type largely of anti-Semitism's own invention, the anarchic, intellectually subversive Jew. While the Jew is the destructive sceptic in Eliot's prose, he or she is most usually the uncomprehending philistine in the poetry and drama. In *Sweeney Agonistes*, the vulgarity of Krumpacker and Klipstein protects them from horrors, in the same way that Bleistein's brutishness exempts him from Burbank's anxieties, and the squatting Jew's degraded condition saves him from Gerontion's anguish. In the prose the Jew is all destructive cerebration; in the poetry, he or she is mentally inert. In the prose, the Jew represents the intellect unfettered by orthodoxy; in the poetry, his or her instinctual drives are unrestrained by self-awareness. While in the prose, it is the Jew's subversiveness that is objectionable, in the poetry it is his or her grossness. In Eliot's work as a whole, the Jew thereby represents extremes of intellectual and physical license, a fantasy of liberation that is rendered in language of disgust and contempt. The Jews of prose and poetry meet, aggravated, in the figure of Rachel *née* Rabinovitch, who may be taken to have repudiated the beliefs and practices of her people in the same way as have 'free-thinking Jews', though she is not an intellectual. They also meet, albeit mitigated, in 'A Song for Simeon'; that Jew between two worlds, no longer of one, incapable of belonging to the other, just as the free-thinking Jew has abandoned his or her own faith while rejecting the Christian faith. It is only the story of Christianity that finds a place for Jews, honorific but subordinate; outside of it, there is nothing but degradation and death for them.

In March 1915 Eliot wrote a letter to his friend Eleanor Hinkley. He was then a graduate student at Merton College, Oxford, and the letter was full of stories about 'Oxford society'. During the course of describing his fellow students, Eliot compared '[t]he more "brilliant" ones' to 'the clever Jew undergraduate mind at Harvard'. This mind displays 'wide but disorderly reading, intense but confused thinking, and utter absence of background and balance and proportion'.[19] The anti-Semitism of Eliot's published prose represents a series of variations on this anti-Semitic cliché masquerading as a judgment. Eliot's contemporaries, and many before him, attributed to Jews a detached, critical intelligence. William Carlos Williams described 'unattached intelligence' as 'the Jewish sphere',[20] and Paul de Man held that the 'Jewish spirit' consisted of 'the ability to assimilate doctrines while maintaining a certain chilly detachment'.[21]

Many of Eliot's remarks about Jews are indebted to this banal ethnography. The sceptical intelligence of Jews is supposed to be corrosive of Christian faith: 'the Jew stands before us in order to represent what every human being basically is. In the Jew the original rebellion, the unbelief, the disobedience of every man comes to light';[22] 'modern Jewry is most certainly a power against religion, a power which bitterly fights Christianity everywhere, uproots Christian faith as well as national feeling.'[23] In modern times the anti-Semitic charge that Jews refused to accept the divinity of Jesus became the charge that they refused to believe in anything at all. Behind the free-thinking Jew of the post-emancipation era stands the disobedient Jew of the Middle Ages. His shadow falls across this account of Renan's, for example, where religious scepticism had become the Jews' defining, paradoxical characteristic:

A peculiar people, in very truth, and created to present all manners of contrasts. This people have given God to the world, and hardly believe in Him themselves. They have created religion, and they are the least religious of peoples. They have founded the hopes of humanity in a kingdom of Heaven, while all its sages keep repeating that we must only occupy ourselves with the things of this earth. The most enlightened nations take seriously what this people have preached, while the latter laugh at the former.[24]

The free-thinking Jew is anticipated in Marlowe's Barabas, the follower of Machevill, who 'count[s] religion but a childish toy / And hold there is no sin but ignorance'.[25] These became anti-Semitic commonplaces: 'Jewish atheists ... are fighting against the Christian religion, ridiculing its dogmas, and insulting its clergy';[26] 'Jewish disbelief' and 'unbelieving circles of Jewry' were common designations in late nineteenth-century Germany and Austria.[27] Jewish sceptics were held responsible for promoting that infidelity to existing institutions which was supposed to lead to revolution: 'The Semites excel in the politics of dissolution.'[28] Those anti-Semites bewildered by modernity feared such Jews and wished them elsewhere, or dead; with Jews gone, the world would be safe again.

In Eliot's early work, Spinoza, one such free-thinking Jew, is 'unquestionably a hero, a symbolic hero of modern Europe'.[29] He represents pure intellect, his philosophy the product of a mind untouched by the demon 'emotion': 'Certain works of philosophy can be called works of art: much of Aristotle and Plato, Spinoza ... clear and beautifully formed thought.'[30] Of that clichéd pair 'the head and the heart' Eliot's examples are reading Spinoza and falling in love,[31] yet he defends Spinoza against the charge of frigidity made by 'emotional people – such as stockbrokers, politicians, men of science – and a few people who pride themselves on being unemotional'.[32] It was Spinoza's ostensible freedom from human attachment, and the geometric harmonies of his thought, that appealed to the Eliot of *The Sacred Wood*. He also invoked Spinoza's 'amor intellectualis Dei' in support of the Kantian aesthetic adumbrated in that book.[33] But Eliot later regarded Spinoza differently. He was susceptible to the romantic notion that Spinoza, whose work offers a refuge from despised 'emotion', paid a high personal price for his detachment. Spinoza's inability to share the convictions of either the Jewish society into which he was born, or the Christian society into which he was exiled, looms large in Eliot's sense of the philosopher. This double alienation is the romance of Spinoza's life: 'I am not altogether sure that Spinoza's isolation was not rather a misfortune to be pitied, than a quality to be admired.'[34]

It is by the development of this theme of isolation that the link between Eliot's praise of Spinoza and his contemptuous dismissal of the generality of free-thinking Jews is disclosed. In his introduction to the Catholic Josef Pieper's *Leisure the Basis of Culture* (1952), Eliot characterises Spinoza's work as a 'one-man philosophy', one which is merely 'a projection of the personality of its author, a disguised imposition of his own temperament with all its emotional bias, upon the reader'. Pieper's mind, by contrast, 'is submissive to ... the great, the main tradition of European thought' and 'his originality is subdued and unostentatious'. Pieper 'accepts explicitly a dogmatic theology' and 'his presuppositions are in full view, instead of being, as with some philosophers who profess complete detachment, concealed from both author and reader'.[35] Spinoza, thus, is doubly at fault where once he was exemplary; his detachment is suspect, and his work is corrupted by an emotional bias. The work is individualistic and dissenting. Its originality is overt and ostentatious, and it hides the premisses from which it is derived.

Blinded by Spinoza's ethnic origin, Eliot failed to discern the philosopher's place in Western philosophy. Spinoza's work cannot be excluded from 'the great, the main tradition of European thought' merely because he was indifferent to Christianity. Eliot mistakes personal detachment for cultural rootlessness; Spinoza was an European philosopher, even though a Jew by origin and a non-Christian by choice. A secular Jew, Spinoza's contribution is within the European intellectual tradition; this is largely, but neither by origin nor wholly, a Christian tradition. He did not, in Santayana's ugly phrase, 'live ... in the crevices of the Christian edifice'.[36] On the contrary. His philosophical relation to the work of Descartes, and his wider intellectual debts, make him a thinker in communion with 'the mind of Europe'.[37] Why does Eliot deny the patent, as in his statement that Spinoza's work conceals its presuppositions, or in his statement that Spinoza stands outside the principal intellectual tradition of Europe?

Eliot imagines 'the Christian intellectual tradition' (let me assume so readily isolable a thing exists) to be the only tradition available to Spinoza, and thus overlooks the Jewish aspect of his thinking. Spinoza remained philosophically indebted to Jewish sources even following his excommunication; intellectual influence cannot so easily be shrugged off as can synagogue membership.[38] (Eliot dismissed Jewish philosophy as 'theological hocus-pocus'.[39]) Even if, which one would deny, Spinoza stood outside 'the main, the great etc.', this does not mean that there was no other tradition for his work. The choice need not be *either* 'the main, the great etc.', *or* a 'projection' of one's own personality. There are other traditions that, furthermore, do not run in parallel lines to each other, but criss-cross repeatedly so that in the end one sees not a collection of separate lines but a pattern to which they all contribute. Indeed, as Judith Shklar has noted, Europe has always had a tradition of traditions.[40] Eliot remained unable to concede this throughout his life. As late as in *Notes* he was still insisting upon the determinative importance of Christianity; in E. M. Forster's summary of its main theme, 'Where there is not Christianity there is nothing'[41] – or only 'strange gods'.

After Strange Gods has a certain notoriety. It is known as the book that was offensive about Jews, the one that Eliot would not allow to be republished. The book is studied not so much for what it says about its subject but for what it discloses about its author. It is regarded as a resource for the biographer, not a text for the critic. Certainly, it is an inferior work. The cultural argument lacks cogency; the literary criticism is often perverse; the anti-Semitism is glib. The book contrives to be both pedantic and mystic, displaying a tension between a surface reasonableness and an underlying, disturbing unreason. Eliot's poetry is dense with examples of a similarly tense combination of civility and panic, but put to more controlled and dramatic effect. In the book it is evidence of a radical uncertainty of purpose, these tensions registering Eliot's imperfect control over both subject and language. The book deploys various defences to this instability, one of which is an ironic admission of weakness. It conceals doubt behind a disingenuous modesty. Eliot also refuses to debate: 'In our time, controversy seems to me, on really fundamental matters, to be futile.'[42] His preface serves as a very selective invitation, welcoming some, barring others. This is only the first of the book's exclusions.

Yet it cannot be detached without deliberate rupture from the generality of Eliot's prose, and to overlook it is to miss a clear statement of his larger critical undertaking. It expressly relates back to 'Tradition and the Individual Talent', and looks forward, by implication, both to *The Idea of a Christian Society* and *Notes*. It is a bridge between the predominantly literary concerns of the former and the ultimately political concerns of the latter. It speculates both on the springs of individual creativity and on favoured forms of communal existence. These questions were of continuous importance to Eliot. The book is unusual only in the manner in which it attempts an answer to each of them. It is not unusual in its anti-Semitism, though here it inaugurates rather than continues the theme. There is no anti-Semitism in 'Tradition and the Individual Talent'; both *The Idea of a Christian Society* and *Notes* disparage Jews.

'Tradition and the Individual Talent' is about the relation of the artist and the critic to tradition. New literary work is written out of an engagement with the old. The artist contributes his work to the ideal order of literary works; the literary critic assesses its place in that order. While the theory is open to many objections, it is a balanced one. It places tradition, artist, and critic, in equilibrium. It is limited to the aesthetic, and tends specifically toward the literary. *After Strange Gods* founders on greater ambitions. It enlarges the notion of 'tradition', regarding it as the sum of a community's social practices, and then poses the question: from what perspective should these practices be criticised? Criticism, the reflexive activity of the mind, has become problematical for Eliot. In 'Tradition and the Individual Talent', he remarks breezily that 'criticism is as inevitable as breathing'.[43] *After Strange Gods* is darker, and more troubled. There he insists that it is the unacknowledged, the tacit, to which men are most deeply attached: 'The assumptions that are only felt are more important than those that can be formulated.'[44] We thus tend to become conscious of traditional practices, says Eliot, only when they start to decay. They are vivid to the extent that we remain unaware of their existence. Consciousness betokens loss; criticism is obituarism. To think is to lament; or to subvert, if the thought bearing upon tradition is external to it, as in the case of free-thinking Jews. The situation for the critic seems desperate. Enter, orthodoxy. The critic's legitimate task is to identify error. By implication, Eliot had adopted 'ecrasez l'hérésie!' as his watchword: 'Tradition by itself is not enough; it must be perpetually criticised and brought up to date under the supervision of what I call orthodoxy.'[45] The agent of that supervision is a clerisy less generously conceived than Coleridge's 'instruments in the great and indispensable work of perpetuating, promoting, and increasing the civilisation of the nation'.[46] Eliot substitutes the narrower 'orthodoxy' for 'civilisation'; *After Strange Gods* is a work of desperately intolerant reaction.

Orthodoxy, Eliot maintains, is not to be confined by any definition: 'As we use the term tradition to include a good deal more than traditional religious beliefs, so I am here giving the term orthodoxy a similar inclusiveness.'[47] So Athanasius and Joyce are both 'orthodox': 'as by Athanasius, orthodoxy may be upheld by one man against the world'; 'the most ethically orthodox of the more eminent writers of my time is Mr. Joyce'.[48] Athanasius, fourth-century bishop and saint, opposed the Arian heresy and suffered exile and persecution for his championship of Christian orthodoxy. Joyce 'left the Church hating it most fervently'.[49] In his early work

Catholicism informs his language while also comprising his enemy. Athanasius and Joyce meet only in a common Catholic origin, not enough to justify imprisoning them in the cell of a common orthodoxy. Eliot wants the force of the Athanasian sanction in his praise of Joyce; the adverb 'ethically' betrays the hopelessness of the manoeuvre. This attempt to squeeze into 'orthodoxy' incommensurable imaginations is a failure. Yet it is as close as Eliot gets in the book to connecting the theological with the aesthetic. Eliot cannot explain how Athanasius and Joyce are both 'orthodox'. He has two ideas and he wants to make them into one. But while he fails to make this connection, he can arrange for an expulsion. If one asks, remarks a commentator, 'what Eliot alleged by way of principle, the answer must be, not very much'.[50] He was adept at identifying heresy in others, though.[51]

Rename *After Strange Gods* 'Orthodoxy and the Critic' and one discloses the book's relation to 'Tradition and the Individual Talent'. Many times the length of the essay, it loses itself in repetition, provocation, scorn, and wayward critical judgments. By the close of the first chapter, which purports to lay out definitions and to define method, there is only confusion and uncertainty. The second and third chapters escape these equivocations by introducing a very old and familiar type of intellectual – the inquisitor. When considering deviations from orthodoxy 'a spirit of excessive tolerance is to be deprecated'. Lacking a coherent notion of orthodoxy, Eliot is forced to think of it in terms of what it excludes: not just the individual talents of Yeats and Lawrence, but the American West, New York, liberalism, and free-thinking Jews. It is a list in which Spinoza would also find a place.

Where better than at the University of Virginia, Eliot asks, to offer a revision of his views on tradition? Virginians, at least, will be able to recollect a tradition. They may even be able to re-establish a native culture, unlike the more shifting, mixed population of certain other American regions. Virginia is another country:

You have here, I imagine, at least some recollection of a 'tradition', such as the influx of foreign populations has almost effaced in some parts of the North, and such as never established itself in the West[52]

The reference to the West is not passing, though it is dismissive. The West has an honorific place in American thought, most clearly articulated in Frederick Jackson Turner's theory of the frontier. It has become a cliché of American historiography. According to Turner the West was responsible for shaping a specifically American culture. It robbed immigrants of European attachments, creating new loyalties, indeed new characters. It encouraged an initial reversion to primitive modes of existence, but then fostered new, complex social forms. The East aped the Old World, the frontier converted the European into the American.[53] It was not just a destroyer of European traditions, it also founded new ones. It was transforming. Continuously invigorated by immigration, the frontier promoted internal trade and national land policies, advancing the power of the national government and encouraging patriotism, stimulated by the menace of the French and native Americans. The West was not what Eliot had in mind when reflecting on how traditions were to be sustained. It was democratic in politics, sectarian in religion, egalitarian in social tendency; against which, Eliot preached submission, Church, and hierarchy. It was a paradox that Eliot's reasoning prevented him from understanding. To its most enthusiastic advocates, its tradition was to be anti-traditional, its reflexes were to be innovative, its custom was to break with the past. It was restless, unsettled, mobile, rather 'Jewish'.[54] It confronts Eliot in two of its most representative figures, the fur trader and the squatter.

In repudiating the West, Eliot dismisses a rival account of the genesis and conservation of a tradition. Insofar as Eliot offers an explanation of American history, it is a catastrophic one, articulated through the North–South divide. Each was defeated – the South by the North, the North by immigration. The frontier theory upsets the North/South distinction, rejecting its claim to be determinative of American history, its culture, and its political institutions. Eliot does not reject the thesis frontally; he does so by rejecting the West's claim to have established any tradition. 'The West' thus becomes an American species of liberalism, corrosive and wholly negative, a mutation Eliot is quick to denounce.[55] In discussing 'tradition', Eliot ignores actual traditions. It is an example of bad theorising, excluding the actual, confusing the general and the ideal, and mistaking the preferred for the possible. His theory has no explanatory power; it is an evasion of reality, not a conceptualising of it. It has far greater pretensions than Turner's, purporting to define the necessary ground rules for every traditional culture. Eliot's remark about the West is a provocation, a denial of one source of American culture. (Of course, a rejection of the West is a rejection of the ideology of the West; it does not matter whether Turner was right.) In this garrulous book the repudiation of the frontier in a sentence is an example of its compact scorn. The Jews comprise another such example, as does New York.

Eliot's inventory of conditions to establish 'the best life for us' is also a picture of an unreconstructed South. It is both blueprint and portrait, both prescriptive and historical, at once a plan for the future and an evocation of the South before the Civil War ('the greatest disaster in the whole of American history'[56]). Stability is necessary; the population should be homogeneous; there must be a proper balance between the urban and the rural, the industrial and the agricultural. It is the local community that is the most permanent, while the concept of the nation is neither fixed nor unvariable. National patriotism, unlike local forms, is abstract, and the precedence of the latter over the former is a law of nature. And in commenting that this final remark 'should carry more weight for being uttered by a Yankee',[57] Eliot unites the programmatic with the elegiac, defending as a form of local patriotism the secessionist loyalties of the South. Eliot associates himself with the defeated protest of the South, describing himself as a Yankee to give the association a quality of unctuous surrender. In further praise of Virginia, Eliot writes of New York:

You are farther away from New York; you have been less industrialised and less invaded by foreign races; and you have a more opulent soil.[58]

When Eliot considered the North generally, he identified migration as an '*influx* of foreign *populations*', while of New York it is the harsher, '*invaded* by foreign *races*'. The shift is not the result of any instinct for synonym; in Eliot's work the tendency is toward repetition, not synonymic variation. It is the book nearing one of its essential enemies, its language thus becoming less measured, and more directly hostile. 'New York': it has the same resonance as 'Viennese' in 'Burbank'. Indeed, as Barnet Litvinoff has observed, 'Vienna resembled a European, land-locked version of New York'[59] in its attraction to Jews from Eastern Europe. New York was a Jewish city to anti-Semites: 'Down in a tall busy street he read a dozen Jewish names on a line of stores … New York – he could not dissociate it now from the slow, upward creep of these people';[60] 'The old-time American … is being chased from the streets by swarms of Polish Jews

... New York is in the process of becoming a cloaca gentium';[61] 'New York to me is a scream – a Kike's dream of a Ghetto. The Lost tribe has taken the island.'[62] Rupert Brooke in a Broadway car: 'The people who surround one are mostly European-born...short, swarthy, gesticulatory, full of clatter, indeterminately alien.'[63] Henry Adams matched this with an equivalent, American disdain: 'there are said to be four-hundred-and-fifty thousand Jews now doing Kosher in New York alone.'[64] Decades later, as if Jewish New York was there to be discovered afresh by each generation of anti-Semites, H. L. Mencken wrote to Pound: 'New York has now become almost wholly Jewish'; Pound took up the theme with another correspondent: 'New York is ganz verjudet.'[65] The Jews had made New York their own; the Virginians had escaped that threat.[66] They were thus likely to endorse Eliot's remarks about liberalism.

Historically, liberalism meant, among other things, the primacy of conscience, which in turn entailed the separation of church and state, the right of religious freedom, the right of civil disobedience, and a scepticism about the benefits of universal suffrage. In 1933 it would have been associated with the defence of constitutional forms of government, the promotion of democracy and the rights of dissent and non-conformity, and the relief of poverty by state intervention. In America, it was experimenting with the New Deal; in Europe, it was on the defensive against Fascism. Eliot's repudiation of liberalism is necessarily a repudiation of all this too:

In a society like ours, worm-eaten with Liberalism, the only possible thing for a person with strong convictions is to state a point of view and leave it at that.[67]

This 'Liberalism' likewise is to be related to the 'Viennese' of 'Burbank', that is, as the citing of a reputation, prejudicially rendered by context (tainted by 'Semite' in the poem, metaphorically associated with the rotting dead in the book). Eliot does not offer a critique; he merely makes a rude verbal gesture. He is as uninterested in the tradition of liberalism, its doctrines and history, as he is in the culture of Vienna or Chicago. Indeed, he does not acknowledge that liberalism has either doctrines or history. It is the sum of everything that corrodes the traditional, that disturbs existing orders, that undermines foundations. It does not protect dissent, it is itself subversion. It does not promote tolerance, it is itself licence. It is the principle of negation, lacking independent life, an 'impossible substitute for the pieties of ordinary existence'.[68] It is the parasite (the worm) that feeds off and then destroys the social body. It is the rat underneath the piles.

This vituperative caricature of liberalism has its origin in the counter-revolutionary polemics of Burke and de Maistre; in its modern forms, it still attracts a scorn amounting to loathing. Maurice Cowling, for example, writes that he 'hate[s] these modes of thinking';[69] Robert Nisbet blames liberalism for 'the contemporary chaos of cultural anarchy, hedonism, narcissism, and generalized flouting of idols'.[70] Detestation of liberalism and all its works seethes in the pronouncements of these conservative academics. There was nothing new in Eliot's attack; liberals themselves were alive to the negative aspects of liberalism.[71] Raymond Williams's praise of Eliot for 'exposing the limitations of an "orthodox" liberalism which has been all too generally and too complacently accepted'[72] was thus too generous. It is in the *Four Quartets*, and not in his prose criticism, that Eliot's conservatism finds its most considered, cogent expression.[73] Indeed, the 'conservatism' of *After Strange Gods* is especially incoherent. Eliot poses the radical's question: What kind of society do we want? But he gives the conservative's answer: a traditional one. It is an incongruous exchange, perhaps to be formulated only in an American context. Americans are used to the idea that their country was invented in 1776; it is, indeed, their national romance.[74] Furthermore, the Southern states are susceptible to the notion that the Confederacy represented a traditional way of life destroyed by the Civil War but capable of being resurrected. These are paradoxical beliefs. Traditional societies are those that 'inventors' are dedicated to destroying: they are the societies that are already there. They cannot be blueprinted, they can only be documented; they are amenable to description by the sociologist, not prescription by the constitutionalist. At most, traditions can be revived; the only traditions that can be created are bogus ones.[75] And even the 'revived' traditions usually contain an element of the contrived: staged pageants, pedagogic displays for the benefit of children, pious or defensive declarations in the face of cultural opposition.

The root problem is the 'whole movement of several centuries towards the aggrandisement and exploitation of personality'.[76] In contemporary fiction the problem is acute. There is also a general point to be made: 'when morals cease to be a matter of tradition and orthodoxy – that is, of the habits of the community formulated, corrected, and elevated by the continuous thought and direction of the Church – and when each man is to elaborate his own ... personality becomes a thing of alarming importance.'[77] Christians sometimes assert that only their own church, divinely underwritten, exists both in and beyond history. Other religious institutions are purely human inventions, historical in essence and therefore perishable. Eliot presses the point further. He implies that there is only one tradition, supported by only one church, and that the alternatives are random, arbitrary inventions of individuals who are preoccupied with 'personality'. (Later, Eliot would work up this implication into the play: *Murder in the Cathedral*.) This is not a contest between a transcendental tradition and other, mercly historical traditions. This shrunken vision disregards loyalties of class and party, cultural and ethnic attachments, and religious commitments that are not Christian commitments. Eliot does not allow for conflict between traditions, either within an individual or a culture. There is one agent of continuity, and one agent of corrosion, alternatively regarded as a composite 'liberalism', or 'the Evil One'. It is liberalism, in all its destructive forms, that must be resisted:

the struggle of our time to concentrate, not to dissipate; to renew our association with traditional wisdom; to re-establish a vital connection between the individual and the race; the struggle, in a word, against liberalism ...[78]

These are words untied from any ascertainable meaning, a prose equivalent of the impassioned rhetoric of 'Gerontion'. It is the urgency of the author's conviction, and not the pressure of any reasoning, that compels assent (if assent is given). The tension between the centripetal and the centrifugal is critical in Eliot's work: it is just that 'struggle' in 'Burbank' which results in the concentrated economy of the anti-Semitism and the diffuse evocation of Venice; or again in 'Gerontion' where a unifying consciousness is at risk of disintegration, the poem dramatising that risk. But in what sense can the struggle to concentrate and not dissipate be described as the 'struggle of our time'? What is 'traditional wisdom'? To what does 'the race' refer? These are bad abstractions, characteristic of debased political speechifying, suitable only for a peroration or as part of a speech deprecating the influence of free-thinking Jews.

In such a context Eliot cannot imagine Jews to be anything other than free-thinkers – liberals by another name. This was and remains

a common identification; according to one nineteenth-century anti-
Semite, 'liberalism is nothing but secularised Judaism.'[79] Eliot echoes
Renan, without the latter's approving intent: 'Every Jew is a liberal.
He is a liberal by nature.'[80] He echoes Meinecke, without the latter's
air of regret: '[The Jews] contributed much to that gradual
depreciation and discrediting of the liberal world of ideas that set in
after the end of the nineteenth century.'[81] To have imagined Jews
otherwise would have been to open up the possibility of a different
tradition, modulated by a different orthodoxy. 'Stiff-necked and
uncircumcised in heart and ears', the Jews resist orthodoxy, just as,
in St Stephen's words, they 'resist the Holy Ghost'.[82] 'Intelligence',
declared one anti-Semite 'is the mortal sin of the Jews ... the monsters
are at home everywhere where intelligence, stupid and criminal
intelligence, arrogates the right to govern alone; born representatives
of atheism, Jacobinism, Enlightenment.... No Jew has yet believed
seriously in God!'[83]

The South Carolinan W. J. Cash wrote in 1941, just eight years
after Eliot gave his lectures at the University of Virginia: 'the Jew,
with his eternal refusal to be assimilated, is everywhere the eternal
Alien; and in the South, where any difference had always stood out
with great vividness, he was especially so.' It was to be expected that
'in the general withdrawal upon the old heritage, the rising insistence
on conformity to it', the Jew 'should come in for renewed
denunciations'.[84] According to one observer, 'Christian anti-Semitism today [1935] is directed less against the orthodox Jews than
against the Jewish free-thinkers.'[85] He had been duped: the
distinction was an anti-Semitic fancy, not to be taken seriously.
Attacking free-thinking Jews was a way of attacking all Jews.

When not writing about Jews, Eliot's use of 'race' was slack: 'the
Christian religion is an essential part of the history of our race ... It is
quite irrelevant to conjecture the possible development of the
European races without Christianity.'[86] The missing term is 'culture'; 'race' substitutes. Eliot could also be dismissive of the political
uses of 'race': 'Mr Brooks['s] race-survival [is] depressingly remi-
niscent of a certain political version of biology';[87] 'we suspect that the
more we know about race the more clearly we shall see that we are all
merely mongrels'.[88] However, in both 'Burbank' and *After Strange
Gods* he adopted a racist anti-Semitism. This postulates conflicting
and mutually exclusive elements,[89] an Aryan racial community and
an opposing Jewish race, which in one version is similarly pure and

in another version is adulterate or 'mongrel'. The poem postulates a Jewish race; the book postulates the threat to racial purity posed by Jewish free-thinkers:

The population should be *homogeneous*; where two or more cultures exist in the same place they are likely either to be fiercely self-conscious or both to become adulterate. What is still more important is *unity of religious background*; and reasons of *race* and *religion* combine to make any large number of free-thinking *Jews* undesirable.

My italicised words indicate the connections in Eliot's argument: 'homogeneous' leads to 'reasons of race' and 'unity of religious background' leads to 'reasons of religion'. These reasons exclude Jews as such. 'Racial' Jews remain Jewish whatever the nature of their beliefs.[90] So, the disparagement of *free-thinking* Jews is an additional piece of anti-Semitic abuse. It does not qualify the offence, it re-enforces it. Jews, *After Strange Gods* implies, are free-thinkers.

Eliot's programme was in keeping with its time. It was patrician anti-Semites who founded the Immigration Restriction League in 1894; the Jewish entrepreneur and the Jewish immigrant, the one assisting the other, were taken to be two aspects of the same degraded material civilisation.[91] Restrictionism was rife in interwar America, and governors of private schools and universities, management boards of country clubs, and partners of law firms limited Jewish access to their places of education and leisure, and their business and professional enterprises. Anti-Semitism was pervasive.[92] In England,[93] as in America, such restrictions were imposed by the institutions themselves;[94] in continental Europe, by contrast, they often had the force of public law.[95] Needless to say, the restrictionist case against Jews was often defended as merely one instance of a more general argument. Eliot's proposal, however, goes beyond these exclusionary practices in two respects.

First, it reaches back to the arguments of those who opposed Jewish emancipation; they 'could conceive of neither state nor society without a Christian foundation ... the Jew had no right to citizenship, to be included in Christian society, so long as he persisted in his ancestral refusal to recognise' Christianity.[96] Isaiah Berlin summarises the thinking of J. G. Hamann, 'the complete and vehement reactionary',[97] on the subject of the Jews thus: 'to tolerate them as an organised religion is a concession to that liberalism and rationalism that constitutes a denial of what men are for, to serve the true God.'[98]

In England, a House of Commons debate on Jewish admission to Parliament led to this intervention:

It has been said that... [Jewish relief] would complete the triumph of liberalism – that it would remove the last remnant of bigotry from the statute-book. Yes, it would be the triumph of liberalism: but what was liberalism? The antagonist and opponent of religion.[99]

Differences of tone aside, this is very close to Eliot's own position. At various times anti-Semites have contended that Jews seduce Christians from the true faith; that they comprise a state within a state; that their practices and beliefs are incompatible with a Christian and latterly a secular society; that they have dual allegiances; that they are an economic burden on the state, or compete unfairly with 'Gentile' businesses. Whatever the specifics, the basic judgment remained the same: 'Relegated to permanent exile, and scattered throughout the entire universe, the Jews outrage and disturb the society of the human race.'[100] Eliot's remark hints at the old complaint that 'the Jews... turned our people away from Christ'.[101] Anti-Semites argue for the exclusion of Jews. They propose limiting their number only when more radical arguments have failed: 'A recovery of the health of our popular life, in all its fields, cultural, moral and economic, and a maintenance of this regained health, are possible only if Jewish influence is either excluded completely or driven back to an extent that makes it safe and tolerable.'[102]

Secondly, it is candid; the 'first rule of most clubs, colleges, and societies that apply "quotas" to restrict Jews', said *Time* magazine, 'is to deny that they would do any such thing'.[103] Eliot proposed to his American audience that they should take pride in their practices, and regard them as steps on the way to creating a traditional society. This was something of a *faux pas*, comparable to that of President Lowell of Harvard when in 1922 he 'openly recommend[ed] what others were doing covertly', that is, restricting Jewish access to universities.[104] Eliot refused the tacit. Harold Nicolson wrote in his diary of a visit to the Woolfs in 1930:

I attack the nomination board at the Foreign Office... The awkward question of the Jews arises. I admit that is the snag. Jews are far more interested in international life than are Englishmen, and if we opened the service it might be flooded by clever Jews. It was a little difficult to argue this point frankly with Leonard there.[105]

Nicolson's 'clever Jews' are Eliot's 'free-thinking Jews', both essentially anti-Semitic formulations, but whereas Nicolson regards the subject as 'awkward', and is embarrassed to discuss it in front of his Jewish host, Eliot shows no such hesitation before either subject or audience. Eliot's anti-Semitism was not the covert, qualified prejudice of his peers. It was prescriptive, and aggressive.

Let me address one point in passing. Ricks asserts that a distinction made by Jewish law between Jewish converts and Jews by birth is Judaism's own acknowledgment of the existence of a Jewish race, or more weakly, an acknowledgment of 'the difficult intertexture of race and religion'.[106] The rule to which he refers prohibits female converts from marrying priests. He is wrong to rely on it for a number of reasons. First, and to the extent that he himself is arguing the existence of a Jewish race, Judaism does not and cannot assist. Since racial identity is something that a religion is incompetent to determine, what Jewish law has to say on the matter is irrelevant. Secondly, one can concede readily that there are contexts in which the assertion of the existence of a Jewish race would not be anti-Semitic, without thereby having to concede that Eliot's assertion is likewise not anti-Semitic. Contexts matter. Thirdly, a distinction between Jewish converts and Jews by birth is not by necessity predicated on race, as an analogy makes obvious: only those American citizens born in the United States are eligible to become president, but that does not mean that the constitution embraces the notion of an American race. Fourthly, the alleged distinction between converts and Jews by birth is in fact a distinction Jewish law makes between Jews of two classes. Converts and certain Jews by birth together comprise the membership of the class whose members may not marry a priest. This class consists of any Jew who either has been a party to an illicit sexual relationship or is the product of such a relationship. The reason for the inclusion of female converts in this class is because neither the circumstances of their birth nor those of their pre-conversion history can be verified (it is believed) with certainty.

As perpetual dissidents, Jews distract attention from the instabilities in orthodoxy's definition. But the attack on them contains an undisclosed irony. It is both the rejection by a dogmatist of sceptics, and a retreat by a sceptic from his own uncertainties. Exclude 'free-thinking Jews' and you exclude doubters, dissenters, and most intellectuals. You might also have to banish a number of poets and novelists. If you are to be rigorous, you might even be compelled to exclude Eliot himself – a possibility of which Eliot sometimes seems almost aware. *After Strange Gods* is a curiously self-cancelling text.

It is thus with relief that critics approach *The Idea of a Christian Society*. This is a more temperate Eliot; there is no discreditable paragraph about 'free-thinking Jews' to trouble the reader. But consider this:

In any future Christian society that I can conceive, the educational system will be formed according to Christian presuppositions of what education ... is for; but the personnel will inevitably be mixed: one may even hope that the mixture may be a benefit to its intellectual vitality. The mixture will include persons of exceptional ability who may be indifferent or dis-believing; *there will be room for a proportion of other persons professing other faiths than Christianity*. The limitations imposed upon such persons would be similar to those imposed by social necessity upon the politician who, without being able to believe the Christian faith, yet has abilities to offer in the public service, with which his country could ill dispense.[107]

The italics are mine. There are some Jews whose exceptional talents it would be a pity to waste, and it is for this reason alone that they are to be allowed to teach in the schools and universities of a Christian society in limited numbers.[108] As for those others of merely ordinary ability, they will have to occupy themselves otherwise, and elsewhere. Too many free-thinking Jews ... Consider, too, the following:

Heresy is often defined as an insistence upon one half of the truth; it can also be an attempt to simplify the truth, by reducing it to the limits of our ordinary understanding, instead of enlarging our reason to the apprehension of truth. Monotheism or tritheism is easier to grasp than trinitarianism.[109]

I take the reference to monotheism to be, or to include, a reference to Judaism. Eliot makes express here what is only implicit in *After Strange Gods*: Jews are heretics.

The lectures that comprise *The Idea of a Christian Society* were given in March 1939, in the moment between the capitulation at Munich and the beginning of World War II, a time of 'emergency'.[110] The book is filled with gloomy foreboding. Though Eliot testifies to his deep shame at the settlement with Hitler, the book is not a defence of the democracies against Nazi totalitarianism. While it anticipates war, it does not itself adopt an adversarial stance. If Fascism is the enemy, it is so only remotely, and not for the vices unique to it. Liberalism remains the true antagonist, as ever in Eliot's criticism;[111]

it is responsible for 'destroying traditional social habits of the people', for 'dissolving their natural collective consciousness into individual constituents', for 'licensing the opinions of the most foolish', and so on.[112] Our culture is 'negative';[113] our circumstances are, or shortly will be, that of 'a state secularised, a community turned into a mob, and a clerisy disintegrated'.[114] A Christian society is unachievable in the United States because of its 'variety of races and religious communions'.[115] So much for Eliot's hopes of Virginia: New York has become America.

After Strange Gods coincided with the inauguration of the Hitlerian persecution, while *Notes* was written in the immediate aftermath of the Holocaust and when the struggle to establish the State of Israel was at its most intense. Not that one would know any of this from reading the books themselves. Though they refer to Jews, these books are uninterested in the circumstances of their empirical lives. Their Jews are abstractions. Likewise *The Idea of a Christian Society*, which also appeared when the predicament of the Jews was acute. The year 1938 was a time of crisis for refugees.[116] 'There are very few of us nowadays who can manage to avoid having our attention drawn to the "refugee problem"',[117] wrote Norman Angell in *You and the Refugee*, a 1939 Penguin Special. 'The persecution of the Jews', asserted Max Plowman in the same year, provided England with 'the opportunity of a moral gesture' of historic dimensions; we must, he said, 'open wide [our] arms and accept these people *at all costs*'.[118] Yet Eliot, in a book that takes as its subject the conditions for and the duties of a Christian society, is silent on the obligation to aid the persecuted. Indeed, it is only in a tone of resigned realism that he concedes 'the necessity of co-operating with non-Christians'.[119] It is as if real Jews were invisible to him.

Lastly, *Notes*. In *After Strange Gods*, Eliot was harshly dismissive of Jews, while in *The Idea of a Christian Society* he muffled his hostility in obliquities. In *Notes*, Jews return, acknowledged by name but marginalised in a footnote. The footnote follows the sentence which reads: 'In certain historical conditions, a fierce exclusiveness may be a necessary condition for the preservation of a culture: the Old Testament bears witness to this.'[120] The 1948 version of this footnote is as follows:

Since the diaspora, and the scattering of Jews among peoples holding the Christian Faith, it may have been unfortunate both for these peoples and for the Jews themselves, that the culture-contact between them has had to be within those neutral zones of culture in which religion could be ignored: and the effect may have been to strengthen the illusion that there can be culture without religion.

Just three years after the liberation of the death camps, this rehearses the recommendation of *After Strange Gods*. Eliot has learnt nothing.[121] Too many free-thinking Jews are undesirable; contact between Jews and Christians is undesirable because it fosters a damaging illusion. But the mix of the redundant, the tentative, the erroneous, and the complacent in the footnote makes for puzzled reading. The redundancy is in the opening clauses, the second adding nothing to the first ('the diaspora' is the way in which one characterises the scattering of the Jews). The tentativeness is evident in Eliot's uncertainty about whether the 'culture-contact' *was* unfortunate. He is wrong to suppose that 'culture-contact' has always failed to take into account the religious dispositions of the engaging parties. Consider: the tutoring of St Jerome in Hebrew by a Jewish scholar;[122] the defence of the Talmud by certain Renaissance humanists;[123] the correspondence on Judaism and Christianity conducted by Menasseh ben Israel with Christian scholars in the seventeenth century, and Franz Rosenzweig with Eugen Rosenstock-Huessy during World War I;[124] the campaign by Christian Zionists for the establishment of a Jewish state.[125] Of more adversarial engagements, consider: the medieval Jewish–Christian disputations;[126] the Mendelssohn–Lavater controversy in eighteenth-century Germany;[127] the interwar polemics by Martin Buber against German neo-Marcionites.[128] In each case, the tenets of Judaism were challenged publicly by Christian polemicists. Studying Judaism was often merely the preliminary to attacking it; for example, in seventeenth-century Leiden the University Chair of Hebrew was called the Chair 'for the Confutation of Judaism'.[129] Christianity was expounded by reference to what it rejected;[130] 'culture-contact' of this kind was just the prelude to a dismissal. Christian-initiated 'culture-contact', which overlooked Jewish sensibilities, thus tended to be under the supervision of anti-Semites; as for the Jews, any 'culture-contact' was fraught with risk, and genuine communication was inhibited by the desire to avoid affronting Christian sensibilities.[131] By the phrase 'has had to be', Eliot complacently endorses the denial of Judaism's continuing legitimacy. Lastly, he overlooks the contribution made by religious Jews to European philosophy, one such 'zone of culture'. The contribution of Maimonides to medieval philosophy,[132] and Levinas's contemporary project of 'translat[ing] into Greek' Jewish ethical principles,[133] are my examples here.

In this chapter of *Notes*, Eliot argues a complex case about the unity of religion and culture. The terms of this argument, however, are limited to intra-Christian differences. These mark the boundaries of his examined 'diversity'. The Jews of the Old Testament maintained their culture, he says, by a fierce adherence to their religion. This is further if extreme evidence of the necessity of religion for culture. Having noticed the Jews in this way, Eliot then pursues them beyond both the Old Testament and the main text of the chapter, into modern times and his footnote. What happens, he asks, when this fierce exclusiveness is abandoned and as a result Jews meet Christians? The illusion is fostered that culture can do without religion. This is because, in an over-fastidious phrase, the 'culture-contact' takes place in a neutral zone. If contact is possible, then why not collaboration? Further, if collaboration is possible, why not a culture generated out of that collaboration? But if Eliot is right, this could not happen.

This is the problem. If one concedes the existence of such zones, what is left of the indispensability of religion? Are these 'neutral zones' themselves illusory? If they are real, then religion ceases to be essential; they must therefore be illusory – but Eliot acknowledges that they are not. In his review of *The Future of an Illusion*, Eliot mocked what he perceived to be Freud's distinction between illusions simpliciter, and illusions that contain some psychological truth.[134] In *Notes*, Eliot needs the flexibility denied to Freud. Without it, the neutrality of these 'zones of culture' becomes chimerical. There cannot be any neutral zone if religion is strictly indispensable to culture.

Eliot would not have exposed himself to so simple an objection if he had limited himself to the Jews of the Hebrew Scriptures and not tried to take in modern Jewry as well. These Jews pose a double challenge, both to the primary need of culture for religion, and to the subsidiary need for *unity* of religious background. They are agents both of secularism and heterodoxy. Jews appear to contribute to a culture without sharing that culture's religion; they also have their own culture without benefit of adherence to Judaism. Free-thinking, they are attached neither to the religion of their birth nor to any other religion. Eliot modified the footnote in the 1962 edition but he did not resolve this core problem:

It seems to me highly desirable that there should be close culture-contact between devout and practising Christians and devout and practising Jews. Much culture-contact in the past has been within those neutral zones of culture in which religion can be ignored, and between Jews and Gentiles both more or less emancipated from their religious traditions. The effect may have been to strengthen the illusion that there can be culture without religion. In this context I recommend to my readers two books by Professor Will Herberg...

These are the differences: the double reference to the diaspora is dropped; contact between the 'devout and practising' of both faiths is recommended in place of deprecating contact between those for whom a 'neutral zone' was possible; it is conceded that both Jews and Gentiles may become detached from their religion; two books by a Jewish sociologist are cited with approval. The changes give a more balanced feel to the footnote, though the reference to 'Jews...more or less emancipated from their religious traditions' returns to the theme of *After Strange Gods*. The last sentence seems to practise what the first sentence preaches – an instance of 'culture-contact' between the devout and practising Anglican, T. S. Eliot, and the identifying if not quite orthodox Jew, Will Herberg. Indeed, one of the recommended books, *Judaism and Modern Man*, is itself a further instance of such 'culture-contact'; the impact of Reinhold Neibuhr's thought on the book's 'historical Judaism' acknowledged in its opening pages.[135] Yet the thesis for which Herberg was celebrated, that Judaism, Protestantism, and Catholicism have become fundamental subdivisions of the 'American religion',[136] a development of which Herberg approved, was unlikely to commend itself to Eliot. So one wonders, is Eliot's recommendation of the books to be taken as endorsements of their arguments, or merely as a deliberate sign of his openness to the work of a Jewish academic? The footnote is too cryptically phrased to provide an answer.

The chapter in *Notes* containing this footnote is entitled 'Unity and Diversity: Sect and Cult', which conveys its own message about the exclusion of Jews, neither sect nor cult. It addresses 'the cultural significance of religious divisions',[137] a subject that demands an extended treatment of the diaspora, but which the terms of Eliot's argument prevent him from undertaking. While Jews are too massive a presence wholly to be ignored, they are too subversive a presence for the body of the chapter. They are thus driven down into a footnote, just as in Eliot's poetry they are driven onto a 'window sill', 'under the flatfish and the squids', in the 'protozoic slime', or simply 'outside the window'. This marginalisation of Jews in *Notes* is indeed gratuitous. The very point made in the footnote is essentially a repetition of a point made earlier in the first chapter. It is one of 'two complementary errors', Eliot observes, to hold 'that culture can be preserved, extended and developed in the absence of religion. This error', he adds, 'may be held by the Christian in common with the infidel.'[138] Who are these 'infidels' but the faithless Jews of the later footnote, capable of being mentioned in the main text only in this oblique, insulting manner? Truly, *Notes* is no advance at all on the exasperated anti-Semitism of *After Strange Gods*.

Jews are troubling; Eliot subdues them by strategies of exclusion. It is one consequence of this exclusion that, when they are being hurt or otherwise harried, their clamouring tends to be inaudible.

PERSECUTED JEWS

In 'Dirge' the dead Bleistein is beyond pain. Though the crabs savage him and disease plagues him, he does not suffer. It is a dishonour that the poem visits upon him, not an injury. Eliot's poem is a torture fantasy that does not imagine the agony of the victim. Compare this scheme for Jews devised by an anti-Dreyfusard: 'A specially trained torturer should first of all cut off their eyelids with a pair of scissors ... When it is thus quite impossible for them to close their eyes, poisonous spiders will be put in the half-shells of walnuts which will be placed on their eyes...'[139] And so on. This sick imagination needs sensate Jews; 'the last thing a sadist wants', as John Casey notes, 'is to possess a corpse'.[140] The fun is in picturing these Jews as defenceless, jerking their heads this way and that, impotently trying to evade the spider stings. The fun in 'Dirge' is rather different; it consists of denying Bleistein the peace of a grave. This is a sadism of disrespect. Eliot makes Bleistein contemptible in death; the crabs that eat his lids feast on a dead man. 'Dirge' is a poem written by a man unable to encompass Jewish distress. One would not be surprised if such a person viewed reports of Nazi persecution sceptically:

There should be someone to point out that this book, although enjoying a cathedratic blessing, is an attempt to arouse moral indignation by means of sensationalism. Needless to say, it does not touch on how we might alleviate the situation of those whose misfortunes it describes, still less on why they, among all the unfortunates of the world, have a first claim on our compassion and help. Certainly no English man or woman would wish to be a German Jew in Germany today; but not only is our title to the moral dictatorship of the world open to question, there is not the least prospect of our being able to exercise it. More particularly, it is noticeable that the jacket of the book speaks of the 'extermination' of the Jews in Germany, whereas the title-page refers only to their 'persecution'; and as the title-page is to the jacket, so are the contents to the title-page, especially in the chapter devoted to the ill-treatment of Jews in German concentration camps.[141]

This *Criterion* review of 1936 is unsigned. Stead believes it to be written by Eliot 'because of the style, the manner of argument and because Eliot did most of the unsigned reviews'.[142] Ricks does not demur: 'whether or not the review was by Eliot [it] had the stamp of his approval and the stamp of his tone'.[143] Bush observes that it displays Eliot's 'own fastidious concern for language and his own conviction that life was a choice between "pyre or pyre"'.[144] I too believe it to be Eliot's; if I am wrong, then I have done him an injustice, for it is a dismal, cruel piece.

It is as if he found the book more objectionable than the wickedness it exposed. The review crawls with impatient distaste, wilfully refusing to do its subject justice. While it seeks to display the working of a mind independent of contemporary cant, it succeeds only in revealing a truculent indifference to human suffering. This indifference is registered in the very way in which the book's title is reproduced at the head of the review:

The Yellow Spot: The Outlawing of Half a Million Human Beings: A Collection of Facts and Documents Relating to Three Years' Persecution of German Jews, Derived chiefly from Nationalist Socialist Sources, very carefully assembled by a Group of Investigators. With an Introduction by the Bishop of Durham. (Gollancz, 1936)

These capitalised words suggest the billboard announcement of a Victorian melodrama or the canvassing of a fairground barker ('Derived chiefly', 'very carefully assembled'). This is not, however, the title on the book's jacket, which is *The Yellow Spot: The Extermination of the Jews in Germany*, or on the spine, which is the simpler *Extermination of the Jews*. More importantly, the typography was a contribution by the journal, the book itself using the lower case throughout (the additional, non-italicised words appear on the book's title-page only, as an explanatory gloss and not as part of the title itself). This is a striking and significant substitution. Eliot used the lower-case *j* to diminish Jews; he used upper-case initials to mock their suffering.

The Yellow Spot is a thorough, unsensationalist report on Nazi anti-Semitism. The first widely circulated publication to claim that Jews were being murdered in Dachau,[145] its analysis is expert, its research meticulous. It reproduces illustrative material in support of its indictment. It is a digest of self-advertising viciousness. For example, cartoon caricatures taken from *Der Stürmer* allege that Jews commit ritual murder; these pictures are pornographic and propagandistic. The authors describe the effect on the Jewish population of the Nuremberg decrees and they quote eye-witness accounts of persecution and painful, humiliating suffering.

Eliot's review understates the seriousness of the book's subject matter, while overstating its defects. Thus the book's contents are said not to justify the alarmism of its jacket or title-page. Yet the book quotes Nazi threats of genocide. The abnormally high suicide rates among Jews is also cited, as are instances of organised violence ending in death. Eliot must, for example, have read this:

After covering about 5 kms. the car ... stopped and we were told there was some engine trouble. We were ordered to leave the car and line up on the side of the road.

Suddenly we heard 4 shots in quick succession, and crying and moaning. Then we were again bundled into the car and brought back ... The bodies of those 'shot while trying to escape' remained in the ditch until Monday afternoon, guarded by a few Storm Troopers. All four of them had been shot in exactly the same way: a revolver bullet through the jugular vein.[146]

This sequence of isolation, deception, and murder, is the sequence of the Holocaust itself. Eliot presses his point: 'as the title-page is to the jacket, so are the contents to the title-page'. But there is no material to justify the suggestion that either the jacket or the title-page overstates the nature of the Nazi Government's intentions towards the Jews of Germany. The harshness of the persecution is fully documented; the sporadic killings proven with eye-witness reliability; the planned destruction of the entire community revealed by ample quotation from the persecutors themselves.

Eliot pursues his objection. He insists that the chapter on the ill-treatment of the Jews in German concentration camps is exaggerated, notwithstanding its epigraph: '[Nazi Party Deputy on the Jews:] Only through the radical extermination of the evil and alien part of our German blood can the future of our people be made eternally secure.'[147] The authors detail, by reference to official sources and eye-witness statements, the systematic and brutal torture of Jews in concentration camps:

a number [of prisoners] were ordered out on parade, and were told that two ... would have to die. The guards stood by with loaded rifles. The prisoners were then ordered to turn right-about and two shots were fired. But no-one was hit, and the guards laughed ... This 'joke' was repeated several times, until one day in June this year the two shots went home. The prisoners were ordered to carry the two dead bodies away.[148]

Eliot objects to what he considers to be a sensationalism of presentation that the facts do not warrant. He is wrong, as the above shows. How can he venture this objection and yet refrain from noting the sensationalism that the book temperately exposes? This, for example, is quoted from the correspondence column of *Der Stürmer*:

The Jewish business apprentice, Willi Wertheim, living at 57, Crotlen-laiderstrasse, Meerane, maintains a race-defiling association with the German embroideress, Charlotte Ahnert. The girl's parents live at 26, Crotlenlaiderstrasse. They agree with the choice of their daughter. The behaviour of the Jew and his degenerate girl friend has long caused public indignation.[149]

Following publication, the girl was imprisoned in a concentration camp. On her release, she was so badly injured that 'she was bandaged all over and could hardly make herself understood'. The young man was continually beaten until he died. 'He was said to have been bound by the feet, thrown to the ground and dragged across cobblestones like a log of wood.' It is the letter to *Der Stürmer* that comprises the sensationalist report attempting 'to rouse moral indignation'. I do not want to labour the point. It is unlikely that anyone, having read both book and review, would dispute the reviewer's glib indifference to Jewish pain. This is a person who, in a fundamental sense, does not know how to speak of the Jewish dead; he is without piety.[150] Drawn elsewhere to examples of martyrdom – Thomas Becket in *Murder in the Cathedral*, Celia in *The Cocktail Party* – Eliot was blind to the martyrdom of German Jewry.

Eliot's refusal to acknowledge the depth of that disaster, even in its early stages, is one such refusal in a long line of anti-Semitic denials of the reality of anti-Semitic persecutions. Dismissing stories of pre-war Nazi persecution, one English apologist wrote: 'the Jews wail more loudly than any other oppressed people',[151] while another dismissed concern about their treatment as 'mawkish sentiment'.[152] Eliot was merely one of a number insisting that Germany was not as represented by these so-called wailing Jews and their friends: 'mountains have been made out of molehills'.[153] The Jews were to be criticised, remarked the popular English historian, Sir Arthur Bryant, for not 'minimis[ing] their sufferings'.[154] During World War II, the English *Catholic Herald* dismissed stories of Jewish persecution.[155] In July 1941 a Ministry of Information instruction stated that atrocity propaganda 'must deal with undisputably innocent people. Not with violent political opponents. And not with Jews.'[156] In 1943 an English pamphlet, 'The Truth About the Jews', denied that any Jews had been killed by the Nazis.[157] In September 1944 a Foreign Office bureaucrat minuted: 'In my opinion a disproportionate amount of the time of this office is wasted in dealing with these wailing Jews.'[158] Another such bureaucrat remarked in January 1945 on the 'notable tendency in Jewish reports ... to exaggerate the number of deportations and deaths'.[159] By confronting but then diminishing or otherwise dismissing Jewish pain, these accounts are related to those 'persecution texts' identified by René Girard – accounts of violence given from the perspective of the persecutors.[160]

Anti-Semitism was a puzzle to Eliot. Reflecting on it, he lapsed into obscurities. In September 1941 he published an article in the *Christian News-letter*[161] which expressed concern about the persecution of the Jews in France. Relying on a newspaper report, Eliot surveyed developments there. The abolition of political parties did not trouble him: there were so many, parliamentary government was a tedious farce. The proscription of Freemasonry was similarly no loss. What gave Eliot 'the gravest anxiety', however, was the news that 'Jews have been given a special status, based on the laws of Nuremberg, which makes their condition little better than that of bondsmen'. On this Eliot commented:

Anti-Semitism there always has been, among the parties of the extreme Right: but it was a very different thing, as a symptom of the disorder of French society and politics for the last hundred and fifty years, from what it is when it takes its place as a principle of reconstruction.

Why was anti-Semitism at that time a 'very different thing'? It was precisely the programme of the 'extreme Right' that was being implemented in Vichy, albeit with the assistance of the Nazis. As two historians of Vichy anti-Semitism have demonstrated, 'without direct German prompting, a local and indigenous French anti-Semitism was at work in Vichy'.[162] The roots of Vichy anti-Semitism lay deep in nineteenth-century French history. In this passage Eliot failed both to grasp the continuity of French anti-Semitism and the likely extent of the collaboration of French anti-Semites with the Nazis.

Eliot's motive in separating out the anti-Semitisms of pre-war and Vichy France derived, I suggest, from an unease concerning the role of his one-time mentor, Charles Maurras, as the bridge between the two. To acknowledge the influences of Maurras, and Action Française, on Vichy persecution of the Jews entailed a parallel acknowledgment of where his own anti-Semitism, itself acquired partly from Maurras, could lead. Eliot criticised a certain kind of anti-Semitism while refusing to bring into focus his own complicity with it. His article was unsatisfactory both as history and political analysis. It overlooked the fact that anti-Semitism was not confined to the Right. It passed over the Dreyfus Affair in silence, not-withstanding its necessary centrality in any account of French anti-Semitism. In insisting upon the difference between 'symptom' and 'principle', Eliot jumbled perspectives. One person's symptom is another's principle; it depends on whether the perspective is sociological or philosophical. French anti-Semitism was both symptom and principle, that is, both an effect of French society and an ideology with many adherents. Eliot continued:

we can only hope that there has been, or that there will be, some organised protest against such injustice, by the French ecclesiastical hierarchy...

Eliot then qualified these unexceptionable sentiments:

unless we are also optimistic enough to hope that these measures are only taken under the strongest pressure from Germany, and that no French government, once that government was master in its own house, would enforce such measures or keep them on its statutes.

The plain sense of this final series of clauses is that if the pressure to enact the Nuremberg-style laws came from Germany, organised protest by the Churches would be unwarranted. Eliot then recoiled from this meaning in the next sentence, adding a second 'unless':

But unless the French Church, and the Protestant bodies in France rise to protest, we must feel serious doubts about the way in which the revival of Christian France, advertised from Vichy, is to be carried out.

Now the pressure from Germany is irrelevant. The snaking of this passage, with its multiple distinctions between different anti-Semitisms, demonstrates the difficulty Eliot seemed to experience when addressing the persecution of the Jews.

THE ANTI-SEMITISM OF POETRY AND PROSE

Eliot had the imagination of an anti-Semite in the highest degree. He was alive to anti-Semitism's resources, insensitive to Jewish pain. Anti-Semitism did not disfigure Eliot's work, it animated it. It was, on occasion, both his refuge and his inspiration, and his exploitation of its literary potential was virtuose. One consequence of this virtuosity is that distinct modulations of anti-Semitism in his work may be identified.

For example, 'Chicago Semite Viennese' ('Burbank') is weightier than the conjunction 'Antwerp...Brussels...London' ('Gerontion'). The former encloses the racial Jew between cities once taken to represent the most disagreeable aspects of modern life. There was the same degradation of work, the same heterogeneity of urban populations, the same combination of agitational politics and large-scale industrial activity. The ascendancy of the one imperial centre matched the decline of the other. By contrast, the European trade centres Antwerp, Brussels, and London, are just places. They are not pregnant with meaning, lapsing into the adjectival to embrace multiple connotations. They are words to be spoken as if in a curse. The landlord is rootless; it is as if he was spawned in one place, patched and peeled in another; he might have originated thus – but three other places would do just as well. While both poems exploit the literary potential of anti-Semitism, only 'Gerontion' resists its solaces, as it resists the solace of Christianity. The anti-Semitism is there, but in a stunted, undeveloped form, indeed, as stunted and undeveloped as the poem's Jew. The 'jew' of 'Gerontion' is not underneath the lot. Kept at bay, he does not dominate the poem as Bleistein and Sir Ferdinand Klein dominate 'Burbank'. 'Gerontion' is characterised by despair; 'Burbank', by a desperate wit. The essential movement of the one is centrifugal, of the other, centripetal. The narrative of 'Burbank' points a moral, its characters are types, the poem's thrusts are directed at a single target. Its language tightens to that hard knot at the poem's centre: 'The jew is underneath the lot'. It makes out a summary case against the Jews. In 'Gerontion' the case is assumed, and the Jews are relegated to a supporting part. They are dismissed, not attacked; placed, rather than challenged.

'Sweeney Among the Nightingales' represents yet another use of anti-Semitism. It is a poem of acute and undefined anxieties. Its animosity is diffused by uncertainties. Its loathing is besieged by doubt, so that the effect of 'Tears at the grapes with murderous paws' is one of a momentarily positive assertion that punctuates a discourse characterised by equivocation and apprehension. As with *After Strange Gods*, this anti-Semitic spasm is a recoil from doubt. In contrast to 'Dirge', a hate poem which fixes Jews as the immutable sum of all that is objectionable, 'Sweeney Among the Nightingales' blurs anti-Semitism into an ungraspable sense of a Jewish threat that is real but elusive. In contrast to 'Burbank', it resists the propositional, and refuses to make a case for the existence of an international Jewish conspiracy. 'The jew is underneath the lot', a statement justified neither by dramatic context nor process of reasoning, breaks with the poem's enclosed, self-sufficient drama and asserts something about Jews in general. The anti-Semitism in 'Sweeney Among the Nightingales' is thus neither dominant, as in 'Burbank', nor subordinate, as in 'Gerontion'. It is diminished. Eliot deflates anti-Semitism's pretensions in an anti-Semitic poem of rare force and verbal dexterity.

When one reviews the anti-Semitism of Eliot's prose, by contrast, there is little to complicate one's dismay and disapproval. The poetry challenges, while the prose merely offends. In the poetry, anti-Semitism is subordinate to Eliot's larger literary purposes; in the prose, it is symptomatic of the fissures and flaws in his reasoning. The poems manipulate anti-Semitic discourse to striking effect; the prose merely arranges certain clichés of anti-Semitism in unsatisfactory combinations. Of all the prose works, anti-Semitism troubles *After Strange Gods* the most. Compare it with 'Gerontion'. While the 'jew' does not explain Gerontion's disintegration, it is the book's fear that Jews can cause the disintegration of whole societies. Though both book and poem unsettle the genres in which they may be located, 'Gerontion' does so as a principle of its construction while *After Strange Gods* does so simply because it cannot help itself. Genre is the target of the first, but the predicament of the second. The book does not know how to describe itself. It is neither sermon, nor literary criticism, nor Modernist prose poem. The anti-Semitism of *The Idea of a Christian Society* and *Notes*, though less disruptive than in *After Strange Gods*, similarly lacks cogency. In his poetry, Eliot deploys anti-Semitic topics with unnerving skill. In the prose, anti-Semitism may be seen plain, its vicious banality unrelieved by literary genius.

However, in theme at least, the anti-Semitisms of Eliot's prose and poetry do converge. If Jews were taken to be 'the descendants of those unclean outcasts who mocked at all that was holy to the Egyptians',[163] then their leprosy ('Gerontion') is to be related to their scepticism (*After Strange Gods*). 'Gerontion' thus practises what *After Strange Gods* preaches, both texts deriving from what has been identified as the anti-Semite's 'aversion to sharing the social space with Jews'.[164] Now consider Rachel's animal nature. The twelfth-century cleric Peter the Venerable, 'hated the Jews because their informed and uncoerced disbelief was the living symbol of the core of rational doubts that confronted him'. Peter resolved this dilemma by holding that Jews were incapable of reason. They were animals: 'Truly, why are you not called *brute animals*? ... The *ass* hears but does not understand; the Jew hears but does not understand.'[165] And then there is Rachel's profession. In their refusal of Christ, Jews were whores: 'Daughter of Jacob ... thou hast dishonoured the King and the King's Son; thou shameless one and harlot! The King was dishonoured in the wilderness and the King's Son in Jerusalem';[166] to another anti-Semite, Jews were 'whorish and shameless'.[167] Consider, too, the sensuality of Klein; to St Ambrose, the Jews were 'carnal creatures, insensitive to the life of the spirit'.[168] Lastly, free-thinking Jews and rats. Fear of anarchists, many of whom were believed to be Jewish, led American legislators to pass panic measures excluding broadly defined categories of aliens. Anarchists, perceived to be mainly Jewish, were described in a Congressional debate of 1918 as 'rats gnawing at the very foundations of our Government'.[169] This cliché lives on in *After Strange Gods* and is invigorated by 'Burbank'. Jews undermine traditional societies; they are like rats. 'The conceptual Jew carried a message', Zygmunt Bauman remarks, that 'alternative to this order here and now is not another order, but chaos and devastation'.[170] Our society is 'worm-eaten with liberalism'; 'Lady Kleinwurm' is a society hostess in an early draft of *The Waste Land*. I propose, then, the following sequence of pairs:

prose, poetry; sceptic Jews, leprous Jews; undesirable Jews, excluded Jews; Rachel the unbeliever, Rachel the beast; the profane Klein, the debauched Klein; free-thinking Jews, rats; the liberal worm, Lady Kleinwurm. Eliot's literary anti-Semitism is spun out of these symmetries.

CHAPTER 6

Making amends, making amendments

Injure, and one should make amends. This is done by repudiating the injurious act and making a suitable act of reparation. Repudiation can take the form of clarifying one's intentions, though this response will often have an implausible, threadbare quality (thus the anti-Semitic Jung: 'My statements have evidently led to all manner of misunderstandings...'[1]). More commonly, repudiation will entail the disowning of intentions: I acknowledge that I meant harm, and now I distance myself from that end. Public insults are cured by similarly public apologies, returning to the injured his or her stolen self-respect. Amends cannot be made on behalf of a wrongdoer, in part because it is the wrongdoer who has to recognise what he or she has done. It entails the 'disciplined remembrance' of the moral significance of his or her offence.[2] When not disciplined, it may lead to 'gestures of disorderly repentance'[3] inadequate to the offence given. It is not easy to make amends, and even an apology can be difficult. Expressions of regret are often stifled by a combination of pride and embarrassment; the narcissistic self-display implicit in certain acts of public recantation may be another deterrent.[4] Remorse without atonement has its own equilibrium; introspection and the private acknowledgment of error do not always lead to amends being made.

If someone persuades him- or herself that the injurer has repented when he or she has not, then he or she is guilty of self-deception; if he or she seeks to persuade others of that false repentance he or she is guilty of deception. However, when the injurer does make amends to the injured, thereby divorcing him- or herself from his or her injurious act, the injured has a duty to forgive. This means no longer adverting to the injury. Even when no amends are made, forgiveness may be appropriate, either because of the good motives of the injurer, or because he or she has already suffered enough for his or her offence, or 'for old time's sake'.[5] In other cases, however, it may not be appropriate; the offence may be such as to dispossess us of the power of forgiveness.[6]

We are capable of making amends because we are moral agents. Eliot would add: and because we are Christians. In the course of a sermon at Magdalene College, Cambridge, in 1948, he said that 'we show our Christianity in the way in which we are aware of our faults and shortcomings, and the way in which we are sorry for them'.[7] While we should hesitate to judge others, Eliot observed, we should be severe in judging ourselves. We can wrong others in spectacular ways, though it is more likely that the wrongs we do will be of the more mundane, everyday kind. Either way, and though we will certainly continue to injure, we should strive to be aware of what it is that we do, and why, and 'then', he concluded, 'be sorry for it'.[8] Certainly, Eliot knew the passion of regret. A deleted passage in *The Waste Land* refers to 'Remorse unbounded, grief intense' that 'Had striven to expiate my fault'.[9] But in both sermon and poem, the consciousness of regret falls short of the desire to make amends.

Being sorry for doing something is not the same as saying sorry to the wronged person, or otherwise remedying the injustice done. Indeed, it is a lesser thing, even when it brings about a transformation of self: 'I began, some years ago, to think that I must eventually make the effort to reconcile myself to Goethe: not primarily to repair an injustice done, for one has committed many such literary injustices without compunction, but because I should otherwise have neglected some opportunity of self-development, which it would be culpable to neglect' ('Goethe as Sage'[10]); 'I am still befouled, / But I know there is only one way out of defilement – / Which leads in the end to reconciliation. / And I know that I must go' (*The Family Reunion*[11]). It doesn't matter to Eliot the critic that hitherto he has denigrated Goethe; it doesn't matter to Eliot the playwright whether Harry truly has killed his wife. What does matter is that the 'opportunity of self-development' should not be missed. The real vice would be to pass up that opportunity. It is this same refined form of self-regard (what Spender calls 'spiritual one-upmanship'[12]) that leads Eliot the critic to celebrate the making of amends for the satisfaction it gives to the penitent: 'To anyone who is capable of experiencing the pleasures of justice, it is gratifying to be able to make amends to a [person] whom one has vaguely depreciated for some years...'('The Second-Order Mind'[13]); and leads Eliot the playwright to make one of his characters suffer a disproportionately intense remorse for having run over a man who was already dead and having submitted to his father's will in not marrying a woman to whom he was anyway unsuited: 'It's hard to make other people realise / The magnitude of things that appear to them petty; / It's harder to confess the sin that no one believes in / Than the crime that everyone can appreciate' (*The Elder Statesman*[14]).

In the first chapter I contended that Eliot's anti-Semitic poetry injures, among others, its Jewish readers. These wounds are 'hurts of intimacy'.[15] They are violations of the bonds that tie us to those texts with which, in Wayne C. Booth's phrase, we keep company.[16] Poets who injure by their poetry therefore should make amends. And, separately but relatedly, they have a continuing responsibility for what they have written, which they may exercise, in appropriate instances, by acts of repudiation. This is why the question of whether Eliot repudiated his anti-Semitism is a pressing one. That he did so seems to have become the received wisdom.[17] It is an attractive thought, and it tempts me. If it were true, it would fulfil a sentimental wish to find an admired poet distancing himself from what one deprecates in his work. I do not despise such a desire. It would also give a certain form to my book. Having exposed the vice in five chapters, I could conclude with the repentance. The conversion narrative is indeed seductive. Further, it would add the rejection of anti-Semitism to the series of repudiations and ostensible repudiations which characterised Eliot's post-war career as a critic. This would further demonstrate just that continuity between Eliot's anti-Semitism and his larger literary projects that throughout this book I have been keen to prove. Finally, it would meet the obligation readily to acknowledge a wrong set right. Failure to make this acknowledgment would itself be a double wrong, both condemning afresh a man who had rehabilitated himself and disregarding a critical moment in his work; one's assessment would be unforgiving and incomplete. Such an omission would be vindictive and make unreliable one's other critical judgments.

Of the Romanian scholar and intellectual Mircea Eliade, a man of international renown who once had been an enthusiastic supporter of his country's fascistic Iron Guard, Norman Manea has observed:

When labelled 'Nazi' or 'anti-Semite', his reaction to the crushing weight of accusations that after all make a brutal simplification of his life story is to withdraw. There is an eloquence as well as a dignity in silence; there is delicacy in evasion, not just cunning; but we cannot avoid seeing that in silence there is much that is also reprehensible. What about publicly retracting one's former beliefs, denouncing the horrors, disclosing the mechanisms of mystification, assuming the guilt? Perhaps very few people are sufficiently lucid and courageous for this, and it is these few who deserve to be called people of conscience.[18]

In this chapter I ask: allowing for differences of circumstance and culpability, was Eliot such a 'person of conscience'?

REPENTING ANTI-SEMITISM

The taking of writers to task for the anti-Semitism of some part of their work, and the response of those writers to that criticism, is a minor theme in literary history. Across the spread of these instances, certain variants can be identified. Each bears a certain relation to the cluster of problems I am investigating in Eliot's literary career. In each case one may posit an author who has published work that is anti-Semitic.

In the first variant, in response to a complaint about that anti-Semitic work the author writes something else in the same or a similar genre. Even when written without conceding the anti-Semitism of the earlier work, that latter work is to be taken as a reflection upon the first, either as a repudiation of it, or a clarification of its intent. This represents a partial making of amends. It can be studied by reference to Dickens. *Our Mutual Friend* answers, or is supposed to answer, *Oliver Twist*.

In the second variant, and again in response to a complaint, a belated acknowledgment that the work is anti-Semitic follows upon a history of denials and evasions. In this case, however, the acknowledgment falls outside that author's published work.

In the third variant there is an ambiguous, impossibly unspecific 'repudiatory' work where the alleged repudiation is obscure to the point of bogusness. Ezra Pound is my example in these second and third instances. A dubious confession to Allen Ginsberg, and passages in the *Pisan Cantos* and elsewhere, supposedly answer the texts of a career anti-Semite.

In the fourth variant the writer expressly rejects anti-Semitism without acknowledging that his or her own earlier work is anti-Semitic; his or her rejection neither engages with that earlier work nor is written in response to a complaint. Indeed, the subsequent work may even be anti-Semitic. I examine this variation by reference to Wyndham Lewis.

In the fifth variant the writer repudiates anti-Semitism by implication of argument; anti-anti-Semitism becomes in the later work one of its intellectual consequences, if not one of its express themes. No complaint has been made of the writer, who offers no acknowledgment of fault. The recent controversy regarding Paul de Man's wartime journalism is the most topical instance here.

Dickens

In 1863 the Jewish Eliza Davis wrote to Dickens protesting the 'great wrong' he had done to the 'Jewish people' by Fagin.[19] *Oliver Twist*'s Fagin is a stage devil, vigorous, menacing, and ugly; 'old' and 'shrivelled', first seen with a 'toasting-fork in his hand', he has a 'villainous-looking and repulsive face' that is 'obscured by a quantity of matted red hair'.[20] Dickens resented Mrs Davis's criticism. If Fagin was a Jew it was because most receivers of stolen goods were Jewish; further, the novel's other villains were Christians.[21] That was his first reply; his second was *Our Mutual Friend*'s Riah. The saintly, submissive Riah defies plausibility; the Fagin-like wickedness has been displaced onto Fledgeby, his non-Jewish landlord. Mrs Davis wrote again, this time thanking Dickens, describing Riah as 'a great compliment paid to myself and to my people'.[22] He is generally considered, however, to be an artistic failure; making amends to Jews is perceived to be difficult, perhaps impossible (the critical reception of *Daniel Deronda* demonstrates the pervasiveness of the sentiment). Belloc deplored even the attempt: 'How unintelligent are the efforts of the writers who would...make amends to the Jews for former persecution by putting imaginary Jew heroes into their books.'[23]

It is sentimental to regard *Our Mutual Friend* as making 'amende honorable' for *Oliver Twist*.[24] Dickens did not, so far as I am aware, ever repudiate his portrayal of Fagin, and David Philipson mistook art for philosophy when he wrote that a 'later judgment must always be supposed to subvert an earlier one, and we are justified in concluding that Dickens's opinion underwent a complete change'.[25] Riah is not to be taken in substitution for Fagin; they are a contrasting pair. The two derive from that debased Romanticism which conceived of Jews as a people naturally living in the extremities of saintliness and evil. Further, on an examination of the two novels, one might conclude either that the creator of the former simply could not be an anti-Semite, given the latter ('I think there cannot be kinder people in the world'[26]), or that he was neither pro- nor anti-Jewish, but simply a novelist indifferently creating Fagins and Riahs out of the fecundity of his imagination. Either of these conclusions is possible in place of the more commonly advanced one that the anti-Semitic author of *Oliver Twist* recanted his opinions in the philo-Semitic *Our Mutual Friend*. The two novels equivocate before these interpretations, *Our Mutual Friend* both denying the existence of, and repudiating, *Oliver Twist*'s anti-Semitism. When Mrs Davis presented Dickens with a Hebrew–English Bible, he again protested that he would not 'wilfully' have done an injustice to the Jewish people 'for any worldly consideration'.[27] In the revised, 1867 edition of *Oliver Twist*, Dickens largely deleted the phrase 'the Jew' or substituted 'Fagin' for it.[28]

Pound

Ezra Pound's anti-Semitism was overt, deep, and practical. It showed itself in many trivial, petty ways. For example, he is said to have objected to the prevalence of Jewish contributors to the *Dial*.[29] On his return visit to America in 1939, it is reported that when he went to Harvard to read his poems he noticed that the audience included many Jews, whereupon he changed his planned programme to include more anti-Semitic poems.[30] In New York City he refused to enter the bookshop of Frances Steloff, one of his chief supporters, simply because she was Jewish.[31] He did not help individual Jews who were victims of persecution, and the factitious distinctions he drew between good and bad Jews were themselves part of the common currency of anti-Semitism. Of course, this does not mean that some have not been taken in by them: 'Hitler jailed no Rothschilds, and Pound thought that the poor Jews whom German resentment drove into concentration camps were suffering for the sins of their inaccessible coreligionists... Correctly or not, [Pound's distinction] attempted a diagnosis, and one tending to decrease rather than encourage anti-Semitism.'[32] To unpack this fatuity:

Hitler jailed and procured the death of many wealthy Jews, including Rothschilds;[33] no Jews within the Third Reich and its satellites were inaccessible to the Nazis; anti-Semitism is incapable of making a true diagnosis; distinguishing between types of Jews was a device in Nazi Germany for justifying the persecution of Jews without limitation; inflicting further pain on A, when A and B are each being injured, brings no relief to B, and thus does not diminish the total harm being done.

There is the massive evidence against Pound of the *Cantos*, the broadcasts, and his post-war sponsorship of Fascist and other ultra-right groups. Pound's work makes distinctions between 'literature' and 'propaganda' untenable. It is not that he abandons fiction for the greater freedom of lies; his fictions lie. The step from the poetry of 'The yidd is a stimulant, and the goyim are cattle'[34] to the broadcast prose of 'hang Roosevelt and a few hundred yids'[35] is insignificant. This observation of Pound's is illuminating:

Where I see scoundrels and vandals, [William Carlos Williams] sees a spectacle or an ineluctable process of nature. Where I want to kill at once, he ruminates, and if this rumination leads to anger it is an almost inarticulate anger, that may but lend colour to style, but which stays almost wholly in the realm of his art. I mean it is a qualificative, contemplative, and does not drive him to some ultra-artistic or non-artistic activity.[36]

This desire to kill, a typically overstated account by Pound of the source of his verbal violence, cannot be sated by artistic activity, and propels him beyond art, while also animating his art. His anti-Semitism is an aspect of this murderous passion, and participates in the millennial war against the Jews waged by their diverse antagonists. The centre of Pound's operations against the Jews is to be found not in the broadcasts but in the *Cantos*. They have a place in Modernist literature; they also have a place in the literature of modern anti-Semitism.

There was huge folly in Pound's anti-Semitism, and great irresponsibility. It was part of his charlatanism, one of his short-cuts to knowledge. 'One can't read everything', he impatiently insisted to Eliot.[37] Anti-Semitism saved Pound, as it saves others, from the efforts and disappointments of thought; 'with one day's reading a man may have the key in his hands', says Pound in Canto LXXIV. It is precisely this, however, that made his anti-Semitism so ineffectual. It lacked system, even elementary cogency. It was sometimes farcical.

It often undid itself in qualifications or exaggerations. The inconsistencies of anti-Semitism are laid bare in Pound's broadcasting, in his essays and articles, and in his poetry.

While Eliot's poetry compresses anti-Semitism, Pound's unpacks it until it sprawls across his work like the loose, untidy contents of a wardrobe. Pound was as incontinent as Eliot was economic. As anti-Semites, the one inclined toward the extravagance of rant, the other, toward the compressed malevolences of slogan and snub. Take Jewish Vienna: while *The Waste Land* renders it 'unreal', and 'Burbank' disarms it by reducing it to an adjective, the *Cantos* brood obsessively on it. Pound struggled with Jews in his poetry; Eliot defeated them every time. Pound's expansiveness exposed him; Eliot's succinctness protected him. Wyndham Lewis observed shrewdly: 'Temperamentally, T. S. Eliot is as "close" as Ezra is exuberant. He is as arrogant as Ezra is modest – as sly as Ezra is open.'[38] Though he didn't mean to, Pound helped make anti-Semitism disreputable,[39] while Eliot gave it new life, and even a measure of intellectual respectability. Though both Pound and Eliot have been criticised for bogus scholarship, it was only in Pound's work that it made common cause with anti-Semitism.

Though hatred of the Jews pervades the *Cantos*, equivocal repudiations of anti-Semitism punctuated Pound's literary career. Just before the war he declared: 'Race prejudice is red herring. The tool of the man defeated intellectually and of the cheap politician. … It is nonsense for the anglo-saxon to revile the jew for beating him at his own game.'[40] Pound would complain when criticised for his Fascism and anti-Semitism; the charges were unjust, 'someone is needed to defend grandpa'.[41] On his release from St Elizabeth's he said: 'I've been making jokes about Jews all my life. Fifty years ago we had jokes about the Scots and the Irish and the Jews, and the best stories you got were from the Jews.'[42] Only joking, pleads Pound. The charge of anti-Semitism is based on rumour, and unsupported by actual evidence: 'And if any man, any individual man, can say he has had a bad deal from me because of race, creed, or color, let him come out and state it with particulars.'[43] The weasel words are 'any individual man', which excludes protests from Jews in general about insults directed at Jews in particular. At about the same time:

I am accused of anti-Semitism. Why do I respect Spinoza, esteem Montaigne as a writer, and endeavour to reestablish the fame of Alexander Del Mar who I think was a Jew. I have utter contempt for Marx and Freud … The work of Freud is a poison invented to counteract another poison concocted by that heretic scoundrel Calvin (the alias of Cauein, or Cohen, philo-usurer) who opposed a Vatican tied to Fugger.[44]

He cannot resist an anti-Semitic jibe even when defending himself from the accusation that he is anti-Semitic. The typically unreflective blindness of these assertions is economically demonstrated thus: 'What I am driving at is that some kike might manage to pin an antisem label on me IF he neglected the mass of my writing.'[45]

He resented his 'antisem label'. Even Louis Zukofsky, while denying Pound the title, convicted him of the offence: '"Jewish internationalism" – there ain't no such thing & exists only in yr. mind tainted by Nazi bigotry – or some other infernal silliness beyond yr. sensible control.'[46] Late in his life, Pound conceded an anti-Semitism of sorts. To Allen Ginsberg: 'the worst mistake I made was that stupid, suburban prejudice of anti-Semitism. All along, that spoiled everything.'[47] Ricks has taken issue, rightly, with 'mistake' and 'suburban'. 'Mistake' is too weak a word for 'the political and spiritual monstrosity of Pound's anti-Semitism'. It is also too weak because it implies that anti-Semitism was an error that could have been corrected without serious impact on his work. If one holds the anti-Semitism to have been constitutive of that work, then the word is impossibly optimistic. 'Suburban' misrepresents anti-Semitism's range and displays a mind irresistibly drawn toward prejudicial thought.[48] 'I am not a demigod', he confesses in Canto cxvi; 'I shared a suburban prejudice', he confesses to Ginsberg. The two remarks are of a piece, deriving from an arrogance that broods on the descent from an ideal of greatness rather than on the injury which that descent did to others. It is an overrated moment in Pound's life: 'It was like a moment of ritual penance, one priest confessing to another of broken taboos.'[49] There was another half-acknowledgment of anti-Semitism, without using the word, in the foreword to *Selected Prose 1909–1965*: 'In sentences referring to groups or races "they" should be used with great care. re USURY: I was out of focus, taking a symptom for a cause. The cause is AVARICE.'[50] Yet note the gap between these qualified admissions about anti-Semitism and the self-damning judgments of those last years. 'How are you, Mr Pound?' asked Richard Stern. Pound replied, 'Senile ... Wrong, wrong, wrong. I've always been wrong. You don't know what it's like to get off on the wrong path.'[51] To Grazia Levi: 'I have come too late to the consciousness of doubt ... Too late came the understanding ...

Too late came the uncertainty of knowing nothing.'[52] 'Pound in these dispirited comments was being much too hard on himself', remarks Davie;[53] this is not a judgment that could be applied to Pound's concessions regarding his anti-Semitism.

These concessions formed no part of the poetry, though Robert Lowell made poetry out of them: 'He showed us his blotched, bent hands, saying, "Worms. / When I talked that nonsense about Jews on the Rome / wireless, she knew it was shit, and still loved me".'[54] (The acknowledgment – limited to the wartime broadcasts, made trivial by 'nonsense', and deferring to the romance of his mistress's devotion to him – hardly suffices.) Though some have tried to read passages in the *Pisan Cantos* as retractions by Pound of his anti-Semitism, they do not mandate such an interpretation.[55] These cantos endorse, and enlarge upon, the anti-Semitism of the previous cantos. Insistently abusive lines such as 'David rex the prime s.o.b.' and 'the yidd is a stimulant', the contemptuous, dismissive 'in the synagogue in Gibraltar / ... / during the preliminary parts of the whatever', the Marcionite 'there is no need for the Xtns to pretend that / they wrote Leviticus' and, endlessly, the passages about usury with quotations from the Hebrew Scriptures, together offer no respite to the persecuted Jews of the earlier cantos. Indeed, the ritual of the Gibraltar synagogue, recounted with some humorous sympathy in Canto XXII, is scornfully alluded to in Canto LXXVI; Pound's return to the theme marks an exacerbated anti-Semitism impatient with detail ('the whatever'). Nor does the subsequent set of cantos, *Thrones*, make any retraction. (Delmore Schwartz justly observed of it that 'Pound has remembered a great deal, but ... has learned nothing.'[56]) Nor, equally, do the final *Drafts and Fragments* (Cantos CX–CXVII), though Davie hints and Casillo expressly affirms, that they do.[57] Casillo argues that Pound 'rejects ... those messianic aspirations which had led him into a protracted and psychologically destructive agon with the Jews'.[58] So even Casillo, whose study of Pound's anti-Semitism is exceptionally thorough and penetrating, cannot resist the pull of the death-bed repentance scene; others have been similarly tempted.[59] Consider: 'As to sin, they invented it – eh? / to implement domination / eh? largely' (Canto CXII); that is, the Jews invented sin in order to rule the world. This fantasy of Jewish conspiracy is glossed correctly by Casillo earlier on in his study; it is later overlooked by him in the last-minute drive to give his book a happy ending.[60]

Wyndham Lewis

Admirers of Wyndham Lewis's work freely concede its anti-Semitism. Essentially trivial, it took the form of personal abuse or a bellicose, political invective. He didn't care much for or about Jews; he routinely said as much. The anti-Semitism in his fiction and poetry is typically casual, unreflective, and slight: 'Is he a Nigger, / A Chink, a Jew, or some yet odder figure?';[61] 'Chacun son Jew! is a good old english saying.'[62] This is an anti-Semitism that lacks commitment. His portrait of Lionel Kein in *The Apes of God* is more hostile to the friend on whom it was based than to Jews as a whole. It is not so much anti-Semitic as anti-Schiff, who told Lewis that he was hurt by it.[63] The contrast here with Eliot's anti-Semitism is striking. Schiff was right to remonstrate on his own behalf; Mrs Millin was equally correct to protest on behalf of Jews in general. It matters to one's sense of the novel that Lionel Kein was modelled on a contemporary man of letters and patron of the arts; it doesn't matter at all to any reading of 'Burbank' whether Sir Ferdinand Klein was the fictional duplicate of an Edwardian financier. Hence Eliot's Jews tend to slide into anonymity, while Wyndham Lewis's bloom into an extravagantly personal eccentricity. The anti-Semitism of his critical prose is as bluff and unreflective as that of his fiction. Though vigorously, even splenetically expressed, it lacks consideration. Again in contrast to Eliot, there is no sign of any pressure of thought behind the anti-Semitism; it is unthinking. Among much that is crude and uninteresting, there is evidence of an indifference to Jewish suffering, and a distaste for the Jewish 'triumph of organization, the subordination of the individual to the race'.[64] His pamphlets of the 1930s reprise anti-Semitism's then standard themes: the un-Britishness of Jews; the Jewish blackening of Hitler's reputation; the involvement of Jews in the Russian Revolution. Only when characterising Jews as instances of the 'type-man' pilloried in his satires did he strike an innovatively anti-Semitic note. Yet it is exactly at this point that the anti-Semitism annuls itself. Identifying Jews as 'types', he also condemned anti-Semites for just this mistake: 'When people fall out ... they always call each other "dirty dagos", "dirty Jews", "dirty Germans" ... Yet that is surely the very moment when they should, instead, insist upon the individual person ... rather than upon vague generalisations ... I don't believe in "Jews", "Dagos", and so on ... They are vulgar myths.'[65]

As early as in *Paleface* (1929), there was this scorn for anti-Semitism, a 'racial superstition'.[66] There were also intermittent signs of a self-censoring tendency. The second edition of *Tarr* omitted '[of the Jews:] the most decayed specimens of the lowest race on earth'.[67] The second edition of *The Caliph's Design* omitted 'a Jew over-raced and over-sexed'.[68] Elsewhere, accompanying praise of Jews and dispraise of anti-Semites,[69] a casual anti-Semitism reappears: 'the fresh-coloured rather jewish-looking face at the window (Jahveh minor) had a gratified glint in his eye'.[70] This is an anti-Semitism without sting. It is simply the only language Lewis knows. In 1939 Lewis published *The Jews: Are They Human?* and answered the question affirmatively; unlike Belloc's *The Jews*, it is not an anti-Semitic book with a chapter on anti-Semitism in it. It urges, for example, the welcoming of Hitler's Jewish refugees. Though the English have recently become 'Jew-conscious', he himself, he says, is not. Neither 'pro-' nor 'anti-Jew', he has no feeling for the Jew either way.[71] The anti-Semite is unintelligent and a bore; his slanders have stuck, notwithstanding the evidence. Though the book has its moments of oblique self-defence ('it is well-nigh impossible to open your mouth without being called a fascist'[72]), it is silent about Lewis's earlier books. Does it therefore make amends? His biographer gives three answers. First, amends were unnecessary because 'Lewis had always been scrupulously fair to the Jews'; secondly, the book made clear Lewis's thinking on Jews; thirdly, it made amends for his earlier 'pinch[es] of malice'.[73] So, there was both nothing to repudiate and something that had to be clarified, and offences for which the making of amends was appropriate. Though any one of these three propositions is arguable, taken together each undermines the other two. Like his biographer, Lewis also got into a tangle when reviewing his work. In *Rude Assignment* (1950), for example, he offered of it a number of incompatible defences, protests, and concessions.

De Man

Paul de Man was born in Antwerp. He lived in Belgium through the Nazi Occupation and only emigrated to the United States in 1948. He began his academic career at Bard College, then taught at Harvard and elsewhere until he reached Yale, where he taught until his death in December 1983. At his memorial service he was praised equally for his influence and his integrity. Thus: 'the future of literary studies depends on reading Paul de Man as best we can, on being true to his example as a reader'; 'he had wit, he had judgment, the classical virtues'; '[he was] a liberator'.[74] Four years later his wartime articles and reviews were discovered. The bulk of them had appeared between December 1940 and November 1942 in the pro-Nazi *Le Soir*; the rest had been published by a Flemish-language collaborationist newspaper. This material, together with the further inquiries into his life that they provoked, revealed that de Man had not only hidden, but in certain respects actually lied about discreditable aspects of his past. His articles had endorsed collaboration with the Nazis and commended collaborationist authors. One of them expressed a certain disdainful anti-Semitism. The discovery of these articles shocked and surprised de Man's friends and colleagues, among them those colleagues who had delivered memorial service tributes. Battle lines were rapidly drawn. In defence of de Man it was argued of the articles themselves that they were ambiguous, distancing themselves from Fascism by strategies of irony and other subtleties; and of the post-war career, that it marked a complete break with Fascism (including anti-Semitism), certain essays even obliquely acknowledging their author's earlier collaborationist complicity. Those unsympathetic to de Man tended to argue the reverse; the articles were pro-Fascist and anti-Semitic, and de Man's post-war work is a development of certain of their themes (one critic even found anti-Semitism in one of his last essays[75]). The debate raised many questions of great interest, and informs certain of the arguments developed in this book.

Though it has been claimed that de Man later disclosed the existence of the articles, the evidence is slight and ambiguous. Derrida believes that de Man's 1955 letter to Harvard's Society of Fellows was a public act of self-accounting, although its misleading phrasing and occasional outright mendacity makes this a difficult proposition to sustain.[76] Harold Bloom has said that de Man told him in 1969 of his wartime career.[77] As for the rest, on de Man's 'ordeal of mutism', Derrida comments: 'Even if sometimes a murmur of protest stirs in me, I prefer, upon reflection, that he chose not to take it on himself to provoke, during his life, this spectacular and painful discussion. It would have taken his time and energy. He did not have very much and that would have deprived us of a part of his work.'[78] (A critic comments: 'Telling the truth should be avoided because it is time-consuming: this is a morally bankrupt argument.'[79]) Hartman makes this 'ordeal' seem even more virtuous, proposing that de Man's silence was a scruple of his superior scepticism: 'He wished to avoid confession, or any religious gesture, preferring to work out his totalitarian temptation in a purely impersonal way.'[80] Felman goes even further, arguing that his work 'performs actively an act of silence not as simple silence but as the absolute refusal of any trivializing or legitimizing discourse' and that de Man thereby 'articulates... the ethical impossibility of a confession that... cannot take place'. This represents 'the most radical and irrevocable assumption of historical responsibility'.[81] I pass over these betrayals of vocation to examine Hartman's claim that in de Man's late essays we may 'glimpse the fragments of a great confession'.[82] My own reading of these essays, insofar as it does not err in the same way as de Man's partisans by fancifully attributing consciousness of personal guilt to his work, points in another direction. I sense an evasion of the burden of confession.

This evasiveness had the effect, for example, of truncating de Man's critical reflections on Heidegger's wartime politics in his 1955 essay 'The Inward Generation';[83] it also, I believe, led de Man in the same essay to propose, wrongly, that Pound came to view his lifetime commitment to a politics of the Right as 'a momentary aberration'.[84] Consider, too, these cryptic remarks from the preface to *Blindness and Insight*: 'I am not given to retrospective self-examination and mercifully forget what I have written with the same alacrity I forget bad movies – although, as with bad movies, certain scenes or phrases return at times to embarrass and haunt me like a guilty conscience.'[85] One's knowledge of de Man's wartime career gives this passage an offensive, teasing quality. If certain phrases in his earlier writings haunted him, one might imagine that this was the direct result of, and not merely analogous with, the promptings of a guilty conscience. De Man investigated the workings of the guilty conscience in 'Excuses (*Confessions*)', a chapter of *Allegories of Reading* that concerns Rousseau's admission in *The Confessions*, and then again in *Reveries of the Solitary Walker*, that he was responsible for a theft which at the time he had blamed on another. This chapter has been mined by critics and supporters of de Man alike for what it might disclose of his posture toward his own shameful secrets. I side with the critics. So far from being obliquely confessional, the chapter mocks the confessional idiom, and displays a deep distaste for Rousseau's 'edifying narrative'.[86] Rousseau's ability to advance sophistries in his own defence while also taking pleasure from his self-abasement offers, indeed, an unattractive spectacle. He thus provides two exemplary texts by reference to which the ethics of confession can be brought into question, even perhaps discredited. In such a context de Man's dictum that 'Confession is not a reparation in the realm of practical justice'[87] may be revealing. Even if confession does not in itself make amends, it is the preliminary to reparation. What de Man is doing in this sentence is seeking to sever the relation between the two.

With these instances in mind, I can now return to Eliot.

MAKING AMENDMENTS

In his later years Eliot would confess mock dismay at once having been taken so seriously on one or other topic. He would tut-tut over the extremism of the judgments of his youth. He would also, however, shift position without acknowledging the shift. He would adopt a posture of recantation that belied an adherence to his original stance. His revisionary judgments often engaged with, without wholly controverting, earlier judgments, while yet exploiting the rhetoric of a more complete disavowal. The second essay on Milton is exemplary of Eliot's sly play with the rhetoric of self-criticism. This game of half-retraction, half-affirmation, established a new theme for Eliot's critics. Not only were they concerned with his opinions, they were now also concerned with his *shifts* in opinion. His changes of mind became objects of study in themselves. And when 'To Criticise the Critic' appeared, these critics in addition had to take into account what Eliot himself had said about those shifts of opinion. Some held that Eliot merely had adopted the 'posture' of recantation;[88] others held that Eliot's positions remained the same, modified only in tone (encouraged by Eliot: 'as we age...we regard the enemy with greater tolerance and even sometimes with sympathy'[89]); a third group regarded Eliot's judgments as being subjected to a constant process of modification or 'second thoughts';[90] and others again viewed Eliot's post-war career as one long retreat – for I. A. Richards, 'Eliot was the great Recanter'.[91]

Did he, then, regret his anti-Semitic work, which mostly remained in print? Regretting an act means wishing that one hadn't committed it. If it is a continuing act, it means bringing it to an end. One stops, and wishes that one had never started. The two go together. For example, Eliot regretted publishing 'Ode' and so ensured that it wasn't republished.[92] He wrote disparagingly of F. W. Bateson in 'The Function of Criticism' and so, when the essay was republished, he altered the paragraph that referred to him.[93] If one regretted doing a certain thing, it would be odd to stop doing it and yet be pleased that one had once done it. It would be odder to wish that one had not done it and yet persist in doing it. Can we say this of Eliot? He was not compulsively unregenerate, lamenting with St Paul 'the evil which I would not, that I do'.[94] He was not comparable to Dante's Guido, who sought absolution for the sin he was about to commit, thereby earning the Devil's reproof that 'absolution minus repentance can't be, / nor repenting and wanting a thing / at once, a complete contradiction'.[95] Still less does one find any weakness of will; there is no reason to suppose that Eliot lacked the necessary resolve to act in accordance with his best judgment.[96] The question can be addressed by considering the suppression of *After Strange Gods* and 'Dirge', the elevation of 'jew' to the upper case in 'Burbank' and 'Gerontion', and changes in phrasing in a footnote to *Notes*.

I should make two preliminary points. First, I will assume in Eliot's favour that, in relation to the changes in typography and phrasing, he wished to diminish the offence given by the unamended texts. Certainly these changes loom large in that small number of alterations made by Eliot to his published work (the bulk consists of the deletion of epigraphs and dedications[97]). Secondly, both the suppressions and the revisions were each either undeclared or underdescribed. They therefore fall between changes forced upon an author and changes that an author clearly flags as having been made because of his or her own change of heart. Pound is a good example of the former kind of author, while Auden is exemplary of the latter kind. Thus, while certain lines in the *Cantos* were deleted or blacked out for fear of litigation, Auden revised his poems in pursuance of a continuing project of self-policing. 'I won't let you reprint ["September 1, 1939"]', he told John Hollander, 'because you know it's bogus.'[98] With a candour that was not Eliot's style, Auden once declared, 'Some poems which I wrote and, unfortunately, published, I have thrown out because they were dishonest, or bad-mannered, or boring.'[99] Auden was by no means the first English poet to revise his work for these, or related, reasons.[100]

'Dirge' was suppressed prior to publication. It was removed from the final text of *The Waste Land* at Pound's suggestion, which in itself is an indication that it was not rejected for its anti-Semitism. (Pound offered to Eliot an inferior poem in honour of *The Waste Land*: 'Bleichstein's dank rotting clothes / Affect the dainty nose'.[101]) Given the continued publication of the other anti-Semitic poems, it would have been inexplicably inconsistent of Eliot to have suppressed it for that reason, or that reason alone. Further, it was omitted along with a number of other poems and passages that were not anti-Semitic.[102] Its suppression should not be treated as an instance of 'the impulse [of anti-Semitism] triumphed over'.[103] I think it similarly unlikely that *After Strange Gods* was allowed to go out of print because of its deprecations regarding free-thinking Jews. For one thing, Eliot's *Selected Prose*, a miscellany of extracts first published in 1953 with Eliot's approval, reproduces a passage from the book's first lecture that anticipates precisely those deprecations.[104] So far as I am aware, Eliot neither disavowed the book's anti-Semitism nor made clear his objections to it. There is reason to suppose that it embarrassed him. The choice of date in the following doesn't seem accidental:

I find myself constantly irritated by having my words, perhaps written thirty or forty years ago, quoted as if I had uttered them yesterday. ... When I publish a collection of essays, or whenever I allow an essay to be published elsewhere, I make a point of indicating the original date of publication, as a reminder to the reader of the distance of time that separates the author when he wrote it from the author as he is today. But rare is the writer who, quoting me, says 'this is what Mr Eliot thought (or felt) in 1933 (or whatever the date was)'.[105]

There has been speculation about the reasons for Eliot's embarrassment. Edmund Wilson put it down to the book's hostile reception.[106] A. D. Moody believes that it was the book's anti-Semitism that troubled Eliot, and in particular the risk that it might be taken to endorse the practices of Nazi Germany: 'There is no reason to suppose that he was thinking of Germany... but it is precisely this which makes [it] so wrong. Eliot himself realised this, and refused to allow *After Strange Gods* to be reprinted. The reason, as he told J. M. Cameron... was that "he regretted the tone and content of the political remarks contained therein".'[107] Yet if Eliot had the anti-Semitic passage in mind he could have said so, in those terms; that passage is not in itself political, though it has political consequences, as do all anti-Semitic proposals; there are other passages in the book better described as 'political', which Eliot could have had in mind. Maud Ellmann claims that Eliot was 'embarrassed by [the book's] anti-Semitism', but does not offer any evidence in support of her claim, other than some generalities in a letter Eliot sent to Pound.[108] Richard Shusterman hopes that Eliot's decision to suppress the book 'reflect[ed] his repentance for its anti-semitism'.[109] Louis Simpson has suggested that Eliot's motive in suppressing it was regret at what he had written about Lawrence.[110] He may be right. It would be in keeping with Eliot's partial revaluation of the novelist in his preface to William Tiverton's *D. H. Lawrence and Human Existence*. According to Helen Gardner, Eliot's proof of evidence in the *Lady Chatterley's Lover* trial repudiated his earlier attack on Lawrence: 'He was prepared to say that when he spoke of [Lawrence] as "a very sick man indeed", he was very sick himself.'[111] The suppression of *After Strange Gods* only becomes evidence of an abandonment of anti-Semitism if it is supported by other instances of disavowal. It is to these instances that I now turn.

Lower-case typography was a Modernist reflex that Eliot bent to an anti-Semitic purpose. This reflex began as a campaign. 'What a battle we made of it merely getting rid of capitals at the beginning of each line!', William Carlos Williams remarked.[112] It was a practice of other Modernists. For example, 'Lewis used lower case type for nationalities, on the grounds that being English was no more worthy of a capital letter than being sick.'[113] Both Joyce (who was not anti-Semitic) and Pound (who was) rendered 'jew' in the lower case.[114] Eliot's sparing and special use can best be brought out by a comparison with 'lower-case cummings'.[115] In 'i sing of Olaf glad and big / whose warmest heart recoiled at war', the lower-case 'i' represents the modesty of the poet before his subject.[116] Similarly, in the closing lines of another poem, 'what i want to know is / how do you like your blueeyed boy / Mister Death', the 'i' defers to the greater power of 'Mister Death' while at the same time challenging its authority with a question.[117] In 'Gerontion', by contrast, the upper case pronoun of the opening phrase 'Here I am' is the assertion of the 'I' against the encroaching Jew. The 'I' strains to be rendered in a super-upper case, and by a reciprocal downward pressure, what should be 'Jew' becomes 'jew'. In such a context, as Gabriel Pearson says, this 'reads like paranoid retaliation'.[118]

This retaliatory act does not, of course, exhaust Eliot's literary anti-Semitism. The poems are replete with such acts, none of which, with the sole exception of a typographical adjustment, has been excluded. If one is prepared to stand by 'Rachel *née* Rabinovitch', it seems an odd scruple to resile from 'The jew is underneath the lot' and substitute 'The Jew is underneath the lot'. Even as staunch an admirer as T. S. Matthews found it difficult to be impressed by the gesture. 'The only observable result' of Eliot's encounter with Mrs Millin was, according to Matthews, 'that in later editions of ['Burbank'] 'jew' was spelled with a capital J'.[119] By recasting the typography of the poems Eliot acknowledged the offence they gave while signalling his refusal to withdraw them. The paltriness of his revisionary gesture thus may be said to add to, rather than lessen, each poem's insults to its Jewish readers, whatever Eliot's actual intentions in this respect may have been.

The question of intentions arises again with the revision to the *Notes* footnote. It seems obvious from the changes made that Eliot wanted to soften its tone. The result, however, was to make essentially the same point though in an ostensibly more welcoming and positive manner. He probably knew that he had botched it, and so in the preface to the paperback edition of *Notes* he tried to anticipate criticism:

These 'Notes' began to take shape towards the end of the Second World War. When it was suggested that they should be reprinted in 'paper back' form, I re-read them for the first time for some years, expecting that I should have to qualify some of the opinions expressed herein. I found to my surprise that I had nothing to retract, and nothing upon which I was disposed to enlarge. One footnote, on p.70, I have re-written: it may still be that I have to say too much too briefly, and that the notion needs further elaboration.

I have lately had occasion to review my literary criticism over forty years and account for developments and changes of opinion, and I propose one day to submit my social criticism to the same examination. For as a man matures, and acquires greater experience of the world, the years may be expected to bring about even greater changes in his views on social and political matters than in his tastes and opinions in the field of literature. I should not now, for instance call myself a 'royalist' tout court, as I once did: I would say that I am in favour of retaining the monarchy in every country in which a monarchy still exists. But that question, as well as others on which my views, or the way in which I would express my views, have changed, or developed, is not touched upon in the present essay.

That is to say, he finds nothing in the book he wishes to retract, and yet he anticipates that his published social criticism (in which category the 1948 *Notes* is prominent) might no longer reflect his current views. By implication, he pleads indulgence for his earlier works as the products of a less mature and callower mind than he now possesses, yet he is quite stubborn about the limited extent to which the 'notion' in the footnote may need further attention (only 'elaboration', not change). The first paragraph begins confidently with a boast about the continuity of his thought, while the second paragraph encourages one to suppose that, had Eliot the time, significant modifications of position would be disclosed. I read the preface, thus, as divided against itself and so at one with the other texts that I have discussed in this part of the chapter: a book that is suppressed but for reasons never adequately given, and two poems that are as offensive as the book but which are allowed to remain in print, albeit with a modified typography. These may be regarded as the gestures of a man who, while unable to break free of an anti-Semitism that had become part of the processes of his thinking, had ceased to be comfortable with his contempt for Jews.

The above represents the sum of steps taken by Eliot to revise his work away from its anti-Semitic tendencies. It has been argued, however, that there are two other texts in which Eliot repudiates anti-Semitism.

THE ROCK AND 'LITTLE GIDDING'

Moody suggests that Eliot's pageant play, *The Rock*, might have been written as a repudiation of the anti-Semitism of *After Strange Gods*.[120] Certainly it comprises an early, though post-*Ara Vos Prec*, repudiation of one kind of anti-Semitism. A church is to be built, and among the distractions, the workers are interrupted by Blackshirts soliciting donations for party funds. The male chorus asks: 'Are you obedient to the Law of God? / Are you with those who reverence the temple?' These questions receive the following dusty response:

> Your vesture, your gesture, your speech and your face,
> Proclaim your extraction from Jewish race.
> ...
>   we must firmly refuse
> To descend to palaver with anthropoid Jews.[121]

This was the first appearance of anti-Semitism in Eliot's work as a subject. It had been a problematic feature of that work since *Ara Vos Prec*. But this is rather different. By putting anti-Semites on the stage Eliot holds their ideology up to scrutiny: 'anthropoid' is a word drawn from an anti-Semite's vocabulary ('the Jew is born of a special category of anthropoid like the black man'[122]). 'Anti-Semitic' becomes a way of describing the work's content, rather than the work itself. Anti-Semitism has become in *The Rock* the subject of Eliot's attention, and not the dark side of his vision. 'Anthropoids' are human in form only. The anti-Semites deny the honour of a human identity to Jews – they may seem to be like other men and women, but they are not. They look like them, but their gestures give them away. They are animals. And the Eliot of *Ara Vos Prec* would add that they have paws. What is the difference between 'descend to palaver with anthropoid Jews' and 'Bleistein's way / A saggy bending of the knees / And elbows'? Though the Jew is similarly anthropoid in each, in the first the language of anti-Semitism stigmatises the speaker while in the second it invigorates the poem. One alienates anti-Semitic language, the other alienates the Jewish reader. Who or what to rebuff? Eliot makes one choice in *The Rock*, and another choice in his anti-Semitic poetry, the more interesting work.

Of course, *The Rock* does not quite jump to the defence of Jews. It is a defence of Christianity, and of its roots in the Hebrew Scriptures. The lines that precede those of the Blackshirts suggest the connection by a reference to the 'Law' and the 'temple'. The rejection of the Blackshirts' anti-Semitism is a rejection of anti-Christian paganism. (Characterising Fascism as neo-pagan was a convenient way of evading its debt to Christian anti-Semitism; it also permitted the characterisation of hatred of the Jews as an expression of anti-Christian resentment.) It is not a plea for modern Jewry, it is an endorsement of Christianity in both its historical and supernatural forms. The Blackshirts refuse their descent from Jews when they refuse to descend to Jews. They deny Christianity's relation to Judaism – Eliot's denial of their denial is as close as he gets to affirmation in his account of Jews. *The Rock* is not Eliot's *Our Mutual Friend*.[123]

Eliot's problem with Jews, which was in part symptomatic of his problem with intellectuals, and in turn derived from uncertainty about his own role, was a modern problem with modern Jews. Eliot's anti-Semitism rejected Jews while embracing their scriptures, both as sources for his own work and more generally. In 'The Man of Letters and the Future of Europe', he displayed some uncertainty, however, on whether this contribution of the Jews' was a cultural one:

for the preservation of any European culture ... a perpetual cultivation of the sources of that culture, in Greece and Rome, and a continual refreshment of them, are necessary. I should say Israel also, but that I wish to confine myself, so far as that is possible, to the cultural, rather than the religious aspect.[124]

This is odd, given the use to which both *The Waste Land* and 'Ash Wednesday' put the Book of Ezekiel. Elsewhere, in a post-war broadcast to Germany entitled 'The Unity of European Culture', Eliot proposed that European literatures have three 'sources which we share in common: that is, the literature of Rome, of Greece, and of Israel'. In another broadcast in the same series, he repeated his reference to 'the ancient civilisations of Greece, Rome and Israel, from which, owing to two thousand years of Christianity, we trace our descent', and asserted that 'we' are the 'common trustees [of] the legacy of Greece, Rome and Israel, and the legacy of Europe throughout the last two thousand years'.[125] He does not suggest that 'Israel', in the form of post-Scriptural Jewry, has played any continuing part in the development of Europe. One inherits a legacy when the legator is dead. Yet what Eliot designates as 'Israel' is a living element, at times dormant, at other times brilliantly active. The contribution of Rabbinic hermeneutics to modern literary criticism is only one such intervention by Jewish tradition in a secular discipline.[126] The anti-Semitism that Eliot rejects is the one that damned the Jews of the Hebrew Scriptures as well as, and as a means of more comprehensively, damning their descendants. The early battles between emancipators and anti-Semites were often fought over just this terrain. The emancipators passed from a defence of Biblical Jewry to a vindication of contemporary Jewry; anti-Semites sought to discredit their Jewish contemporaries by writing slightingly of the Jews of the Bible.[127]

Eliot's argument had, of course, a context. Indeed, it stumbled into a passionately contested debate about Jewish history. On one side were Jews and their friends; the other side was dominated by anti-Semites. It was customary for modern Jewish apologetics to point out the Jewish contribution to the West, partly to challenge those who insisted upon its indivisibly Christian nature, and partly as an assertion of pride at a time of humiliation and torment. Though often failing to distinguish between a Jewish contribution and a contribution by a person who happened to be Jewish, their efforts were a corrective to those who dismissed the Jews as an irrelevance in the development of the West, and a rebuke to anti-Semites.[128] Quite independent of this, there is a whole discourse regarding the contribution of the Jews to world history that starts in the eighteenth century, becomes a feature of nineteenth-century thought, and then is put to hostile use in the twentieth century. The key figure in this later history is H. S. Chamberlain, whose *Foundations of the Nineteenth Century* pitted Asiatic Jews against Aryans. In just this way did the nineteenth-century distinction between the Hebraic and the Hellenic degenerate, until the polarisation was such that anti-Semites began to urge that the world could not accommodate both 'races'. Chamberlain's work was a station on the road to the Holocaust.[129] Eliot's remarks are not part of this latter discourse, because they locate the Jews within a European context; but equally they fall outside the tradition of Jewish and philo-Semitic apologetics because of their failure to acknowledge that the Jewish contribution is a continuing one.

Eliot's confusion is evident in the various positions he adopted on this question. I identify four such positions: 'Israel' represents a religious, but not a cultural resource; 'Israel' is a cultural resource, but a closed one; free-thinking Jews do continue to make cultural interventions, but of a deleterious kind; though *free-thinking* Jews are harmful, there is some scope for beneficial 'culture-contact' between 'devout and practising' Jews and their Christian counterparts. These are, respectively, the positions adopted in: 'The Man of Letters and the Future of Europe'; 'The Unity of European Culture'; *After Strange Gods*, and the original footnote in *Notes*; the revised footnote in *Notes*. There is one common feature, and that is a tendency to limit the 'Jewish contribution': it is either purely religious and not cultural; cultural but not living; living but harmful; or else it is such that it requires no more than a footnote to assess. Plainly, Eliot did not think either deeply or coherently about Judaism or Jewish history, which is hardly surprising, given that anti-Semitism was his principal tutor.

At least Eliot had the right name for the heresy of seeking to dissociate Christianity from its Jewish origin. Simone Weil's 'rejection of Israel', Eliot observed, 'made her a very heterodox Christian'. She was guilty of 'something very like the Marcionite heresy'. By 'denying the divine mission of Israel', she also rejected 'the foundation of the Christian Church'.[130] (Here we are meant to infer that it was Israel's mission to found the Church; having done so, it should have dissolved itself.) Marcion, a second-century heretic, rejected the Old Testament and insisted that the refusal of the Jews to follow Jesus meant that they worshipped another God. The message of the Bible and the message of Christ were irreconcilable. It was Tertullian who gave orthodox Christianity's answer to Marcion in a work that was no less deeply hostile to Jews than Marcion's. The God of the Jews is not a different God to the one whom Christians worship, Tertullian insisted. It is the same God; and He has rejected the Jews. (As Newman put it, 'Judaism ... was rejected when it rejected the Messiah'.[131]) Tertullian contests Marcion by making God an anti-Semite.[132] A defence of Judaism is thus sometimes necessary in the greater defence of Christianity. Origen attacked the pagan Celsus: 'he thinks he will more easily prove Christianity to be untrue if he can show its falsehood by attacking its origin in Judaism'.[133] Weil remarked in a letter: 'I have never been able to understand how it is possible for a reasonable mind to regard the Jehovah of the Bible and the Father who is invoked in the Gospel as one and the same Being.'[134] She took a sympathetic interest in Marcion's teachings. Levinas puts it simply: 'She hate[d] the Bible.'[135] The desire to sever Christianity from its Jewish origins is a project of many anti-Semites, nor is this project confined to the intellectually disreputable among them, proven by the example of Schopenhauer in whose work it is a minor but recurring theme. It was developed most fully in the present century by the liberal Protestant theologian Harnack, whose 'neo-Marcionism' attracted support from those 'German Christians' seeking to free Christianity from 'alien Semitic sensibilities';[136] F. H. Bradley counted himself among those 'who do not think that Christianity is called upon to wrap itself any longer in "Hebrew old clothes"'.[137] I take Eliot's phrase 'the divine mission of Israel' to refer to Israel's role as precursor of Christianity. It is a chilly approval, and one that is consistent with, though not in itself evidence of, a certain kind of anti-Semitism.[138] The 'chosen people' become the 'rejected people'.[139]

In recognising the historical relation between Judaism and Christianity, he was sometimes ready to acknowledge the existential reality of Judaism too. The little footnote in the 1962 edition of *Notes* does this, as did Eliot conversationally when he praised the Jewish thinker Martin Buber.[140] It was more usual, however, for him to note 'the futility of non-Christian lives' and 'the incredibility of every alternative to Christianity that offers itself'.[141] This verbal exclusion of Jews seems to have been a reflex for him. In a radio broadcast, for example, he paused to define his use of 'we': 'we – I mean our ancestors for twelve or fifteen generations'. 'We', he then commented, could have had the benefits of science without giving up 'the belief in holy living and holy dying, in sanctity, chastity, humility, austerity, asceticism, the belief in... Christian tragedy'.[142] In 'The Humanism of Irving Babbitt', he remarked: 'For us, religion is of course Christianity';[143] in 'Religion and Literature' a sentence begins: 'It is our business, as Christians ...'.[144] In 'Modern Education and Classics': 'I am only here concerned with readers who are prepared to prefer a Christian civilization...'.[145] The Jewish faith was invisible to him; we must choose either 'a Christian or secularist philosophy'.[146] And there is the larger question: where do Jews fit in a Christian society? In an article written during 1941 he commented that the ambition to create a Christian Britain is 'the greatest we can take to ourselves'.[147] Jews can play no part in that 'we'. They can only watch, and wait, until the ambition is achieved and they are left – where? Eliot does not say.

'Little Gidding' contains an account of a chance meeting between the poet and a stranger in the dawn following a London blitz. The two walk companionably together, 'in a dead patrol'. Eliot addresses this 'familiar compound ghost', another poet, whose reply acknowledges a common vocation, '[t]o purify the dialect of the tribe', and warns of the exasperations of old age, among which is 'the awareness / Of things ill done and done to others' harm / Which once you took for virtue'. It is a considerable speech, in turn pedagogic and personal. The ghost discloses his own condition to the poet while also instructing him. In this 'hallucinated scene after an air-raid',[148] there are echoes of 'Gerontion' both in phrasing and in its description of the ruins of old age, where both 'body and soul begin to fall asunder'. By contrast with that poem, however, this is a true dialogue with a disclosed interlocutor, and what the stranger has to say is received as true wisdom, in the manner of Dante's encounter with his teacher, Brunetto Latini, in the seventh circle of Hell. Obliquely confessional, the ghost anticipates, and thereby expresses, Eliot's own regret. This is a revelatory moment in a body of work that strives to resist the temptations of self-disclosure. These lines play a variation on Yeats's 'Vacillation'. The poet is oblivious to the beauties of the seasons; he is burdened by the weight of his recollected wrongs:

> Things said or done long years ago,
> Or things I did not do or say
> But thought that I might say or do,
> Weigh me down, and not a day
> But something is recalled,
> My conscience or my vanity appalled.[149]

Eliot didn't like the poem, deprecating in *After Strange Gods* its tone of 'regret' and 'resignation'.[150] He was wrong about this; the poem is simply realistic about the poet's inability to make good the harm that he has done, and the regret that he feels as a result. It is a hard thing to have to accept that it is too late to remedy the injustices one has committed. Eliot just doesn't see this, and 'Little Gidding' is an aggravated version of this misreading. It refuses to acknowledge any responsibility to those the poet has injured and thereby seeks to avoid just that tone of 'regret' Eliot so disliked in Yeats's poem. 'Vacillation' looks back to a landscape filled with those wounded by the poet; 'Little Gidding' looks forward to the poet's purgation in the 'refining fire'. It anticipates a redemption that leaves the poet's injured without justice.

It doesn't matter, therefore, precisely what wrongs have been done, because the poem is not burdened by the need to make amends for them. There is harshness in the self-criticism, but no particularity. It is nothing less than '*all* that you have done, and been' that shames. Anything and everything may be encompassed by this – recall Pound's 'Wrong, wrong, wrong. I've always been wrong.' For Ricks to suggest that 'the awareness / Of things ill done' shows Eliot's dismay at the anti-Semitism of his work thus seems desperate, and desperately implausible:

Eliot – who believed in redemption and whose art is redemptive – came to contemplate the painful admission 'Of things ill done and done to others' harm / Which once you took for exercise of virtue'. The unpublished 'Dirge' about a drowned Jew might then be seen to count for less, even to matter exactly as the impulse triumphed over, an ugliness of spirit the contemplation of which could precipitate beauty and justice, crystallised in the due limpid indifference within 'Death by Water': 'Gentile or Jew ...'[151]

There is a sleight of hand here. Though Ricks does not expressly argue that the lines from 'Little Gidding' refer to the poet's anti-Semitism, he creates the impression that they might. If, however, they refer to anything specific at all, it is probably to the sins of rectitude, offences 'which once you took for exercise of virtue'. Eliot may have regretted, for example, the persecutory zeal with which he pursued Lawrence and Yeats in *After Strange Gods*. The lines should not, I think, be taken as expressing regret for his literary anti-Semitism. If such was Eliot's intention, then he failed. It was impossibly vague, deplorably reticent. A line from Baudelaire's 'Au Lecteur', an important poem to the Eliot of *The Waste Land*, is pertinent: 'Nos péchés sont têtus, nos repentirs sont lâches'.[152] Reluctantly, I am driven to conclude that Eliot, on this hard question at least, cannot be described as a person of conscience.

DENIALS AND EVASIONS

Of course, it would not have been easy for Eliot to have repudiated the anti-Semitism in his œuvre. Quite apart from the shaming self-display such a repudiation would have entailed, it was too integral to his work for him to have been able to take its measure. It seems that he could not admit that he had anything to apologise for; he understood neither the challenge to readers posed by poems made out of anti-Semitism's vile materials nor the offence that anti-Semitism could give. Furthermore, disowning it would have meant disavowing too much else. Reject the anti-Semitic texts, and many others would be pulled out in their wake. That Eliot's revisions should have been so paltry is thus not surprising.

The Healy correspondence

In May 1940 Eliot exchanged correspondence with an American critic, J. V. Healy.[153] Healy had written to Eliot about Pound's anti-Semitism, commenting on Eliot's own 'tendencies in that direction'. Eliot asked for the evidence, and Healy responded with *After Strange Gods*. By 'free-thinking Jews', Eliot then explained, he meant Jews who have abandoned one religion without adopting another. They are as undesirable in large numbers as free-thinkers of 'any [other] race'. These Jews are 'only a special case'. Judaism, Eliot continued, is 'unfortunately' not 'very portable'. Without 'its traditional practices, observances and Messianism, it tends to become a mild and colourless form of Unitarianism'. The Jew separated from his faith is to be distinguished from the 'free-thinking European' or 'American of European race', because these latter 'retain ... many of the moral habits ... of Christianity'. This is because they are 'the descendants of Christians'. The Jew, by contrast, 'is much more deracinated', a deracination which is 'dangerous' and tends toward 'irresponsibility'. These views, Eliot insisted, derive not from prejudice but from the 'recognition' of 'an historical social situation'.

If 'free-thinking Europeans' are 'descendants of Christians' then Jews cannot be Europeans. The letter thus goes further than either *After Strange Gods* or *Notes* (fuller than the former; more dismissive than the latter), and is alarming in its implications and confusions.

What could Eliot have meant when he wrote that Judaism is 'not very portable'? For many centuries, it has been a religion of exile, practised by observance, prayer, and study. It has centres of learning, but no monasteries or convents. A synagogue can be maintained wherever ten Jews assemble to pray. When Jews are forced to move, they take their books with them. Their religion travels in those books, which 'carry us through history', says Levinas, and which are, 'even more deeply than the earth, our support'.[154] So far from free-thinking Jews losing the habits and conventions of their faith, such Jews have a place within Jewish life, though not always a comfortable one.[155] Why, in any event, are 'free-thinking Jews' a '*special* case'? His animus infected a letter intended to be self-exculpatory. 'Deracination' has a special resonance in anti-Semitic discourse. When Eliot used it, he invoked a whole tradition of fear, hatred, and abuse.[156]

The comparison of Judaism with Unitarianism is startling, though an American context domesticates the connection. On occasion, adherents of these two faiths were subjected to similarly discriminatory treatment early in America's history.[157] By the close of the last century, American Jewry had developed strong links with Unitarianism. Reform rabbis annually met with Unitarian ministers in a Liberal Congress of Religion. Many Jews in communities too small to maintain a synagogue were active in the Unitarian Church. Nevertheless, though Unitarians were energetic proselytisers amongst Jews, they attracted few Jewish converts.[158] Given that the theological link between the two is the common denial of Christ's divinity, Eliot's comparison is evidence of his inability to conceive of Judaism in anything other than negative terms.

In his reply, Healy focused on Eliot's use of 'race'. Eliot would have had a fair point if he had not written 'reasons of *race* and religion'. The word 'race' introduces ethnological and genetic distinctions. Furthermore, it was 'unfortunate' that Eliot should have 'pick[ed] on Jews' when they were being 'hounded and tortured'. Eliot's answer was brief. He acknowledged that while 'the whole tone of *After Strange Gods* is of a violence which I now deprecate', the remark about Jews is not one of those statements that he would now wish to qualify.[159] There the exchange ended. Eliot's letters are muddled, notwithstanding the formal exactness of his phrasing. (This is not wholly surprising; there is a rhetoric of precision in Eliot's criticism which ought not to be confused with the real thing.) It seems that Eliot did no better when challenged by Leslie Fiedler:

I wrote to [Eliot], asking him about the obsessive hostility betrayed in [his anti-Semitic poetry]. I was expecting, I think, a recantation, an apology at least, since at the moment at which I opened our correspondence the full horror of the Holocaust had been revealed. He began in his response by trying – rather unconvincingly, it seemed to me – to assure me that he was, of course, opposed to the Nazis' 'Final Solution', that, indeed, he considered anti-Semitism a 'heresy'; but he then went on to write, in a cliché almost as offensive as spelling the name of my people without a capital letter, that some of his best friends were Jews. And he concluded by unctuously expressing the hope that I was a faithful attendant of a synagogue in Missoula, Montana, which is to say, not, at least, 'free-thinking'.[160]

This modern-day Eliza Davis hoped for, but did not receive, an apology.

The Bollingen award

The 1949 Bollingen poetry prize was the first of what was intended to be an annual award administered by the Library of Congress. Eliot was one of the jurors. The jury's duty was to recommend to the Bollingen Foundation the awarding of the prize to 'the author of the book of verse which ... represents the highest achievement of American poetry in the year for which the award is made'.[161] Pound's *Pisan Cantos* won. The award was controversial; not simply honouring a poem composed by an anti-Semitic poet, it honoured a poem that itself was anti-Semitic. The press release announcing the award was defensive:

The fellows are aware that objections may be made to awarding a prize to a man situated as is Mr Pound. In their view, however, the possibility of such objection did not alter the responsibility assumed by the Jury of Selection. This was to make a choice for the award among the eligible books, provided any one merited such recognition, according to the stated terms of the Bollingen Prize. To permit other considerations than that of poetic achievement to sway the decision would destroy the significance of the award and would in principle deny the validity of that objective perception of value on which civilized society must rest.[162]

That is, the prize is a repudiation of the politics of the prize-winner. One shows one's strength by praising one's enemy. By concentrating on what was objectionable about the poet, and ignoring what was objectionable about the poem, the press release misrouted the ensuing debate toward Pound's career as a man of letters, and away from the *Pisan Cantos* themselves.

The statement of the jury, with which Eliot has to be associated, was Eliot's sole public declaration on the affair. He admired only limited parts of the *Cantos*, his general view being largely adverse.[163] He was 'thoroughly discomfited by the affair. At first he thought of resigning from the jury but then decided not to do so. He refused to give any interviews to the press about the matter.'[164] Privately, he complained about 'the degree of terrorization men of letters appear to suffer'.[165] His distress may have been aggravated by the attention his own anti-Semitic work received.[166] The *Saturday Review of Literature* accused him of anti-Semitism, proposing that 'this rootless expatriate' be dropped from the jury.[167] It was contended in the *Partisan Review* that Eliot's vote for Pound derived from their shared perspective on Jews; though Eliot's anti-Semitism was 'different in kind' to that of Pound, it was similarly essential to his poetry and 'social ideas'.[168]

Some of the jurors supported Pound for reasons unrelated to the merits of the poem; the motives of others were unclear. It has been said that Eliot, e.e. cummings,. Auden, and Allen Tate intended to embarrass the Department of Justice.[169] The majority jurors and their critics limited the debate to variations on the following exchange: 'Pound is a Fascist and a traitor' – 'He may be, but this has nothing to do with his poetry.' Both sides were at ease in their parallel gestures of apodictic dismissal. Pound's conduct during the war was a matter of record; the distinction between the merit of an artefact and the morality of its maker is easily grasped. These were comfortable positions to take up, offering opportunities for indignation without intellectual risk. Both sides could fight their campaigns within impregnable redoubts. There could be no doubt about the viciousness of Pound's broadcasts; likewise there could be no doubt about the quality of Pound's poetry. One side refused to acknowledge the relevance of the war record; the other side, the relevance of the poetry. How could one award a national prize to a traitor? How could one deny it to him merely because he was a traitor? Latent in the former position was a sub-Romantic sense that Pound had betrayed the poet's calling by his conduct; similarly latent in the latter position was a post-Romantic conviction that it is not just the poet's opinions that are irrelevant to an assessment of his poetry, but the opinions of the poem too. Indeed, while the one side appeared to insist that poets had to have opinions of a particular kind, the other side seemed to doubt whether poems could have opinions at all.[170]

The defenders of the award emphasised the self-referential aspect of poetry, commonly understood to be its defining characteristic as against prose. Poetry is about itself, while prose is about the world; poetry's ostensible statements are warped by context, prose's statements are not; and so on. As for those critics of the award who were not content merely to damn the poem because of its (contingent, to the majority jurors) association with the poet, their polemics raised questions of a different kind. If one grants that poetry does have a relation with the world, and that it may therefore bear upon religion or politics, how does this concession shape the proper evaluation of that poetry? If poetry is not self-subsisting, is the value of a poem affected by the opinions it expresses? And, a different but related question, is assent to those opinions a necessary precondition for the reading of that poem? The defenders of the award conceived of poetry as autotelic, while its antagonists regarded it as intimate with the world, with which they believed it to have a direct relation; a world to which, indeed, they insisted it refers, and about which it makes statements.

Eliot anticipated these arguments with arguments of his own that the majority jurors would have endorsed:

when we are considering poetry we must consider it primarily as poetry and not another thing ... [it] is not the inculcation of morals, or the direction of politics, and no more is it religion or an equivalent of religion, except by some monstrous abuse of words ... a poem, in some sense, has its own life ...[171]

This is from the 1928 preface to the new edition of *The Sacred Wood*. The essays contended for 'the integrity of poetry', defending it against those for whom it must be judged as 'another thing'. However, Eliot had, he said:

passed on to another problem not touched upon in this book: that of the relation of poetry to the spiritual and social life of its times and other times ... poetry ... certainly has something to do with morals, and with religion, and even with politics perhaps, though we cannot say what.

Eliot was wrong to imply that one can pass from the one to the other as if they were two different stages of a single journey. If poetry truly is to be regarded as autotelic, then the question of its relation to its times is a trivial one. It is a matter of biographical anecdotes, cultural 'backgrounds', and other such contingencies. If, conversely, one acknowledges poetry's relation with politics, whatever one's uncertainties about the nature of that relation, then its relation to its times will be of determining importance. Analysis unavoidably favours the intrinsic or the extrinsic; a poem cannot be divided into two equal halves.

What we may regard as Eliot's second 'problem', the one identified in the preface, yielded both *For Lancelot Andrewes* (1928) and *After Strange Gods*. Indeed, the latter is to that second problem what the essays themselves in *The Sacred Wood* are to the first. This second problem did not receive the same disciplined attention as the first. Eliot's speculations tended toward either the vapid or the eccentric. Lumping together politics, morals, and religion, he failed to make necessary distinctions. These three do not comprise an indivisible whole, nor is each of them without its measure of fractured and contradictory complexity. Nevertheless, any concession to the view that poetry has even 'something perhaps' to do with politics should have made it difficult (perhaps impossible) to vote for Pound. By doing so, Eliot had reverted to the position described in the preface. His vote for Pound marked a regression to the first of his two problems. It represented an evasion of the project outlined by the 1928 preface. It also represented an evasion of the challenge posed by the anti-Semitism of the *Pisan Cantos*.

The Brinnin letter

John Brinnin was the director of the New York Poetry Center. Eliot gave public readings there three times in the early 1950s at Brinnin's invitation. The first two occasions passed without incident. When the third was planned, there were protests.[172] The Center was part of the

Young Men's and Women's Hebrew Association. Some thought it wrong that Eliot should be given hospitality. Brinnin, who didn't agree, but would not (or could not) ignore these sentiments of opposition, contrived a means by which Eliot could express hostility to anti-Semitism. He was asked to endorse a petition condemning Soviet persecution of dissident Jewish intellectuals. He complied, by letter, and got his third invitation.

The letter begins by thanking Brinnin for the opportunity of going 'on record' about anti-Semitism. A simple endorsement of the need to take a public stand against Soviet persecution is not enough. One has to go deeper, and analyse the nature of Soviet anti-Semitism, more sophisticated than the Nazi variant. The Soviets escape international opprobrium by inventing judicial pretexts for their persecution rather than by relying on a doctrine of racial superiority. The anti-Semitic drive of the Soviets is typical of all such efforts, whatever the identity of the government responsible. Hysteria dominates: even the incitement of the masses is not wholly 'deliberate' in the sense of being dictated by policy alone. Anti-Semitic sentiment is exploited, not invented; and it is shared by rulers and masses. It is a genuine but pernicious response to a profound national dilemma. Eliot regards this state persecution, symptomatic of a crisis both economic and religious, as 'true anti-Semitism'. It is to be distinguished from the Moslem antagonism to Jews, which is derived from the adversarial nature of the relations between the two peoples. (He at last resolves the difficulty with 'race' and 'religion'; 'people' is the new term.) Eliot ends with a warning. Governments who deny the rights of their own citizens, making pariahs of them, will 'have to pay the full price for so doing', though what that price is Eliot does not say. Witnesses to persecution will not be exempt from punishment. The ostensibly 'uninvolved' must share in the expiation. This, he adds in a final, defensive piece of autobiography, is a conviction he has long held.

There is a great deal that is admirable about this letter. It is both dignified and touching. There is an evident desire to please,[173] allied to an old habit of careful, qualified exposition. Refusing to sign the petition would have reopened the whole miserable question of his anti-Semitism in the least justifiable of circumstances; merely signing and then returning it would have been supine. The letter meets both objections, demonstrating Eliot's wish to address the question of anti-Semitism in a rather wider perspective than the simple sponsorship of a petition would demand. Linked to this is the desire to establish the depth of his own antagonism to the prejudice, and the period during which he has felt it.

But his analysis of anti-Semitism is deeply tendentious. He so defines it as to exclude religious hostility as a true form of the prejudice. Christian anti-Semitism is not mentioned; Moslem anti-Semitism (about which Eliot was wrong[174]) draws the fire. That anti-Semitism existed before the nation–state was invented escapes Eliot's attention. And it is not an answer to say that Eliot was limited by the nature of the request to him, because he deliberately went beyond its remit, extending his appraisal to anti-Semitism in general. He did not confine himself to the specific instance of contemporary Soviet persecution (though even if he had purported to do so, the pre-1917 origins of Russian anti-Semitism would have led honest discussion of the issue into broader considerations). The letter emerges from a theoretical void. It has been composed by a man who so radically dissociates the present from the past that to talk about making amends is to assume a continuity of doubtful existence. The letter practises its own special kind of exclusion. This time it is an inverted exclusion. Instead of excluding Jews from the class of possible readers, or members of a community, it excludes Eliot from the class of anti-Semites. It doesn't help situate his own relations with Jews. By its definition of anti-Semitism, it omits Eliot from the ranks of anti-Semites. Behind the sweep of Eliot's condemnation, there is a silent movement of self-exculpation. He quietly defends himself, while noisily attacking others.

By defining anti-Semitism as a purely national phenomenon, or as a sin, he tried to protect himself from censure. He did not meet the challenge, he ducked it. The Brinnin letter does not make amends. Eliot declares himself innocent of the charge. An exercise in partisan definition takes the place of an apology.

The '*TLS*' correspondence

On 2 August 1957 the *Times Literary Supplement* published an anonymous review entitled 'Classic Inhumanism'. It examined the 'men of 1914' (Pound, Wyndham Lewis, Joyce, and Eliot), T. E. Hulme's influence on them, and the classical revival that Hulme predicted by virtue of their work. The reviewer praised a biography of Wyndham Lewis for showing the connection between this revival and certain right-wing tendencies in France (a connection which explained the political development of Pound), Wyndham Lewis's praise of Hitler, and Eliot's 'unambiguous signs of anti-Semitism'.

Eliot responded the following week. Querying the reviewer's account of his relation to Hulme, and his allegedly self-confessed 'romanticism', Eliot added: 'I should also like to know on what grounds I have been charged with Fascism and anti-semitism, and whether your reviewer himself believes such charges.' On 16 August the reviewer replied:

In the pages of *Criterion* for the decade 1928–38 are to be found the evidences that are sometimes used to support the charge of Fascism against Mr Eliot. The case is brought up again in the *Modern Monthly* for 1933 and in Albert Mordell's 'T. S. Eliot's Deficiencies as a Social Critic', 1951. As for my own view, I agree with Mr S. E. Hyman that Mr Eliot's premises lead him 'not quite to fascism, but to a kind of tentative and embarrassing flirtation with it'.

Responding again, Eliot was quick to spot the silence on the question of anti-Semitism: 'I invited your reviewer to state the grounds for the accusation of Fascism and anti-semitism. To the second charge he does not return.' As to the first charge, Eliot countered by: citing *The Rock* and *Murder in the Cathedral*; dismissing as 'too vague to be taken seriously' the reviewer's reference to the *Criterion*; insisting that his essay 'The Literature of Fascism' gave 'no ground for the charge'. As if to crush the reviewer altogether, Eliot then put the Hyman quotation in context:

Mr Geoffrey Wagner, author of the book on Wyndham Lewis which your reviewer was reviewing, also cites Mr Hyman. But what Mr Wagner says is this (p. 89, footnote): 'Stanley Edgar Hyman, *The Armed Vision* (New York, Knopf, 1948) p. 87 explores the (obviously absurd) idea of Eliot being in any way a Fascist.'

It seemed that Eliot had won the argument. He certainly had the last word with the reviewer, who however could have pointed out both that Hyman provides documentary justification for his 'accus[ation]'[175] and that Wagner concludes only that 'it would be uncharitable' to associate Eliot 'directly with Fascism'.[176] The reviewer might also have pointed out that Eliot's 1928 essay on Fascism dealt only with the Italian variant, that in any event it is not to be regarded without qualification as a guide to Eliot's views in the 1930s, and that in the following year Eliot 'confessed' to a 'preference for fascism in practice' over communism.[177] Without strain, he could also have cited the evidence of Eliot's 'unambiguous signs of anti-Semitism'. In the event, it was Christopher Logue who obliged, in a letter of 6 September.

Having cited the usual passages, and one more obscure passage on the British Union of Fascists ('the aims set forth in [their] statement of policy are wholly admirable'), he continued:

> It may be said that one must dig deep to resurrect these, surely, 'youthful passions'. The above quotations are only a sample, however, and the judgment does not stand or fall by them alone. Only in the full spread of Mr Eliot's writings can be seen the social and political notions he represents, and even then the reader must translate them from an ideal to a practical form before their ramifications are clear.

This was both generous and slightly opaque. No digging, deep or otherwise, is needed to find the anti-Semitic poems, which could then, and still can, be found both in the collected and selected editions of Eliot's poetry. Logue did not make clear whether his insistence on context and 'translation' was likely to be exculpatory of Eliot or lead to a harsher condemnation. In a curious inversion of the argument debated in chapter 1, he maintained that Eliot's words of 'polite menace' mattered far *more* when first published than in 1957, both because of the major threat that Fascism then posed and because of Eliot's standing at that time as 'a moral and intellectual leader'. Logue concluded with 'things ill done ...'.

Eliot would have none of it. In the next week's issue he rounded on Logue in a tone of persecuted condescension:

> Sir – Your correspondent Mr Christopher Logue has supported the accusations of your reviewer with all but two of the pieces of 'evidence' which those who share his frame of mind are wont to produce against me.

Adducing those 'pieces' (one of which was the passage from *Notes*), Eliot offered Logue a mock compliment for finding a quotation 'which I have not seen used before' in support of the charge of Fascism. Restoring the quotation to its context, he mitigated the bad impression that, standing alone, it undoubtedly makes. That was as far as he could go on the subject. He had nothing at all to say about the anti-Semitic quotations. There are several things wrong with this letter. Putting quotation marks around 'evidence' does not refute that evidence. Referring to those other accusers who 'share [Logue's] frame of mind' is to murmur conspiracy in a most unhappy context. Indicating that the charge of anti-Semitism is not new to him, and thereby implying that this repetition somehow devalues the charge, is perverse. Adducing the footnote to *Notes*, which he was shortly thereafter to revise, is positively to invite the censure of later readers. If it was as harmless as the rest, why change it? And if Logue's letter prompted the thought that it was anti-Semitic, why not admit it? Most importantly of all, the letter discloses an unattractive method of dealing with the charge. The tactic is first to embarrass the accuser into withdrawal by calling for evidence, but if produced, to sidestep the issue.[178] This makes a nonsense, however, of the original request. Eliot is so quick to patronise Logue – helping to make his case for him – he overlooks the fact that Logue's first letter asked an ostensibly genuine question about the relevant material. The letter stressed his forgetfulness: 'I sometimes meet with quotations from my own writings which I fail to identify.' Eliot's tactic was both devious and inept. If he was so familiar with the 'evidence' cited to support the charge, why ask for it in the first place?[179]

INSENSITIVITIES

For Eliot to have been sensitive to the anti-Semitism of his own work, he would have had also to be sensitive to the anti-Semitism of the work of others. He seems not to have been.

Let me begin by comparing Eliot's reading of 'Gerontion' at a poetry recital in September 1943 with Faber's rejection in July 1944 of *Animal Farm* for publication. Invited with other poets to read from his own poetry at the Wigmore Hall, Eliot chose 'The Journey of the Magi' and 'Gerontion'.[180] Many Jews were beyond insult by then. When Eliot rose to recite his poems, the British press knew and had reported upon the fate of Jews under Nazi rule 'down to the last detail'. The existence of the gas chambers had become 'a common item of news'.[181] Just three months before Eliot read his lines about 'the jew' squatting on a window sill, spawned in an Antwerp estaminet, the press had reported the final destruction of the Warsaw Ghetto, one of the last, precarious ledges for Jews in Occupied Europe. On 18 June that year, David Low's cartoon 'How the Beastly Business Begins' appeared in the *Evening Standard*. It shows Jews in terminal distress. On the left, three Jews are hanging from gallows; on the right they are filing into a building with 'GAS' marked over the entrance; in the foreground, mostly women and small children lie dead or despairing on the ground. The cartoon has a bubble insert of two women gossiping, one marked 'Ignorance', the other marked 'Bigotry': 'It must be the fault of the Jews.'[182] At the recital itself, Louis MacNeice read 'Bar-Room Matins',[183] which scorns the public's glib appetite for news in the traditional language of a church service, and concludes: 'Die the soldiers, die the Jews, / ... / Give us this day our daily news.'

After consideration of Orwell's manuscript, Eliot told him: 'We [i.e., Geoffrey Faber, the Chairman, and Eliot] have no conviction ... that this is the right point of view from which to criticise the political situation at the present time.'[184] In the months preceding George Orwell's submission of his novel, Leningrad had been relieved, the Russians had entered Rumania, and they had recovered the Crimea. In the month in which Eliot wrote to Orwell, the Russians recovered Belorussia and took Lublin, establishing the Polish Committee of National Liberation in the teeth of opposition from the Polish government in London.[185] Here is a man capable of rejecting *Animal Farm* on grounds of expediency and timing and yet equally capable of reciting 'Gerontion' at a time when to be a Jew was likely to be catastrophic, and when countless Jews were being done to death in Treblinka, Auschwitz, and Belsen, many of whom were from Antwerp, Brussels, and Vienna, if not London. Eliot was guilty of precisely that wartime British anti-Semitism which Orwell analysed as 'not at present lead[ing] to open persecution, but [which] has the effect of making people callous to the sufferings of Jews in other countries'.[186]

Insensitive to the anti-Semitism of his own work, Eliot was similarly insensitive to the anti-Semitism of others. Charles Maurras is my example. Born in 1886, in time to intervene in the Dreyfus affair, Maurras died in 1952, late enough to witness the consequences of the political positions he had adopted, and for him to find himself, like Dreyfus, imprisoned for life for betraying his country to the Germans. Facing the Lyons court in 1945, after the verdict was delivered, he exclaimed: 'C'est la revanche de Dreyfus.'[187] His appeal to the thuggish Right can be attributed to the simplicity of his hatreds, and the romance of his enthusiasms; his appeal to intellectuals is due both to his allegiances and to the sceptical manner in which he defended them. The violence of his slanders and the celebrated classicism of his style, the tacit support for street brawling and the sophistication of his reasoning, his ability to lead a political organisation and yet also find space in cultural journals, gave him enormous prestige among those predisposed to be impressed by what he stood for, and even among those who were not. He united his admirers in the facility with which he reconciled the claims of reason with those of reaction. This was done regularly, and with great fluency in the columns of the Action Française's daily newspaper. A supporter of the Catholic Church and a Royalist, he was, however, condemned by both Pope and pretender. He was willing to discuss the possibility of a coup, but drew back from it when it seemed possible. He perfected his stance of reaction by opposing not only the republic itself, but also the political alternatives to it.[188] Though the Action Française was the principal influence on the ideology of Vichy, Maurras himself equivocated about collaboration with, while opposing resistance to, the Germans.[189] His politics were self-cancelling: a hater of both Germany and democracy, the one drove him away from Fascism, the other into its embrace. He always enjoyed, however, the consolations of anti-Semitism. Hatred of the Jews led him out from every impasse.

Maurras was one of a limited number of influences that had completed their work on Eliot before his arrival in England. To Eliot, Maurras was an example of how an intellectual might stand against the given tendencies of the time. He was a literary stylist of some distinction, and master of a number of idioms, from the polemical to the discursive. He argued a strong case for the indivisible unity of France endangered by 'individualism and multiplicity of beliefs',[190] a theme echoed by Eliot in his own reflections on tradition and orthodoxy, which also have the effect of tending to exclude Jews, and Jewish history and culture. And as against another mentor of Eliot, Irving Babbitt, he was an anti-Semite.[191] At one time Eliot planned to write a book on him. In 1928 he was still addressing him as 'Cher Monsieur et Maître'.[192] He translated Maurras for the *Criterion*, thereby introducing him to many of its readers.[193] His book on Dante took as its epigraph a quotation from Maurras. There is an allusion to one of his works in 'Triumphal March'. Eliot defended Maurras against criticism that he was an anti-Christian thinker.[194] His endorsement rarely was unqualified, however. He deprecated Maurras's 'extravagances'; he was 'quite clear that the Action Française... was much too intemperate and vituperative for his taste';[195] he was sharp about Maurras's hatred of Germany, his dislike of England, and his failure to grasp the importance of

economics. Eliot described Maurras as 'a free-thinker and product of
the post-Revolution bourgeoisie'.[196] In his last published account of
Maurras he described him as:

a man who I held in respect and admiration, although some of his views
were exasperating and some deplorable – but a great writer, a genuine lover
of his country, and a man who deserved a better fate than that which he had
in the end to meet... if Charles Maurras had confined himself to literature,
and to the literature of political theory, and had never attempted to found
a political party, a *movement* – engaging in, and increasing the acrimony of
the political struggle – if he had not given his support to the restoration of
the Monarchy in such a way as to strengthen instead of reducing animosities
– then those of his ideas which were sound and strong might have spread
more widely, and penetrated more deeply, and affected more sensibly the
contemporary mind.[197]

Eliot ignored the ideological nature of Third Republic politics and
pleaded a special case. Maurras's political theorising was inseparable
from the incitements of his column. He was politically engaged long
before founding Action Française. His most significant political act
was a journalistic intervention in the Dreyfus Affair; when the cause
of the anti-Dreyfusards seemed bleakest, he came to the defence of
Colonel Henry, who had killed himself when arrested for forgery. For
years, he was obsessed with the thought of Léon Blum's murder:
'now, there is a man to be shot in the back'.[198] It has been proposed
that Maurras laid the foundations of political anti-Semitism at the
turn of the century.[199] To have praised him as 'a genuine lover of his
country' without acknowledging that that 'country' was an ideological construct that excluded a number of substantial minorities
who were citizens of it, was praise too easily given. Eliot's censure,
almost lost in qualifications, was superficial. There were stronger
objections to make to Maurras's political activism than to claim that
it thereby inhibited the dissemination of his 'sound and strong' ideas.
When reaching for an example of Maurrassian unwisdom, Eliot went
to the form that Maurras's Royalism took, and not to anti-Semitism,
about which he was silent.

Sympathising with the Pope's decision of 1940 to interdict the
Action Française newspaper, Eliot guessed that its heresy was the
belief that only the monarchical form of government was compatible
with Catholicism. 'Perhaps', he added, the Pope was 'also condemning a dangerous intolerance which classified Jews, Protestants
and Freemasons in one comprehensive condemnation'.[200] But why

'dangerous'? And to whom? Apparently for the odd reason that this intolerance makes an error of classification. It rejects all three – Jews, Protestants, and Freemasons – without discrimination. Would an intolerance that condemned Protestants, but not Jews or Freemasons, be less dangerous? The phrase has a special resonance. 'Dangerous intolerance' may be the balancing evil to the 'excessive tolerance' deprecated in *After Strange Gods*. Eliot praised Maurras in the same article for his 'incessant journalistic battle against political corruption'. Though he conceded it was waged 'somewhat indiscriminately and with excessive violence', there is no mention that his targets were invariably Jewish, nor that Maurras's inaugural battle was against the victim, not the perpetrator, of corrupt practices. Responding to an obituary notice on Maurras, Eliot challenged its account of Maurras's career and opinions, but passed in silence over its charge that Maurras was an anti-Semite. Maurras had been described as 'the fierce, unrelenting editor of *L'Action Française*, with his Fascism, his anti-Semitism and his gang of would-be young toughs ... a Catholic Royalist, excommunicated by the Pope and denounced by the Pretender. His peculiar, though certainly sincere brand of patriotism led him into collaboration with the occupiers of his country.'[201] This notice was, Eliot wrote, 'in some respects, capable of modification'.[202] Describing Maurras as a 'Catholic Royalist' was questionable; it was 'misleading to term [him] a Fascist'; the Camelots du Roy were not so tough; but on Maurras's anti-Semitism, no 'modification' was proposed.

CONCLUSION

In or about 1950, the Jewish poet and man of letters Emanuel Litvinoff read to a London audience his poem 'To T. S. Eliot'. Eliot was present. When Litvinoff had finished:

Most of the audience began to clap ... but Stephen Spender rose angrily and shouted that Litvinoff had grossly insulted Tom Eliot who was the most gentle of men. He continued with great emotion and spoke with great rapidity. Perhaps I did not hear Spender properly but he seemed to say something like: 'As a poet I'm at least as much a Jew as Litvinoff, and Tom isn't anti-Semitic in the least.' In the confusion of anger, Spender was not entirely coherent but there was no mistaking his gutsy aggression towards Emanuel Litvinoff's attitude as it was forcibly expressed in the poem addressed to Eliot. For his part, Eliot, in the chair behind me, his head down, muttered generously, 'It's a good poem, it's a very good poem.'[203]

Eliot was right. The poem is accurate about his reputation and impressive in its outraged adoption of the language of his poetry. It is a work divided by love and dismay, in which Litvinoff wrestles to find in the language of his despiser the means by which he may both honour and challenge him. Eliot made poetry out of anti-Semitism; Litvinoff made a poem out of Eliot's poetry of anti-Semitism, countering Eliot's texts with his own. 'To T. S. Eliot' is a work of resistance as well as respect. I wish my book to be regarded as another such work.

Notes

1. INTRODUCTION

1 Wilson 1977, 549. Cf.: 'I never heard such [anti-Semitic] sentiments from his own lips' (Read 1971, 35); 'in the thirty-five years of my acquaintance with him I never heard him utter an antisemitic remark' (Spender 1975, 60); 'I never once heard him make an uncharitable remark about Jews' (Chiari 1972, 35). Loewenstein (1993, 24, 31) quotes Eliot remarking that Hitler 'made an intelligent antisemitism impossible for a generation'; this is a misattribution. Her source (Watson 1977, 122–3) attributes the remark to a friend of Eliot's and *not* to Eliot himself.

2 Gombrich 1984, 177; Matthews 1974, 114.

3 It would seem that Matthews's account is, at best, a melodramatic and telescoped version of the truth. Millin wrote to Eliot about his anti-Semitism; Eliot responded, perplexed and hurt. Their correspondence is part of the Sarah Gertrude Millin Collection at the William Cullen Library, University of Witwatersrand, Johannesburg. I am grateful to Lavinia Braun for this information. For an account of Millin's own noxious racism, see Coetzee 1988, ch. 6.

4 Wilson 1977, 548.

5 Levenson 1986, 163.

6 'Poetry and Drama': Eliot 1971b, 79.

7 Shapiro 1960, 37.

8 Donoghue 1989, 234.

9 Pound 1978b, 177.

10 Nicolson 1958, 35.

11 Kenner 1985b, 22.

12 Ackroyd 1985, 299, 323.

13 Schwartz 1970, 312–31. Cf.: '[p]eople went out and read or refused to read what Eliot wrote about. They also took their Eliot neat, undiluted with other reading ... No modern critic has had anything like the effect of Eliot on the literary people' (Blackmur 1955, 167–8); '[Eliot was] the bishop of modern poetry, the lawgiver who had dominated classrooms for a generation' (Kazin 1979, 212).

14 Lewis 1987, 55.

15 Extracted from Grant 1982, 69.

16 Aldington 1967, 167.

17 Winters 1987, 490.

18 Breslin 1985, 37–8.

19 Eliot 1964, 153.

20 Robbins 1951, 19. Cf.: '[on "A Cooking Egg":] he [Eliot] did not later continue in a view so unjust. He knew well that all sorts of people made money out of the war' (Bradbrook 1988).

21 Ricks 1988, 39.

22 Spender 1975, 60.

23 Wilk 1986, 11; Maccoby 1983/4; Trotter 1984, 46–7. By contrast, it has been proposed that Eliot's 'remarks' about Jews are confined, in the poetry, to 'Gerontion', 'Burbank', and 'Dirge' (Moody 1980, 370). Coote (1993, 639) proposes that another *Ara Vos Prec* poem, 'Whispers of Immortality', is anti-Semitic. He regards, I suppose, 'Grishkin' as Jewish. I think he is mistaken.

24 Maccoby 1983/4, 7.

25 Trotter 1984, 44–7.

26 Robertson Smith 1972, 23.

27 Bedient 1986, 43.

28 Wolin 1993, 272–300.

29 Baldick 1987.

30 Leavis 1967, 72. 'Reading in [Leavis's] book about Eliot and Pound, I did not think to ask ... if great writers could be anti-Semites and snobs' (Miller 1993, 139).

31 Spender 1938 [1935], 167.

32 MacNeice 1938, 166.

33 Davie 1977, 117. 'The only lesson [Eliot] might teach us – of inhuman accuracy and self-control in publishing only those poems we need never be sorry for – this we shall never learn because the lesson is too hard' (ibid., 120).

34 Mencken 1989.

35 Read 1971, 35. Cf.: 'In a couple of places in the poems..."anti-Semitic" is an accurate description' (Lentricchia 1994, 281).

36 'I have found only one other prejudicial reference to Jews by de Man' (quoted in Prendergast 1990, 322). A later version drops the 'only': 'I have found one other prejudicial reference to Jews' (Hartman 1989, 24).

37 Kojecky 1971, 12 and 197.

38 'I had hoped that the concessions to the [Nazi] occupier or the ideological contagion (which I had already expected: one did not accept to publish in that context without paying the price, that is, without accepting *what we know today* to be unacceptable) would take minimal and in some sort negative forms: more those of omission or of abstention' (Derrida 1989, 170; my italics). This exculpation continues for another ninety pages.

39 Chace 1973, 111. Sartre correctly challenges the notion that 'anti-Semitic opinion ... [is] a molecule that can enter into combination with other molecules of any origin whatsoever without undergoing any alteration'. It is not possible, he maintains, to be 'a good father and a good husband, a conscientious citizen, highly cultivated, philanthropic, *and* in addition an anti-Semite' (Sartre 1965, 8). Anti-Semitism, however 'moderate', taints the whole person.

40 Brooke-Rose 1971, 252.

41 De Man 1989, 164.

42 Raine 1990.

43 Crawford 1987, 207.

44 Randall 1934, 168–9.

45 For example: 'Many centuries later, when Christians received the birthright which Jewry had thrown away by resorting to usury and hence denying the Fatherhood of God'; 'It is distinguished from certain other "exiled" German reviews by a freedom from communist or Jewish propaganda'; 'however much there may be of degenerate Judaism in the corresponding "bourgeois" pseudo-Calvinistic attribution of a peculiar sanctity to Business ...' (Wilson 1935, 343; Randall 1938, 398; Prior 1939, 313). Eliot's anti-Semitism is not thus to be assessed. There are also passages in the *Criterion* sympathetic to Jews: '[a review of a book by a Jewish theologian:] very valuable as a corrective to those who find in the Jews a perfect subject for crude generalisation'; 'Hundreds of intellectuals have been deprived of the possibility of expressing their views. No writer who is not a member of *Reichsschrifttumskammer* can hope for publication. Only Arians [*sic*], i.e., those who are not Jews, can belong' (MacNeice 1934, 163; Rychner 1936, 489).

46 Lyotard 1990, 3.

47 Greenblatt 1992, 56.

48 Sartre 1965, 17.

49 Misrahi 1972, 8.

50 ibid., 17. Sartre's phenomenology of anti-Semitism fails, however, to account for the anti-Semite 'who, far from being mediocre, has a touch of genius' (Hook 1949, 470). Relatedly, it fails to account for a poetry of anti-Semitism; this is because Sartre adheres to a Symbolist account of poetry (as defined in *What is Literature?*) that makes him blind to the possibility of its existence (Sartre 1983, 4–5, 10).

51 Ackroyd 1985, 56.

52 Poliakov 1974–5, III, 34–5.

53 The first accusation against Jews of ritual murder was made in Norwich in 1144: Poliakov 1974–5, I, 58.

54 Langmuir 1990, 40. For a note on the historiography of English anti-Semitism, see Kushner 1990, 191–2.

55 Ashton 1933, 38, 56, 34, 120.

56 Belloc 1922, viii; on the limits of tolerance, see, for example, Kushner 1990, 200–1.

57 For an examination of the factors inhibiting anti-Semitism, see: Sarna 1986, 125; Borden 1984, chs. 3 and 5; Poliakov 1974–5, III, 43; Gartner 1988, 319; Dobkowski 1979, 115; Jaher 1994, 86–7.

58 Naomi Cohen 1984, 221–31, 267–71.

59 Ginsberg 1993, 79.

60 Lears 1983, 275, 133.

61 Quoted in McCormick 1988, 27.

62 Quoted in Higham 1975, 130. Identifying America as 'Jewish' was an anti-Semitic commonplace: 'Americanism is nothing else … than the Jewish spirit distilled' (Sombart 1962, 62); 'The crude cult of money is a North American, and at the same time, Jewish trait' (quoted in Pulzer 1964, 240).

63 Quoted: Gartner 1988, 315.

64 Adams 1986, 250.

65 Dobkowski 1979, 117. 'Since the taint of finance afflicted even an Adams (living on inherited income), he complained wittily that he himself was getting more Jewish every day … a displaced person in industrialised America, Adams felt himself a curiosity as much as any Jew'; 'When he felt out of place in New England, Lowell likened himself to the Hebrew Joseph who had also lived among a younger generation who knew him not. Moreover, when he felt less noble, in a mood self-ridicule, he would describe himself as the Jew who hated pork or pulled a sharp trade. Oddly, Lowell, who had grown up in homogeneous New England, established a personal identity which involved both an attraction toward and a revulsion from Jews' (Solomon 1989, 38, 41, 18).

66 Adams 1961, 3.

67 Thus, populist anti-Semitism 'tended to be linked with Anglophobia, in the belief that the London money market exploited the United States' (Lipset and Raab 1971, 94).

68 Byrnes 1950, 261, 274. 'As French antisemites were well aware, they were participating in a phenomenon which had European dimensions, but French antisemitism has also its own particular internal history. Its mutation into an organized movement and ideology can be dated fairly precisely from the early 1880s' (Wilson 1982, 170).

69 Eliot 1987, 16.

70 Marrus 1989, 9.

71 Poliakov 1985, IV, 38–42.

72 ibid., 40.

73 Byrnes 1950, 111.

74 Marrus and Paxton 1981, 33; on the anti-Semitism of French intellectuals, see Mehlman 1983. Robert Wistrich asks 'which other European nation (with the exception of Germany) can vaunt so illustrious a literary legacy of antisemitism as that which extends from Voltaire and the Encyclopaedists through Drumont, Barrès, Maurras to Bernanos, Drieu de la Rochelle and Giraudoux?' (Preface: Weinberg 1987, ix).

75 Burns 1992, 92.
76 Birnbaum 1992, 262.
77 Lindemann 1991, 85.
78 Eliot 1926, 5.
79 Benda 1929, 113–14.
80 For example: '[Eliot] proved to be very cordial...he even suggested publishing...one of my most overtly Jewish poems...he expressed to me on several occasions after 1933 his horror of the antisemitic outrages... in Nazi Germany' (Roditi 1991, 72). The moral distinction postulated between the anti-Semitic invective of poetry and its author's personal civility lacks substance. It has been advanced in the most implausible contexts: '[Pound's] behaviour had always been exemplary and never had he wronged any Jews' (de Rachewiltz 1971, 297–8).
81 The 'curious shift from a faith in the Jews to a fear of them', that is, from a conviction of their power to an anxiety about it, is analysed in its American context in Wilson 1957, 77. Cf.: 'Nothing, in fact, is – to believe the anti-Semite – too colossal for the Jew to have achieved' (Zangwill 1937, 102).
82 Trachtenberg 1983, 193.
83 Quoted in Dobkowski 1979, 51.
84 ibid., 91.
85 ibid., 183.
86 ibid., 48.
87 Quoted in Griffiths 1980, 64.
88 Quoted in Valentin 1971, 118. Cf.: 'The Chief Constable spread his hands in an odd Jewish gesture as if frankness was all he had ever wanted' (Power 1992, 217).
89 Modder 1960, 120–1.
90 Sigg 1989, 197.
91 Riding and Graves 1969, 239.
92 Glanz 1970, 309–10.
93 Quoted in Katz 1988, 285.
94 Dostoievsky 1985, 641;
95 Kipling 1987, 200.
96 '[Jews] resorted to clipping the coin': Pound 1978a, 219; cf. Glassman 1975, 106, 114.
97 Casillo 1988, 260.
98 Mond had bought the *English Review* in 1910, sacking Ford Madox Ford to Pound's great rage. Pound attacked Mond as a 'manufacturing, political hebrew' (quoted in Carpenter 1988, 297–8).
99 Murray 1948, 234.
100 Cumberland 1795, 11
101 Kipling 1987, 194.
102 Quoted in Dobkowski 1979, 194.
103 Eliot 1982, 105.
104 Quoted in Modder 1960, 45.

105 Gilman 1986, 244; 'In the history of nineteenth-century German philosophy there is a distinct relationship between anti-semitism and anti-feminism' (Figes 1978, 121).

106 Pulzer 1964, 221.

107 Mosse 1985, 109.

108 Poliakov 1974–5, III, 379.

109 Lewis 1939, 58–68.

110 Lewis 1931, 41.

111 Lyndall Gordon's use of 'context' in her biography of Eliot is opportunistic and exculpatory: 'Eliot's view of women had much more to do with traditional and literary prejudices than with the reality of his marriage, however unsuitable' (Gordon 1978, 76–7). In a later essay, however, she argues 'the emotions in Eliot's letters to Pound, with their undisguised anti-Semitism and misogyny, would help us to understand that the quatrains were rooted in the peculiar circumstances of Eliot's life: the misogyny connected with his hellish marriage, the anti-Semitism with anxieties over money' (Gordon 1985, 175).

112 Wistrich 1990, 517; Gay 1978, 196; Janik and Toulmin 1973, 71–3; Gilman 1986, 245.

113 Freud 1977, 198.

114 Eliot 1917a, 17.

115 Eliot 1971a, 39. I take her to be a Jewish society hostess. Lyndall Gordon, whose grasp of Eliot's anti-Semitism is weak, misses this connection: 'Pound undoubtedly improved particular passages: his excisions of the anti-Semitic portrait of Bleistein and the misogynistic portrait of Fresca curtailed Eliot's excessive animus' (Gordon 1978, 105).

116 Quoted in Wilson 1982, 486.

117 Gilman 1993, 155.

118 Schwartz 1993, 281–2.

119 A literary cliché: De Beauvoir 1975, 196–200.

120 Kristeva 1982, 53.

121 In 1892 an American anti-Semite fulminated against the 'red-eyed Jewish millionaires' in control of the party of Thomas Jefferson (quoted in Ginsberg 1993, 77–8).

122 Wharton 1985, 14, 256.

123 Sartre 1969, 288. This formulation relies on Bergson's epigram 'percevoir signifie immobiliser'. Eliot, addressing the same point in an early Harvard essay, 'drew the logical conclusion from this belief in change as the criterion of life that to pin things down is to render them lifeless' (Douglass 1986, 59, 66).

124 Ackroyd 1985, 143. Eliot wrote: 'On the Ilford murder your attitude has been in striking contrast with the flaccid sentimentality of other papers I have seen.' In the same letter (8 January 1923), he praised the newspaper's 'remarkable series of articles ... on Fascismo' (quoted in

Weis 1990, 292). Thompson was hanged, along with her lover, for the murder of her husband.

125 Eliot 1917a, 9.

126 ibid., 117.

127 ibid., 111.

128 Kenner, indifferent to Eliot's misogyny, trivialises the drowning theme: '[the drowned woman] is part of the public mythology of an era when one of the police-court shamans of the British people was the man who drowned a succession of wives, by a method which left no marks of a struggle, in order to realize their insurance money' (Kenner 1985a, 197). In fact Eliot's drownings must be put in the context of a whole series of literary murders and failed murders (Gilbert and Gubar 1987, chs. 1–2 *passim*; on the persistence of this theme from the medieval test for witches of immersion by water to the undrownable Alex in the film *Fatal Attraction*, see Smith 1989, 27).

129 Gilbert and Gubar 1987, 4.

130 Eliot 1988a, 47.

131 *Sweeney Agonistes*. Neville Coghill was shocked when he saw the play: 'It seemed to justify the ways of Crippen to woman ... there appeared to be no alternative for Sweeney than to murder Doris'. Eliot later told Coghill that, without questioning the legitimacy of the interpretation, it was not what he had intended (Coghill 1948, 85–6).

132 Eliot 1934a, 16 (my italics).

133 'Negroes' had the upper case in certain American editions (Robbins 1951, 209, n. 47). However, the Centenary Edition of *Collected Poems* 1909–1962, published in the United States by Harcourt Brace Jovanovich, has the word in the lower case. By radical contrast to what I argue here, Eric Sigg proposes that Eliot 'pa[id] attention to black people and to what they and their culture had to offer' (Sigg 1994, 27).

134 See Brooks 1988, 55–64, and Read 1971, 20, The scatological racism of Eliot's privately distributed 'Bolo' verse (Eliot 1990, 23) is not so culturally-specific: see Gilman 1985, ch. 4.

135 Eliot 1934a, 15, 21.

136 Warren 1977, 248. Though Warren deprecates this view, he leaves his readers in no doubt about his commitment to segregation: 'Let the negro sit beneath his own vine and fig tree' (ibid., 264). In the antebellum South 'the negro ... occupied an acknowledged, if limited and humble, place' (ibid., 247); the Civil War and the Reconstruction put paid to that.

137 Hegel 1977, 9. On the importance of not confusing racism or xenophobia with anti-Semitism see, for example, Lyotard 1993, 159; for an attempt to construct a general model of 'racialized discourse', see Goldberg 1993; for an attempt to relate the anti-Semitism of one author to the misogyny of another, see Harrowitz 1994.

138 This is a common enough anti-Semitic practice (a related example is

the contrasting of 'good' with 'Jewish' capital). Anti-Dreyfusards in 'intellectual' occupations protested their anti-intellectual credentials. These protests lapsed into the oxymoronic: 'Doctor L. F., disgusted by these eunuchs called Intellectuals'; 'A non-intellectual teacher'; 'an archivist who is not an intellectual' (quoted in Wilson 1982, 151).

139 Miller 1993, 81. Cf.: 'The contradiction between mockery of the victim and self-denigration is … a definition of Wagner's anti-Semitism … this idiosyncratic hatred is of the type that Benjamin had in mind when he defined disgust as the fear of being thought to be the same as that which is found disgusting' (Adorno 1991, 23–4). Miller goes almost as far – which is too far – in his more elegant account of Eliot's anti-Semitism.

140 Veblen 1975, 473–4.

141 Lears 1983, 312.

142 On the Jamesian, see, for example, Mayer 1989, 105–7; on the Theophrastan: 'His natural instinct was to write poetry which was as close to fiction as possible – to depict externals, to anatomise social life by a process of selection and concentration … His main interest was in people and the creation of caricature … He was … interested in externals' (Ackroyd 1985, 51, 104).

143 Olsen 1985, 12; the phrase is used by Olsen to identify the distinguishing feature of literature in general.

144 Bauman 1991, 39.

145 Cf.: Donoghue 1994, 95.

146 Quoted in Sigg 1989, 73. The passage is from Eliot's preface to Harry Crosby's *Transit of Venus: Poems* (1931).

147 I use 'topos', 'commonplace', and 'cliché' interchangeably. For a discussion of the distinctions that can be drawn between these three terms, see Wierenga 1991, 158–60.

148 See Curtius 1973, ch. 5.

149 Rosenberg 1960, 301.

150 Unger 1961, 44.

151 Modder 1960, 51–64, and chs. 7–13 *passim*.

152 'Epistle to Cobham': Pope 1966, 285.

153 Quoted in Carpenter 1982, 58.

154 Quoted in Wheen 1990, 64.

155 Quoted in Untermeyer 1990, 55.

156 Sitwell 1957, 241.

157 Quoted in Graham 1988, 132.

158 Auden 1979, 92.

159 Williams 1973, 195. Cf.: '[Agatha:] When the loop in time comes – and it does not come for everybody – / The hidden is revealed, and the spectres show themselves. [Gerald:] I don't in the least know what you're talking about. / You seem to be wanting to give us all the hump' (*The Family Reunion*, I, 1).

160 Bloom 1988, 166.

161 Matthews 1974, 113. Eliot did not always take the accusation so seriously. Spender (1985, 107) recalls him, 'in a very good mood', quoting the Russian press: 'I am a reactionary, anti-Semitic, pornographic hyena.'

162 Levy and Scherle 1969, 81. By contrast, for example, William Simpson's *Jews and Christians To-day* (1940) acknowledges that anti-Semitism is a sin of which Christians are entirely capable. In *Notes*, Eliot remarked: 'Every sin that can be imagined has been practised' (1963a, 80).

163 Gager 1985, 151.

164 Simon 1986, xv, 217.

165 Wistrich 1991, 16.

166 Stow 1988, 72.

167 Schweitzer 1988, 884.

168 Quoted in Wistrich 1991, 16.

169 Cohn-Sherbok 1992, 25.

170 On Luther's anti-Semitism see, for example, Cohen 1991.

171 Hilberg 1961, 5–6.

172 Wistrich 1991, 27.

173 ibid., 20.

174 Trachtenberg 1983, 166.

175 Cohen 1984, 13.

176 Jaher 1994, 140.

177 Byrnes 1950, 209.

178 Pulzer 1964, 273.

179 Frey 1988, 618.

180 Asbury 1988, 562.

181 'Lancelot Andrewes': Eliot 1970, 12–13.

182 Langmuir 1990, 7.

183 Klein 1978, 7.

184 ibid., 25.

185 Orwell 1970, IV, 465. 'Although Bakunin prefaced his [book] with the customary denial that the author was a vilifier or enemy of the Jews, this did not prevent him from freely deploying the usual anti-Jewish barbs' (Rose 1992b, 62). For a consideration of this 'disjuncture between self-description and behaviour', see Smith 1994, 59–60.

186 Muggeridge 1989, 243. Hartman, blithely disregarding his larger critical principles, makes de Man the beneficiary of this argument: 'It remains important ... to place oneself in that era and ask basic questions about motives and attitudes' (Hartman 1989, 15). I endorse the following criticism: 'This is an odd injunction, given deconstruction's criticism of that branch of empathetic hermeneutics that believes you can recover the intentions and meanings ... of historical actors, grasp the past from the point of view of the past' (Prendergast 1990, 335; these comments relate to an earlier version of Hartman's essay, but the point remains valid in relation to both versions).

187 Empson 1984, 196. Who is this 'one' who should not take offence? The best one can say for this argument is that Herbert Read's is worse: '[Eliot] has been accused of anti-Semitism ... all of us, if we are honest with ourselves, must confess to a certain spontaneous xenophobia. It is an instinct that the educated man controls or eradicates, and in this respect Eliot was as controlled as the best of us' (Read 1971, 35).

188 Matthews 1974, 113. It is a common view: 'Eliot was not so much anti-Semitic as he was the unwitting victim of the myths of his class and kind' (Brinnin 1982, 269); 'there can be no doubt that [Eliot] adopted the automatic anti-Jewish attitude of his class and generation' (McCormick 1988, 361). A stronger variant of this argument proposes that the poet or playwright was compelled to submit to the prejudices of his times. This leads to the proposition that the writer's anti-Semitism was not genuinely held. Thus: 'Shakespeare bowed his great genius to the prejudices of an ignorant age' (quoted in Blau and Baron 1963, 675). Such a case could not, of course, be made for Eliot.

189 LaCapra 1983, 23–71.

190 'The critic may certainly consider the relation between the literary work and truth and values, but only in order to discover – or rather to decide, because he or she knows the answer in advance since this is critical dogma – that the work is irretrievably incoherent, that it can affirm nothing and that it subverts its own values. This is what's called deconstructing a text' (Todorov 1988, 97). There is a more tentative version: 'if [the poems under discussion] carry messages about history they do so in a medium which diffuses or ironises the messages'. Poems that do not do so will usually be those 'we judge not to be good'. This slides from ontology to value; no longer constitutive of all poetry, reading for a diffusing/ironising of the message becomes the means by which good poetry is found. If one is to avoid misreading poetry as non-poetry, or good poetry as bad poetry, one needs to be careful when investigating 'the interaction between [poems] and their historical contexts' (Kermode 1990b, 66–7). I reject the formula: (good) poetry ironises, bad/non-poetry affirms.

191 Katz 1980, 53.

192 Perkins 1993, 128.

193 Often, from within the same group. For example, while Adrienne Monnier and Sylvia Beach were aiding Jewish refugees in wartime France, Natalie Barney, another 'woman of the Left Bank', regarded Jewish greed as the cause of World War Two (Benstock 1987, 412–14).

194 Nadel 1989.

195 Forster 1965, 25–6. In 1940, when Forster heard of a friend's anti-Semitism, he wrote to him pointing out its evil effects: Furbank 1979, II, 236.

196 Murry 1948, 234.

197 Bedford 1987, II, 371, 2.

198 'Years later [Woolf] would remember "How I hated marrying a Jew"' (Edel 1981, 186).

199 '[A]nti-Semitic slurs were freely sprinkled in Rupert's letters, usually harping on the Jews as rootless, intellectually destructive outsiders' (Delaney 1988, 23–4).

200 His biographer reports 'the loudly expressed anti-Semitism of [his] later years' (Alexander 1982, 125).

201 Loewenstein 1993, ch. 6.

202 Wright 1985, 122–5.

203 Orwell 1970, IV, 509. Cf.: 'I can think of passages in Villon, Shakespeare, Smollet, Thackeray, H. G. Wells, Aldous Huxley, T. S. Eliot and many another which would be called anti-semitic if they had been written since Hitler came to power'; 'I can think of passages which if written now [1945] would be stigmatised as anti-semitic, in the works of Shakespeare [etc., etc.]' (Orwell 1970, III, 113, 385). Yet there were occasions when Orwell did identify Eliot as an anti-Semite: 'Neo-Tories [like Eliot] ... are always liable to succumb to anti-semitism, at least intermittently' (Orwell 1970, III, 422, 426).

204 Levinas 1990, 128–9.

205 Ellmann 1987, 81.

206 Finkielkraut 1994, 14.

207 Ricks 1988, 75.

208 Chiari 1982, 42.

209 Ettinger 1976a, 954.

210 Grosser and Halperin 1979, 248–9.

211 It was brave (and tactless) of J. M. Cameron to add this footnote in his contribution to a celebratory volume marking Eliot's seventieth birthday: 'Hindsight is, of course, easy. But the general intentions of the Nazis were known before 1933; the furnaces of Auschwitz were already on the drawing-board' (Cameron 1958, 145).

212 Levin 1981, 170. The reference to Jefferson is somewhat pious. Jefferson was 'a Virginian with strong parochial loyalties' who held 'to the values of agrarian society' (Hofstadter 1948, 25). He was also a slave owner. Still, he championed the rights of Jews both in 1776, in a debate over naturalisation in Virginia, and in 1785 when they gained protection under the Virginia Act for Religious Toleration. He consistently appointed Jews to public office. He took pride, as expressed in a letter to Isaac Harby, that his university 'set the example of ceasing to violate the rights of conscience by any injunctions on the different sects respecting their religions' (Sarna 1987, 69).

213 Litvinoff 1980, 715–16.

214 Quoted in Gilbert 1987, 64.

215 Steinberg 1990, 72.

216 Marshall 1990.

217 For examples see Bernard Lewis 1986, 93; Griffiths 1980, 65.

218 Saperstein 1989, 21.

219 Grossman 1988, 178.

220 Quoted in Poliakov 1974–5, I, 71.

221 Quoted in Dinnerstein 1987, 237.

222 *Chaplinsky* v. *New Hampshire* 315 U.S. 568 (1942); *Brandenburg* v. *Ohio* 395 U.S. 444 (1969): cited in Schneider 1992, 272.

223 Quoted in Emerson 1970, 395.

224 Cf.: Roth 1994, 121. The texts themselves are 'dagger poems' of a violence to make one impatient with analysis, as in these remarks of Irving Howe: 'When I read LeRoi Jones calling for "dagger poems in the slimy bellies of their owner jews"…then I know I am in the presence of a racist hoodlum, inciting people to blood. And I am not going to be deflected from that perception by talk about rhythm, metaphor, and diction' (quoted in Stern 1991, 297).

225 Finkielkraut 1994, 13. Unlike Finkielkraut, however, I believe this to be true of anti-Semitism generally, not merely of its Nazi version.

226 Todorov 1993, xiii.

227 Austin 1980, chs. 8 to 9. This is not the place in which to explore the subtleties and difficulties of Austin's work, save to acknowledge that Austin himself considered poetry to be special: 'The normal conditions of reference may be suspended, or no attempt made at a standard perlocutionary act, no attempt to make you do anything, as Walt Whitman does not seriously incite the eagle of liberty to soar' (ibid., 104).

228 Ewart 1989, 44.

229 Eliot 1963a, 59.

230 'Religion and Literature': Eliot 1951, 397.

231 Plutzik 1974, 338.

232 Quoted in Bickel 1975, 72. The phrase is from Holmes's celebrated dissent in *Gitlow* v. *New York* 268 U.S. 673 (1925).

233 Donoghue 1989, 233.

234 Cf.: 'There is much talk of Eliot's anti-Semitism, especially by critics who have no scruple in presenting themselves as hating Christianity' (Donoghue 1994, 215; see also 89). It is as if Donoghue is too angry on Eliot's behalf to be coherent. Is Eliot to be regarded a Christian martyr, persecuted on the pretext of an alleged anti-Semitism by those who hate his faith?

235 Jay 1992.

236 ibid., 15.

2. 'GERONTION', CRITICISM, AND THE LIMITS OF THE DRAMATIC MONOLOGUE

1 Ransom 1971, 136–60.

2 Honnighausen 1988, ch. 4.

3 Trachtenberg 1983, 47, 208.

4 Pound 1973, 270.

5 Pound 1981, 45. The lines were changed in Pound's *Collected Shorter Poems*: 'Let us be done with pandars and jobbery, / Let us spit upon those who pat the big-bellies for profit' (Pound 1984, 145). The change is unacknowledged.

6 Quoted in Wertheimer 1987, 158.

7 Quoted in Weinzierl 1974, 237.

8 Quoted in Wilson 1982, 491.

9 Quoted in Katz 1980, 62.

10 Quoted in Wilson 1982, 597.

11 Quoted in Dinnerstein 1994, 42.

12 McClelland 1970, 244–5.

13 Pound 1978a, 219.

14 'Limbo': Heaney 1972, 70.

15 Quoted in Wilson 1982, 389.

16 Quoted in Holmes 1979, 40.

17 Quoted in Poliakov 1974–5, III, 372.

18 Gilman 1991, 100.

19 Quoted in Mehlman 1983, 24.

20 Jaher 1994, 58.

21 Quoted in Poliakov 1974–5, III, 49.

22 Quoted in Samuel 1967, 213.

23 Quoted in Holmes 1979, 38.

24 Ashton 1933, 23.

25 Augustine 1961, 169.

26 Quoted in Schorske 1987, 128.

27 Quoted in Roberts 1994, 299.

28 Quoted in Poliakov 1977, IV, 289.

29 Borden 1984, 85.

30 Wertheimer 1987, 25–6: 'government officials continued to link Eastern Jews with vermin and plague – an association that was to have a long and catastrophic history in Germany'.

31 Quoted in Singerman 1987, 107.

32 Holmes 1979, 37–48.

33 Gilman 1991, 40.

34 Carey 1992, 13.

35 Edelmann 1986, 3.

36 Quoted in Poliakov 1974–5, III, 89.

37 Quoted in Litvinoff 1988, 101.

38 Josephus 1818, iv, 310–11.

39 Tacitus 1975, 273.

40 Poliakov 1974–5, I, 104; Roth 1970, 211.

41 Nolte 1969, 170.

42 Wilson 1982, 478–9.

43 Quoted in Gilman 1991, 100–1.
44 Quoted in Hitchens 1991, 87. The leper theory was 'eagerly appropriated by [nineteenth-century] anthropologists to support their "Aryanism"' (Litvinoff 1988, 145).
45 Quoted in Poliakov 1974–5, III, 359.
46 Mankowitz 1949, 130. Even the hostile Karl Shapiro backs away from the subject: 'Eliot's anti-Semitism, which I am not going to discuss...' (Shapiro 1960, 51).
47 The page before the title page, Mankowitz 1967. Interviewed in *The Jewish Quarterly*, Mankowitz described himself as 'a Jewish writer, writing in the English language' (Sonntag 1980, 81).
48 Quoted in Wilson 1982, 710.
49 Pearson 1970, 86.
50 ibid., 87.
51 ibid., 90. Another critic reaches a similar if milder conclusion: 'The poem is funny, but at everyone's expense' (Crawford 1987, 116). Ricks responds: 'It should be retorted that the groups, races, and classes in the poem cannot equally afford the expense' (Ricks 1988, 36). This is well said, though inadequate as a retort. There is a distinction between denying that the poem's target is 'everyone' and denying that 'everyone' can afford the attack equally. Ricks takes the latter position, I adopt the former.
52 Shapiro 1960, 35.
53 Quoted in Alexander Bloom 1986, 147.
54 Fiedler 1991, 63.
55 Howe 1982, 57.
56 Howe 1991, 31.
57 Kazin 1979, 67.
58 Henry Roth, quoted in Fiedler 1991, 64.
59 Ozick 1993, 16–17.
60 Honorific references, however, certainly: see, for example, Roditi 1932.
61 Hook 1987, 212; Alexander Bloom 1986, 31.
62 Diana Trilling 1982, 411–29; Klingenstein 1991, 95–8.
63 Graff 1987, 61.
64 Schwartz 1984, xii.
65 Oren 1985, 121.
66 Salusinszky 1987, 86.
67 Booth 1988, 395. cf.: '[of Columbia:] The English department was especially protected against "outsiders"; it was felt that the Anglo-Saxon tradition could not be entrusted to Jewish instructors' (Diana Trilling 1993, 268).
68 Salusinszky 1987, 61.
69 Asphodel 1989, 229.
70 Dinwiddy 1958, 94, 96.
71 Quoted in Alexander Bloom 1986, 149.

72 Browning 1981, ii, 481.

73 Edgeworth 1817, 263.

74 Trilling 1967, 26–7.

75 Mordell 1951, 13.

76 Drew 1949, 50.

77 Porteus 1948, 222.

78 Bailey 1939, 21.

79 Mayer 1989, 228.

80 Howarth 1964, 50.

81 Chiari 1972, 48.

82 Smith 1956, 54. A recent, further instance: '[of "Burbank" and the other quatrain poems:] It attacks targets without apology...there is nothing stuffy about it and it is not afraid to be unfair' (Mays 1994, 117).

83 Nott 1958, 125.

84 Richards 1930, 277. Cf.: 'Notable is the distinct Eliotic bias, despite disclaimers, expressed in the expectation that the reader dissociate himself from the bias of the "personal" yet retain the "genuine" content of experience which constitutes personality... masterly reading is the normative pursuit of an adjustment of interests and an abatement of differences' (Freund 1987, 34, 37). Though it is to Leavis's credit that he insisted upon a specifically *literary* criticism of Eliot's poetry, distinct from Anglo-Catholic edifications (Leavis 1976, 278–92; Leavis and Leavis 1969, 52). Jewish Leavisites may have believed that consistency required them likewise to disengage themselves from that poetry's anti-Semitism. Consider, for example, this: 'As a literary critic I believed in the doctrine that a work of art lived or died by the laws of its own being – aesthetic laws – and I believed that it must not be judged by any other standards, whether moral or political. A poem or a novel might contain offensive sentiments (anti-Semitism, for example)... but it could still be a great work from a strictly literary point of view, and it was the responsibility of a serious critic to make his judgments on the basis of literary values alone' (Podhoretz 1980, 23).

85 Eliot 1964, 87–102; 'the suspicion remains, even when he wrote the opposite, that he connected intensity of expression with right belief, and considered Dante, for example, a better poet than Shakespeare' (Cowling 1980, 110). Eliot later restated his view: '[the] philosophical system must be tenable: a poem arising out of a religion which struck us as wholly vile, or out of a philosophy which seemed to us pure nonsense, simply would not appear to be a poem at all' ('Goethe as Sage': Eliot 1971b, 225). In his second Milton paper he insisted that any 'entry' made by 'our theological and political dispositions' into a consideration of Milton's poetry 'as poetry' would be 'unlawful' ('Milton II': Eliot 1971b, 148).

86 Cf.: 'The charge [against Pound] of anti-Semitism is familiar, and there

were once Arab attacks on the "Divina Commedia"...as anti-Mohammedan' (Kenner 1985b, 255). Kenner intends us to consider Jewish critics of Pound and 'Arab' critics of Dante as similarly absurd. Compare also: '[on the question of Eliot's anti-Semitism:] the projects of literary criticism and literary history...do not require that writers be models of decency' (Lentricchia 1994, 281). It seems I run the risk of being convicted of misunderstanding the nature of these 'projects'. So be it!

87 'The Function of Criticism': Eliot 1951, 25.

88 'The Perfect Critic': Eliot 1960, 14–15. Modern criticism has adopted this as a principle. See, for example, Murray Krieger's stipulation that the reader must 'surrender [his or her] own contexts' on reading poetry (Krieger 1981, 17).

89 Kant 1973, 42.

90 Nietzsche 1969, 104.

91 Klein 1987, 268–71; Maccoby: 1973, 68–79; 1974, 7–10; 1983/4, 3–7. In confronting Eliot's anti-Semitism, however, they aimed higher than other critics; they, and the few others like them, led the way for those of us who now address this topic.

92 Jews tell jokes about (other) Jews who attribute all their misfortunes to anti-Semitism. L. B. Berger, a deservedly obscure Jewish poet, finds anti-Semitism contributing to the rejection of his poetry: 'T. S. Eliot, of Faber and Faber, his anti-Semitism a matter of record, thanked him for submitting a copy of "The Collected Poems", but... Infuriatingly, the letter was signed by a secretary in Mr Eliot's absence' (Richler 1991, 122). The secretary signing the letter is a further mark of Berger's unimportance. There is comic poignancy in Berger's dismay. Such is his reverence for Eliot, even a letter of rejection from him would be precious.

93 Howe 1982, 165.

94 Atlas 1977, 126, 163, 288–9. Robert Fitzgerald's chronicle of the 1949–51 Princeton Seminars has Schwartz showing an 'obsessive' interest in Eliot, but does not record what he said about the poet. Fitzgerald speculates that the cool response Schwartz received may have led him to postpone publication of his projected book on Eliot, which never appeared (Fitzgerald 1985, 67–8).

95 Schwartz 1939, 437. Eliot wrote to thank Schwartz for his article; Schwartz 'endowed [the letter] with a sort of talismanic value' (Atlas 1977, 154). The other three essays are 'T. S. Eliot as the International Hero', 'T. S. Eliot's Voice and His Voices', and 'The Literary Dictatorship of T. S. Eliot' (Schwartz 1970, 120–8, 129–43, 312–31). Irving Howe has recalled that while neither Schwartz nor Philip Rahv (of *Partisan Review*) commented on Eliot's anti-Semitism in print, both deplored it in conversation (Howe 1991, 30). My point, exactly.

96 Schwartz 1984, 68.

97 Atlas 1977, 163.

98 Salusinszky 1987, 34, 46–7. He has also been criticised, from the perspective of normative Judaism, for erecting 'an artistic anti-Judaism'; he is an 'idol-maker' (Ozick 1984, 178–99).

99 Bloom 1982, 3.

100 Bloom 1985, 1.

101 Salusinszky 1987, 62.

102 ibid., 50.

103 ibid., 64.

104 Bloom 1982, 17.

105 Bloom 1970, 37.

106 ibid., 179. Cf: 'I began my teaching career nearly forty years ago in an academic context dominated by the ideas of T. S. Eliot; ideas that roused me to fury, and against which I fought as vigorously as I could' (Bloom 1995, 517).

107 Bloom 1976, 95. He gets Eliot wrong here, however: see ch. 4.

108 On the contrast between Bloom and Eliot, see Handelman 1982, 187–90.

109 *Literary criticism*: Cullingford 1981, 158; Handelman 1982, 189; Eagleton 1983, 40; Ozick 1984, 187; Solotaroff 1987, 29; Fromm 1991, 80; Hartman 1994, 13. *Fiction*: Richler 1969, 113; Lodge 1978, 31; Roth 1988, 183; Bainbridge 1991, 34; Stone 1992, 28. Frederic Raphael's 1963 novel, *Lindmann*, quotes lines from 'Burbank' about rats and Jews as an epigraph, and pays Eliot mock deference by crediting him with these libels thus: 'Thomas Stearns Eliot OM'.

110 Jay 1993, 546.

111 Robbins 1991, 18.

112 Derrida 1978, 65.

113 Sidney Hook remarks, 'In retrospect, and in the present climate of opinion, it may be difficult to explain the absence of moral indignation on the part of Jewish students when they were passed over for others who "belonged". This discrimination was something we took for granted' (Hook 1987, 211).

114 Perl 1989, xii. This attempt to claim Eliot for post-modernism is unpersuasive. Louis Menand has argued, correctly, that Eliot's irony did not disable him from making positive judgments (Menand 1987, 7).

115 ibid., 103 (my italics).

116 ibid., 135. Perl's endnote (211) ascribes a passage in the pre-war *The Idea of a Christian Society* (1939, 63–4) to the post-war *Notes*. This allows him to rebut Steiner's criticism that Eliot alluded to the Holocaust only once, in 'an oddly condescending footnote' (Steiner 1978, 34).

117 ibid., xiii. Cf.: 'the most obvious limitation of my study is its lack of attention to the Christian aspect of Eliot's critical thought. Two points are offered to extenuate this omission. First, as "a free-thinking", secular Jew (the sort Eliot once viciously condemned as a corruptive danger that western society could not tolerate), I consider my capacity

for understanding Eliot as a Christian to be limited. Secondly...'
(Shusterman 1988, 3).

118 Cf.: '[Helmut Newton] freely admits to an admiration for fascistic
iconography. But then, being a Jew who had to emigrate to Australia
during the War, he can, in his own words, "afford to"' (Palmer 1991,
16); '[in response to the charge that Jung was anti-Semitic:] I am a
Jewess and my husband is a Jew. Does anyone here believe that I would
defend Dr Jung if he were anti-Semitic?' (quoted in Maidenbaum and
Martin 1991, 242).

119 'William Blake': Eliot 1951, 305–16.

120 ibid., 322.

121 Blake 1967, 183–5.

122 'Wrath' and 'tree' figure in Blake's poetic vocabulary: Damon 1973,
410–11, and 452–3.

123 Blake 1967, 58.

124 Matthew 12: 38–9. Cf.: Luke 11: 29.

125 Barthes 1990, 5.

126 'Four Elizabethan Dramatists': Eliot 1951, 117.

127 Pound has these two poems in view in his review of Eliot's first
collection: 'Since Browning there have been very few good poems of
this sort. Mr Eliot has made two notable additions to this list' (Pound
1960, 419–20). If these two poems are additions to the list, 'Gerontion'
puts a line under it. It is a poem about the impossibility of writing like
Browning in the twentieth century. Bloom describes Eliot as Browning's
'secret student', by which he also means antagonist (Bloom 1988, 186).
I agree.

128 On 'counter-statements', see Fowler 1985, 174.

129 Genesis 22. All further quotations in this section are from the same
chapter.

130 Abraham should have replied to this putative divine voice: 'That I
may not kill my good son is absolutely certain. But that you who appear
to me are God is not certain and cannot become certain, even though
the voice were to sound from the very heavens'... [For] that a voice
which one seems to hear *cannot* be divine one can be certain of... in case
when it is commanded is contrary to moral law. However majestic or
supernatural it may appear to be, one must regard it as a deception'
(quoted: Fackenheim 1980, 34).

131 Genesis 15: 18.

132 Fackenheim 1980, 54. But there is also the religious response, which
complicates matters: 'If religion is taken seriously in its own right, can
one fail to entertain the idea of sacrifice? If it is taken radically, can one
simply exclude the notion of total sacrifice?' Fackenheim concludes
that one cannot, though it is a 'scandal' (ibid., 55).

133 Kierkegaard 1987, 54–5.

134 Hegel 1971, 187.

135 Genesis 27: 1, 18; Genesis 31: 11; Genesis 37: 13; Genesis 46: 2; Exodus 3: 4; Isaiah 6: 8.
136 As the textbooks note, the poem's first line borrows from A. C. Benson's *Edward Fitzgerald*: 'Here he sits, in a dry month, old and blind, being read to by a country boy, longing for rain' (Southam 1981, 51; Smith 1956, 63; Williamson 1967, 107). By substituting 'Here I am' for 'Here he sits', Eliot diminishes pity into self-pity, and begins the poem's work of destruction upon its form.
137 Stephen Heath overlooks this in his symptomatic account of the poem. He regards it merely as a literary statement of the threat posed to a man by a woman's aberrant behaviour (Heath 1982, 27). By contrast, Elaine Showalter situates 'Hysteria' in the context of the World War I 'discovery' of male hysteria: 'Men's quarrels with the feminine element in their own psyches became externalised as quarrels with women, and hysteria expressed itself in part as fear or anger towards the neurotic woman' (Showalter 1991, 173). This 'hysteria' is represented in another of Eliot's poetic engagements with a neurotic woman, 'The Portrait of a Lady': 'Inside my brain a dull tom-tom begins…'
138 Tennyson 1971, 89–90.
139 'In Memoriam': Eliot 1951, 331.
140 ibid., 331. But compare Eliot's later remark, made perhaps with 'Gerontion' in mind, that 'dramatic monologue cannot create a character' ('The Three Voices of Poetry': 1971b, 95). This says much about his own view as a poet of the form as a poet, though it is simply perverse as a critical judgment.
141 Browning 1981, I, 781.
142 ibid., II, 680.
143 ibid., I, 705.
144 ibid., II, 481.
145 Luke 2: 25–35.
146 MacIntyre 1988, 11 (my italics).
147 Gardner 1985, 124. She is right, however, to insist upon Simeon's Jewishness. Lyndall Gordon, by contrast, overlooks this in a lather of biographical fancy: 'In "A Song for Simeon" [Eliot] hoped that [the choice souls of the future] would acknowledge and re-enact, with greater success, his lonely watch' (Gordon 1978, 140). This mis-conceived reading is consistent with – indeed, made possible by – Gordon's failure to address the anti-Semitism in Eliot's poetry.
148 Moody 1980, 135.
149 The phrase is Konig's (1986, 17), who applies it to Ahasuerus, the Wandering Jew.
150 Jay 1983, 99. For a contrasting view, which stresses the continuities between Eliot's poetry and the dramatic monologues of Tennyson and Browning, see Christ 1984, 46–50.
151 Ricks 1987, 154; see also Griffiths 1989, 219–20.

152 Bush 1985, 33.
153 Ricks 1988, 29.
154 Danto 1986, 117–33. Danto makes certain remarks about obscenity in art which bear, by analogy, on my discussion of anti-Semitism: 'one could not mention an obscenity without through that act *using* the obscenity: obscenity was a kind of solvent that ate through the device even of quotation or display, so that the effort at mere imitation of the obscene utterance was doomed: there was no allowed distance of the sort that had long since insinuated itself in dramatic representation, separating the words the actor spoke from those the character spoke, even when phonically identical' (ibid., 122). Anti-Semitism is a similarly strong 'solvent'.
155 Ricks 1988, 30.

3. 'SWEENEY AMONG THE NIGHTINGALES', 'BURBANK', AND THE POETICS OF ANTI-SEMITISM

1 Collingwood 1965, 122.
2 Norris 1991, 208.
3 Rorty 1991, 129–32.
4 De Man 1986b, 6.
5 Graff 1979, 5.
6 Russo 1989, 541.
7 Abrams 1991, 104.
8 Cf.: Sidney 1971, 31.
9 Tabachnick 1969, 754.
10 Brooks 1962, 729–41. The privileging of irony by the New Critics became a reflex, and was thus liable to be overstated: 'Irony may be regarded', remarked John Crowe Ransom, 'as the ultimate mode of the great minds' (quoted in Gelpi 1990, 9). Irony continues to enjoy a good press: see Rorty 1989, ch. 4.
11 Objecting to Auden's 'apophthegm' (from 'In Memory of W. B. Yeats'), Richard Ellmann observes that 'events cannot be separated from the emotions to which they give birth, nor roused human feelings from subsequent events' (Ellmann 1989, 85). It is for this reason that Keats's account of 'the poetical Character' is unsatisfactory: 'It has as much delight in conceiving an Iago as an Imogen. What shocks the virtuous philosopher, delights the cameleon Poet. It does no harm from its relish of the dark side of things any more than from its taste for the bright one; because they both end in speculation' (Keats 1987, 157).
12 Cohen 1991, 306.
13 Eliot 1918, 114.
14 Quoted in Mendes-Flohr and Reinarz 1980, 261. The falsely metaphoric becomes falsely literal in Nazi anti-Semitism: 'The discovery of the Jewish virus is one of the greatest revolutions which has been undertaken

in the world. The struggle we are waging is of the same kind as in the past century, that of Pasteur and Koch. How many diseases can be traced back to the Jewish virus? We shall regain our health only when we exterminate the Jews' (quoted in Lang 1990, 16).

15 Ricks 1988, 31.

16 Quoted ibid., 32.

17 Prologue: Marlowe 1979, 9.

18 Weininger 1906, 309.

19 De Man 1988, 45.

20 Derrida 1989, 205–10. Derrida considers the article to be 'nonconformist'. He is wrong. The disdain for 'vulgar anti-Semitism' probably stemmed from an instinct of self-defence. De Man had praised modern literature in earlier columns. Only vulgar anti-Semites, he contended, could take that to mean that he was endorsing the Jewish contribution to that literature. Flesch, making a related point, interprets the article as striking a bargain with the Nazis: 'the Nazis can have the Jews if they leave literature, especially French literature, alone' (Flesch 1989, 179).

21 Cohn 1967; Holmes 1979, ch. 9.

22 Though *The Times* later changed its mind: Cohn 1979, 155. During his detention at St Elizabeth's, Pound urged visitors to read the 'Protocols' (Tytell 1987, 304). In a wartime radio broadcast, he alleged that the 'Protocols' deliberately had been 'garbled' so that it could later be claimed that they were 'a forgery, and the kike is slandered'. In a later broadcast he put the point more succinctly: 'Certainly they are a forgery, and that is the one proof we have of their authenticity' (Pound 1978a, 198, 283).

23 Hegel 1971, 190.

24 Ricks suggests implausibly that withholding the new surname is more sinister than Rachel herself: 'But in Eliot's line the surname which is now Rachel's is remarkably – just because unremarkedly – withheld in a way that is sinisterly inconceivable in any world of social remark; what is sinister is such a dark way of speaking, much more than any darkness possessed by Rachel' (Ricks 1988, 31). This is fanciful. Rachel's 'tear[ing] at grapes with murderous paws' cannot be regarded as less sinister than the failure to follow convention when naming her.

25 I apply Occam's Razor to Ricks's reading of the poem: 'if everything in some science can be interpreted without assuming this or that hypothetical entity, there is no ground for assuming it' (Russell 1961, 462–3). Russell says that he has found it most useful in logical analysis. It also has its uses in literary criticism.

26 This is a critical reflex: 'the strange or deviant is brought within a discursive order and thus made to seem natural ... If all else failed, we could read a sequence of words with no apparent order as signifying absurdity or chaos and then, by giving it an allegorical relation to the world, take it as a statement about the incoherence and absurdity of our own language ... Much of Robbe-Grillet can be recuperated if we

read it as the musings or speech of a pathological narrator' (Culler 1975, 136–7). This is a misreading of Robbe-Grillet (Heath 1972, 67–8, 119–20), just as it misreads 'Sweeney Among the Nightingales'.

27 Yeats 1936, xxii.

28 Chesterton 1940, 95 (my italics).

29 Holmes 1979, 63.

30 Pound 1978a, 257.

31 Dinnerstein 1987, 62. In 1933 she tried, but failed, to relax the immigration rules that kept out German Jewish refugees (Kraut and Breitman 1987, 177). When challenged with her alleged Jewishness, she responded, 'If I were a Jew, I would make no secret of it. On the contrary, I would acknowledge it' (quoted in Dinnerstein 1991, 221). Anti-Semites were convinced that Jews powerfully influenced the Roosevelt administration (Shapiro 1987, 134).

32 Arnold 1969, 167–8. It is evidence of Gwendolyn's unthinking anti-Semitism early on in *Daniel Deronda* that she can dismiss Rachel as 'that thin Jewess' (Eliot 1967, 84).

33 Quoted in Dijkstra 1986, 387.

34 Quoted in Wilson 1982, 593.

35 Dijkstra 1986, 277, 401.

36 Quoted in Wilson 1982, 548.

37 ibid., 591, 594.

38 Casillo 1988, 222.

39 Joyce 1972, 80. On 'Joyce and the mystique of the Jewish woman', see Nadel 1989, 154–80.

40 Du Maurier 1947, 541.

41 Glossop 1923, 34.

42 Baudelaire 1986, 96. Eliot was dismissive of Baudelaire's 'stock of imagery': 'His prostitutes, mulattoes, Jewesses, serpents, cats, corpses form a machinery which has not worn very well' ('Baudelaire': Eliot 1951, 424).

43 See Bristow 1982, which reproduces a warning notice to 'young women travelling alone' on the 'Brazil and River Plate' steamer service.

44 Simon 1986, 216–18.

45 Jaher 1994, 71. On medieval bestiaries, and their anti-Semitic applications, see Lazar 1991, 55–6.

46 Wilson 1982, 485.

47 Mosse 1985, 117.

48 Browning 1981, I, 706.

49 Swinburne 1992, 81.

50 Quoted in Katz 1978, 86.

51 Hooker 1983, 225. It is noteworthy, however, that 'rabin' in 'Rabinovitch', a status name, means 'rabbi' (see Hanks and Hodges

1988, 440). In some sense it confers a certain quintessential 'Jewishness' on Rachel. 'Rabbi' has been a term of abuse since Jesus said 'Be not ye called Rabbi!' (Matthew 23: 8; and see Alexander 1991, 81).

52 Marcus 1974, 142–4.
53 Jaher 1994, 166.
54 One critic reads 'Sweeney Among the Nightingales' as asserting that 'a Jewess ought not to marry a Gentile' (Harrison 1967, 151). I disagree: the poem asserts the pointlessness of such marriages because Rachel remains identifiably Jewish.
55 Quoted in McCormick 1988, 360.
56 Quoted in Poliakov 1985, IV, 275. This is a 'rhetoric of specious nomenclature' (Kaplan 1986, xii).
57 Kadish 1992, 34–5.
58 Quoted in Kristeva 1982, 181.
59 Bering 1992, 50–1.
60 Belloc 1922, 100.
61 Quoted in Carpenter 1988, 482.
62 Eliot 1988a, 206.
63 Dostoievsky 1985, 430.
64 Hitchens 1991, 49.
65 Lentricchia 1983, 324.
66 Mallarmé 1965, 96.
67 Lecercle 1990, 114, 117.
68 Sartre 1965, 10.
69 Blanchot 1993, 124.
70 Quoted in Wilson 1982, 478.
71 Mallarmé 1965, 62–5.
72 Kermode 1971b; Wilson 1982.
73 Quoted in Wilson 1982, 554. Wilson distinguishes the leading writers who sided with the anti-Semites from those others who were the theoreticians of the movement: 'those who elaborated antisemitic ideology were writers of lesser prestige and status, but men with a sense of their status as writers none the less' (606–7). Huysmans, Alphonse Daudet, Edmond de Goncourt, and others, were fellow-travellers of anti-Semitism. Huysmans's anti-Semitism was, nevertheless, violent and extreme (Griffiths 1966, 76–7, 309–10).
74 Symons 1958, 81.
75 Eliot 1978, 42.
76 Eliot 1927b, 195.
77 'The Unity of European Culture': Eliot 1963a, 112. In the foreword to Joseph Chiari's *Symbolisme from Poe to Mallarmé*, Eliot observed: '[w]ithout [the Symboliste] aesthetic I do not think that the work of some other modern writers would be quite what it is (I am thinking of Rilke, for example, and *some* of my own *later* work)' (vii: my italics).

78 Davie 1970, 63.
79 Wilson 1974, 23.
80 ibid., 23.
81 Davie 1970, 79.
82 Richards 1971, 99–101.
83 Kermode 1971b, 80.
84 Said 1992, 65.
85 Rosenberg 1973, 246.
86 Notwithstanding the example of Huysmans, and trivial instances such as Rimbaud's 'A vendre ce que les Juifs n'ont pas vendu, ce que noblesse ni crime n'ont goûté' (Rimbaud 1962, 295).
87 Kermode 1967, 39.
88 Spender 1975, 60.
89 Orwell 1970, II, 187.
90 'Lack of dependence on logical structure distinguishes symbolist poetry from simple expository prose; but this is also true of poetry in general. In this sense, then, all poetry is *symbolist* poetry' (Brooks 1948, 67); 'The empire of signs is prose; poetry is on the side of painting, sculpture, and music ... Doubtless, emotion, even passion – and why not anger, social indignation, and political hatred? – are at the origin of [a poem by Rimbaud]. But they are not expressed there, as in a pamphlet or confession ... It is true that the prose-writer and the poet both write. But there is nothing in common between these two acts of writing except the movement of the hand which traces the letters. Otherwise their universes are incommunicable ...' (Sartre 1983, 4–5, 10). Symbolist poetry becomes the type of all poetry in Sartre's analysis and represents 'the discovery that words may have meanings though they have no referents' (Davie 1970, 78).
91 Richards 1926, 232
92 Quoted in Glaser 1978, 224.
93 Brooke 1931, 9–10.
94 Besant 1903, 200.
95 Lewis 1939, 40.
96 Quoted in Kushner 1989, 124.
97 Quoted in Lindemann 1991, 222. In John Peal Bishop's poem 'This is the Man' (quoted in Dobkowski 1979, 235), the poet sits with his girlfriend. An ugly and dishevelled Jew passes them and then doubles back to kiss the woman's hand: 'Semitic snout / Returned and upturned eyes came / back, and while I stared there speechless bent and / kissed your hand.' As with 'Burbank', there is the easy familiarity that the Jew shows toward the woman, and the same incongruity of a Jewish chivalry (in 'Burbank' evidenced by Klein's title, in 'This is the Man' evidenced by the Jew's gesture).
98 Tennyson 1971, 41.
99 Gross 1992, 209.

100 Sartre 1965, 24.
101 Gilman 1986, 119.
102 Eliot 1935b, 611.
103 Wagner 1973, 27.
104 ibid., 32–3.
105 Quoted in Langmuir 1990, 27.
106 Quoted in Dinnerstein 1988, 320.
107 Quoted in Jaher 1994, 225.
108 Quoted in Holmes 1979, 66. Jews are infernal: 'Demons escaped from hell, / Race of the Jews, detestable men, / More accursed that Lucifer / And more wicked than all the devils' (quoted in Poliakov 1974–5, I, 192).
109 Polenberg 1989, 14.
110 Quoted in Wilson 1982, 155.
111 Pulzer 1964, 62.
112 ibid., 242.
113 Quoted in Wilson 1982, 485.
114 Quoted in Kushner 1989, 110.
115 Quoted in Poliakov 1985, IV, 51.
116 Quoted in Kushner 1989, 110.
117 Quoted in Blakeney 1985, 186.
118 Quoted in Holmes 1979, 38.
119 ibid., 18.
120 Pound 1978a, 345.
121 ibid., 115.
122 ibid., 111.
123 ibid., 253.
124 Pound 1973, 71.
125 Gilman 1993, 15.
126 Eliot 1971a, 5, 23.
127 Quoted in Kushner 1989, 4.
128 James 1975, 176.
129 Quoted in Dobkowski 1979, 158.
130 Kramnick and Sheerman 1993, 252.
131 Santayana 1987, 257.
132 Quoted in Blakeney 1985, 14.
133 Quoted in Holmes 1979, 55.
134 This enjambment is 'perhaps the most brilliant technical stroke of all the poems in the Gautier stanza' (Gross 1968, 185). Thus does literary virtuosity partner a contemptuous anti-Semitism in Eliot's work.
135 Ricks 1988, 35.
136 Brooks regarded this line, and Keats's 'Beauty is truth, truth beauty', as challenges to his poetics: '"Beauty is truth, truth beauty" has precisely the same status, and the same justification, as Shakespeare's "Ripeness is all". It is a speech "in character" and supported by

dramatic context' (Brooks 1968, 135). The critics compete to capture for poetry lines typically read as contextless prose. Eliot dismissed 'Beauty is truth' but defended 'Ripeness is all' ('Dante': Eliot 1951, 270).

137 Bush 1985, 25–6.
138 Longenbach 1991, 56, 58.
139 I have adapted a sentence from Macherey 1978, 133. It has long been regarded a mark of sophistication in Marxist literary theory to reject any simple equation of literature and ideology. This has led to a tendency to disregard, or otherwise play down or excuse, the objectionable nature of certain texts. Wyndham Lewis is a beneficiary of just this tendency (see Jameson 1979, *passim*).
140 Bloom 1977, 386.
141 Krieger 1981, 18–19.
142 Kermode 1990b, 66, on Auden's 'Spain, 1937'.
143 McGann 1989, 117, 123. This is a commonplace of modern criticism, usefully applicable to otherwise intractably objectionable texts. Thus, with Wyndham Lewis's 'protofascist' work in view, Frederic Jameson proposes that 'great art distances ideology by the way in which, endowing the latter with figuration and with narrative articulation, the text frees its ideological content to demonstrate its own contradictions' (1979, 22–3).
144 Redman (1991, 244) argues this of an article by Pound.
145 Rorty 1991, 107.
146 Barthes 1977, 41.
147 Eliot 1987, 6.
148 Quoted in Bredin 1987, 28. '[On Céline:] That object, the Jew, gives thought a focus where all contradictions are explained and satisfied' (Kristeva 1982, 178).
149 'From Poe to Valery': Eliot 1978, 39.
150 ibid., 40.
151 Pearson 1970, 83–101.
152 'East Coker', II.
153 Kermode, writing about Mallarmé, Hulme and Pound, expresses it thus: 'In varying degrees they all obscurely wish that poetry could be written with something other than words, but since it can't, that words may be made to have the same sort of physical presence "as a piece of string". The resistance to words in their Image is explained by the fact that words are the means of a very different sort of communication; they are so used to being discursive that it is almost impossible to stop them discoursing' (Kermode 1971b, 151).
154 'From Poe to Valery': Eliot 1978, 39.
155 Pearson 1970, 83. Karl Shapiro anticipated Pearson's thesis: '[Eliot] begins as an uneasy Symbolist; he knows something is wrong with Symbolism and that it hasn't worked' (Shapiro 1960, 96). Chace

comments that 'Eliot's partisan activities [may be seen] in part as an awkward emergence from the Symbolist quarantine' (Chace 1973, xviii).

156 Pearson 1970, 93.
157 ibid., 83, 93, 94.
158 Levy and Scherle 1969, 81.

4. 'DIRGE', 'A COOKING EGG', *THE WASTE LAND*, AND THE AESTHETICS OF UGLINESS

1 Quoted in Ellmann 1989, 49.
2 Pound 1960, 45.
3 Lewis 1987, 185. On the 'first step[s] of art into the land of the ugly', see Butler 1994, 106–23.
4 Stead 1983, 126.
5 Sheridan 1970, 202.
6 Gilman 1991, 68–9.
7 Lacoue-Labarthe 1990, 69.
8 Hegel 1971, 202.
9 Quoted in Levinas 1990, 236.
10 Poliakov 1985, IV, 297.
11 'Dante': Eliot 1951, 169 (my italics).
12 Eliot 1964, 106 (my italics).
13 Quoted in Wellek 1983, III, 168 (my italics).
14 Levenson 1986, 162.
15 Grant 1982, I, 98.
16 Sigg 1989, 38.
17 Long 1988, 101.
18 Smith 1956, 54. 'Beauty' was the reviewers' criterion: 'The established poets receive full-length reviews, in which they are invariably praised for the quality of "beauty"their poetry displays. In the same year [1909] Ezra Pound's *Personae* is dismissed in a few lines for lacking that quality' (Stead 1983, 56). Those who praised the early Pound did so in the language of his detractors: '"In Praise of Ysolt" is ... beautiful ... The beauty of it is the beauty of passion, sincerity and intensity' (quoted in Sullivan 1970, 37).
19 Gross 1968, 185.
20 Quoted in Ricks 1988, 28. Steiner echoes Fiedler, and no doubt many other similarly perplexed critics: 'what was I to do when I discovered similar slanders at the heart of their [i.e., Eliot's and Pound's] greatest poems, preserved still in present-day anthologies for classroom use, thanks in large part (it is a final irony) to a generation of Jewish critics and pedagogues – including me' (Fiedler 1991, 10).
21 Ricks 1988, 29.
22 ibid., 39.

23 'The idea of the microcosm, the notion that the structure of the universe can be reflected on a smaller scale in some particular phenomenon, has always been a favorite in the history of esthetics' (Gilbert and Kuhn 1972, 5–6). '[Plotinus's] theory ... does not start as a theory of beauty, much less as a theory of art or poems. It is a theory of the world and God, of all being and all knowing, and only as an incident or an analogy does it find a place for art' (Wimsatt and Brooks 1970, I, 122–3).

24 Quoted in Ruthven 1979, 1.

25 ibid., 1.

26 Wellek 1981, I, 188 (quoting Herder).

27 Quoted in Butler 1994, 46.

28 Kermode 1971a, 241: 'Simone Weil explains the difference from destruction: decreation is not a change from the created to nothingness, but from the created to the uncreated. "Modern reality", commented [Wallace] Stevens, "is a reality of decreation, in which our revelations are not the revelations of belief".' Kermode then oddly describes decreation as 'a creative act like that of God'.

29 This second 'school ... takes [*The Waste Land*] to be ... an account of "the trials of a life in the process of becoming exemplary"' (Menand 1987, 91). Lyndall Gordon's *Eliot's Early Years*, for example, is influenced by her inspirational reading of *The Waste Land*.

30 Swinburne 1989, 23, 71.

31 Shelley 1971, 233–4.

32 Coleridge 1973, 367.

33 Fussell 1982, 226.

34 Fowler 1989, 75.

35 Rorty 1989, 94.

36 Eliot 1934a, 13.

37 Arnold 1888, 1–55.

38 Eliot 1964, 131.

39 ibid., 124, 131. Wyndham Lewis, whose view was akin to Eliot's on this critical point, was derisive of Eliot's theoretical posture: 'Mr Eliot is precluded on account of his role as theologian, from pointing out the common or garden foolishness of this salvation by poetry of ... Mr Richards ... For it is theologically a "deadly error": and so the fact that it is *absurd* sinks into insignificance' (Lewis 1987, 76–7; Russo 1989, 346–51).

40 Richards 1926, 235.

41 Eliot 1960, viii–x. Arnold's dictum 'poetry is at bottom a criticism of life' was 'useful as a protest against the view that literature is only an *amusement*' (Wellek 1981, iv, 164; my italics). In *The Use of Poetry*, Eliot described poetry as a 'mug's game' and defined the poet's proper ambition as seeking a part in society 'as worthy as that of a music-hall comedian' (Eliot 1964, 154). This 'mordant debunking of the poet's putative status as world legislator, prophet and saviour' derives its point

from its 'deflationary contrast to the over-lofty claims made for poetry since romanticism' (Shusterman 1988, 134).

42 Eliot 1964, 141. Eliot did not maintain this position consistently. Elsewhere in *The Use of Poetry*, 'we find occasional declarations of essentialism, that there is something special that is common to and permanent in all poetry' (Shusterman 1988, 79).

43 Krieger 1981, 36. All further quotations in this paragraph are from the same page.

44 Davie 1992, 201.

45 Arnold 1914, 64–5.

46 Buckley 1959, 32.

47 Reeves 1948, 42.

48 Moore 1948, 50.

49 Ricks's book was published in October 1988. A month later, Channel 4 broadcast a discussion between, among others, Ricks and Steiner on Eliot's anti-Semitism. It was on this occasion that Steiner referred to the two versions of the footnotes in *Notes*. In June 1989, Craig Raine, reviewing a book of essays by Chinua Achebe, took issue with Steiner's account of these footnotes. In a letter to the *London Review of Books* (22 June) responding to the review, Steiner extended to Eliot's prose his original criticism of the anti-Semitic 'ugliness' of some of Eliot's poetry. He commented of the first version of the footnote in *Notes* (on 'culture-contact' between Jews and Christians) that it 'only makes matters much *uglier*' (my italics).

50 Plimpton 1977, 353.

51 Of 'Beauty is truth': 'Dante': Eliot 1951, 270.

52 Hastings 1985, 29.

53 Blake 1988, 65. Cf.: 'Blake managed, in phrases of a peremptory simplicity, to reduce humanity to poetry and poetry to Evil' (Bataille 1985, 79).

54 Frye 1971, 127.

55 Cixous 1989, 7–8.

56 Bataille 1985, 197. Sade, for example, 'went as far as the imagination allows: there was nothing respectable which he did not mock, nothing pure which he did not soil, nothing joyful which he did not frighten' (ibid., 121). Similarly, Frederic Jameson, wrestling with the question of why one 'should be expected to find aesthetic pleasure' in Wyndham Lewis's work, whose 'impulses are often so ugly or ideologically offensive', detects merit in these impulses 'com[ing] before us ... released from the rationalizing censorship of a respectable consciousness intent on keeping up appearances' (1979, 20–1).

57 'If people find themselves thinking that Jews are swine who deserved what the Nazis did to them, then that is something for which they should be ashamed, not merely because of what it shows about them, but also for the sake of those who suffered under the Nazis; for in thinking what

they did they placed themselves in a concrete moral relation to them. If they said that it was, after all, *merely* a thought, they would betray their moral coarseness' (Gaita 1991, 319).

58 Rushdie 1992, 396.

59 Aristotle 1972, 4. Responding to the question 'Can the ugly, if represented in a way appropriate to it, be beautiful in art?', Plutarch argued that it remains ugly, but we take pleasure in it by reason of the intelligence involved in obtaining the likeness (Bosanquet 1949, 108; Gilbert and Kuhn 1972, 103). This position was later adopted by Addison, among others (Wimsatt and Brooks 1970, II, 255).

60 Hegel 1975, I, 44.

61 Matthiessen 1959, 97–8.

62 Quoted in Wellek 1983, IV, 443.

63 Watkins 1958, 25.

64 Quoted in Wellek 1981, II, 254.

65 Augustine 1972, 455–6.

66 Nietzsche 1967, 141.

67 Croce 1972, 79.

68 Kayser 1981, 105, 188 *passim*.

69 Broch 1984, 179–80.

70 Lewis 1987, 88–93, 115; Lewis 1989, 151. Lewis enlisted Eliot as a satirist, and thereby misrepresented him: 'Sweeney, the enigmatical Mrs Porter, Prufrock, Klipstein and Burbank, are authentic figures of Satire and nothing else' (Lewis 1987, 15).

71 Kenner 1985a, ch. 2, 63–80; see also Longenbach 1991, 41–66.

72 Quoted in McCormick 1988, 366.

73 Eliot 1988a, 363 (my italics). He was right. Even Riding and Graves (*A Survey of Modernist Poetry* ([1928] 1969, 235) describe 'Burbank' as 'humorous'.

74 Eliot 1988a, 363; in a letter to Mary Hutchinson, he described the poems as '*very serious!*' (ibid., 310).

75 Poe 1981, 184. Cf.: 'Nothing could be more traditional than this conception of Beauty as a female body: naked, immobile, and mute. Indeed, the beauty of female muteness and reification reaches its highest pitch when the woman in question is dead' (Johnson 1989, 124).

76 Empson 1984, 195–6.

77 Hegel, 1975, I, 434.

78 Wagner 1973, 27.

79 Kristeva 1982, 109.

80 Quoted in Wilson 1982, 489.

81 Syrus 1982, 39. This theme has a classical resonance: 'Sophocles has Philoctetes declare that when deprived of friends and of a polis, he became "a corpse among the living"' (MacIntyre 1988, 96).

82 Poliakov 1974–5, I, 185.

83 Tacitus 1975, 273–4.
84 Quoted in Poliakov 1985, IV, 7.
85 Bonfil 1988, 93.
86 Quoted in Poliakov 1974–5, III, 70.
87 Quoted in Dobkowski 1979, 9.
88 Quoted in Oberman 1984, 99.
89 Quoted in Trachtenberg 1983, 50.
90 Lewis 1939, 17, 54.
91 Dickens 1976, 107.
92 Fitzgerald 1973, 232.
93 Lewis 1980, 168.
94 Du Maurier 1895, 12.
95 Defoe 1976, 113.
96 Rosenberg 1970, 210.
97 Quoted in Zimmermann 1988, 249.
98 Poliakov 1974–5, I, 223.
99 Meinecke 1963, 15.
100 Joyce 1973a, 55–6.
101 'Une Saison En Enfer': Rimbaud 1962, 299.
102 Danto 1981.
103 Quoted in McCormick 1988, 308.
104 Joyce 1983, 6.
105 Sartre 1965, 49.
106 Cf.: Bate 1971, 10–11.
107 Schopenhauer 1966, I, 208.
108 'Philip Massinger': Eliot 1951, 206 (my italics). The essay first appeared in *The Sacred Wood*, the volume's title underlining the violence of Eliot's poetic-critical project. Watson (1962, 187–8) suggests that it comes from Frazer: 'In this sacred grove there grew a certain tree round which ... a grim figure might be seen to prowl ... He was a priest and a murderer: and the man for whom he was looking was sooner or later to murder him and hold the priesthood in his stead. Such was the rule of the sanctuary. A candidate for the priesthood could only succeed to office by slaying the priest, and having slain him, he retained office till he was himself slain' (Frazer 1987, 1). Eliot is the candidate, murderer, and thief.
109 'It has come to be practically a sort of rule in literature that a man, having once shown himself capable of original writing, is entitled thenceforth to steal from the writing of others at discretion' ('Shakespeare', quoted in Poirier 1988, 140).
110 Hardy 1970.
111 'The Metaphysical Poets': Eliot 1951, 289.
112 Ellmann 1987, 95, 101, 102.
113 Eliot 1971a, 121. 'It is worth noting, in view of Pound's subsequent [*sic*] anti-Semitic phase, that he opposed the introduction of Bleistein into

The Waste Land, writing "doubtful" under two emphatic question marks on the fair copy of these additional verses in Eliot's hand' (Levin 1981, 43–4). This begs the question: did Pound think the poem 'doubtful' because of its anti-Semitism? I doubt it. Ricks, unequivocal about Pound's anti-Semitism, merely records the jotting, reserving the scruples over publication to Eliot alone (Ricks 1988, 38–9).

114 Pole 1983, 219–31.
115 Lewis 1939, 110.
116 Douglas 1985, 35–6.
117 Quoted in Wilson 1982, 457.
118 Kipling 1987, 200.
119 Quoted in Holmes 1979, 217.
120 Quoted in Wilson 1982, 486.
121 Quoted in Holmes 1979, 17.
122 Lewis 1939, 34.
123 Quoted in Holmes 1979, 90–1.
124 Quoted in Byrnes 1950, 209.
125 Quoted in Litvinoff 1988, 310.
126 Marx 1975, 421–2.
127 Quoted in Litvinoff 1988, 441.
128 Wilson 1982, 153.
129 Douglas 1985, 40.
130 Wilson 1982, 486.
131 Quoted in Ricks 1988, 72.
132 Leavis 1967, 77. For an account of the part played by disgust in the fiction of the period, written from a somewhat different perspective to my own, see Trotter 1993, ch. 14.
133 Quoted in Rose 1992b, 77 (my italics).
134 Adams 1988, v, 276.
135 Quoted in Lears 1983, 275.
136 Eliot 1982, 68.
137 Mond was a vigorous litigant. In 1910 he sued his parliamentary opponent over allegations of mistreatment of his workforce (Searle 1987, 132). Shortly after the outbreak of World War I he sued over a letter addressing him as a 'German swine' (Goodman 1982, 97). Three months before the publication of 'A Cooking Egg', Mond sued on the libel that he had allotted shares to Germans during the war (Lebzelter 1978, 50–1; Holmes 1979, 144). Eliot flattered Mond in the *Criterion*. Disparaging H. G. Wells's praise of 'experts', he remarked: 'It is possible that Lord Melchett might be able to rule British industry entirely to its advantage.' But, added Eliot, this is not because he is an 'expert' but because he is 'the independent and intelligent Alfred Mond' (Eliot 1929a, 380).
138 Quoted in Poliakov 1985, IV, 191.
139 Quoted in Holmes 1979, 59. Karl Kraus juxtaposed satirically 'feudal

and Jewish-sounding titles', mocking the 'ennobled *nouveaux riches* from Jewish families' (Timms 1989, 350). The ennoblement of some Edwardian Jews greatly distressed anti-Semites. Belloc wrote a series of novels about a Jewish financier, I. Z. Barnett, 'the Peabody Yid', who is elevated to the peerage with the title of Lord Lambeth and who later becomes the Duke of Battersea. 'He is one of Belloc's most amusing creations' (Wilson 1986, 127). Like H. G. Wells's Sir Reuben Lichtenstein, Jews such as Klein 'were not so much a new British gentry as "pseudomorphous" after the gentry' (Wells 1973, 25).

140 Pound 1978a, 212.
141 See Washington 1993 *passim*.
142 ibid., 100.
143 Eliot 1969, 294.
144 Murray 1993, ch. 6.
145 Gibbon 1854, iv, 47.
146 Adams 1961, 341.
147 Bernal 1991, 337.
148 Wells 1991, 64, 59, 70, 116.
149 Quoted in Bernal 1991, 341.
150 Quoted in Rose 1992a, 238.
151 Joyce 1973a, 471.
152 Gilbert 1952, 86.
153 Joyce 1973b, 156.
154 Eliot 1971a, 123.
155 Cook 1986.
156 Joyce 1973a, 39.
157 Adorno 1986, 75.
158 Nabokov 1983, 251.

5. FREE-THINKING JEWS, PERSECUTED JEWS, AND THE ANTI-SEMITISM OF ELIOT'S PROSE

1 Eliot 1935a, 433.
2 Carlebach 1978, 322–3.
3 Pound 1940, 76.
4 'Some indications of Muslim perceptions of Jews and Judaism may be gathered from the ways in which these appear in certain common themes of Muslim discourse. One, frequently encountered in classical times, is the attribution of a Jewish origin or ancestry in order to discredit an individual, a group, a custom, or an idea' (Lewis 1984, 103).
5 'The Literature of Politics': Eliot 1978, 138.
6 Wilson 1967, 388.
7 Blake 1966, 502–3.
8 Eliot 1987, 259.
9 Mosse 1985, facing page 34. An article of mine on Eliot in *The Times*

(1988) prompted a reader to complain that, among those national and ethnic groups that attract hostility, only the Jews protested about their treatment: 'nobody sends for the police or the men in white coats for anti-Saxonism, anti-Frankism...' Only the Jews are protected, and 'unremittingly' protect themselves, from 'any expression of the foibles of the rest of humanity' (Smith 1988).

10 Eliot 1917b, 151. Eliot wrote to Pound about the Bodenheim family, 'being Semites I suppose they will survive somehow'. Eliot tried to help Bodenheim, who had failed in London literary society and then returned to America. Writing to his mother, Eliot described Bodenheim as 'an odd American Jew... rather pathetic, although foolish'. In a letter to Bodenheim following the latter's departure from England, the tone is kind and without condescension (Eliot 1988a, 384, 391, 431–2).

11 Moore 1987, 103–7.

12 Eliot 1988a, 400.

13 ibid., 184, 190.

14 'The Dry Salvages', v.

15 'Lancelot Andrewes': Eliot 1970, 19.

16 'Euripedes and Professor Murray': Eliot 1951, 75.

17 'Thoughts After Lambeth': ibid., 364, 370.

18 Eliot 1928d, 353. 'The superficiality of the Jewish parvenu in the realm of culture is a set theme in anti-Semitic discourse within psychoanalysis' (Gilman 1991, 197).

19 Eliot 1988a, 92.

20 Williams 1969, 32.

21 'Leur cérébralité, leur capacité d'assimiler les doctrines en gardant vis-à-vis d'elles une certain froideur' (De Man 1988, 45). For Barrès, Jewish 'reasoning was too clear, impersonal, like a bank account' (Wilson 1982, 611).

22 Quoted in Jansen 1988, 77.

23 Quoted in Mendes-Flohr and Reinharz 1980, 279.

24 Quoted in Almog 1988, 258.

25 Marlowe 1979, 9.

26 Quoted in Modras 1988, 189.

27 Pulzer 1964, 130, 249.

28 Quoted in Wilson 1982, 350. According to Weininger: 'Jews... lack deep-rooted and original ideas. The Jews are the essential unbelievers; not even believing in themselves. The Jew has no center. He is critical, not a critic. He is not merely a materialist; he doubts all and any truths. He is irreligious; indeed, his religion is not even a real religion' (Gilman 1991, 136).

29 Eliot 1927a. Eliot began his review: 'The figure of Spinoza has been almost more important in the last hundred years than the philosophy of Spinoza.' The 'modern Europe' which made a hero of Spinoza was, Eliot insisted throughout the interwar period, 'negative' (see, for

example, Eliot 1982, 47). On the importance of Spinoza to the Victorian moralists, see Baker 1975, 47, n. 44.

30 'The Possibility of a Poetic Drama': Eliot 1951, 66–7; in 'William Blake' Eliot linked Spinoza with Montaigne in possessing 'a peculiar honesty, which, in a world too frightened to be honest, is peculiarly terrifying': ibid., 317.

31 'The Metaphysical Poets': ibid., 287.

32 'The Perfect Critic': Eliot 1960, 15.

33 ibid., 14–15.

34 Eliot 1928c. In a letter to his mother (29 March 1919), Eliot wrote: 'I know a great many people, but there are many more who would like to know me, and I can remain isolated and detached' (Eliot 1988a, 280).

35 Introduction, Pieper 1952, 16–17.

36 Santayana 1987, 502. The view from which this remark derives was a commonplace. Compare Belloc: 'the European thing is essentially a Catholic thing, and ... European values would disappear with the disappearance of Catholicism' (quoted in Wilson 1986, 109). Spinoza was a problem for philosophically-minded anti-Semites. Weininger insisted that though the philosopher was 'incomparably the greatest Jew of the last nine hundred years', he lacked 'genius' (quoted in Gilman 1991, 134).

37 'Tradition and the Individual Talent': Eliot 1951, 16. On Spinoza's relation to Descartes, see Hampshire 1953, 62; on his intellectual debts, see Jaspers 1974, 111.

38 If one looks 'behind the geometrical method', one finds Spinoza's Jewish learning (Wolfson 1969, I, 12–13). Even in his attack on the notion of the Chosen People of Israel, Spinoza 'put himself in the line of the ancient Jewish free-thinkers' (Poliakov 1974–5, II, 273–4). Schopenhauer makes the same point in typically offensive fashion, asserting that 'Spinoza ... could not get rid of the Jews' (Schopenhauer 1966, II, 645).

39 Eliot 1989, 178–9.

40 Shklar 1984, 4. As with Spinoza, so with Blake. Unable or unwilling to acknowledge Spinoza's indebtedness to any tradition other that the one he himself valued, Eliot was similarly unregarding of Blake's indebtedness to the antinomian tradition (on which, see Thompson 1993 *passim*).

41 Forster 1965, 266.

42 Eliot 1934a, 13.

43 Eliot 1951, 13.

44 Eliot 1934a, 13.

45 ibid., 62. Pound dismissed *After Strange Gods* as Eliot's 'Heresy book' (Pound 1934c, 130). Cf.: 'The role of Jews in tempting or aiding Christians to become heretics was, according to canon law, the most justifiable reason for inquisitorial jurisdiction over them' (Cohen 1984, 91).

46 Coleridge 1972, 39–40.
47 Eliot 1934a, 21.
48 ibid., 30, 38.
49 Quoted in Ellmann 1959, 175.
50 Cowling 1980, 108.
51 When Eliot gave up hunting heretics, his use of the word was more relaxed: 'I question [Graham Greene's] orthodoxy – but correctness is a better word – in dealing with the issues' (Levy and Scherle 1969, 39). 'Heresy' always had a certain elasticity of meaning for him: 'a more satisfactory symbol or sign [of the German mind] ... would be Protestantism; and specifically Lutheran Protestantism. If we choose to go back further, we might discern simply a tendency to heresy. When I speak of these terms ... I am not directly concerned with religious beliefs ... I am speaking from a cultural or a sociological point of view' (Eliot 1945a, 167).
52 Eliot 1934a, 15. Fifteen years later, Eliot was still deprecating the 'stream of mixed immigration' into the United States after the Civil War (Eliot 1963a, 45).
53 Turner's celebration of the frontier was certain to antagonise Eliot: 'The frontier is the line of most rapid and effective Americanisation. The wilderness masters the colonist. It finds him a European in dress, industries, tools, modes of travel, and thought ... It strips him of the garments of civilisation ... It puts him in the log cabin ... and runs an Indian palisade around him ... Little by little he transforms the wilderness, but the outcome is not the old Europe ... here is a new product that is American ... the advance of the frontier has meant a steady movement away from the influence of Europe, a steady growth of independence on American lines' (quoted in Pierson 1968, 17).
54 '[T]he mobility and vitality which characterise the Children of Israel and make them objects of envy, scarcely offended a Christian majority which was evincing exactly the same qualities. In the nineteenth century, the American myth of the frontier seemed to be creating a new wandering people' (Poliakov 1974–5, III, 44).
55 Turner was wrong about frontier life. The pioneers of the West were settlers, not nomads, establishing patterns of mutual help, and communal endeavour. He neglected this collective dimension (Boatright 1968, 46). Eliot thus erred in dismissing the frontier, even on his own terms.
56 Eliot 1934a, 16.
57 ibid., 20.
58 ibid., 16.
59 Litvinoff 1988, 195.
60 Fitzgerald 1973, 232.
61 Quoted in Poliakov 1985, IV, 228; on the anti-Semitism of New York guidebooks and the 'New York novel', see Jaher 1994, 222–3, 236.
62 Quoted in Dobkowski 1979, 137. For southern anti-Semites, New York

'harbored all that was evil in American life. It was the centre of American liberalism and Harlem, as well as the home of large numbers of supposedly unassimilated immigrants, [and] of the major civil rights organisations... agrarian spokesmen... described cities in general, and New York in particular, as unnatural, parasitical, materialistic, pagan, alien and corrupt' (Shapiro 1987, 140–1).

63 Brooke 1931, 16.

64 Quoted in Howe 1976, 406.

65 Quoted in Redman 1991, 176–7.

66 Consider, in this context, these remarks of the novelist Katherine Anne Porter: 'I am an old American. My people came to Virginia in 1648, so we have had time to become acclimatized... we are people based in English as our mother tongue, and we do not abuse it or misuse it, and when we speak a word, we know what it means. These others have fallen into a curious kind of argot, more or less originating in New York, a deadly mixture of academic, guttersnipe, gangster, fake-yiddish, and dull old wornout dirty words – an appalling bankruptcy in language, as if they hate English and are trying to destroy it along with all other living things they touch' (quoted in Stern 1991, 294–5). 'These others'? Though the quotation does not make this altogether clear, it is not hard to see that by this phrase she intends Jews, and those tainted by Jews.

67 Eliot 1934a, 13.

68 Scruton 1980, 81.

69 Cowling 1980, xvii.

70 Nisbet 1982, 214.

71 For example: 'The modern State... starts from the basis of an authoritarian order, and the protest against that order... is the beginning of Liberalism. Thus Liberalism appears at first as a criticism, sometimes even as a destructive and revolutionary criticism. Its negative aspect is for centuries foremost' (Hobhouse [1911] 1964, 14).

72 Williams 1985, 237.

73 See, for example, Collini 1993, 346.

74 Rorty 1994, 109.

75 This has to be the case within Eliot's terms of reference. Outside those terms (where Eliot's authority is not invoked, and his work apparently not studied – though see Shils 1981), the sociology and history of 'invented traditions' flourishes: see the essays collected in Hobsbawm and Ranger 1984. America is particularly interesting in this context: 'The basic political problem of the U.S.A, once secession had been eliminated, was how to assimilate a heterogeneous mass... of people who were Americans not by birth but by immigration. Americans had to be made' (Hobsbawm 1984, 279).

76 Eliot 1934a, 53.

77 ibid., 54.

78 ibid., 48.

79 Valentin 1971, 62.
80 Quoted in Nolte 1969, 70.
81 Meinecke 1963, 15.
82 Acts 7:51.
83 Quoted in Poliakov 1974–5, III, 297.
84 Cash 1973, 342; cf. Dinnerstein 1994, ch. 9.
85 Coudenhove-Kalergi 1935, 244.
86 'The Humanism of Irving Babbitt': Eliot 1951, 473, 476. Praising the Elizabethan dramatists, and their audience, Eliot remarked on a 'homogeneity of race, of sense of humour and sense of right and wrong' (Eliot 1964, 52).
87 Eliot 1942, 115.
88 Eliot 1928c.
89 Taylor 1985, 149.
90 It is only by ignoring 'race' in Eliot's sentence that Brooks is able to propose that 'as far as [Eliot's] argument is concerned, *free-thinking* is the key phrase. Thus, even the ultra-conservative Old South got along with its God-fearing Jews very well' (Brooks 1988, 62–3).
91 Ginsberg 1993, 79; Dinnerstein 1994, 44–5.
92 Buckley 1992, 6.
93 Endelman 1990, 194–6.
94 Synnott 1987, 233–71. Research has shown that 'social club discrimination is [still] widely accepted, even among the least prejudiced third of the [American] population' (Selznick and Steinberg 1969, 184).
95 Katzberg 1988, 340.
96 Katz 1980, 55.
97 Berlin 1993, 126.
98 ibid., 52.
99 Quoted in Feldman 1994, 30.
100 Quoted in Poliakov 1974–5, I, 212.
101 Quoted in Poliakov 1985, IV, 69.
102 Quoted in Pulzer 1964, 228.
103 Quoted in Dinnerstein 1988, 317.
104 Higham 1975, 160.
105 Nicolson 1971, 50.
106 Ricks 1988, 42.
107 Eliot 1982, 63.
108 Robbins, whose outrage often leads him to overstate the case against Eliot, misreads the passage to include the proposing of restrictions on the number of pupils as well as staff (Robbins 1951, 19–20). This interpretation is made impossible by 'personnel' in the first sentence.
109 Eliot 1982, 74.
110 ibid., 42.
111 As early as 'The Function of Criticism' (1923), Eliot was attacking 'Whiggery' (Eliot 1951, 29). And on the outbreak of war, Eliot insisted

that 'either Germanism will win, or something that is neither Liberalism or Totalitarianism: Liberalism is not even a starter in this race' (Eliot 1939c).

112 Eliot 1982, 49.

113 ibid., 47.

114 ibid., 67.

115 ibid., 69–70.

116 Marrus 1985, 166.

117 Angell 1939, 11.

118 Plowman 1942, 225–6.

119 Eliot 1982, 73.

120 Eliot 1948a, 70.

121 Though the footnote does *not* propose 'that the Jews [had] some historical responsibility for the Holocaust' (Steiner 1988), it makes it impossible to assert 'the doom of the Jews under the Nazis transformed [Eliot's] literary suspicion into horror and compassion' (Kirk 1971, 211). Just after the war, Emilio Cecchi discussed with Eliot the death camps: 'Eliot wondered whether the gates of such hells ... can really be considered to be closed for ever. Or whether mankind, now capable of reaching such extremes of frightfulness, has a weaker resistance to new and infernal suggestions' (Cecchi 1948, 76). These musings derive from a generalised sense of human sinfulness and are appropriate to the poet of the *Four Quartets*. Eliot did not understand the Holocaust as an event in the history of anti-Semitism. Steiner wonders of *Notes*: 'How was it possible to ... plead for a Christian order when the Holocaust had put in question the very nature of Christianity and of its role in European history?' (Steiner 1978, 34). Yet Eliot would not have accepted the premiss of Steiner's question.

122 Curtius 1973, 72–3, and Simon 1986, 230.

123 Dubnow 1967–73, III, 672–6.

124 Glassman 1975, 110; Rosenstock-Huessy and Rosenzweig 1971.

125 Rappaport 1980, 134–49.

126 Maccoby 1982a *passim*.

127 Altmann 1973, 194–263.

128 Mendes-Flohr 1987, 156–9.

129 Ettinger 1976b, 11.

130 Maccoby 1982b, 149.

131 Rubenstein 1992, 14–15.

132 Husik 1973, 306–7.

133 Friedlander 1990, 89; Handelman 1991, 265.

134 Eliot 1928d, 352.

135 Herberg 1970, vi–vii.

136 Ausmus 1987, 139.

137 ibid., 67.

138 Eliot 1963a, 29–30.

139 Quoted in Wilson 1982, 589.
140 Casey 1991, 137. As a leader of Pamyat, the anti-Semitic Russian movement, was recently heard to remark, the practice of desecrating Jewish graves misses the essential target: 'You should take it not out on the dead, but on the living' (quoted in Selbourne 1993, 187). Wounding Jewish sensibilities, and violating their dead, is not enough. For an analysis of the 'profound offense' caused by the violation of a corpse, see Feinberg 1985, 54–7, 72–7, and 95.
141 Eliot 1936, 759–60. The book was reviewed more intelligently elsewhere. For example, in the *New English Weekly* (with which Eliot was closely associated), it was praised as 'a fully-documented account of what has happened, and is happening, in Germany, based mainly on German official documents, and reports and articles from the German Press. Some of the extracts are authenticated in the present writer's personal knowledge, and documents and papers in his own possession. The whole vile picture stands out clearly, and ought to be a poignant warning to the ... anti-Semite whither his doctrines and prejudices lead him' (Elwell-Sutton 1936, 6). This social credit journal was not a particular friend to the Jews. See also Sharf 1964, 76–7, summarising other reviews of the book, none of which adopted Eliot's line.
142 Stead 1986, 206.
143 Ricks 1988, 4, 226.
144 Bush 1985, 226 (the phrase is from 'Little Gidding', IV).
145 Kramnick and Sheerman 1993, 353.
146 *The Yellow Spot* 1936, 51.
147 ibid., 257.
148 ibid., 269–70.
149 ibid., 267–8.
150 Cf.: Casey 1988, 178; he celebrates Eliot's work for comprising 'a lesson in the enormous intellectual and moral effort that is required *really* to remember the dead'.
151 Quoted in Griffiths 1980, 71; see also Kushner 1994a, 40.
152 Quoted in Roberts 1994, 293.
153 Quoted in Griffiths 1980, 76–8.
154 Quoted in Roberts 1994, 302.
155 Kushner 1989, 80.
156 ibid., 139.
157 ibid., 158.
158 Wasserstein 1988, 178.
159 ibid., 351. Many people were impatient with 'the quantity of books depicting the plight of Jewish refugees' (Kushner 1989, 115). In its current form, this impatience leads to understatements of the significance of the Holocaust (see Dawidowicz 1981), and in the most aggravated version of that form, it amounts to a denial of the

Holocaust's historical reality (Seidel 1986; Vidal-Nacquet 1992; Lipstadt 1993).

160 Girard 1989, 9.
161 Eliot 1982, 137–9. All further quotations in this section are from the same source. For an instance of this journal's rather crass (but rare?) wartime anti-Semitism, see Kushner 1994b, 166.
162 Marrus and Paxton 1981, xii.
163 Bein 1990, 42.
164 Katz 1986, 7.
165 Langmuir 1990, 207.
166 Quoted in Cohn-Sherbok 1992, 26.
167 Quoted in Osborne 1993, 130.
168 Quoted in Simon 1986, 216.
169 Quoted in Polenberg 1989, 159.
170 Bauman 1991, 39.

6. MAKING AMENDS, MAKING AMENDMENTS

1 Quoted in Masson 1988, 148; on Jung and anti-Semitism, see Maidenbaum and Martin 1991 *passim*. He did not, or did not adequately, acknowledge the wrongs he had done; in a private conversation with Rabbi Leo Baeck after the war, he is reported to have said 'I slipped up' (ibid., 219, 224). This remark has assumed too great a significance for Jung's defenders (ibid., 256, 269) – comparable to the significance attached to Pound's conversation with Allen Ginsberg (which I examine later in this chapter). It was not public; it was not specific; it did not reflect the gravity of the offence.
2 Gaita 1991, 52, 58.
3 Heller 1993, 156.
4 Said 1994, 84.
5 Murphy and Hampton 1990, 26–9.
6 Arendt 1959, 217.
7 Eliot 1948b, 6.
8 Ibid., 8. The need for self-examination was an Eliot theme. In a letter written at the outbreak of war, he wrote: 'We cannot effectively denounce the enemy without understanding him; we cannot understand him unless we understand ourselves, and our own weaknesses and sins' (Eliot 1939b, 291).
9 Eliot 1971a, 117. But remorse is not enough: 'The idea of reparation is prominent in Homer... and the need for it, for gestures that compensate and heal, must surely be recognised in any society if the notion of holding oneself responsible is to have any content' (Williams 1993, 90).
10 Eliot 1971b, 210.
11 Eliot 1969, 337.

12 Spender 1975, 200.
13 Eliot 1920, 586.
14 Eliot 1969, 573.
15 Murphy and Hampton 1990, 17.
16 Booth 1988.
17 For example: 'T. S. Eliot would apologize for any distress he had caused amongst his Jewish readers' (Coren 1993, 213). No evidence is offered to support this statement.
18 Manea 1994, 104.
19 Kaplan 1989, 472–3. Twenty years earlier Maria Edgeworth published *Harrington* in response to a letter from an American Jew complaining about an anti-Semitic portrait in one of her novels. She described *Harrington* as an act of 'atonement' and 'reparation' (Ragussis 1989, 113).
20 Dickens 1976, 105.
21 Extracted from Wall 1970, 161. It has been misdescribed as a 'letter of apology', which it is not, or not simply (Rosenberg, 1960, 134).
22 Quoted in Naman 1980, 80. In 1868, at the request of the *Jewish Chronicle*, Dickens agreed to drop the story of the murder in *Oliver Twist* from his forthcoming public readings (Salbstein 1982, 208).
23 Belloc 1922, 135–6.
24 Modder 1960, 223. '[H]e at last made amends, not only by a personal contribution to a well-known Anglo-Jewish charity, but also by fashioning a benevolent Jew, Mr Riah' (Panitz 1981, 111); 'when Eliza David [sic] took him to task for maligning her race, he was genuinely contrite and strove to make amends with the character of Riah, a creature as impossibly good as Fagin was impossibly bad' (Trilling 1982, 71).
25 Philipson 1889, 96–7.
26 Dickens 1975, 579. This is Lizzie's declaration, which the novel endorses.
27 Quoted in Kaplan 1989, 472–3.
28 'Note on the Text': Dickens 1976, 28.
29 Torrey 1984, 106.
30 ibid., 154.
31 Putnam 1987, 158.
32 Kenner 1975, 465.
33 Kazin 1988, 48.
34 Canto LXXIV.
35 Quoted in Carpenter 1982, 617.
36 Pound 1960, 392.
37 Pound 1934b. This was part of an exchange with Eliot following Pound's review of *After Strange Gods* (Pound 1934a). Chace regards Pound's 'predilection for single and specific causes' as consistent with his anti-Semitism (Chace 1973, 81). William Carlos Williams called Pound 'a lazy animal in many ways' (O'Connor and Stone 1959, 9).

38 Lewis 1987, 57.

39 Guy Davenport visited Pound at St Elizabeth's: 'He talked as I suspected he would talk. And it was from Pound himself that I first saw how whacky the anti-Semitism was. It made no sense that I could see' (Davenport 1984, 174).

40 Pound 1978b, 242–3. Two sentences before, however, Pound writes that 'The red herring is scoundrel's device *and usurer's stand-by*' (my italics). That is, this device is most commonly used by the Jews. Pound's repudiation of anti-Semitism itself prompts an anti-Semitic smear.

41 Reck 1968, 146.

42 Heymann 1967, 256.

43 Plimpton 1977, 54. This is a familiar line, advanced, for example, by Belloc: 'There is not in the whole mass of my written books and articles ... a single line in which a Jew has been attacked as a Jew or in which the vast majority of their race, suffering and poor, has received, I will not say an insult from my pen, but anything which could be construed even as dislike' (quoted in Wilson 1986, 188).

44 Quoted in Heymann 1967, 265. Praise of Spinoza is supposed by some to save reputations: '[Heidegger] was able to tell his students and listeners in the summer term of 1936 that the work of Spinoza was not "Jewish philosophy" but a Cartesian philosophy (which was a courageous act at the time) ...' (Lacoue-Labarthe 1990, 48, and see also 134).

45 Quoted in Heymann 1967, 223. Pound was criticised for his anti-Semitism in the *New English Weekly*: 'In a six-cylinder fury, / Against excessive usury, / Ezra is attacking jewry; / he forgets the few – / Who've never known what penury / is, or smelt a Jew' (Duncan 1939, 252). Pound replied: 'Did I not coin the term "Aryo-kike" / to designate just those usurious Aryan bastards / whom, quo ante / Our eminent brother Dante / Had also found need to stigmatise' (Pound 1939, 292).

46 Ahearn 1987, 184.

47 Miles 1990, 403.

48 Ricks 1988, 54.

49 Tytell 1987, 337.

50 Pound 1973, 6.

51 Quoted in Ackroyd 1980, 105.

52 Quoted in Davie 1975, 10.

53 ibid., 11–12.

54 Lowell 1971, 119. In another version, 'Olga' replaces 'she' (Lowell 1984).

55 For example: 'There is no doubt that he said much which he subsequently regretted: "How mean thy hates / Fostered in falsity"' (Cookson 1985, 69). But contrast: '[the *Pisan Cantos*] are also remarkable in that they reflect no regret, no remorse, no self-doubt. When Pound cries "Pull down thy vanity", he is referring not to his own, but to the

vanity of his American captors' (Torrey 1984, 11); 'Pound on Vanity had been, as usual, a dramatic impersonation, a monologue in the style of a period' (Simpson 1975, 85).

56 Schwartz 1972, 447.

57 Davie 1975, 11–12.

58 Casillo 1988, 333. 'Drafts and Fragments' is 'an act of public contrition, a poetic last will and testament, that is very moving' (Leibowitz 1972, 475).

59 For example, John Harrison, who concludes his chapter on Pound by praising him for having the courage to admit that 'the principles by which [he]...lived and thought...are perhaps mistaken principles', notwithstanding that the chapter itself contains all the evidence necessary to refute precisely this sentimental proposition (Harrison 1967, 142).

60 'In Canto 113...[Pound] probably refers to the Jews, who gave the world (but themselves rejected) the idea of original sin, and whom Pound blames for man's pernicious fear of moral transgression and punishment' (Casillo 1988, 32). This is a Nietzschean doctrine; there is nothing, incidentally, 'suburban' about it. 'What is Jewish, what is Christian morality? Chance robbed of its innocence; misfortune dirtied by the concept "sin"'; 'The concept "Hell" will master even Rome' (Nietzsche 1972, 136, 181–2). Steiner has adopted this argument: 'Hitler's jibe that "conscience is a Jewish invention" provides a clue', he contends, to the Holocaust (Steiner 1978, 36). Pound gives all this a vulgar twist, proposing that sin was invented as an instrument of domination.

61 Lewis 1979, 79.

62 Lewis 1931, 42.

63 Meyers 1980, 177.

64 Quoted in Wagner 1957, 77.

65 Lewis 1981, 311–12. I ascribe to Lewis these opinions of Zagreus, one of the novel's characters. The novel mocks a number of such myths about Jews. For example, the ingenuous Dan Boleyn reflects: 'for it was known that [Jews] were the lowest of the low and very dirty' (ibid., 475). These musings define his fatuous naïveté.

66 Lewis 1929, 18.

67 Wagner 1957, 77.

68 Lewis 1986b, 69, 174.

69 For example: 'the Jews were the most moral nation the world has ever seen'; 'we so often describe Gentile villainies as "Jewish" that conscience obliges me to insert a caveat' (Lewis 1986a, 13, 209); '[anti-Semitism is] one of the City Man's substitutes for thought'; 'The Jews are an alibi for all the double-dealers, plotters and intriguers, fomenters of war, und so weiter. A useful tribe, they take the rap for everything' (Lewis 1983, 62).

70 Lewis 1983, 109.
71 Wyndham Lewis made the same point after the war: '[The Jews] certainly are maligned. They have their own advocates in plenty; I am only interested in justice' (ibid., 62).
72 Lewis 1939, 29.
73 Bridson 1972, 211–12, quoting Lewis 1931, 42. Meyers argues that Lewis 'recanted... in *The Jews: Are They Human?* and *The Hitler Cult*' (Meyers 1980, 192).
74 Brooks et al. 1985, 4, 7, 9.
75 Rapaport 1989, 360–2: 'Hegel on the Sublime' (de Man 1987, 139–53).
76 Derrida 1989, 225–6; Lehman 1991, 198–201. De Man misstated both the number and the nature of the articles, and he misrepresented his relation to the collaborationist Hendrik de Man, which was that of nephew, not son.
77 Chase 1989, 78.
78 Derrida 1989, 227, 229.
79 Wiener 1991, 18.
80 Hartman 1989, 18. But contrast Hartman at de Man's Memorial Service: 'his writings... have more of a personal stamp than we may presently see' (Brooks 1985, 7).
81 Quoted in Macdonald 1992, 165. This has been described as 'an astonishing – and morally sickening – attempt to prove that convenient silence and amnesia are really the most powerful provocation to, and demonstration of, real remembering, at the same time as confirming "the radical impossibility of witnessing" "the original" – i.e., the atrocity of Nazism' (Cunningham 1994, 70). In *Testimony*, Felman argues that (a) de Man's 'unspoken autobiographical story' testifies to 'the impossible confession of the Holocaust', and (b) Lanzmann's *Shoah* 'leads us... to a retrieval of the possibility of speaking and to a recovery and a return of the voice' (Felman and Laub 1992, xix). There is something deeply depressing about Felman's eagerness to honour *both* de Man *and* Lanzmann in such a context. Compare Lyotard on Heidegger's comparable silences: 'These silences cannot be interpreted as a kind of speech that, in what it "gives to be understood", is more generous than perennial talk... It is a mute silence that leads nothing be heard. A leaden silence' (1990, 52). That it is possible to combine moral scrupulousness with a high regard for de Man's achievement is demonstrated by – and in – de Graef 1993.
82 Hartman 1989, 20. 'Might it be that in order to "save" deconstruction one [i.e. Hartman] is reduced to resorting to language that ought to make any deconstructor blush?' (Mehlman 1989, 325).
83 De Man 1989, 17; cf.: 'De Man does not say enough: he does not explicate Heidegger's political attitude, he does not explicitly condemn it, and he does not confess and condemn his own commitment to a similar politics' (de Graef 1993, 124).

84 De Man 1989, 14.
85 De Man 1986a, xii. 'Literary History and Literary Modernity', a chapter in the book, has been read as 'full of references to a hidden past' (Wiener 1991, 6) and as evidencing a 'will to obliterate [that] past' (Hirsch 1991, 73).
86 De Man 1979, 279. Eliot similarly deprecated Rousseau's *Confessions* and its modern derivatives: 'Nowadays "confessions", of an insignificant sort, pour from the press; everyone "met son coeur à nu", or pretends to; "personalities" succeed one another in interest' ('Dante': Eliot 1951, 272).
87 De Man 1979, 280. This is an 'exemption of the self from guilt' (MacIntyre 1990, 212).
88 Leavis 1986, 125.
89 'To Criticize the Critic': Eliot 1978, 16.
90 Blackmur 1955, 163.
91 Quoted in Russo 1989, 275.
92 'Eliot will not allow ["Ode"] to be reprinted' (Smith 1956, 37). Edmund Wilson reportedly recalled 'that when Eliot was asked why he omitted "Ode" from all further collections, he replied, "An oversight"; obviously untrue, said Wilson' (Matthews 1974, 44).
93 'In the first version of "The Function of Criticism" I am referred to with a shudder as "a Mr. Bateson"; in the final version in *On Poetry and Poets* the offensive "a" has disappeared' (Bateson 1969, 5).
94 Romans 7: 19.
95 Dante 1994, 166.
96 Davidson 1969, 93.
97 Stevie Smith spotted a revision: 'In [*Murder in the Cathedral*] Mr Eliot uses this rendering, "on earth peace, good will toward men", but in the film script this becomes "peace on earth to men of good will", which is a limitation and shrinkage of charity, for all men need good will, and most of all those who do not have it' (Smith 1958, 174).
98 Hollander 1989, 141. There was a nineteenth-century precedent for this. Matthew Arnold dropped 'Empedocles on Etna' from his 1853 *Poems* because it failed to meet art's requirements: Arnold 1971, 306; Trilling 1974, 150.
99 Auden 1966, 15.
100 Tennyson, for example, 'ever sensitive to public criticism of his writing' (Cunningham 1994, 154), deleted the phrase 'the canker of peace' from the passage in 'Maud' about the start of the Crimean War.
101 Eliot 1988a, 498.
102 At one time Eliot was anxious for these poems to remain private. Sending the manuscript of *The Waste Land* to John Quinn, he wrote: 'Naturally, I hope that the portions which I have suppressed will never appear in print'; in an earlier letter to his patron, he wrote: 'I beg you

fervently to keep them to yourself and see that they are never printed' (quoted in Matthews 1974, 74).

103 Ricks 1988, 39–40.

104 Eliot 1963b, 204. '[Though Eliot] never actually recanted any of the obnoxious statements he made in [*After Strange Gods*], ... he did give the impression that he was rather sorry he had made them' (Matthews 1974, 113).

105 'To Criticize the Critic': Eliot 1978, 14 (my italics).

106 Wilson 1977, 548–9.

107 Moody 1980, 371.

108 Ellmann 1987, 35.

109 Shusterman 1988, 3.

110 Simpson 1975, 172.

111 Gardner 1980, 55.

112 Williams 1967, 148. He 'objected ... to [Harriet Monroe's] replacement by capitals of the lower-case letters he had used at the beginning of lines' (Symons 1987, 127). Cf.: 'I was wearing a navy blue beret (the real McCoy, made in France) and had already written my first poem in lower-case letters' (Richler 1994, 40).

113 Wagner 1957, 34, n. 7.

114 A piece of sophistry:

> the code is: a Jew is not a jew ... That is, 'jew' is associated with, is perhaps synonymous with, 'usurer', but not all Jews are usurers, so they are not jews. Likewise, usurers who are *not* racially or culturally Jews, financiers such as J. P. Morgan and the American 'patrician', August Belmont, are in fact 'jews'. The Rothschilds, favourite target of European anti-semitism, happen to be both. Most Jews, like most non-Jews, are victims of usura. This line of reasoning lies, for example, behind the first page of Canto 52, where we hear that the sins of 'a few big jews', 'real jews', cause the anti-semitic prejudice or 'vengeance' under which 'poor yitts' suffer (Kearns 1989, 105).

This silly argument, which refutes itself with 'poor yitts', is part of the pathology of Pound studies.

115 'Perhaps at some time in the future, though it is extremely unlikely, we'll be able to shed the lower case and embellish the new language with Caps. But for the moment cummings has the right idea' (Williams 1969, 267).

116 cummings 1988, 25.

117 ibid., 4. This *i* represents 'a casualness, a humility, a denial of the idea of personal immortality responsible for "I"' (Riding and Graves 1969, 60).

118 Pearson 1970, 88. Proposing that 'Eliot's Jew [is] ... another Leopold Bloom' is therefore misconceived (Smith 1956, 60). Eliot was not alone in using the lower case denigratively. Gertrude Stein's *The Autobiography*

of Alice B. Toklas refers to the 'few stray irish poets' who hung around Sylvia Beach's Paris bookshop (Fitch 1985, 127).

119 Matthews 1974, 163.

120 Moody 1980, 371.

121 Part I, 44.

122 Quoted in Wilson 1982, 458.

123 Cf.: 'He might have seen his error even as [*After Strange Gods*] was being published, for early in 1934 he drafted the scene which ends part I of *The Rock*, in which the totalitarian ideologies are satirised, and the Blackshirts chant anti-semitic abuse at the Chorus' (Moody 1980, 371). This assumes that Eliot would have seen the connection between Nazi policy towards the Jews and the anti-Semitic passage in his book. I think this is unlikely.

124 Eliot 1945b, 341.

125 'The Unity of European Culture': Eliot 1963a, 113, 123, 124.

126 See, for example, Handelman 1982, and Hartman and Budick 1986.

127 Poliakov 1974–5, III, 61, 67.

128 For example: Bentwich, *The Jews and a Changing Civilisation* (1934); Sachs, *Beauty and the Jew* (1937); Roth, *The Jewish Contribution to Civilisation* (1938); and Salomon, *The Jews of Britain* (1939). Stefan Zweig commented: 'I am aware that I incur the risk of being accused of Jewish pretentiousness when I emphasize the fact that so many of the Nobel prize winners have been Jews, but a Jew cannot, nowadays, afford to be squeamish' (Zweig 1937, 164). Listing Jewish Nobel laureates became standard in 1930s works seeking to counter anti-Semitism (for example, Valentin 1971 [1936], 206). The case for the continuing vitality of the Jewish people has to be made anew each generation: see, for example, Rabinowicz 1974, on Arnold Toynbee's characterisation of the Jews as a 'fossil of the Syriac civilisation'.

129 Mosse 1985, 105–8.

130 Preface: Weil 1987, viii. Lewis Golden, the Treasurer of the London Library and a sponsor of the T. S. Eliot Centenary Fund, thus rather missed the point when he wrote to *The Times* in Eliot's defence: 'In [*Notes*] he more than once mentions that our culture is based on the legacy of Greece, Rome and Israel. That is not surprising, for everyone knows of the profound respect Eliot had for Simone Weil' (Golden 1988).

131 Newman 1974, 127.

132 Gager 1985, 163–4.

133 Quoted in Rokéah 1988, 59.

134 Quoted in Hellmann 1982, 50–1.

135 Levinas 1990, 133. By 'Bible' Levinas means the Hebrew Scriptures.

136 Mendes-Flohr 1987, 150–4.

137 Bradley 1988, 317.

138 The super-Marcionite Pound objected to Eliot's poem 'The Cul-

tivation of Christmas Trees'. Eliot had 'abandon[ed]' the 'Muses' for 'Moses' (quoted in Langbaum 1987, 196). Pound thought Eliot soft on the Jews and insensitive to the malignancy of their influence. He 'grumbl[ed] that while his friend Henry Swabey had translated Lancelot Andrewes's Latin tracts against usury, Eliot had been interested only in Andrewes's sermons' (Reck 1968, 80).

139 Cf.: Newman 1974, 118, 248.
140 Levy and Scherle 1969, 39.
141 Eliot 1948b, 5.
142 Eliot 1932, 429.
143 Eliot 1951, 480.
144 ibid., 399.
145 ibid., 515.
146 Eliot 1939a.
147 Eliot 1982, 122.
148 'What Dante Means to Me': Eliot 1978, 128.
149 Yeats 1990, 301. Bush quotes these lines, but without drawing any express comparisons. He merely says that Eliot was 'deeply immersed' in Yeats's work (Bush 1985, 235; likewise Gardner 1980, 68).
150 '... the austerity of Mr Yeats's later verse on the whole, should compel the admiration of the least sympathetic. Though the tone is often of regret, sometimes of resignation: [quotes lines from "Vacillation"] and though Mr Yeats is still perhaps a little too much the weather-worn Triton among the streams, he has arrived at greatness against the greatest odds; if he has not arrived at a central and universal philosophy he has at least discarded, for the most part, the trifling and the eccentric, the provincial in time and place' (Eliot 1934a, 46–7).
151 Ricks 1988, 39–40. Ricks's gloss on these lines is a commonplace of Eliot apologetics: 'Eliot's sorrow at "the shame of motives late revealed"... probably reflects... remorse at having set down, in his early writings, phrases of prejudice' (Kirk 1971, 211); 'It may... be no excessive tolerance to apply to Eliot's earlier deprecations the splendid and moving lines in "Little Gidding"' (Unger 1961, 44). Even Simpson, in an otherwise clear-sighted account of Eliot's anti-Semitism, cannot resist the picture of the repentant sinner: 'For both [his reactionary politics and his anti-Semitism] he is still responsible – and he holds himself responsible. In "Little Gidding" he speaks of...', etc. (Simpson 1975, 158–9).
152 Baudelaire 1986, 53.
153 This correspondence is at the Harry Ransom Humanities Research Center, University of Texas at Austin. Ricks quotes from it, making a number of points about the letter similar to my own. However, for him it 'is not corroded with ill-will [although it is] not persuasive' (Ricks 1988, 44). I disagree. I believe it to be as hostile as the passage from *After Strange Gods* that it purports to defend.

154 Levinas 1989, 296.

155 Goodman 1976; Levine 1936.

156 For example, in late nineteenth-century France, 'the rootless, migrant wanderer par excellence in anti-Semitic and Nationalist writing was the Jew'. Barrès's novel *Les Déracinés* was an influential instance of this theme (Wilson 1982, 627).

157 Borden 1984, 28. And later, 'Unitarians and desynagogued Jews led liberal causes' (Updike 1990, 127).

158 Glazer 1972, 53, 101–2; Berlin 1989, 41, 65–7; on Unitarian anti-Semitism, however, see Jaher 1994, 214–15. The links between Judaism and Unitarianism redeem from eccentricity Empson's hunch about Eliot's anti-Semitism (Empson 1984, 197). He proposes that Eliot's rejection of his family's Unitarianism, and his hostility to his father, alchemised an anti-Semitism in which the substitution of 'Bleistein' for 'father' in 'Full fathom five your Bleistein lies' becomes significant. His parents' Unitarianism, in denying the doctrine of the incarnation, repudiated the mysterious and dogmatic part of a religion whose mysteries and dogmas were for Eliot its most central portion. Voltaire commented: 'When I see Christians cursing Jews, methinks I see children beating their fathers' (quoted in Poliakov 1974–5, III, 95). A practising psychoanalyst has observed:

> At some point in the course of analytic treatment almost all non-Jewish patients will manifest varying degrees of anti-Semitism ... These fear and hate reactions become directed toward the analyst in the process of transference ... During these anti-Semitic stages of analysis, the Jew who is hated and feared by the patient in the person of his analyst usually represents to him a deformed image of his father. (Loewenstein 1988, 38)

159 ·A year after publication Eliot wrote to Spender that the book was 'more interesting than his early work', although he was 'severe' with it, and added that he 'was not guiltless' of failing to 'read every scrap' of 'one's authors' (Spender 1978, 255).

160 Fiedler 1991, 11.

161 O'Connor and Stone, 1959, 44.

162 ibid., 45.

163 Eliot wrote to Leavis:

> I agree with you about Pound & the aridity of the Cantos, with the exception of at least one item and a few lines from at least one of the so-called Pisan Cantos where it seems to me also that a touch of humanity breaks through; I mean the lovely verse of 'Bow [*sic*] down thy vanity' and the reference to the Negro who knocked him up a table when he was in the cage at Pisa. And of course Pound's incomparable sense of rhythm carries a lot over. But I do find the Cantos, apart from that exceptional moment, quite arid and depressing. (quoted: Carpenter 1988, 912)

164 Ackroyd 1985, 297.

165 Kenner 1985b, 5.

166 Ackroyd 1985, 297. Another juror, Katherine Anne Porter, whose anti-Semitism was kept largely private, escaped similar attack only to experience it later, on publication of *Ship of Fools* (Givner 1982, 450). Solotaroff identifies the novel's repellent Jew as 'the stage Jew of the modern literary tradition whom other Christian writers of sensibility (among them T. S. Eliot) have dragged out of the ghetto to represent the vulgar and menacing dislocations of traditional order'. He follows this with a quotation from 'Gerontion' (Solotaroff 1970, 115).

167 Quoted in Ackroyd 1985, 297.

168 Davis 1949, 514. Edmund Wilson speculated at the time on Eliot's position on the affair: 'He will undoubtedly deplore Pound's language, but Eliot is anti-Semitic himself and was at one time inclined toward Fascism' (Wilson 1977, 485).

169 Tytell 1987, 302.

170 'With Pound ... the loyalty is not to dogmas of Fascism but to the poet's vision of a tragic disorder which lies far deeper in our lives and in our time' (Archibald MacLeish, quoted in Graff 1980, 175; cf.: 'the passage in Pound from the broadcasts to the cantos is a passage from betrayal to renewed fidelity': Lecercle 1990, 119). What would be, in prose, loyalty to Fascism instead becomes, in poetry, fidelity to a tragic vision. MacLeish contrasts the barbarous dogmas of prose with the transmuted visions of poetry. That which would be objectionable as dogma is transfigured by poetry into vision, and made innocent. What rightly we reject from the ideologue we must accept from the poet. The effect of this reasoning is to insist that those who complain about Fascism in Pound's poetry are wilfully blind. They tramp over the work in complaining boots instead of harvesting its meaning. It was left to the more robust Donald Davie, a few years later, to assert of Pound's poetry that 'the development from imagism in poetry to fascism in politics is clear and unbroken' ([1952] 1992, 86).

171 Eliot 1960, viii–x. Hartman is scathing about the 'practical criticism' derived from Eliot's characterisation of poetry: 'The student was... admonished to respect the mystery of [literary] texts... Literature was *not* politics, *not* religion, *not* philosophy, *not* science, *not* rhetoric, etc. These were real but extrinsic factors; instead an intrinsic approach to the mode of existence of the literary work of art had to be found ... Yet no theorist of the time was able to define the differentiating "nothing"' (Hartman 1980, 285). The 'not... not... not' echoes Eliot's string of negatives. Eliot's 'nothing' is, first, poetry as a 'superior amusement', and then, marking the abandonment of any attempt at definition, poetry as having 'in some sense, a life of its own', whatever that might mean.

172 Brinnin 1982, 269–71.

173 A certain willingness to ingratiate himself can be detected in his private correspondence, and perhaps explains the following exchange of letters

with Groucho Marx. The comedian wrote to Eliot telling him that he was planning to visit Israel in late 1963. Eliot responded: 'I envy you going to Israel and I wish I could go there too if the winter climate is good as I have a keen admiration for that country' (Marx 1969, 126).

174 See Ben-Shammai 1988; Grossman 1988.

175 Hyman rounds up the usual suspects: *After Strange Gods*, passages from the *Criterion* and elsewhere. He concludes that 'All of this adds up, not quite to fascism, but to a kind of tentative and embarrassed' – not 'embarrassing', as the reviewer, and then Eliot, writes – 'flirting with it' (Hyman 1955, 71–2).

176 Wagner 1957, 87–9.

177 Eliot 1929b, 690. This reviewed essays by Barnes (on Fascism) and Rowse (on Communism) that followed Eliot's 'The Literature of Fascism', which appeared in the *Criterion* the previous year. Eliot concluded: 'my chief purpose ... is to affirm my previous contention that neither fascism nor communism is new or revolutionary as *idea*' (ibid., 691). The vintage of Fascism was one of the least important, or interesting, of its challenges. This eccentricity of approach was one reason for Eliot's lack of influence on the political culture of the 1930s.

178 'I mentioned that colleagues and students of mine would from time to time ask me if Eliot was anti-Semitic, sometimes just assuming that he was. Eliot agreed completely with my way of handling such questions. First, by asking what evidence there was, and then by examining and evaluating the line of prose or verse which appeared to them to have such a connotation' (Levy and Scherle 1969, 81). Eliot could not get beyond the first stage. Wilson commented on the controversy in a letter to Van Wyck Brooks: 'Aiken tells me that Eliot has now made an ineffective rebuttal ... What is curious here is that Eliot should be so vague about himself' (Wilson 1977, 548).

179 The *TLS* debate ended with a letter from Albert Mordell, whose article had been cited by the reviewer:

> If Eliot says he was not a Fascist, I think we should take him at his word ... As a Jew, I was also pleased to learn that he disavowed the charge of anti-Semitism against him. I did not myself call him an anti-Semite, and I do not believe he was one even though he made some disparaging remarks here and there about Jews. Anti-Semitism means discrimination and even persecution. And of course Eliot does not believe in either. (Mordell 1957)

Yet six years earlier Mordell had written of *After Strange Gods* that Eliot had 'introduced the Hitler racial theory of the advantages of a homogeneous population' (Mordell 1951, 13).

180 The two poems were later published, along with others, by the Arts and Letters Committee of the National Council of Women in 1945 as *Poets' Choice: A Spoken Anthology*. The initial letter of 'jew' was printed in the lower case.

181 Sharf 1964, 179. On 17 December 1942, Eden announced to the House of Commons: 'the German authorities, not content with denying to persons of Jewish race in all the territories over which their barbarous rule has been extended the most elementary rights, are now carrying into effect Hitler's oft-repeated intention to exterminate the Jewish people in Europe.' Eden went on to identify the policy of forced transportation, the labour camps, and the mass executions of the infirm. He concluded: 'The number of victims of these bloody cruelties is reckoned in many hundreds of thousands' (quoted in Wasserstein 1988, 172–3).

182 Wasserstein 1988, 118.

183 *Poets' Choice*, 20; the poem was written in July 1940 (MacNeice 1979, 178–9).

184 Eliot's letter of rejection is in Crick 1980, 315. Crick suggests that 'it is a simplification to say that T. S. Eliot turned down *Animal Farm*. It was rejected by the firm, a different and not wholly consistent animal' (ibid., 316). Symons is more robust: 'during the war he did not flinch from the implication of accepting Stalin's Russia as an ally when he rejected *Animal Farm*' (Symons 1987, 251).

185 Calvocoressi and Wint 1979, 901–2.

186 Orwell 1970, III, 287. In 1945 he commented: 'Many English people have heard almost nothing about the extermination of German and Polish Jews during the present war. Their own antisemitism has caused this vast crime to bounce off their consciousness' (ibid., 420).

187 Nolte 1969, 88.

188 Of Maurras's election to the Academie Française: 'Of course I voted for him. One does not often have the chance to vote against the Republic, against the King, and against the Pope, all at one and the same time' (quoted in Weber 1962, 409; see also Zeldin 1973, II, 1148).

189 Hamilton 1971, 230–1.

190 Griffiths 1966, 309. Griffiths could be paraphrasing a programmatic and optimistic version of *After Strange Gods*: '[Maurras] saw the only solution ... to be a reversion to traditional national values; and he saw all exceptions to these values as dangerous to the country. The Jews, like the other "métèques", based their lives on other values and traditions and formed states within a state. Only by a restoration of the purity of the French race could France be saved.'

191 Babbitt mocked anti-Semitic paranoia: 'Mr Henry Ford would no doubt dismiss such utterances as part of the great Jewish plot to destroy Gentile civilisation. It was not a Jew, however, but Madame de Staël who declared ...' (Babbitt 1979, 27). Though he found Maurras 'romantically anti-romantic' (Weber 1962, 480), both men vigorously and repetitively condemned Rousseau for modernity's evils (Nolte 1969, 167; Nevin 1984, 43; Stromberg 1982, 101).

192 Ackroyd 1985, 76.

193 Tredell 1994, 345; in conversation with C. H. Sisson.
194 Eliot 1928b, 195–203. Writing to the *Church Times*, Eliot questioned 'whether the Christian and Catholic idea and the Fascist idea are ... compatible'. Though typically circumspect, he encouraged the inference that they were not (Eliot 1934c).
195 'The Humanism of Irving Babbitt': Eliot 1951, 480; Tomlin 1988, 46–7. In his 1916 Oxford University Extension Lectures, Eliot remarked of Maurras that his 'reaction fundamentally sound, but / Marked by extreme violence and intolerance' (quoted in Svarny 1988, 21).
196 Eliot 1982, 134–5. In 'To Criticize the Critic', Eliot divided his literary criticism into three periods. In the first, 'The influence of Babbitt (with an infusion later of T. E. Hulme and of the more literary essays of Charles Maurras) is apparent in my recurrent theme of Classicism versus Romanticism' (Eliot 1978, 17). Note the double limitation: only until 1918 (when his 'second period' began), and just the 'more literary' aspect of Maurras's work.
197 'The Literature of Politics': Eliot 1978, 142–3.
198 Birnbaum 1992, 237.
199 ibid., 248.
200 Eliot 1982, 134.
201 Ryan 1953.
202 Eliot 1953.
203 Abse 1974, 130–2; cf. Abse 1994, 179–81.

List of works cited

The date of publication given is that of the edition used, not the date of first publication. The place of publication is London, unless otherwise stated.

Abrams, M. H. (1991), *Doing Things with Texts* (New York: W. W. Norton).
Abse, Dannie (1974), *A Poet in the Family* (Hutchinson).
  (1994) *Intermittent Journals* (Bridgend: Seren).
Ackroyd, Peter (1980), *Ezra Pound and His World* (Thames & Hudson).
  (1985), *T. S. Eliot* (Abacus).
Adams, Henry (1961), *The Education of Henry Adams* (Boston: Houghton Mifflin).
  (1982; 1988), *Letters*, vols. I–VI, ed. J. C. Levenson *et al.* (Cambridge, MA: Belknap Press).
  (1986), *Mont Saint Michel and Chartres* (Penguin).
Adorno, Theodor (1986), *Aesthetic Theory* (Routledge & Kegan Paul).
  (1991), *In Search of Wagner* (Verso).
Ahearn, Barry, ed. (1987), *Pound/Zukofsky* (Faber & Faber).
Aldington, Richard (1967), 'Stepping Heavenward', in *Soft Answers* (Carbondale: Southern Illinois University Press).
Alexander, Edward (1991), *The Jewish Idea and Its Enemies* (New Brunswick: Transaction Publishers).
Alexander, Peter (1982), *Roy Campbell* (Oxford: Oxford University Press).
Almog, Shmuel (1988), 'The Racial Motif in Renan's Attitude to Jews and Judaism', in *Antisemitism Through the Ages*, ed. Shmuel Almog (Oxford: Pergamon).
Altmann, Alexander (1973), *Moses Mendelssohn* (Routledge & Kegan Paul).
Angell, Norman (1939), *You and the Refugee* (Penguin).
Arendt, Hannah (1959), *The Human Condition* (New York: Doubleday Anchor).
Aristotle (1972), 'On the Art of Poetry', in *Classical Literary Criticism* (Penguin).
Arnold, Matthew (1888), *Essays in Criticism: Second Series* (Macmillan).
  (1914), *Essays* (Oxford: Oxford University Press, 1914).
  (1969), *Poetical Works* (Oxford University Press, 1969).

(1971), 'Preface to *Poems* 1853', in *English Critical Texts*, ed. D. J. Enright and Ernst De Chickera (Oxford: Clarendon).

Asbury, B. A. (1988), 'Four Theologians', in *Remembering for the Future*, I–II and S. V. (Oxford: Pergamon).

Ashton, H. S. (1933), *The Jew at Bay* (Phillip Allan).

Asphodel (1989), 'A Pin in the Darkness', in *Generations of Memories*, Jewish Women in London Group (Women's Press).

Atlas, James (1977), *Delmore Schwartz* (New York: Farrar, Strauss & Giroux).

Auden, W. H. (1966), *Collected Shorter Poems 1927–1957* (Faber & Faber).
(1979), *Selected Poems* (Faber & Faber).

Augustine, St (1961), *Confessions* (Penguin).
(1972), *City of God* (Penguin).

Ausmus, Harry J. (1987), *Will Herberg* (Chapel Hill: University of North Carolina Press).

Austin, J. L. (1980), *How To Do Things With Words* (Oxford: Oxford University Press).

Babbitt, Irving (1979), *Democracy and Leadership* (Indianapolis: Liberty Classics).

Bailey, Ruth (1939), *A Dialogue on Modern Poetry* (Oxford University Press).

Bainbridge, Beryl (1991), *An Awfully Big Adventure* (Penguin).

Baker, William (1975), *George Eliot and Judaism* (Salzburg: Institüt fur Englische Spreche und Literatur, Universität Salzburg).

Baldick, Chris (1987), *The Social Mission of English Criticism 1848–1932* (Oxford: Clarendon).

Barthes, Roland (1977), *Writing Degree Zero* (New York: Hill & Wang).
(1990), *New Critical Essays* (Berkeley: University of California Press).

Bataille, Georges (1985), *Literature and Evil* (Marion Boyars).

Bate, W. Jackson (1971), *The Burden of the Past and the English Poet* (Chatto & Windus).

Bateson, F. W. (1969), 'Editorial Comment', *Essays in Criticism*, January.

Baudelaire, Charles (1986), *The Complete Verse* (Anvil Press Poetry).

Bauman, Zygmunt (1991), *Modernity and the Holocaust* (Polity).

Bedford, Sybille (1987), *Aldous Huxley* I–II (Paladin).

Bedient, Calvin (1986), *He Do The Police In Different Voices* (Chicago: University of Chicago Press).

Bein, Alex (1990), *The Jewish Question* (Associated Universities Press).

Belloc, Hilaire (1922), *The Jews* (Constable).

Benda, Julien (1929), *Belphegor* (Faber & Faber).

Ben-Shammai, Haggai (1988), 'Jew-Hatred in the Islamic Tradition and the Koranic Exegesis', in *Antisemitism Through the Ages*, ed. Shmuel Almog (Oxford: Pergamon).

Benstock, Shari (1987), *Women of the Left Bank* (Virago).

Bentwich, Norman (1934), *The Jews and a Changing Civilisation* (John Lane).

Bering, Dietz (1992), *The Stigma of Names* (Polity).

Berlin, George, L. (1989), *Defending the Faith* (New York, State University of New York Press).

Berlin, Isaiah (1993), *The Magus of the North* (John Murray).

Bernal, Martin (1991), *Black Athena* (Vintage).

Besant, Walter (1903), *East London* (Chatto & Windus).

Bickel, Alexander M. (1975), *The Morality of Consent* (New Haven, CT: Yale University Press).

Birnbaum, Pierre (1992), *Anti-Semitism in Modern France* (Oxford: Blackwell).

Blackmur, R. P. (1955), 'In the Hope of Straightening Things Out', in *The Lion and the Honeycomb* (New York: Harcourt Brace & World).

Blake, Robert (1966), *Disraeli* (Methuen).

Blake, William (1967), *Poetry and Prose*, ed. Geoffrey Keynes (Nonesuch Library).

(1988), *The Oxford Authors* (Oxford: Oxford University Press).

Blakeney, Michael (1985), *Australia and the Jewish Refugees 1933–1948* (Sydney: Croom Helm Australia).

Blanchot, Maurice (1993), *The Infinite Conversation* (Minneapolis: University of Minnesota Press).

Blau, Joseph L., and Baron, Salo W., eds. (1963), *The Jews of the United States 1790–1840*, 3 vols. (New York: Columbia University Press).

Bloom, Alexander (1986), *Prodigal Sons* (New York: Oxford University Press).

Bloom, Harold (1970), *Yeats* (New York: Oxford University Press).

(1976), *Poetry and Repression* (New Haven, CT: Yale University Press).

(1977), *Wallace Stevens* (Ithaca, NY: Cornell University Press).

(1982), *The Breaking of the Vessels* (Chicago: University of Chicago Press).

ed. (1985), *T. S. Eliot* (New York: Chelsea House).

ed. (1986), *T. S. Eliot's* The Waste Land (New York: Chelsea House).

(1988), *Poetics of Influence* (New Haven, CT: Henry R. Schwab).

(1989), *Ruin the Sacred Truths* (Cambridge, MA: Harvard University Press).

(1995) *The Western Canon* (Macmillan)

Boatright, Mody C. (1968), 'The Myth of Frontier Individualism', in *Turner and the Sociology of the Frontier*, ed. Richard Hofstadter and Seymour Martin Lipset (New York: Basic Books).

Bonfil, Robert (1988), 'The Devil and the Jews in the Christian Consciousness of the Middle Ages', in *Antisemitism Through the Ages*, ed. Shmuel Almog (Oxford: Pergamon).

Booth, Wayne C. (1988), *The Company We Keep* (Berkeley: University of California Press).

Borden, Morton (1984), *Jews, Turks, and Infidels* (Chapel Hill: University of North Carolina Press).

Bosanquet, Bernard (1949), *A History of Aesthetic* (Allen & Unwin).

Bradbrook, Muriel (1988), Letter, *The Times*, 13 August.

Bradley, F. H. (1988), *Ethical Studies* (Oxford: Clarendon).

Bredin, Jean-Denis (1987), *The Affair* (Sidgwick & Jackson).

Breslin, James E. B. (1985), *William Carlos Williams* (Chicago: University of Chicago Press).

Bridson, D. G. (1972), *The Filibuster* (Cassell).

Brinnin, John Malcolm (1982), *Sextet* (André Deutsch).

Bristow, Edward J. (1982), *Prostitution and Prejudice* (Oxford: Clarendon).

Broch, Hermann (1984), *Hugo von Hofmannsthal and His Time* (Chicago: University of Chicago Press).

Brooke, Rupert (1931), *Letters from America* (Sidgwick & Jackson).

Brooke-Rose, Christine (1971), *A ZBC of Ezra Pound* (Faber & Faber).

Brooks, Cleanth (1948), *Modern Poetry and the Tradition* (Editions Poetry London).

(1962), 'Irony as a Principle of Structure', in *Literary Opinion in America*, vol. II, ed. Morton Dauwen Zabel (New York: Harper Torchbooks).

(1968), *The Well-Wrought Urn* (University Paperbacks).

(1988), 'T. S. Eliot and the American South', in *T. S. Eliot: Essays from The Southern Review*, ed. James Olney (Oxford: Clarendon).

Brooks, Peter, *et al.*, eds. (1985), 'The Lesson of Paul de Man', *Yale French Studies*, 69 (New Haven, CT: Yale University Press).

Browning, Robert (1981), *The Poems* I–II, ed. J. Pettigrew (Penguin).

Buckley, Vincent (1959), *Poetry and Morality* (Chatto & Windus).

Buckley, William F. (1992), *In Search of Anti-Semitism* (New York: Continuum).

Burns, Michael (1992), *Dreyfus* (Harper Perennial).

Bush, Ronald (1985), *T. S. Eliot* (New York: Oxford University Press).

Butler, Christopher (1994), *Early Modernism* (Oxford: Clarendon).

Byrnes, Robert F. (1950), *Anti-Semitism in Modern France* (New Brunswick, NJ: Rutgers University Press).

Calvocoressi, Peter, and Wint, Guy (1979), *Total War* (Penguin).

Cameron, J. M. (1985), 'T. S. Eliot as a Political Writer', in *T. S. Eliot*, ed. Neville Braybrooke (Rupert Hart-Davis).

Carey, John (1992), *The Intellectuals and the Masses* (Faber & Faber).

Carlebach, Julius (1978), *Karl Marx and the Radical Critique of Judaism* (Routledge & Kegan Paul).

Carpenter, Humphrey (1982), *W. H. Auden* (Boston: Houghton Mifflin).

(1988), *A Serious Character: The Life of Ezra Pound* (Faber & Faber).

Casey, John (1988), 'Our Duty to the Dead', in *Conservative Thoughts*, ed. Roger Scruton (Claridge).

(1991), *Pagan Virtue* (Oxford: Clarendon).

Cash, W. J. (1973), *The Mind of the South* (Penguin).

Casillo, Robert (1988), *The Genealogy of Demons* (Evanston, IL: Northwestern University Press).

Cecchi, Emilio (1948), 'A Meeting With Eliot', in *T. S. Eliot*, compiled by Richard March and Tambimuttu (PL Editions Poetry).

Chace, William M. (1973), *The Political Identities of Ezra Pound and T. S. Eliot* (Stanford, CA: Stanford University Press).

Chase, Cynthia (1989), 'Trappings of an Education', in *Responses*, ed. Werner Hamacher *et al.* (Lincoln: University of Nebraska Press).

Chaucer, Geoffrey (1975), *The Prioress' Prologue and Tale*, ed. James Winny (Cambridge: Cambridge University Press).

Chesterton, G. K. (1940), *The End of the Armistice* (Sheed & Ward).

Chiari, Joseph (1956), *Symbolisme from Poe to Mallarmé* (Rockliff).

(1972), *T. S. Eliot: Poet and Dramatist* (Vision).

(1982), *T. S. Eliot* (Enitharmon).

Christ, Carol T. (1984), *Victorian and Modern Poetics* (Chicago: University of Chicago Press).

(1991), 'Gender, Voice and Figuration in Eliot's Early Poetry', in *T. S. Eliot*, ed. Ronald Bush (Cambridge: Cambridge University Press).

Cixous, Hélène (1989), 'The Scene of the Unconscious', in *The Future of Literary Theory*, ed. Ralph Cohen (New York: Routledge).

Coetzee, J. M. (1988), *White Writing* (New Haven, CT: Yale University Press).

Coghill, Nevill (1948), 'Sweeney Agonistes', in *T. S. Eliot*, compiled by Richard March and Tambimuttu (PL Editions Poetry).

Cohen, Derek (1991), 'Shylock and the Idea of the Jew', in *Shylock*, ed. Harold Bloom (New York: Chelsea House).

Cohen, Jeremy (1984), *The Friars and the Jews* (Ithaca, NY: Cornell University Press).

(1991), 'Traditional Prejudice and Religious Reform: The Theological and Historical Foundations of Luther's Anti-Judaism', in *Anti-Semitism in Times of Crisis*, ed. Sander Gilman and Steven T. Katz (New York: New York University Press).

Cohen, Naomi (1984), *Encounter with Emancipation* (Philadelphia: Jewish Publication Society).

Cohn, Norman (1967), *Warrant for Genocide* (Eyre & Spottiswoode).

Cohn-Sherbok, Dan (1992), *The Crucified Jew* (Fount).

Coleridge, Samuel Taylor (1972), *On the Constitution of the Church and State* (J. M. Dent).

(1973), *Poetical Works*, ed. E. H. Coleridge (Oxford: Oxford University Press).

Collingwood, R. G. (1965), *The Principles of Art* (Oxford: Oxford University Press).

Collini, Stefan (1993), *Public Moralists* (Oxford: Clarendon).

Cook, Eleanor (1986), 'T. S. Eliot and the Carthaginian Peace', in *T. S. Eliot's* The Waste Land, ed. Harold Bloom (New York: Chelsea House).

Cookson, William (1985), *A Guide to the Cantos of Ezra Pound* (Croom Helm).

Coote, Stephen (1993), *The Penguin Short History of English Literature* (Penguin).

Coren, Michael (1993), *The Invisible Man* (Bloomsbury).

Coudenhove-Kalergi, Heinrich (1935), *Anti-Semitism Throughout the Ages* (Hutchinson).

Cowling, Maurice (1980), *Religion and Public Doctrine in Modern England* (Cambridge: Cambridge University Press).

Crawford, Robert (1987), *The Savage and the City in the Work of T. S. Eliot* (Oxford: Clarendon).

Crick, Bernard (1980), *George Orwell* (Secker & Warburg).

Croce, Benedetto (1972), *Aesthetic* (Peter Owen).

Culler, Jonathan (1975), *Structuralist Poetics* (Routledge & Kegan Paul).

Cullingford, Elizabeth (1981), *Yeats, Ireland, and Fascism* (Macmillan).

Cumberland, Richard (1795), *The Jew* (C. Dilly).

cummings, e.e. (1988), *selected poems 1923–1958* (Faber & Faber).

Cunningham, Valentine (1994), *In the Reading Gaol* (Oxford: Blackwell).

Curtius, Ernst Robert (1973), *European Literature and the Latin Middle Ages* (Princeton, NJ: Princeton University Press).

Damon, S. Foster (1973), *A Blake Dictionary* (Thames & Hudson).

Dante (1994), *Hell* (Chatto & Windus).

Danto, Arthur C. (1981), *The Transfiguration of the Commonplace* (Cambridge, MA: Harvard University Press).

 (1986), *The Philosophical Disenfranchisement of Art* (New York: Columbia University Press).

Davenport, Guy (1984), *The Geography of the Imagination* (Pan).

Davidson, Donald (1969), 'How is Weakness of the Will Possible?', in *Moral Concepts*, ed. Joel Feinberg (Oxford: Oxford University Press).

Davie, Donald (1970), 'Eliot and Pound: A Distinction', in *Eliot in Perspective*, ed. Graham Martin (Macmillan).

 (1975), *Pound* (Fontana/Collins).

 (1977), *The Poet in the Imaginary Museum* (New York: Persea).

 (1992), *Purity of Diction in English Verse and Articulate Energy* (Penguin).

Davis, Robert Gorham (1949), 'The Question of the Pound Award', *Partisan Review*, May.

Dawidowicz, Lucy S. (1981), *The Holocaust and the Historians* (Cambridge, MA: Harvard University Press).

De Beauvoir, Simone (1975), *The Second Sex* (Penguin).

Defoe, Daniel (1976), *Roxana* (Oxford University Press).

De Graef, Ortwin (1993), *Serenity in Crisis: A Preface to Paul de Man 1939–1960* (Lincoln: University of Nebraska Press).

Delaney, Paul (1988), *The Neo-Pagans* (Hamish Hamilton).

De Man, Paul (1979), *Allegories of Reading* (New Haven, CT: Yale University Press).

 (1986a), *Blindness and Insight*, 2nd edn (Methuen).

 (1986b), *The Resistance to Theory* (Minneapolis: University of Minnesota Press).

 (1987), 'Hegel on the Sublime', in *Displacement*, ed. Mark Krupnick (Bloomington: Indiana University Press).

(1988), *Wartime Journalism, 1939–1943*, ed. Werner Hamacher *et al.* (Lincoln: University of Nebraska Press).

(1989), *Critical Writings 1953–1978* (Minneapolis: University of Minnesota Press).

De Rachewiltz, Mary (1971), *Discretions* (Faber & Faber).

Derrida, Jacques (1978), *Writing and Difference* (Routledge & Kegan Paul).

(1989), *Memoires for Paul de Man*, revised edition (New York: Columbia University Press).

Dickens, Charles (1975), *Our Mutual Friend* (Penguin).

(1976), *Oliver Twist* (Penguin).

Dijkstra, Bram (1986), *Idols of Perversity* (New York: Oxford University Press).

Dinnerstein, Leonard (1987), *Uneasy at Home* (New York: Columbia University Press).

(1988), 'Antisemitism in the United States 1918–1945', in *Remembering for the Future*, I–II and S. V. (Oxford: Pergamon).

(1991), 'Antisemitism in Crisis Times in the United States: The 1920s and 1930s', in *Anti-Semitism in Times of Crisis*, ed. Sander Gilman and Steven T. Katz (New York: New York University Press).

(1994), *Antisemitism in America* (New York: Oxford University Press).

Dinwiddy, Hugh (1958), 'Reading T. S. Eliot with Schoolboys', in *T. S. Eliot*, ed. Neville Braybrooke (Rupert Hart-Davis).

Dobkowski, Michael N. (1979), *The Tarnished Dream* (Westport: Greenwood Press).

Donoghue, Denis (1989), 'The Idea of a Christian Society', *Yale Review*, September.

(1994), *The Old Moderns* (New York: Knopf).

Dostoievsky, Feodor (1985), *The Diary of a Writer* (Salt Lake City, UH: Gibbs M. Smith).

Douglas, Mary (1985), *Purity and Danger* (Ark).

Douglass, Paul (1986), *Bergson, Eliot & American Literature* (Lexington: University Press of Kentucky).

Drew, Elizabeth (1949), *T. S. Eliot* (New York: Scribner's).

Dubnow, Simon (1967–73), *History of the Jews*, I–V (South Brunswick: Yoseloff).

Du Maurier, George (1895), *Trilby* (Osgood/McIlvaine).

(1947), *Novels* (Pilot).

Duncan, Ronald (1939), 'Poem', *New English Weekly*, 2 February.

Eagleton, Terry (1983), *Literary Theory* (Oxford: Blackwell).

Edel, Leon (1981), *Bloomsbury* (Penguin).

Edelmann, R. (1986), 'Ahasuerus, the Wandering Jew: Origin and Background', in *The Wandering Jew*, ed. Galit Hasan-Rokem and Alan Dundes (Bloomington: Indiana University Press).

Edgeworth, Maria (1817), *Harrington and Ormond: Tales*, I–III (R. Hunter; Baldwin, Craddock & Joy).

Eliot, George (1967), *Daniel Deronda* (Penguin).
Eliot, T. S. (1917a), 'Eeldrop and Appleplex', *Little Review*, May and September.
  (1917b), 'Reflections on Contemporary Poetry', *Egoist*, November.
  (1918), 'Studies in Contemporary Criticism', *Egoist*, October.
  (1920), 'The Second-Order Mind', *Dial*, December.
  (1926), 'The Idea of a Literary Review', *Criterion*, January.
  (1927a), Review, *Times Literary Supplement*, 21 April.
  (1927b), 'A Commentary', *Monthly Criterion*, September.
  (1928a), 'Isolated Superiority', *Dial*, January.
  (1928b), 'The Action Française, M. Maurras and Mr Ward', *Criterion*, March.
  (1928c), 'The Idealism of Julien Benda', *Cambridge Review*, 6 June.
  (1928d), Review of *The Future of an Illusion*, *Criterion*, December.
  (1929a), 'A Commentary', *Criterion*, April.
  (1929b), 'Mr Barnes and Mr Rowse', *Criterion*, July.
  (1932), 'Religion and Science: A Phantom Dilemma', *Listener*, 23 March.
  (1934a), *After Strange Gods* (Faber & Faber).
  (1934b), *The Rock* (Faber & Faber).
  (1934c), Letter, *The Church Times*, 2 February.
  (1935a), 'A Commentary', *Criterion*, April.
  (1935b), 'A Commentary', *Criterion*, July.
  (1935c), 'Notes on the Way', *Time and Tide*, 5 January.
  (1936), Review of *The Yellow Spot*, *Criterion*, July.
  (1939a), 'On Reading Official Reports', *New English Weekly*, 11 May.
  (1939b), Letter, *New English Weekly*, 14 September.
  (1939c), 'A Commentary', *New English Weekly*, 5 October.
  (1942), 'A Letter to the Editors', *Partisan Review*, March–April.
  (1945a), Letter, *New English Weekly*, 8 March.
  (1945b), 'The Man of Letters and the Future of Europe', *Sewanee Review*, July–September.
  (1948a), *Notes Towards the Definition of Culture*, 1st edn (Faber & Faber).
  (1948b), *A Sermon Preached in Magdalene College Chapel* (Cambridge: Cambridge University Press).
  (1951), *Selected Essays* (Faber & Faber).
  (1953), Letter, *Time and Tide*, 17 January.
  (1957a), Letter, *Times Literary Supplement*, 9 August.
  (1957b), Letter, *Times Literary Supplement*, 23 August.
  (1957c), Letter, *Times Literary Supplement*, 13 September.
  (1960), *The Sacred Wood* (Methuen).
  (1962), 'Poetry and Propaganda', *Literary Opinion in America*, vol. 1, ed. Morton Dauwen Zabel (New York: Harper Torchbooks).
  (1963a), *Notes Towards the Definition of Culture*, 2nd edn (Faber & Faber).
  (1963b), *Selected Prose*, ed. John Hayward (Penguin, 1963).
  (1964), *The Use of Poetry and the Use of Criticism*, 2nd edn (Faber & Faber).
  (1969), *The Complete Poems and Plays of T. S. Eliot* (Faber & Faber).

(1970), *For Lancelot Andrewes* (Faber & Faber).

(1971a), '*The Waste Land*': *A Facsimile and Transcript*, ed. Valerie Eliot (Faber & Faber).

(1971b), *On Poetry and Poets* (Faber & Faber).

(1978), *To Criticize the Critic* (Faber & Faber).

(1982), *The Idea of a Christian Society and Other Writings* (Faber & Faber).

ed. (1987), *A Choice of Kipling's Verse* (Faber & Faber).

(1988a), *The Letters of T. S. Eliot*, vol. i, ed. Valerie Eliot (Faber & Faber).

(1988b), *Collected Poems 1909–1962* (San Diego: Harcourt Brace Jovano-vich).

(1988c), *Selected Poems* (San Diego: Harcourt Brace Jovanovich).

(1989), 'The Development of Leibniz' Monadism', *Monist* (October 1916); Appendix 1, *Knowledge and Experience in the Philosophy of F. H. Bradley* (New York: Columbia University Press).

(1990), 'Columbiad: Two Stanzos', in *The Faber Book of Blue Verse*, ed. John Whitworth (Faber & Faber).

Ellmann, Maud (1987), *The Poetics of Impersonality* (Brighton: Harvester).

Ellmann, Richard (1959), *James Joyce* (Oxford: Oxford University Press).

(1989), *a long the riverrun* (Penguin).

Elwell-Sutton, A. S. (1936), 'Anti-Semitism', *New English Weekly*, 16 April.

Emerson, Thomas I. (1970), *The System of Freedom of Expression* (New York: Vintage).

Empson, William (1969), *The Structure of Complex Words* (Chatto & Windus).

(1984), *Using Biography* (Chatto & Windus).

Endelman, Todd M. (1987), 'Conversion as a Response to Antisemitism', in *Living with Antisemitism*, ed. Jehuda Reinharz (Hanover: University Press of New England).

(1990), *Radical Assimilation in English Jewish History 1656–1945* (Blooming-ton: Indiana University Press).

Ettinger, S. (1976a), 'The Modern Period', in *A History of the Jewish People*, ed. H. H. Ben-Sasson (Cambridge, MA: Harvard University Press).

(1976b), 'The Origins of Modern Anti-Semitism', in *The Catastrophe of European Jewry*, ed. Y. Gutman and L. Rothkirchen (Jerusalem: Yad Vashem).

Ewart, Gavin (1989), *Penultimate Poems* (Hutchinson).

Fackenheim, Emil L. (1980), *Encounters Between Judaism and Modern Philosophy* (New York: Schocken).

Feinberg, Joel (1985), *Offense to Others* (Oxford: Oxford University Press).

Feldman, David (1994), *Englishmen and Jews* (New Haven, CT: Yale University Press).

Felman, Shoshana, and Laub Dori, M. D. (1992), *Testimony* (Routledge).

Fiedler, Leslie (1991), *Fiedler on the Roof* (Boston: David R. Godine).

Figes, Eva (1978), *Patriarchal Attitudes* (Virago).

Finkielkraut, Alain (1994), *The Imaginary Jew* (Lincoln: University of Nebraska Press).

Fitch, Noel Riley (1985), *Sylvia Beach and the Lost Generation* (Penguin).

Fitzgerald, F. Scott (1973), *The Beautiful and the Damned* (Penguin).

Fitzgerald, Robert (1985), *Enlarging the Change* (Boston: Northeastern University Press).

Flesch, William (1989), 'Ancestral Voices', in *Wartime Journalism 1939–1943*, ed. Werner Hamacher *et al.* (Lincoln: University of Nebraska Press).

Forster, E. M. (1965), *Two Cheers for Democracy* (Penguin).

Fowler, Alastair (1985), *Kinds of Literature* (Oxford: Oxford University Press).

(1989), *A History of English Literature* (Oxford: Basil Blackwell).

Frazer, J. G. (1987), *The Golden Bough*, abbreviated edn (Macmillan).

Freud, Sigmund (1977), *Case Histories*, vol. I (Penguin).

Freund, Elizabeth (1987), *The Return of the Reader* (Methuen).

Frey, Robert Seitz (1988), 'The Holocaust and the Suffering of God', in *Remembering for the Future*, I–II and S. V. (Oxford: Pergamon).

Friedlander, Judith (1990), *Vilna on the Seine* (New Haven, CT: Yale University Press).

Fromm, Harold (1991), *Academic Capitalism and Literary Value* (Athens: University of Georgia Press).

Frye, Northrop (1971), *Anatomy of Criticism* (Princeton, NJ: Princeton University Press).

Furbank, P. N. (1979), *E. M. Forster*, vols. I–II (Oxford: Oxford University Press).

Fussell, Paul (1982), *Abroad* (Oxford: Oxford University Press).

Fyvel, Tosco (1983), *George Orwell* (Hutchinson).

Gager, John G. (1985), *The Origins of Anti-Semitism* (New York: Oxford University Press).

Gaita, Raimond (1991), *Good and Evil* (Macmillan).

Gardner, Helen (1980), *The Composition of Four Quartets* (Faber & Faber).

(1985), *The Art of T. S. Eliot*, 3rd edn (Faber & Faber).

Gartner, Lloyd P. (1988), 'The Two Continuities of Antisemitism in the United States', in *Antisemitism Through the Ages*, ed. Shmuel Almog (Oxford: Pergamon).

Gay, Peter (1978), *Freud, Jews, and Other Germans* (New York: Oxford University Press).

(1987), *A Godless Jew* (New Haven, CT: Yale University Press).

Gelpi, Albert (1990), *A Coherent Splendor* (Cambridge: Cambridge University Press).

Gibbon, Edward (1854), *The History of the Decline and Fall of the Roman Empire*, vols. I–VII (Henry G. Bohn).

Gilbert, Katherine Everett, and Kuhn, Helmut (1972), *A History of Esthetics* (New York: Dover).

Gilbert, Martin (1987), *The Holocaust* (Fontana).

Gilbert, Sandra M., and Gubar, Susan (1987; 1988), *No Man's Land*, vols. I–II (New Haven, CT: Yale University Press).

Gilbert, Stuart (1952), *James Joyce's 'Ulysses'* (Faber & Faber).

Gilman, Sander L. (1985), *Difference and Pathology* (Ithaca, NY: Cornell University Press).

(1986), *Jewish Self-Hatred* (Baltimore: Johns Hopkins University Press).

(1991), *The Jew's Body* (Routledge).

(1993), *Freud, Race, and Gender* (Princeton, NJ: Princeton University Press).

Ginsberg, Benjamin (1993), *The Fatal Embrace* (Chicago: University of Chicago Press).

Girard, René (1989), *The Scapegoat* (Baltimore: Johns Hopkins University Press).

Givner, Joan (1982), *Katherine Anne Porter* (New York: Simon & Schuster).

Glanz, Rudolf (1970), 'Jewish Names in Early American Humour', in *Studies in Judaica Americana* (New York: Ktav).

Glaser, Hermann (1978), *The Cultural Roots of National Socialism* (Croom Helm).

Glassman, Bernard (1975), *Anti-Semitic Stereotypes Without Jews* (Detroit, MI: Wayne State University Press).

Glazer, Nathan (1972), *American Judaism* (Chicago: University of Chicago Press).

Glossop, Reginald (1923), *The Jewess of Hull* (Odhams).

Goldberg, David Theo (1993), *Racist Culture* (Oxford: Blackwell).

Golden, Lewis (1988), Letter, *The Times*, 11 August.

Gombrich, E. H. (1984), *Tributes* (Oxford: Phaidon).

Goodman, Jean (1982), *The Mond Legacy* (Weidenfeld & Nicolson).

Goodman, Saul L., ed. (1976), *The Faith of Secular Jews* (New York: Ktav).

Gordon, Lyndall (1978), *Eliot's Early Years* (Oxford: Oxford University Press).

(1985), 'T. S. Eliot', in *The Craft of Literary Biography*, ed. Jeffrey Meyers (Macmillan).

Graff, Gerald (1979), *Literature Against Itself* (Chicago: University of Chicago Press).

(1980), *Poetic Statement and Critical Dogma* (Chicago: University of Chicago Press).

(1987), *Professing Literature* (Chicago: University of Chicago Press).

Graham, Desmond (1988), *Keith Douglas* (Oxford: Oxford University Press).

Grant, Michael, ed. (1982), *T. S. Eliot: The Critical Heritage*, vols. I–II (Routledge & Kegan Paul).

Greenberg, Clement (1949), 'The Question of the Pound Award', *Partisan Review*, May.

Greenblatt, Stephen J. (1992), 'Marlowe, Marx, and Anti-Semitism', *Learning to Curse* (Routledge & Kegan Paul).

Griffiths, Eric (1989), *The Printed Voice of Victorian Poetry* (Oxford: Clarendon).

Griffiths, Richard (1966), *The Reactionary Revolution* (Constable).

(1980), *Fellow Travellers of the Right* (Constable).

Gross, Harvey (1968), *Sound and Form in Modern Poetry* (Ann Arbor: University of Michigan Press).

Gross, John (1992), *Shylock* (Chatto & Windus).

Grosser, Paul E., and Halperin, Edward G. (1979), *Anti-Semitism* (Secaucus: Citadel).

Grossman, Avraham (1988), 'The Economic and Social Background of Hostile Attitudes Toward the Jews in the Ninth and Tenth Century Muslim Caliphate', in *Antisemitism Through the Ages*, ed. Shmuel Almog (Oxford: Pergamon).

Hamilton, Alastair (1971), *The Appeal of Fascism* (Anthony Blond).

Hampshire, Stuart (1953), *Spinoza* (Penguin).

Handelman, Susan A. (1982), *The Slayers of Moses* (Albany: State University of New York Press).

(1991), *Fragments of Redemption* (Bloomington: Indiana University Press).

Hanks, Patrick, and Hodges, Flavia (1988), *A Dictionary of Surnames* (Oxford: Oxford University Press).

Hardy, Thomas (1970), 'Barbara of the House of Grebe', in *A Group of Noble Dames* (Heron).

Harrison, John R. (1967), *The Reactionaries* (New York: Schocken).

Harrowitz, Nancy A. (1994), *Antisemitism, Misogyny, & the Logic of Cultural Difference* (Lincoln: University of Nebraska Press).

Hartman, Geoffrey (1980), *Criticism in the Wilderness* (New Haven, CT: Yale University Press).

(1989), 'Looking Back on Paul de Man', in *Reading De Man Reading*, ed. Lindsay Walters and Wlad Godzich (Minneapolis: University of Minnesota Press).

(1994), 'Darkness Visible', in *Holocaust Remembrance*, ed. Geoffrey Hartman (Oxford: Basil Blackwell).

Hartman, Geoffrey, and Budick, Sanford, eds. (1986), *Midrash and Literature* (New Haven, CT: Yale University Press).

Hastings, Michael (1985), *Tom and Viv* (Penguin).

Heaney, Seamus (1972), *Wintering Out* (Faber & Faber).

Heath, Stephen (1972), *The Nouveau Roman* (Elek).

(1982), *The Sexual Fix* (Macmillan).

Hegel, G. W. F. (1971), *Early Theological Writings* (Philadelphia: University of Pennsylvania Press).

(1975), *Aesthetics*, vols. I–II (Oxford: Clarendon).

(1977), *Phenomenology of Spirit* (Oxford: Clarendon).

Heller, Agnes (1993), 'The Limits to Natural Law and the Paradox of Evil', in *On Human Rights*, ed. Stephen Shute and Susan Hurley (New York: Basic Books).

Hellmann, John (1982), *Simone Weil* (Waterloo, IA: Wilfrid Laurier University Press).

Herberg, Will (1970), *Judaism and Modern Man* (New York: Atheneum).

Herr, Moshe David (1988), 'The Sages' Reaction to Antisemitism in the Hellenistic-Roman World', in *Antisemitism Through the Ages*, ed. Shmuel Almog (Oxford: Pergamon).

Heyman, C. David (1967), *Ezra Pound* (New York: Seaver).

Higham, John (1975), *Send These To Me* (New York: Atheneum).

Hilberg, Raul (1961), *The Destruction of the European Jews* (W. H. Allen).

Hirsch, David H. (1991), *The Deconstruction of Literature* (Hanover: Brown University Press).

Hitchens, Christopher (1991), *Class, Blood and Nostalgia* (Vintage).

Hobbes, Thomas (1974), *Leviathan* (Penguin).

Hobhouse, L. T. (1964), *Liberalism* (Oxford University Press).

Hobsbawm, Eric (1984), 'Mass-Producing Traditions in Europe 1870–1914', in *The Invention of Tradition*, ed. Eric Hobsbawm and Terence Ranger (Cambridge: Cambridge University Press).

Hofstadter, Richard (1948), *The American Political Tradition* (New York: Vintage).

Hollander, John (1989), 'Remembering Auden', in *Encounters*, ed. Kai Erikson (New Haven, CT: Yale University Press).

Holmes, Colin (1979), *Anti-Semitism in British Society 1876–1939* (Edward Arnold).

Honnighausen, Lothar (1988), *The Symbolist Tradition in English Literature* (Cambridge: Cambridge University Press).

Hook, Sidney (1949), 'Reflections on the Jewish Question', *Partisan Review*, May.

(1987), *Out of Step* (New York: Carroll & Graf).

Hooker, Joan Fillmore (1983), *T. S. Eliot's Poems in French Translation* (Epping: Bowker).

Hopkins, Kenneth (1971), *A Dull Head Among Windy Space: The Eliot Cult* (North Walsham: Warren House).

Howarth, Herbert (1964), *Notes on Some Figures Behind T. S. Eliot* (Boston: Houghton Mifflin).

Howe, Irving (1976), *The Immigrant Jews of New York* (Routledge & Kegan Paul).

(1982), *A Margin of Hope* (New York: Harcourt Brace Jovanovich).

(1991), 'An Exercise in Memory', *New Republic*, 11 March.

Husik, Isaac (1973), *A History of Mediaeval Jewish Philosophy* (New York: Atheneum).

Hyman, Stanley Edgar (1955), *The Armed Vision* (New York: Vintage).

Jaher, Frederic Cople (1994), *A Scapegoat in the Wilderness* (Cambridge, MA: Harvard University Press).

James, Henry (1975), 'Glasses', in *Affairs of the Heart* (Pan).

Jameson, Frederic (1979), *Fables of Aggression* (Berkeley: University of California Press).

Janik, Allan, and Toulmin, Stephen (1973), *Wittgenstein's Vienna* (New York: Touchstone).

Jansen, Hans (1988), 'Anti-Semitism in the Amiable Guise of Theological Philo-Semitism in Karl Barth's Israel Theology Before and After Auschwitz', in *Remembering for the Future*, I–II and S. V. (Oxford: Pergamon).

Jaspers, Karl (1974), *Spinoza* (New York: Harcourt Brace Jovanovich).

Jay, Gregory S. (1983), *T. S. Eliot and the Poetics of Literary History* (Baton Rouge: Louisiana State University Press).

Jay, Martin (1992), 'The Aesthetic Alibi', *Salmagundi*, Winter.

(1993), *Downcast Eyes* (Berkeley: University of California Press).

Johnson, Barbara (1989), *A World of Difference* (Baltimore: Johns Hopkins University Press).

Josephus, Flavius (1818), 'Against Apion', in *Works*, vol. IV, trans. William Whiston (William Allason & J. Maynard).

Joyce, James (1972), *Dubliners* (Penguin).

(1973a), *Ulysses* (Penguin).

(1973b), *The Critical Writings*, ed. Ellsworthy Mason and Richard Ellmann (New York: Viking).

(1983), *Giacomo Joyce* (Faber & Faber).

Julius, Anthony (1988), 'The Mark against Eliot', *The Times*, 9 August.

Kadish, Sharman (1992), *Bolsheviks and British Jews* (Frank Cass).

Kant, Immanuel (1973), *The Critique of Judgement* (Oxford: Clarendon).

Kaplan, Alice Yaeger (1986), *Reproductions of Banality* (Minneapolis: University of Minnesota Press).

Kaplan, Fred (1989), *Dickens* (Sceptre).

Katz, Jacob (1978), *Out of the Ghetto* (New York: Schocken).

(1980), *From Prejudice to Destruction* (Cambridge, MA: Harvard University Press).

(1986), *The Darker Side of Genius* (Hanover: University Press of New England).

(1988), 'The Preparatory Stage of the Modern Antisemitic Movement (1873–1879)', in *Antisemitism Through the Ages*, ed. Shmuel Almog (Oxford: Pergamon).

Katzberg, Nathaniel (1988), 'Hungarian Antisemitism', in *Antisemitism Through the Ages*, ed. Shmuel Almog (Oxford: Pergamon).

Kayser, Wolfgang (1981), *The Grotesque in Art and Literature* (New York: Columbia University Press).

Kazin, Alfred (1979), *New York Jew* (New York: Vintage).

(1988), 'Homer to Mussolini', in *Ezra Pound*, ed. Marcel Smith and William A. Ulmer (Tuscaloosa: University of Alabama Press).

Kearns, George (1989), *Pound: The Cantos* (Cambridge: Cambridge University Press).

Keats, John (1987), *Letters of John Keats*, ed. Robert Gittings (Oxford University Press).

Kenner, Hugh (1975), *The Pound Era* (Faber & Faber).

(1985a), *The Invisible Poet: T. S. Eliot* (Methuen).

(1985b), *The Poetry of Ezra Pound* (Lincoln, NE: University of Nebraska Press).

Kermode, Frank (1967), *The Sense of an Ending* (Oxford University Press).

(1971a), 'A Babylonish Dialect', in *T. S. Eliot*, ed. Allen Tate (Penguin).

(1971b), *Romantic Image* (Fontana).

(1990a), *An Appetite for Poetry* (Fontana).

(1990b), *Poetry, Narrative, History* (Oxford: Basil Blackwell).

Kierkegaard, Soren (1987), *Fear and Trembling* (Penguin).

Kipling, Rudyard (1987), *Puck of Pook's Hill* (Penguin).

Kirk, Russell (1971), *Eliot and His Age* (New York: Random House).

Klein, A. M. (1987), *Literary Essays* (Toronto: University of Toronto Press).

Klein, Charlotte (1978), *Anti-Judaism in Christian Theology* (Society for Promoting Christian Knowledge).

Klingenstein, Susanne (1991), *Jews in the American Academy 1900–1940* (New Haven, CT: Yale University Press).

Kojecky, Roger (1971), *T. S. Eliot's Social Criticism* (Faber & Faber).

Konig, Eduard (1986), 'The Wandering Jew', in *The Wandering Jew*, ed. G. Hasan-Rokem and A. Dundes (Bloomington: Indiana University Press).

Kramnick, Isaac, and Sheerman, Barry (1993), *Harold Laski* (Hamish Hamilton).

Kraut, Alan M., and Breitman, Richard D. (1987), 'Anti-Semitism in the State Department', in *Anti-Semitism in American History*, ed. David A. Gerber (Urbana: University of Illinois Press).

Krieger, Murray (1981), *Theory of Criticism* (Baltimore: Johns Hopkins University Press).

Kristeva, Julia (1982), *Powers of Horror* (New York: Columbia University Press).

Kushner, Tony (1989), *The Persistence of Prejudice* (Manchester: Manchester University Press).

(1990), 'British anti-Semitism 1918–1945', in *The Making of Anglo-Jewry*, ed. David Cesarani (Oxford: Blackwell).

(1994a), 'The Fascist as "Other"? Racism and Neo-Nazism in Contemporary Britain', *Patterns of Prejudice*, 28:1.

(1994b), *The Holocaust and the Liberal Imagination* (Oxford: Basil Blackwell).

LaCapra, Dominick (1983), *Rethinking Intellectual History* (Ithaca, NY: Cornell University Press).

Lacoue-Labarthe, Phillipe (1990), *Heidegger, Art and Politics* (Oxford: Basil Blackwell).

Lang, Berel (1990), *Act and Idea in the Nazi Genocide* (Chicago: University of Chicago Press).

Langbaum, Robert (1987), *The Word from Below* (Madison: University of Wisconsin Press).

Langmuir, Gavin I. (1990), *Toward a Definition of Antisemitism* (Berkeley: University of California Press).

Lazar, Moshe (1991), 'The Lamb and the Scapegoat: The Dehumanization of the Jews in Medieval Propaganda Imagery', in *Anti-Semitism in Times of Crisis*, ed. Sander Gilman and Steven T. Katz (New York: University Press).

Lears, Jackson (1983), *No Place of Grace* (New York, Pantheon).

Leavis, F. R. (1967), *New Bearings in English Poetry* (Penguin).
　(1975), *The Living Principle* (Chatto & Windus).
　(1976), *The Common Pursuit* (Penguin).
　(1986), 'T. S. Eliot's Influence', in *Valuation in Criticism* (Cambridge: Cambridge University Press).

Leavis, F. R., and Leavis, Q. D. (1969), *Lectures in America* (Chatto & Windus).

Lebzelter, Gisela C. (1978), *Political Anti-Semitism in England 1918–1939* (Macmillan).

Lecercle, J.-J. (1990), 'Textual Responsibility', in *The Political Responsibility of Intellectuals*, ed. Ian Maclean *et al.* (Cambridge: Cambridge University Press).

Lehman, David (1991), *Signs of the Times* (André Deutsch).

Leibowitz, Herbert (1972), 'The Muse in Chains', in *Ezra Pound: The Critical Heritage*, ed. Eric Homberger (Routledge & Kegan Paul).

Lentricchia, Frank (1983), *After the New Criticism* (Methuen).
　(1994), *Modernist Quartet* (Cambridge: Cambridge University Press).

Lessing, Gotthold Ephraim (1970), *Nathan the Wise* (J. M. Dent).

Levenson, Michael H. (1986), *A Genealogy of Modernism* (Cambridge: Cambridge University Press).

Levin, Bernard (1988), 'How Eliot Caught the Plague', *The Times*, 15 August.

Levin, Harry (1981), 'Ezra Pound, T. S. Eliot and the European Horizon', in *Memories of the Moderns* (Faber & Faber).

Levinas, Emmanuel (1989), *The Levinas Reader*, ed. Sean Hand (Oxford: Basil Blackwell).
　(1990), *Difficult Freedom* (Athlone).

Levine, Israel (1936), *Faithful Rebels* (Soncino).

Levy, William Turner, and Scherle, Victor (1969), *Affectionately, T. S. Eliot* (J. M. Dent).

Lewis, Bernard (1984), *The Jews of Islam* (Routledge & Kegan Paul).
　(1986), *Semites and Anti-Semites* (Weidenfeld & Nicolson).

Lewis, Matthew (1980), *The Monk* (Oxford: Oxford University Press).

Lewis, Wyndham (1929), *Paleface* (Chatto & Windus).

(1931), *Hitler* (Chatto & Windus).

(1939), *The Jews: Are They Human?* (Allen & Unwin).

(1979), *Collected Poems and Plays*, ed. Alan Munton (Manchester: Carcanet).

(1981), *The Apes of God* (Santa Barbara, CA: Black Sparrow).

(1983), *Self-Condemned* (Santa Barbara, CA: Black Sparrow).

(1986a), *Rotting Hill* (Santa Barbara, CA: Black Sparrow).

(1986b), *The Caliph's Design* (Santa Barbara, CA: Black Sparrow).

(1987), *Men Without Art* (Santa Rosa, CA: Black Sparrow).

(1989), *The Art Of Being Ruled* (Santa Rosa, CA: Black Sparrow).

Lindemann, Albert S. (1991), *The Jew Accused* (Cambridge: Cambridge University Press).

Lipset, Seymour Martin, and Raab, Earl (1971), *The Politics of Unreason* (Heinemann).

Lipstadt, Deborah (1993), *Denying the Holocaust* (New York: Free Press).

Litvinoff, Barnet (1988), *The Burning Bush* (Collins).

Litvinoff, Emanuel (1980), 'To T. S. Eliot', in *Voices Within The Ark*, ed. Howard Schwartz and Anthony Rudolf (New York: Avon).

Lodge, David (1978), *Changing Places* (Penguin).

Loewenstein, Andrea Freud (1993), *Loathsome Jews and Engulfing Women* (New York: New York University Press).

Loewenstein, Rudolph M. (1988), 'Anti-Semites in Psychoanalysis', in *Error Without Trial: Psychological Research on Antisemitism*, ed. Werner Bergman (Berlin: Walter de Gruyter).

Logue, Christopher (1957), Letter, *Times Literary Supplement*, 6 September.

Long, Michael (1988), 'The Politics of English Modernism', in *Visions and Blueprints*, ed. Edward Timms and Peter Collier (Manchester: Manchester University Press).

Longenbach, James (1991), '*Ara Vos Prec*: Satire and Suffering', in *T. S. Eliot*, ed. Ronald Bush (Cambridge: Cambridge University Press).

Lowell, Robert (1971), *Notebook* (Faber & Faber).

(1984), *Poems*, ed. Jonathan Raban (Faber & Faber).

Lyotard, J.-F. (1990), *Heidegger and 'the jews'* (Minneapolis: University of Minnesota Press).

(1993), *Political Writings* (University College London Press).

Maccoby, Hyam (1973), 'The Anti-Semitism of T. S. Eliot', *Midstream*, 19:5, May.

(1974), 'Anti-Semitism in the Work of Eliot and Pound: A contrast', *Books*, Autumn.

(1982a), *Judaism on Trial* (Associated Universities Press).

(1982b), *The Sacred Executioner* (Thames & Hudson).

(1983/4), 'An Interpretation of T. S. Eliot', *European Judaism*, 17:22, Winter.

Macdonald, Heather (1992), 'The Holocaust as Text', *Salmagundi*, Autumn.

Macherey, Pierre (1978), *A Theory of Literary Production* (Routledge & Kegan Paul).

MacIntyre, Alasdair (1988), *Whose Justice? Which Rationality?* (Duckworth).
(1990), *Three Rival Versions of Moral Inquiry* (Duckworth).

MacNeice, Louis (1934), Review, *Criterion*, October.
(1938), *Modern Poetry* (Oxford: Oxford University Press).
(1979), *Collected Poems* (Faber & Faber).

Magny, Claude Edmonde (1948), 'A Double Note on T. S. Eliot and James Joyce', in *T. S. Eliot*, compiled by Richard March and Tambimuttu (PL Editions Poetry).

Maidenbaum, Aryeh, and Martin, Stephen A., eds. (1991), *Lingering Shadows: Jungians, Freudians, and Anti-Semitism* (Boston: Shambala).

Mallarmé, Stéphane (1965), *The Penguin Poets*, ed. Anthony Hartley (Penguin).

Manea, Norman (1994), *On Clowns* (Faber & Faber).

Mankowitz, Wolf (1949), 'Notes on "Gerontion"', in *T. S. Eliot*, ed. B. Rajan (Dennis Dobson).
(1967), *The Penguin Wolf Mankowitz* (Penguin).

Marcus, Jacob R. (1974), *The Jew in the Medieval World* (New York: Atheneum).

Marlowe, Christopher (1979), *The Jew of Malta*, ed. T. W. Craik (Ernest Benn).

Marrus, Michael R. (1985), *The Unwanted* (New York: Oxford University Press).
(1989), *The Holocaust in History* (Penguin).

Marrus, Michael R., and Paxton, Robert O. (1981), *Vichy France and the Jews* (New York: Basic Books).

Marshall, Robert (1990), *In the Sewers of Lvov* (Collins).

Marx, Groucho (1969), *The Groucho Letters* (Sphere).

Marx, Karl (1975), *Early Writings* (Penguin).

Masson, Jeffrey (1988), *Against Therapy* (Fontana).

Matthews, T. S. (1974), *Great Tom* (Weidenfeld & Nicolson; New York: Harper & Row).

Matthiessen, F. O. (1959), *The Achievement of T. S. Eliot*, 3rd edn (Oxford University Press).

Mayer, John T. (1989), *T. S. Eliot's Silent Voices* (New York: Oxford University Press).

Mays, J. C. C. (1994), 'The Early Poems', *The Cambridge Companion to T. S. Eliot*, ed. A. David Moody (Cambridge: Cambridge University Press).

McClelland, J. S., ed. (1970), *The French Right* (Jonathan Cape).

McCormick, John (1988), *George Santayana* (New York: Paragon House).

McGann, Jerome J. (1989), *Towards a Literature of Knowledge* (Oxford: Clarendon).

Mehlman, Jeffrey (1983), *Legacies of Anti-Semitism in France* (Minneapolis: University of Minnesota Press).

(1989), 'Perspectives: On de Man and *Le Soir*', in *Responses*, ed. Werner Hamacher *et al.* (Lincoln: University of Nebraska Press).

Meinecke, Freidrich (1963), *The German Catastrophe* (Boston, MA: Beacon).

Menand, Louis (1987), *Discovering Modernism* (New York: Oxford University Press).

Mencken, H. L. (1989), *The Diary of H. L. Mencken*, ed. Charles A. Fecher (New York: Knopf).

Mendes-Flohr, Paul R. (1987), 'Buber and the Metaphysics of Contempt', in *Living with Antisemitism*, ed. Jehuda Reinharz (Hanover: University Press of New England).

Mendes-Flohr, Paul R., and Reinharz, Jehuda, eds. (1980), *The Jew in the Modern World* (New York: Oxford University Press).

Meyers, Jeffrey (1980), *The Enemy* (Routledge & Kegan Paul).

Miles, Barry (1990), *Ginsberg* (Viking).

Miller, Karl (1993), *Rebecca's Vest* (Hamish Hamilton).

Millett, Kate (1979), *Sexual Politics* (Virago).

Misrahi, Robert (1972), *Marx et la question juive* (Paris: Gallimard).

Modder, Montagu Frank (1960), *The Jew in the Literature of England* (New York: Meridian).

Modras, Ronald (1988), 'The Catholic Church in Poland and Antisemitism, 1933–1939', *Remembering for the Future*, I–II and S. V. (Oxford: Pergamon).

Moody, A. D. (1980), *T. S. Eliot: Poet* (Cambridge: Cambridge University Press).

Moore, Marianne (1987), *The Complete Prose* (New York: Elisabeth Sifton / Penguin).

Moore, Nicholas (1948), 'Three Poems for Mr Eliot', in *T. S. Eliot*, compiled by Richard March and Tambimuttu (PL Editions Poetry).

Mordell, Albert (1951), *T. S. Eliot's Deficiencies as a Social Critic / T. S. Eliot – Special Pleader as Book Reviewer and Literary Critic* (Girard: Haldeman-Julius).

(1957), Letter, *Times Literary Supplement*, 20 September.

Mosse, George L. (1985), *Toward the Final Solution* (Madison: University of Wisconsin Press).

Muggeridge, Malcolm (1989), *The Thirties* (Weidenfeld & Nicolson).

Muir, Edwin (1934), 'Mr Eliot on Evil', *Spectator*, 9 March.

Murphy, Jeffrey G., and Hampton, Jean (1990), *Forgiveness and Mercy* (Cambridge: Cambridge University Press).

Murray, Oswyn (1993), *Early Greece* (Fontana).

Murry, John Middleton (1948), *Looking Before and After* (Sheppard Press).

Nabokov, Vladimir (1983), *Lectures on Literature* (Picador).

Nadel, Ira B. (1989), *Joyce and the Jews* (Macmillan).

Naman, Anne Aresty (1980), *The Jew in the Victorian Novel* (New York: AMS Press).

Nevin, Thomas R. (1984), *Irving Babbitt* (Chapel Hill: University of North Carolina Press).

Newman, John Henry (1974), *An Essay on the Development of Christian Doctrine* (Penguin).

Nicolson, Harold (1958), 'My Words Echo', in *T. S. Eliot*, ed. Neville Braybrooke (Rupert Hart-Davis).

(1971), *Diaries and Letters 1930–1939*, ed. Nigel Nicolson (Collins).

Nietzsche, Friedrich (1967), *The Birth of Tragedy* (New York: Vintage).

(1969), *On the Genealogy of Morals* (New York: Vintage).

(1972), *The Anti-Christ* (Penguin).

(1973), *Beyond Good and Evil* (Penguin).

Nisbet, Robert (1982), *Prejudices* (Cambridge, MA: Harvard University Press).

Nolte, Ernst (1969), *Three Faces of Fascism* (New York: Mentor).

Norris, Christopher (1991), *Spinoza and the Origins of Modern Critical Theory* (Oxford: Basil Blackwell).

Nott, Kathleen (1958), *The Emperor's Clothes* (Bloomington: Indiana University Press).

Oberman, Heiko A. (1984), *The Roots of Anti-Semitism in the Age of Renaissance and Reformation* (Philadelphia: Fortress).

O'Connor, W. V., and Stone, E. (1959), *A Casebook on Ezra Pound* (New York: Thomas Y. Crowell).

Olsen, Stein Haugom (1985), *The Structure of Literary Understanding* (Cambridge: Cambridge University Press).

Oren, Dan A. (1985), *Joining the Club* (New Haven, CT: Yale University Press).

Orwell, George (1970), *The Collected Essays, Journalism and Letters*, I–IV, ed. Sonia Orwell and Ian Angus (Penguin).

Osborne, Lawrence (1993), *The Poisoned Embrace* (Bloomsbury).

Ozick, Cynthia (1984), *Art and Ardor* (New York: E. P. Dutton).

(1993), 'T. S. Eliot at 101', in *What Henry James Knew* (Jonathan Cape).

Palmer, Andrew (1991), 'With the Naked Eye', *Independent*, 11 November.

Panitz, Esther L. (1981), *The Alien in Their Midst* (Associated Universities Press).

Pearson, Gabriel (1970), 'Eliot: An American Use of Symbolism', in *Eliot in Perspective*, ed. Graham Martin (Macmillan).

Perkins, David (1993), *Is Literary History Possible?* (Baltimore: Johns Hopkins University Press).

Perl, Jeffrey M. (1989), *Skepticism and Modern Enmity* (Baltimore: Johns Hopkins University Press).

Philipson, David (1889), *The Jew in English Fiction* (Cincinnati: Robert Clarke).

Pieper, Josef (1952), *Leisure the Basis of Culture*, with an introduction by T. S. Eliot (Faber & Faber).

Pierson, George Wilson (1968), 'The Frontier and American Institutions', in *Turner and the Sociology of the Frontier*, ed. Richard Hofstadter and Seymour Martin Lipset (New York: Basic Books).

Plimpton, George, ed. (1977), *Writers at Work*, 2nd series (Penguin).

Plowman, Max (1942), *The Right to Live* (Andrew Dakers).

Plutzik, Hyman (1974), 'For T. S. E. Only', in *Jewish-American Literature*, ed. Abraham Chapman (New York: New American Library).

Podhoretz, Norman (1980), *Breaking Ranks* (New York: Harper & Row).

Poe, Edgar Allen (1981), *The Complete Poetry and Selected Prose*, ed. Allen Tate (New York: New American Library).

Poirier, Richard (1988), *The Renewal of Literature* (Faber & Faber).

Pole, David (1983), *Aesthetics, Form and Emotion* (Duckworth).

Polenberg, Richard (1989), *Fighting Faiths* (Penguin).

Poliakov, Leon (1974–5; 1985), *The History of Anti-Semitism* (vols. I–III: Routledge & Kegan Paul; vol. IV: New York: Vanguard).

(1977), *Jewish Bankers and the Holy See* (Routledge & Kegan Paul).

Pope, Alexander (1966), *Poetical Works*, ed. Herbert Davis (Oxford University Press).

Porteus, Hugh Gordon (1948), 'Resurrection in the Crypt', in *T. S. Eliot*, compiled by Richard March and Tambimuttu (PL Editions Poetry).

Pound, Ezra (1934a), Review of *After Strange Gods*, *New English Weekly*, 8 March.

(1934b), Letter, *New English Weekly*, 10 May.

(1934c), Letter, *New English Weekly*, 24 May.

(1939), Letter, *New English Weekly*, 2 February.

(1940), Letter, *New English Weekly*, 30 May.

(1960), *Literary Essays of Ezra Pound*, ed. T. S. Eliot (Faber & Faber).

(1973), *Selected Prose 1909–1965*, ed. William Cookson (Faber & Faber).

(1975), *Cantos* (Faber & Faber).

(1978a), '*Ezra Pound Speaking*', ed. Leonard W. Doob (Westport: Greenwood Press).

(1978b), *Guide to Kulchur* (Peter Owen).

(1981), 'Salutation the Third', *Blast* 1, ed. Wyndham Lewis (Santa Barbara, CA: Black Sparrow).

(1984), *Collected Shorter Poems* (Faber & Faber).

(1985), *Pound/Lewis*, ed. Timothy Materer (Faber & Faber).

(1987), *Pound/Zukofsky*, ed. Barry Ahearn (Faber & Faber).

Power, M. S. (1992), *Come the Executioner* (Penguin).

Prendergast, Christopher (1990), 'Making the Difference: Paul de Man, Fascism and Deconstruction', in *Intellectuals: Aesthetics, Politics, Academics*, ed. Bruce Robbins (Minneapolis: University of Minnesota Press).

Prior, Arthur N. (1939), Letter, *Criterion*, January.

Pulzer, Peter G. (1964), *The Rise of Political Anti-Semitism in Germany and Austria* (New York: John Wiley).

Putnam, Samuel (1987), *Paris was our Mistress* (Plantin).

Rabinowicz, Oskar K. (1974), *Arnold Toynbee on Judaism and Zionism* (W. H. Allen).

Ragussis, Michael (1989), 'Representation, Conversion, and Literary Form: *Harrington* and the Novel of Jewish Identity', *Critical Inquiry*, Autumn.

Raine, Craig (1990), *Haydn & The Valve Trumpet* (Faber & Faber).

Randall, A. W. G. (1934), Review of *My Life as German and Jew* by Jakob Wasserman, *Criterion*, October.

   (1938), 'Review of German Periodicals', *Criterion*, January.

Ransom, John Crowe (1971), 'Gerontion', in *T. S. Eliot*, ed. Allen Tate (Penguin).

Rapaport, Herman (1989), 'De Man Ce Soir', in *Responses*, eds. Werner Hamacher *et al.* (Lincoln: University of Nebraska Press).

Raphael, Frederic (1989), *Lindmann* (Fontana).

Rappaport, Solomon (1980), *Jew and Gentile* (New York: Philosophical Library).

Read, Herbert (1971), 'T. S. E. – A Memoir', in *T. S. Eliot*, ed. Allen Tate (Penguin).

Reck, Michael (1968), *Ezra Pound* (Rupert Hart-Davis).

Redman, Tim (1991), *Ezra Pound and Italian Fascism* (Cambridge: Cambridge University Press).

Reeves, James (1948), 'Cambridge Twenty Years Ago', in *T. S. Eliot*, compiled by Richard March and Tambimuttu (PL Editions Poetry).

Richards, I. A. (1926), *Principles of Literary Criticism*, 2nd edn (Routledge & Kegan Paul).

   (1930), *Practical Criticism* (Kegan Paul, Trench, Trubner).

   (1971), *The Philosophy of Rhetoric* (Oxford University Press).

Richler, Mordecai (1969), *Cocksure* (Panther).

   (1991), *Solomon Gursky Was Here* (Vintage).

   (1994), *This Year in Jerusalem* (Chatto & Windus).

Ricks, Christopher (1987), *The Force of Poetry* (Oxford: Oxford University Press).

   (1988), *T. S. Eliot and Prejudice* (Faber & Faber).

Riding, Laura, and Graves, Robert (1969), *A Survey of Modernist Poetry* (New York: Haskell House).

Rimbaud, Arthur (1962), *Collected Poems* (Penguin).

Robbins, Jill (1991), *Prodigal Son / Elder Brother* (Chicago: University of Chicago Press).

Robbins, Rossell Hope (1951), *The T. S. Eliot Myth* (New York: Henry Schuman).

Roberts, Andrew (1994), *Eminent Churchillians* (Weidenfeld & Nicolson).

Roditi, Edouard (1932), 'Judaism and Poetry', *Jewish Review*, 2, September–December.

   (1991), Letter, *Jewish Quarterly*, Summer.

Rokéah, David (1988), 'The Church Fathers and the Jews in Writing

Designed for Internal and External Use', in *Antisemitism Through the Ages*, ed. Shmuel Almog (Oxford: Pergamon).

Rorty, Richard (1989), *Contingency, Irony and Solidarity* (Cambridge: Cambridge University Press).

(1991), *Essays on Heidegger and Others* (Cambridge: Cambridge University Press).

(1994), 'After Philosophy, Democracy', interview in *The American Philosopher* with Giovanna Borradori (Chicago: University of Chicago Press).

Rose, Paul Lawrence (1992a), *German Question / Jewish Question* (Princeton, NJ: Princeton University Press).

(1992b), *Wagner* (Faber & Faber).

Rosenberg, Edgar (1960), *From Shylock to Svengali* (Stanford, CA: Stanford University Press).

Rosenberg, Harold (1970), *The Tradition of the New* (Paladin).

(1973), *Discovering the Present* (Chicago: University of Chicago Press).

Rosenstock-Huessy, Eugen, and Rosenzweig, Franz (1971), *Judaism Despite Christianity* (New York: Schocken).

Roth, Cecil (1938), *The Jewish Contribution to Civilisation* (East and West Library).

(1970), *A History of the Jews* (New York: Schocken).

Roth, Philip (1988), *The Counterlife* (Penguin).

(1994), *Operation Shylock* (New York: Vintage International).

Rousseau, Jean-Jacques (1953), *The Confessions* (Penguin).

(1979), *Reveries of the Solitary Walker* (Penguin).

Rubenstein, Richard L. (1992), *After Auschwitz*, 2nd edn (Baltimore: Johns Hopkins University Press).

Rushdie, Salman (1992), 'In Good Faith', in *Imaginary Homelands* (Granta).

Russell, Bertrand (1961), *History of Western Philosophy* (Allen & Unwin).

Russo, John Paul (1989), *I. A. Richards* (Routledge).

Ruthven, K. K. (1979), *Critical Assumptions* (Cambridge: Cambridge University Press).

Ryan, Desmond (1953), 'Letter from Paris', *Time and Tide*, 3 January.

Rychner, Max (1936), 'German Chronicle', *Criterion*, April.

Sacher, Harry, and Bentwich, Norman, eds. (1932–4), *The Jewish Review*, vols. I–VIII (The Soncino Press).

Sachs, Joseph (1937), *Beauty and the Jew* (Edward Goldston).

Said, Edward (1992), *Musical Elaborations* (Vintage).

(1994), *Representations of the Intellectual* (Vintage).

Salbstein, M. C. N. (1982), *The Emancipation of the Jews in Britain* (Associated Universities Press).

Salomon, Sidney (1939), *The Jews of Britain* (Hutchinson).

Salusinszky, Imre (1987), *Criticism in Society* (New York: Methuen).

Samuel, Maurice (1967), *Blood Accusation* (Weidenfeld & Nicolson).

Santayana, George (1987), *Persons and Places* (Cambridge, MA: MIT Press).

Saperstein, Marc (1989), *Moments of Crisis in Jewish–Christian Relations* (SCM Press).

Sarna, Jonathan D. (1986), 'American Anti-Semitism', in *History and Hate*, ed. David Berger (Philadelphia: Jewish Publication Society).

(1987), 'The "Mythical Jew" and the "Jew Next Door" in Nineteenth Century America', in *Anti-Semitism in American History*, ed. David A. Gerber (Urbana: University of Illinois Press).

Sartre, Jean-Paul (1965), *Anti-Semite and Jew* (New York: Schocken).

(1969), *Being and Nothingness* (Methuen).

(1983), *What is Literature?* (University Paperbacks).

Schneider, Ronna Greff (1992), 'Hate Speech in the United States', in *Striking a Balance*, ed. Sandra Coliver (Article 19).

Schopenhauer, Arthur (1966), *The World as Will and Representation*, vols. I–II (New York: Dover).

Schorske, Carl E. (1987), *Fin-De-Siècle Vienna* (Cambridge: Cambridge University Press).

Schwartz, Delmore (1939), '*The Criterion*, 1922–39', *Kenyon Review*, 1:4, Autumn.

(1970), 'The Literary Dictatorship of T. S. Eliot', in *Selected Essays*, ed. Donald A. Dike and David H. Zucker (Chicago: University of Chicago Press).

(1972), 'Ezra Pound and History', in *Ezra Pound: The Critical Heritage*, ed. Eric Homberger (Routledge & Kegan Paul).

(1984), *Letters of Delmore Schwartz*, ed. Robert Phillips, with introduction by Karl Shapiro (Princeton, NJ: Ontario Review Press).

(1993), *Delmore Schwartz and James Laughlin: Selected Letters*, ed. Robert Phillips (New York: W. W. Norton).

Schweitzer, Frederick M. (1988), 'The Tap-Root of Anti-Semitism', in *Remembering for the Future*, I–II and S. V. (Oxford: Pergamon).

Scruton, Roger (1980), *The Meaning of Conservatism* (Penguin).

Searle, G. R. (1987), *Corruption in British Politics 1895–1930* (Oxford: Clarendon).

Seidel, Gill (1986), *The Holocaust Denial* (Leeds: Beyond the Pale Collective).

Selbourne, David (1993), *The Spirit of the Age* (Sinclair-Stevenson).

Selznick, Gertrude J., and Steinberg, Stephen (1969), *The Tenacity of Prejudice* (New York: Harper & Row).

Shakespeare, William (1964), *The Merchant of Venice*, ed. John Russell Brown (Methuen).

(1971), *The Tempest*, ed. Frank Kermode (Methuen).

Shapiro, Edward S. (1987), 'Anti-Semitism Mississippi Style', in *Anti-Semitism in American History*, ed. David A. Gerber (Urbana: University of Illinois Press).

Shapiro, Karl (1960), *In Defense of Ignorance* (New York: Random House).

Sharf, Andrew (1964), *The British Press and Jews Under Nazi Rule* (Oxford University Press).

Shelley, Percy Bysshe (1971), 'A Defence of Poetry', in *English Critical Texts*, ed. D. J. Enright and Ernst De Chickera (Oxford: Clarendon).

Sheridan, Richard Brinsley (1970), *The Plays* (Oxford University Press).

Shils, Edward (1981), *Tradition* (Faber & Faber).

Shklar, Judith (1984), *Ordinary Vices* (Cambridge: Belknap).

Showalter, Elaine (1991), *The Female Malady* (Virago).

Shusterman, Richard (1988), *T. S. Eliot and the Philosophy of Literary Criticism* (Duckworth).

Sidney, Philip (1971), 'An Apology for Poetry', in *English Critical Texts*, ed. D. J. Enright and Ernst De Chickera (Oxford: Clarendon).

Sigg, Eric (1989), *The American T. S. Eliot* (Cambridge: Cambridge University Press).

(1994), 'A Product of America', *The Cambridge Companion to T. S. Eliot*, ed. A . David Moody (Cambridge: Cambridge University Press).

Simon, Marcel (1986), *Verus Israel* (Oxford: Oxford University Press).

Simpson, Louis (1975), *Three on the Tower* (New York: William Morrow).

Simpson, William W. (1940), *Jews and Christians To-Day* (Epworth).

Singerman, Robert (1987), 'The Jew as Racial Alien', in *Anti-Semitism in American History*, ed. David A. Gerber (Urbana: University of Illinois Press).

Sitwell, Edith (1957), *Collected Poems* (Macmillan).

Smith, Anna Marie (1994), *New Right Discourse on Race & Sexuality* (Cambridge: Cambridge University Press).

Smith, Grover (1956), *T. S. Eliot's Poetry and Plays* (Chicago: University of Chicago Press).

Smith, Joan (1989), *Misogynies* (Faber & Faber).

Smith, R. V. (1988), Letter, *The Times*, 11 August.

Smith, Stevie (1958), 'History or Poetic Drama?', in *T. S. Eliot*, ed. Neville Braybrooke (Rupert Hart-Davis).

Smith, W. Robertson (1972), *The Religion of the Semites* (New York: Schocken).

Solomon, Barbar Miller (1989), *Ancestors and Immigrants* (Boston: Northeastern University Press).

Solotaroff, Theodore (1970), *The Red Hot Vacuum* (Boston: Nonpareil).

(1987), *A Few Good Voices in My Head* (New York: Harper & Row).

Sombart, Werner (1962), *The Jews and Modern Capitalism* (New York: Collier).

Sonntag, Jacob, ed. (1980), *Jewish Perspectives* (Secker & Warburg).

Southam, B. C. (1981), *A Student's Guide to the Selected Poems of T. S. Eliot* (Faber & Faber).

Spender, Stephen (1938), *The Destructive Element* (Jonathan Cape).

(1975), *Eliot* (Fontana).

(1978), *The Thirties and After* (Fontana).

(1985), *Journals 1939–1983*, ed. John Goldsmith (Faber & Faber).

Stead, C. K. (1983), *The New Poetic* (Hutchinson).

(1986), *Pound, Yeats, Eliot and the Modernist Movement* (Macmillan).

Steinberg, Jonathan (1990), *All or Nothing* (Routledge).

Steiner, George (1978), *In Bluebeard's Castle* (Faber & Faber).

(1988), Letter, *London Review of Books*, 22 June.

Stern, Guy (1991), 'The Rhetoric of Anti-Semitism in Postwar American Literature', in *Anti-Semitism in Times of Crisis*, ed. Sander Gilman and Steven T. Katz (New York: New York University Press).

Stone, Robert (1992), *A Flag for Sunrise* (New York: Vintage).

Stow, Kenneth R. (1988), 'Hatred of the Jews or Love of the Church', in *Antisemitism Through the Ages*, ed. Shmuel Almog (Oxford: Pergamon).

Stromberg, Roland N. (1982), *Redemption by War* (Lawrence, KS: Regents Press).

Sullivan, J. P., ed. (1970), *Ezra Pound* (Penguin).

Svarny, Erik (1988), '*The Men of 1914*' (Milton Keynes: Open University Press).

Swinburne, Algernon Charles (1992), 'Dolores', in *The Dedalus Book of Femmes Fatales*, ed. Brian Stableford (Sawtry: Dedalus).

Swinburne, Richard (1989), *Responsibility and Atonement* (Oxford: Clarendon).

Symons, Arthur (1958), *The Symbolist Movement in Literature* (New York: E. P. Dutton).

Symons, Julian (1987), *Makers of the New* (André Deutsch).

Synnott, Martha Graham (1987), 'Anti-Semitism and American Universities', in *Anti-Semitism in American History*, ed. David A. Gerber (Urbana: University of Illinois Press).

Syrus, Publilius (1982), 'Sententiae', in *Minor Latin Poets*, vol. I, trans. J. Wight Duff and Arnold M. Duff (Heinemann).

Tabachnick, A. (1969), 'The Yiddish Translation of Eliot's *Waste Land*', in *The Way We Think*, vols. I–II, ed. Joseph Leftwich (South Brunswick: Thomas Yoseloff).

Tacitus (1975), *The Histories* (Penguin).

Taylor, Simon (1985), *Prelude to Genocide* (Duckworth).

Tennyson (1971), *Poems and Plays*, ed. T. Herbert Warren, revised by F. Page (Oxford: Oxford University Press).

Thackeray, William Makepiece (1872), 'Rebecca and Rowena', in *Works*, vol. VIII (Smith, Elder).

Thompson, E. P. (1993), *Witness Against the Beast: William Blake and the Moral Law* (Cambridge: Cambridge University Press).

Timms, Edward (1989), *Karl Kraus* (New Haven, CT: Yale University Press).

Tiverton, Father William (1951), *D. H. Lawrence and Human Existence* (Rockliff).

Todorov, Tzvetan (1988), 'Poetic Truth: Three Interpretations', *Essays in Criticism*, April.

(1993), *On Human Diversity* (Cambridge, MA: Harvard University Press).

Tomlin, Frederick (1988), *T. S. Eliot* (Routledge).

Torrey, E. Fuller (1984), *The Roots of Treason* (San Diego: Harcourt Brace Jovanovich).

Trachtenberg, Joshua (1983), *The Devil and the Jews* (Philadelphia: Jewish Publication Society of America).

Tredell, Nicholas (1994), *Conversations with Critics* (Manchester: Carcanet).

Trilling, Diana (1982), 'Lionel Trilling: A Jew at Columbia', an appendix to Lionel Trilling, *Speaking of Literature and Society*, ed. Diana Trilling (Oxford: Oxford University Press).

(1993), *The Beginning of the Journey* (New York: Harcourt Brace).

Trilling, Lionel (1967), *Beyond Culture* (Penguin).

(1974), *Matthew Arnold* (Allen & Unwin).

(1982), *Speaking of Literature and Society* (Oxford: Oxford University Press).

Trollope, Anthony (1970), *Mr Scarborough's Family* (Oxford: Oxford University Press).

Trotter, David (1984), *The Making of the Reader* (Macmillan).

(1993), *The English Novel in History 1895–1920* (Routledge).

Tytell, John (1987), *Ezra Pound* (New York: Anchor).

Unger, Leonard (1961), *T. S. Eliot* (Minneapolis: University of Minnesota Press).

Untermeyer, Louis (1990), 'Irony de Luxe', in *T. S. Eliot: Critical Assessments*, vols. I–II, ed. Graham Clarke (Christopher Helm).

Updike, John (1990), *Self-Consciousness* (Penguin).

Valentin, Hugo (1971), *Antisemitism Historically and Critically Examined* (Freeport: Books for Libraries Press).

Veblen, Thorstein (1975), 'The Intellectual Pre-Eminence of Jews in Modern Europe', in *The Portable Veblen*, ed. Max Lerner (New York: Viking).

Vidal-Nacquet, Pierre (1992), *Assassins of Memory* (New York: Columbia University Press, 1992).

Wagner, Geoffrey (1957), *Wyndham Lewis* (Routledge & Kegan Paul).

Wagner, Richard (1973), 'Judaism in Music', in *Stories and Essays*, ed. Charles Osborne (Peter Owen).

Wall, Stephen, ed. (1970), *Charles Dickens* (Penguin).

Warren, Robert Penn (1977), 'The Briar Patch', in *I'll Take My Stand* (Baton Rouge: Louisiana State University Press).

Washington, Peter (1993), *Madame Blavatsky's Baboon* (Secker & Warburg).

Wasserstein, Bernard (1988), *Britain and the Jews of Europe 1939–1945* (Oxford: Oxford University Press).

Watkins, Vernon (1958), 'Ode', *T. S. Eliot*, ed. Neville Braybrooke (Rupert Hart-Davis).

Watson, George (1962), *The Literary Critics* (Penguin).

(1977), *Politics and Literature in Modern Britain* (Macmillan).

Weber, Eugen (1962), *Action Française* (Stanford: Stanford University Press).

Weil, Simone (1987), *The Need for Roots* (Ark).

Weinberg, Henry H. (1987), *The Myth of the Jew in France 1967–1982* (Oakville: Mosaic).

Weininger, Otto (1906), *Sex and Character* (Heinemann).

Weinzierl, Erika (1974), 'On the Parthenogenesis of the Anti-Semitism of Sebastian Brunner 1814–1893', in *Yad Vashem Studies on the European Jewish Catastrophe and Resistance*, vol. X (Jerusalem: Yad Vashem).

Weis, René (1990), *Criminal Justice* (Penguin).

Wellek, René (1981; 1983; 1986), *A History of Modern Criticism 1750–1950* (vols. I–IV: Cambridge: Cambridge University Press; vols. V–VI: Jonathan Cape).

Wells, H. G. (1973), *Tono-Bungay* (Collins).

(1991), *A Short History of the World* (Penguin).

Wertheimer, Jack (1987), *Unwelcome Strangers* (New York: Oxford University Press).

Wharton, Edith (1985), *The House of Mirth* (Penguin).

Wheen, Francis (1990), *Tom Driberg* (Chatto & Windus).

Wiener, Jon (1991), *Professors, Politics and Pop* (Verso).

Wierenga, Lambert (1991), 'The Rhetoric of the Commonplace', in *Toward a Definition of Topos*, ed. Lynette Hunter (Macmillan).

Wilk, Melvin (1986), *Jewish Presence in T. S. Eliot and Franz Kafka* (Atlanta: Scholars).

Williams, Bernard (1993), *Shame and Necessity* (Berkeley: University of California Press).

Williams, Raymond (1973), *Drama from Ibsen to Brecht* (Penguin).

(1985), *Culture and Society* (Penguin).

Williams, William Carlos (1967), *Autobiography* (New York: New Directions).

(1969), *Selected Essays* (New York: New Directions).

Williamson, George (1967), *A Reader's Guide to T. S. Eliot*, 2nd ed (Thames & Hudson).

Wilson, A. N. (1986), *Hilaire Belloc* (Penguin).

Wilson, Edmund (1957), *A Piece of My Mind* (W. H. Allen).

(1967), *The Bit Between My Teeth* (New York: Noonday Press).

(1974), *Axel's Castle* (Collins).

(1977), *Letters on Literature and Politics 1912–1972*, ed. Elena Wilson (New York: Farrar, Straus & Giroux).

Wilson, R. McNair (1935), Review, *Criterion*, January.

Wilson, Stephen (1982), *Ideology and Experience* (Farleigh Dickinson University Press).

Wimsatt, William K., and Brooks, Cleanth (1970), *Literary Criticism*, vols. I–IV (Routledge & Kegan Paul).

Winters, Yvor (1987), 'T. S. Eliot or the Illusion of Reaction', in *In Defense of Reason* (Athens: Swallow Press/Ohio University Press).

Wistrich, Robert (1990), *The Jews of Vienna in the Age of Franz Joseph* (Oxford: Oxford University Press).

(1991), *Anti-Semitism* (Thames Methuen).

Wolfson, Harry Austryn (1969), *The Philosophy of Spinoza*, vols. I–II (New York: Schocken).

Wolin, Richard, ed. (1993), *The Heidegger Controversy* (Cambridge, MA: The MIT Press).

Wright, Patrick (1985), *On Living in an Old Country* (Verso).

Yeats, W. B., ed. (1936), *The Oxford Book of Modern Verse 1892–1935* (Oxford: Oxford University Press).

(1990), *The Poems*, ed. Daniel Albright (J. M. Dent).

Zangwill, Israel (1937), *Speeches, Articles and Letters* (Soncino).

Zeldin, Theodore (1973), *France 1848–1945*, vols. I–II (Oxford: Clarendon).

Zimmerman, Moshe (1988), 'From Radicalism to Antisemitism', in *Antisemitism Through the Ages*, ed. Shmuel Almog (Oxford: Pergamon).

Zweig, Arnold (1937), *Insulted and Exiled* (John Miles).

Poets' Choice (n.d.) The Arts and Letters Committee of the National Council of Women of Great Britain.

The Yellow Spot (1936) (Gollancz).

Index